THE **James T. Bialac** NATIVE AMERICAN ART COLLECTION

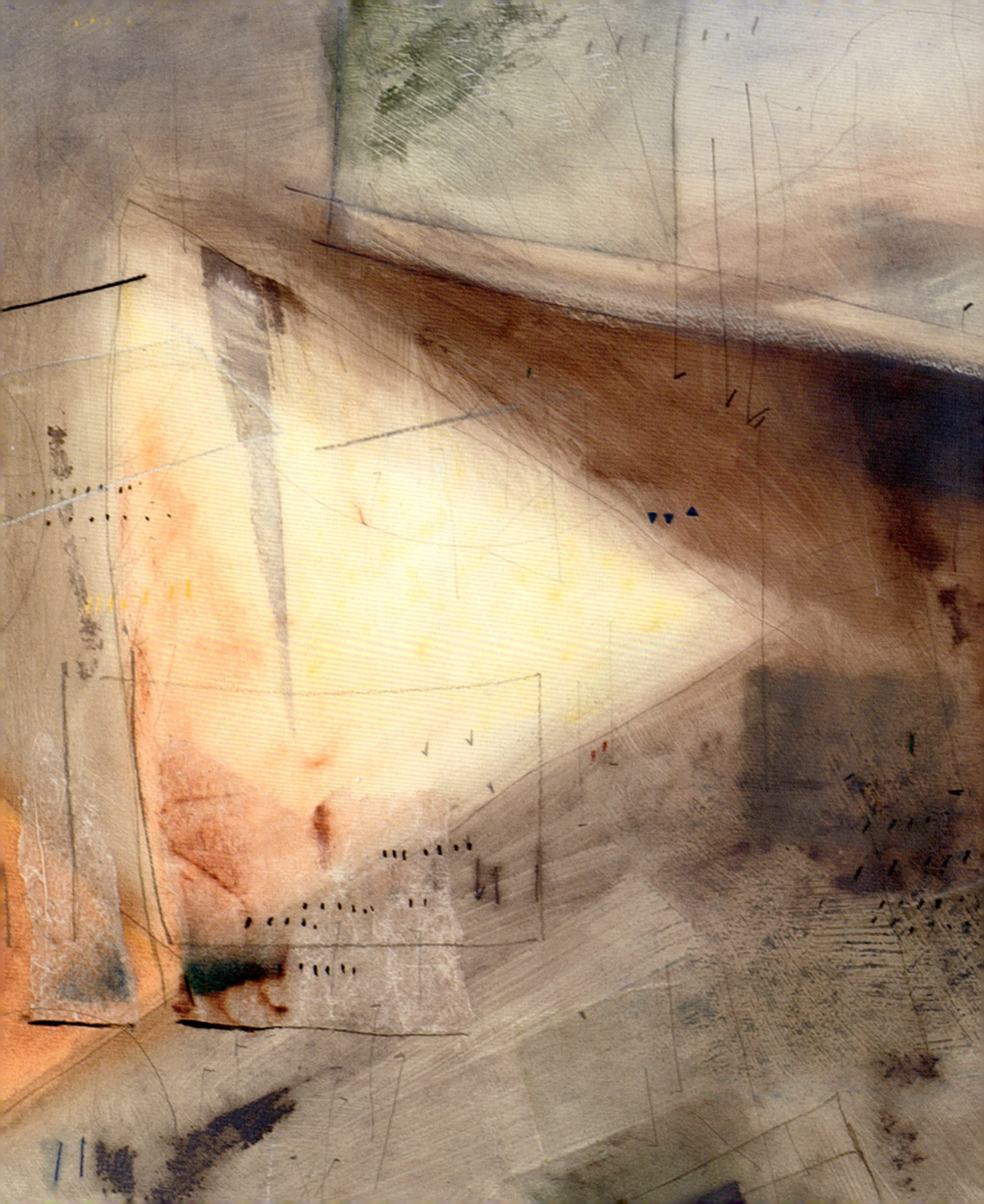

THE **James T. Bialac** NATIVE AMERICAN ART COLLECTION

SELECTED WORKS

MARK ANDREW WHITE, GENERAL EDITOR

UNIVERSITY OF OKLAHOMA PRESS : NORMAN
IN COOPERATION WITH THE FRED JONES JR. MUSEUM OF ART

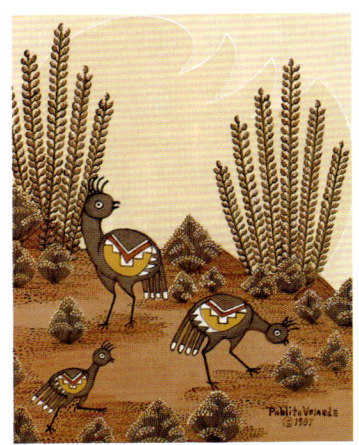

LIBRARY OF CONGRESS CATALOGING-IN-PUBLICATION DATA

The James T. Bialac Native American Art Collection : Selected Works.

    pages cm

 Includes bibliographical references and index.

  ISBN 978-0-8061-4299-9 (hardcover : alk. paper)—

  ISBN 978-0-8061-4304-0 (pbk. : alk. paper)

1. Indian art—Catalogs. 2. Bialac, James T.—Art collections—Catalogs.

3. Art—Private collections—Oklahoma—Norman—Catalogs.

4. Fred Jones Jr. Museum of Art—Catalogs.

N6538.A4J36 2012

704.03'970074—dc23

2012003005

PP. II–III: DETAIL OF PLATE 109 (P. 129); P. IV: PLATE 10 (P. 21);
P. V: DETAIL OF PLATE 115 (P. 138); PP. VI–VII: DETAIL OF PLATE 91 (P. 107);
P. VIII: DETAIL OF PLATE 147 (P. 166); P. X: DETAIL OF PLATE 92 (P. 108);
PP. XII–1: DETAIL OF PLATE 114 (P. 136)

The paper in this book meets the guidelines for permanence and durability of the Committee on Production Guidelines for Book Longevity of the Council on Library Resources, Inc. ∞

Copyright © 2012 by the University of Oklahoma Press, Norman, Publishing Division of the University. Manufactured in China.

1 2 3 4 5 6 7 8 9 10

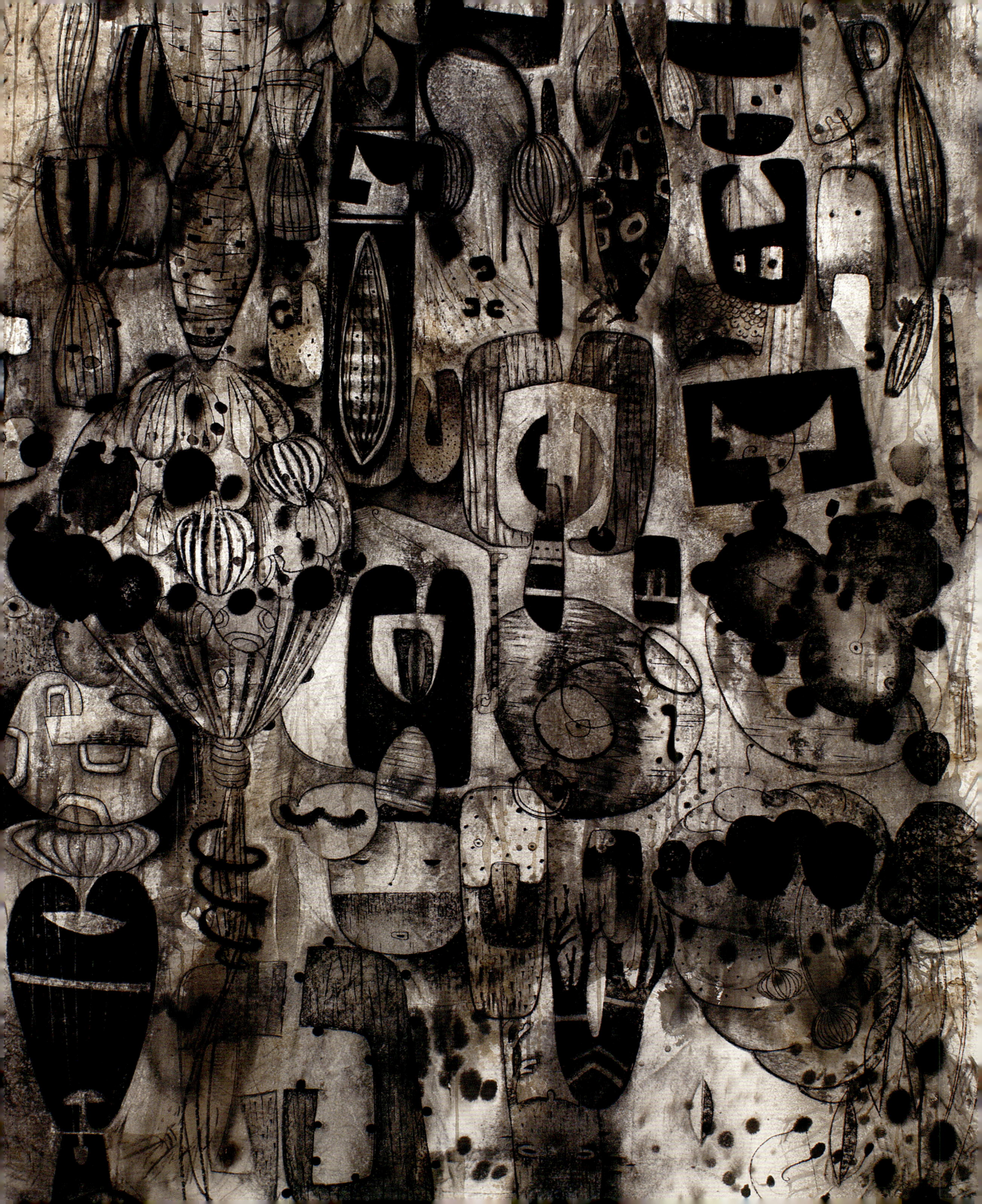

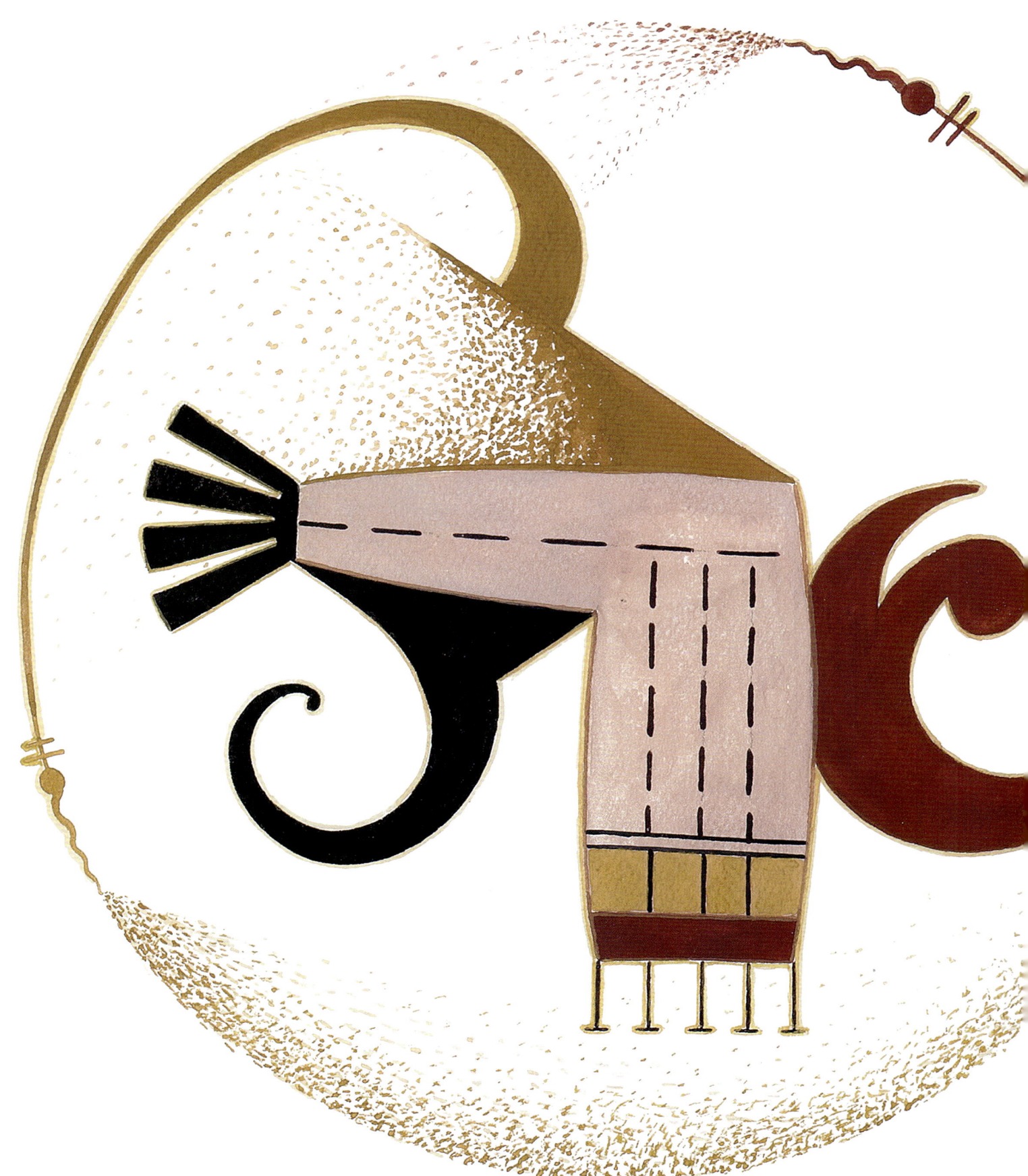

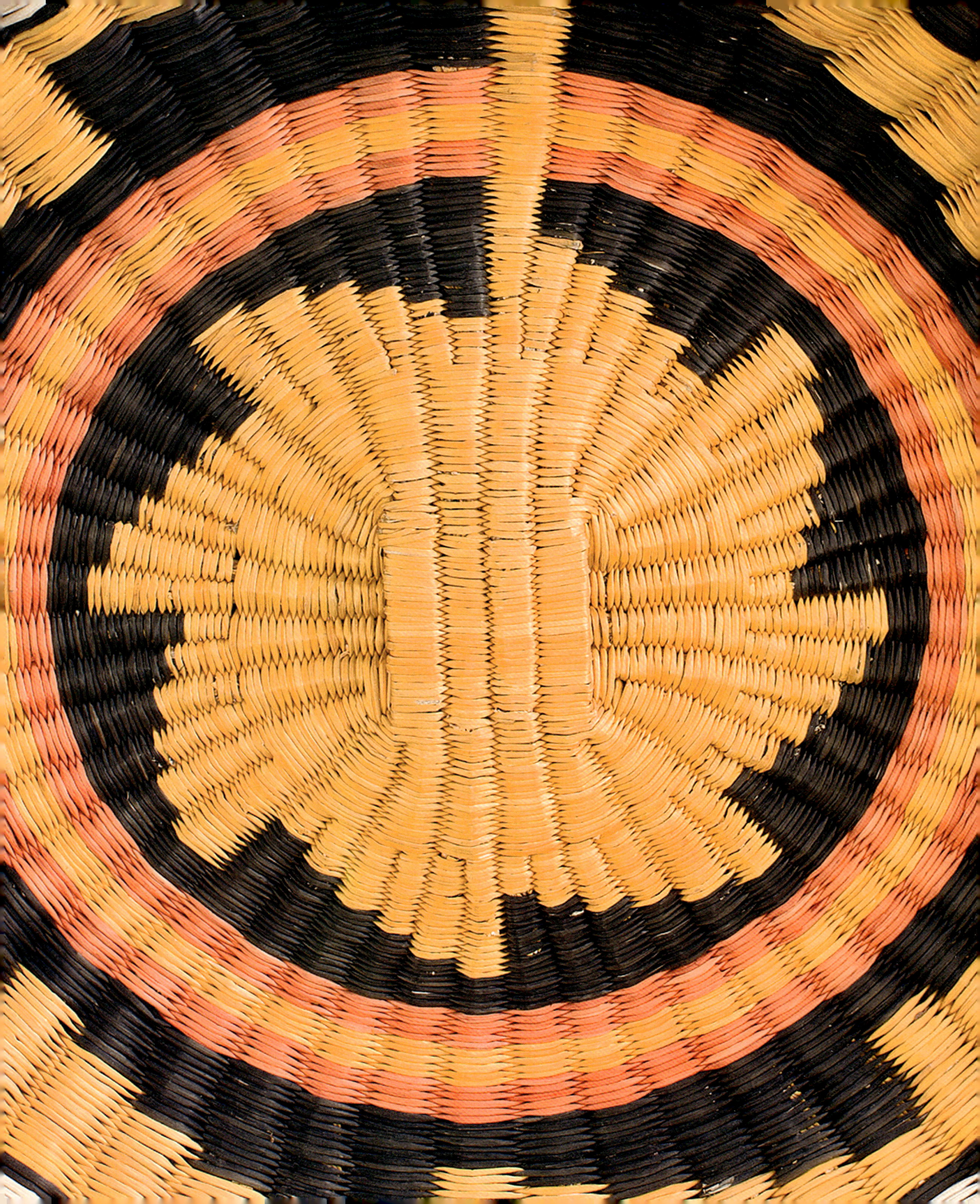

Foreword DAVID L. BOREN

NATIVE AMERICAN ART has long occupied a place of honor at the University of Oklahoma. In the mid-1920s, Oscar B. Jacobson, head of the OU School of Art and the first director of what became the Fred Jones Jr. Museum of Art on our campus, became aware of a group of young Kiowa artists from western Oklahoma and helped introduce their distinctive work to the world. In the years that followed, as the university's school of art trained and encouraged new generations of Native artists, its museum of art collected and exhibited their work. The recent creation of a new Ph.D. program in art history, focusing on the art of the American West and Native American art, the first of its kind in the nation, represents the ongoing commitment of the University of Oklahoma to the serious study of this vital subject.

The collections, exhibitions, and programs of the Fred Jones Jr. Museum of Art play an increasingly important role in furthering the educational mission of the University. Over the years, the many gifts and bequests given to our museum have not only enlarged and enhanced its collections but also have extended and magnified the museum's influence on and service to our students, faculty, and community. In 2010, James T. Bialac, the generous spirit we celebrate with this book, joined in this honored tradition by giving the university the largest and most significant gift of Native American art in its history. The extraordinary donation of more than 4,000 works of art, including 2,600 paintings and works on paper, 1,000 kachinas, and 100 pieces of jewelry, collected with care and discrimination over nearly a half century, is remarkable for its quality and beauty as well as its quantity.

The addition of the James T. Bialac Native American Art Collection has advanced the Fred Jones Jr. Museum of Art to the front rank of museums with extensive holdings of indigenous art. Virtually every significant American Indian artist of the twentieth and twenty-first centuries is represented in this assemblage, many of them by more than one work. The tribal affiliations of these talented creators span North America. Such an omnibus holding as this not only offers vast possibilities for exhibitions, programs, and publications but also presents unparalleled opportunities for students, faculty, and outside scholars to encounter and work with real objects.

The works depicted on the pages that follow merely sample Jim Bialac's superb collection. Future catalogues will deal more comprehensively with the various media and artists represented in this choice gathering of creativity. We thank Jim Bialac again for entrusting the University of Oklahoma with his legacy and believe that his decision to share both his collection and his passion with us will produce untold benefits for the University family for many years to come.

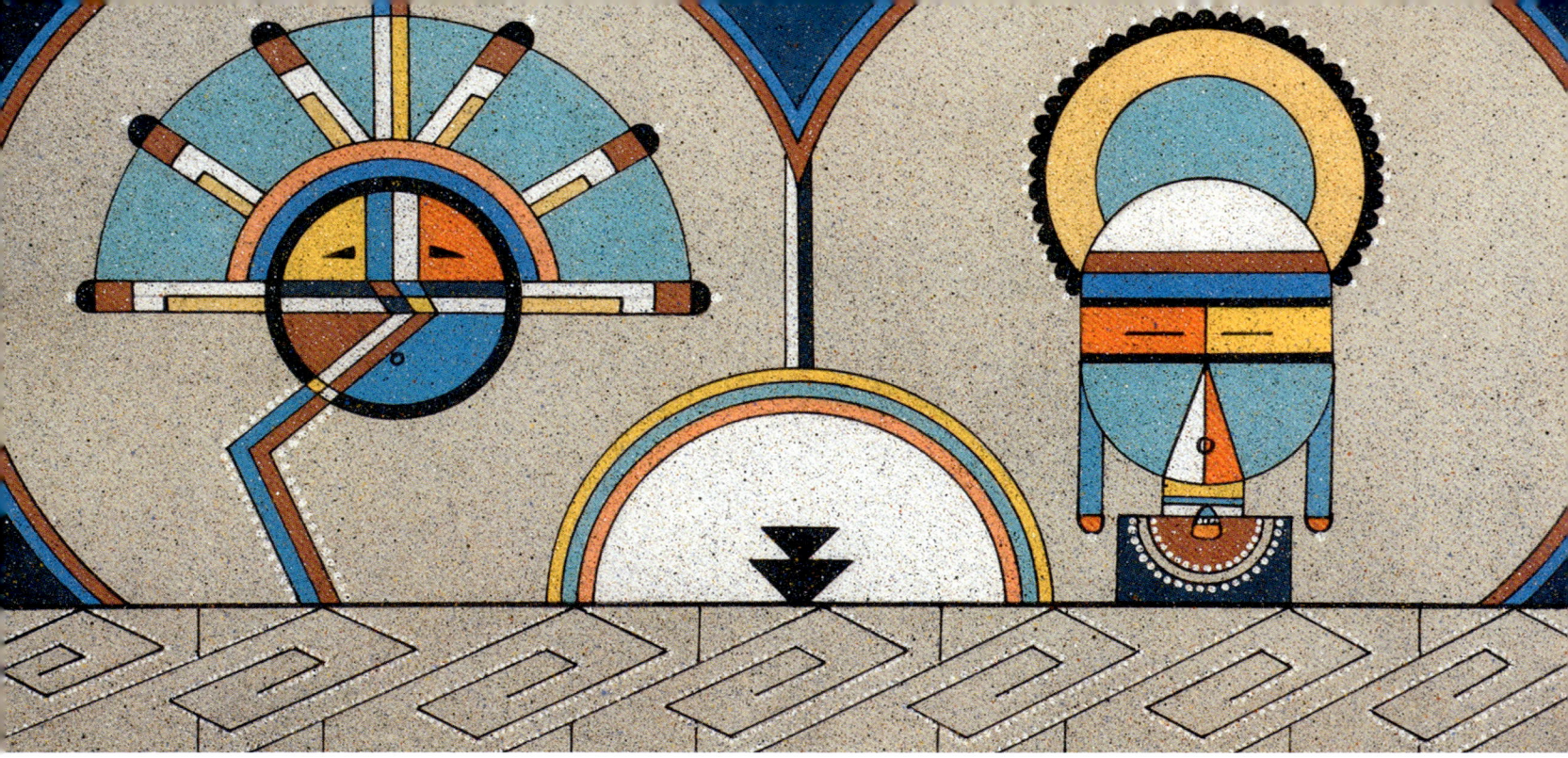

Preface and Acknowledgments

I FIRST MET JAMES BIALAC in 2009, when I visited him at his home in Phoenix, Arizona. I was there to speak with him about his collection of Native American art and to view it for the first time. Our conversation was fascinating, and I was overwhelmed with the scope of his treasures: nearly four thousand works of art, including paintings, sculptures, prints, kachinas, jewelry, ceramics, rattles, baskets, and textiles

According to my colleague Jackson Rushing, Mr. Bialac's collection was, by all definitions, one of the most important private collections of Native American art in the country. Dr. Rushing and I both knew how important it would be for the Fred Jones Jr. Museum of Art at the University of Oklahoma to welcome this extraordinary collection and to make it available to students and the

general public for generations to come. Mr. Bialac heard about our museum through his longtime friend Rennard Strickland, who had already bequeathed his collection of Native American art to the university. Dr. Strickland was able to convey to Mr. Bialac the depth of the University of Oklahoma's commitment, under the exceptional leadership of President David and First Lady Molly Shi Boren, to art and education. In fact, President Boren had already been aware of Mr. Bialac's collection before I made my trip to Phoenix, and when I returned, he asked me to work with Mr. Bialac on the donation agreement.

The James T. Bialac Collection was officially bequeathed to the university in March 2010. On that occasion Mr. Bialac was acknowledged in front of the Board of Regents, and the collection was transferred to the

University of Oklahoma in March of the following year. A part of it is now displayed on the first floor of the Stuart Wing in the James T. Bialac Gallery of Native American Art, as well as throughout the permanent collection of the museum. The unique and beautiful stained glass window by Fritz Scholder (*Pottery Motifs*) embellishes the wall of the Cy and Lissa Wagner Gallery, visible day and night along Boyd Street. More than three hundred works are displayed at Andrew M. Coats Hall, University of Oklahoma College of Law, for the benefit of students. Other works will be displayed across campus as time goes on.

Mr. Bialac's open mind and generosity also allowed us to make history through our negotiation of a long-term loan with three Arizona institutions: the University of Arizona, Arizona State University, and the Arizona Supreme Court. Under the stewardship of the University of Oklahoma, works from the Bialac Collection will be displayed at these Arizona locations for the appreciation of students and the broader public.

It is finally worth mentioning that the conservation of art always has been one of Mr. Bialac's greatest concerns. He therefore gave us his collection in impeccable condition—another impressive legacy of his donation for all viewers to keep in mind as they are viewing the Bialac Collection.

I would like first and foremost to thank President and Mrs. Boren for their ongoing support of Native American art and their commitment to education. I am also grateful to Regent Jon R. Stuart, his wife Dee Dee Stuart, and the Stuart Family Foundation for making it logistically possible to transfer the Bialac Collection to Oklahoma. I would further like to express my gratitude to the catalogue's contributors: Mary Jo Watson, Christy Vezolles, Mark Andrew White, Edwin L. Wade, Rennard Strickland, W. Jackson Rushing III, and Christina E. Burke. B. Byron Price, director of the University of Oklahoma Press, deserves special thanks for his support and assistance in the publication of this catalogue. And special thanks as well to Carol Haralson, for her beautiful design of the volume.

I would also like to thank Heather Ahtone for her help with this publication. Heather joined the museum staff in January 2012 as the James T. Bialac Assistant Curator of Native American and Non-Western Art. With President Boren's commitment to the study of American Indian culture and Mr. Bialac's generous gift to the University of Oklahoma, it became important to have a curator on staff dedicated to the scholarly representation of this increasingly large portion of the collection.

Finally, I would like to thank my staff, especially the Registration Department under the leadership of Miranda Callander, and the Preparation Department, including Brad Stevens, for making this adventure possible.

GHISLAIN D'HUMIÈRES

Wylodean and Bill Saxon Director, Fred Jones Jr. Art Museum

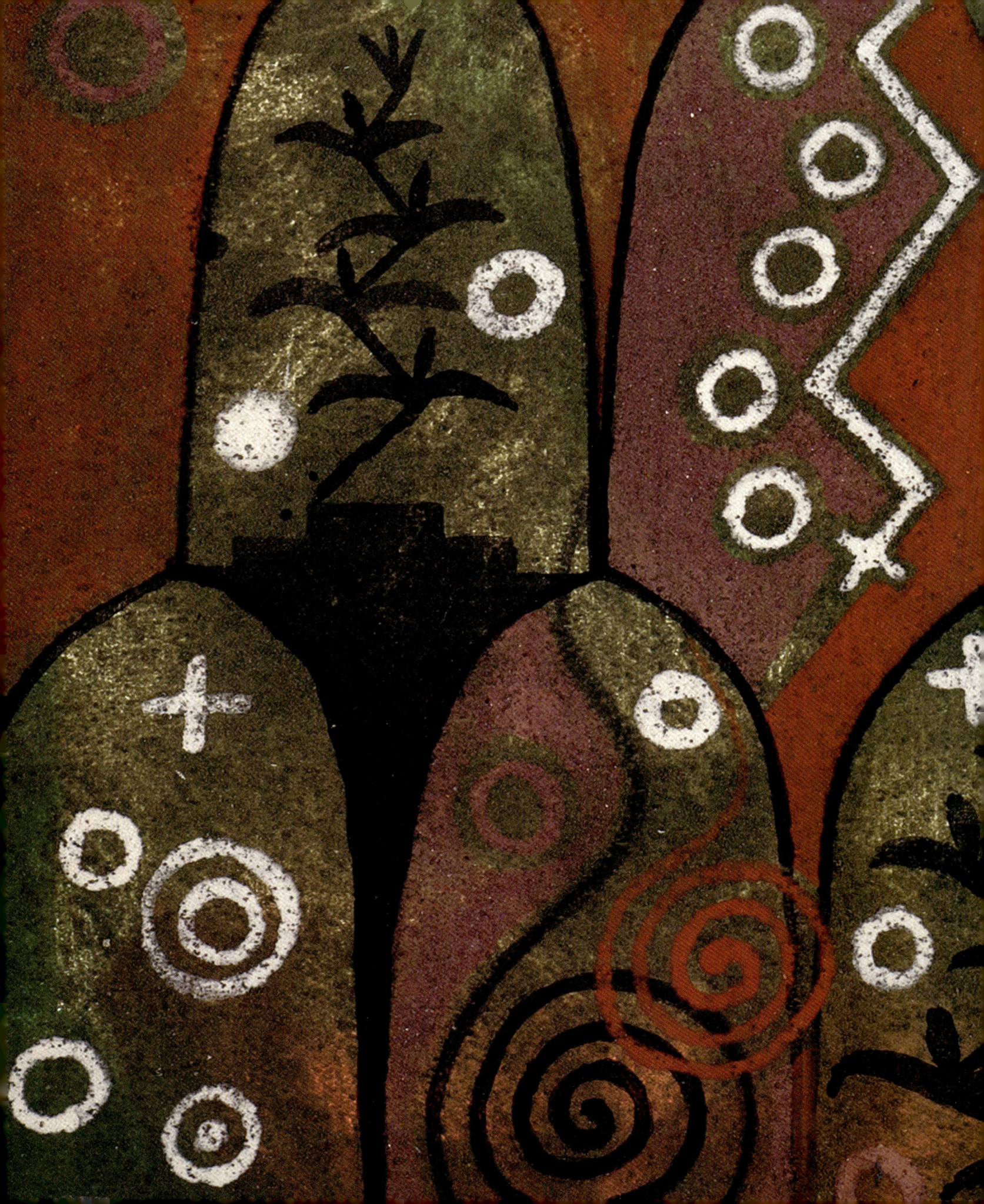

THE **James T. Bialac** NATIVE AMERICAN ART COLLECTION

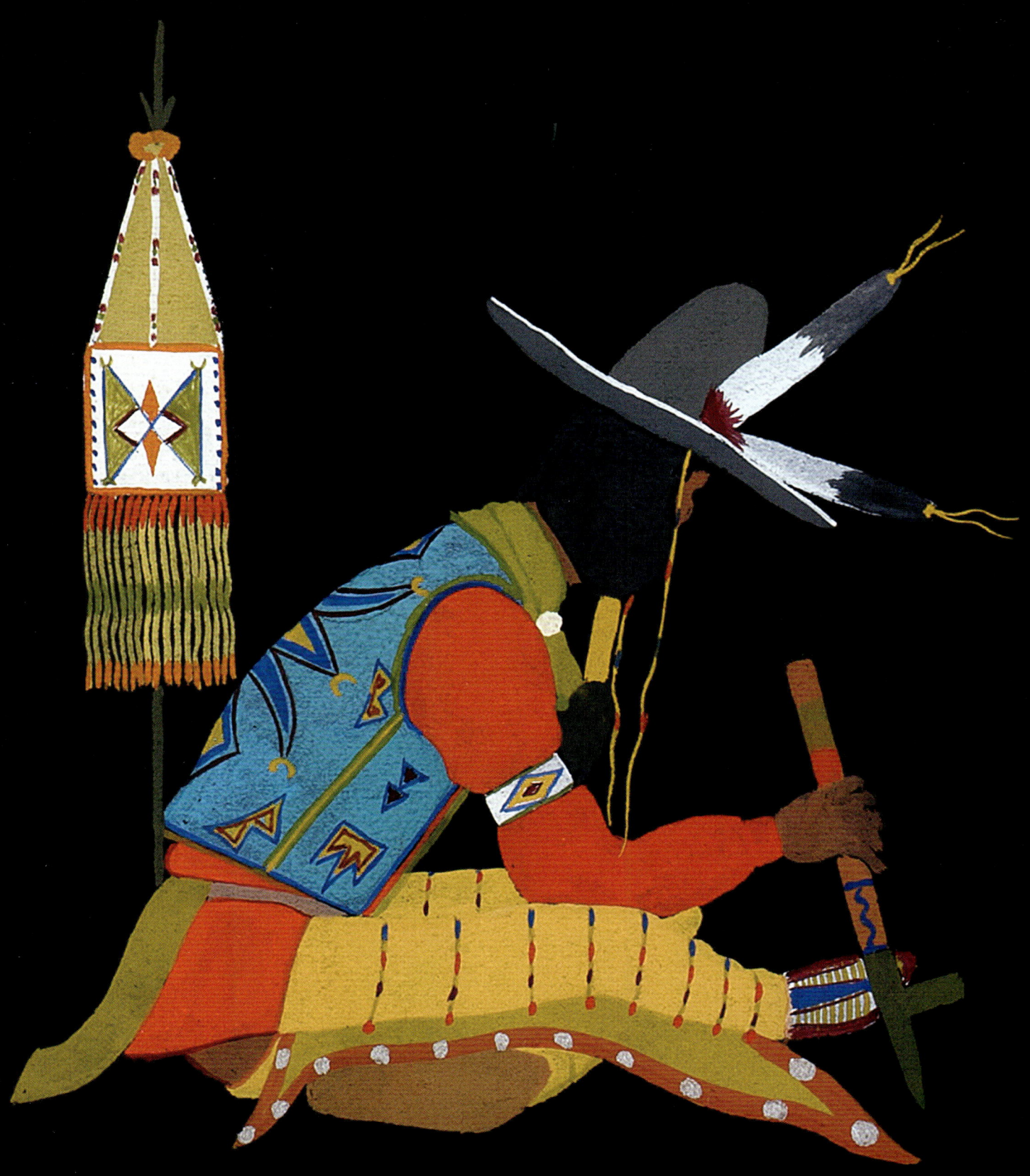

Introduction

A TRADITION OF APPRECIATION: NATIVE AMERICAN ART
AT THE UNIVERSITY OF OKLAHOMA

Mary Jo Watson

HOME TO NEARLY FORTY Native American tribes as well as immigrants from all parts of the world, Oklahoma is a land of diverse cultures. From its founding in 1890, the University of Oklahoma has honored the region's unique multicultural heritage—perhaps most visibly in the university's strong support of Native art and artists. This tradition of support began with Oscar B. Jacobson, the university's first director of the School of Art. A native of Sweden, Jacobson began his tenure at the university in 1915 and quickly recognized the fine qualities of Native art. His career at OU is identified with a determination to promote Native artists and expand public appreciation of their work.

In the 1920s, Jacobson began championing individual artists, especially a small group of Kiowa artists brought to his attention by Susie Peters, a young field matron at the Kiowa Agency in Anadarko. He exhibited the work of these Kiowa painters at the International Art Congress in Prague, Czechoslovakia, resulting in further high-profile showings. Through his promotional efforts, the names of Monroe Tsatoke, Stephen Mopope, Lois Smoky, and others would become

PLATE 1

MONROE TSATOKE

U.S., Kiowa, 1904–1937

Contemplation, 1929

Watercolor on paper, 8¼ x 6½ in.

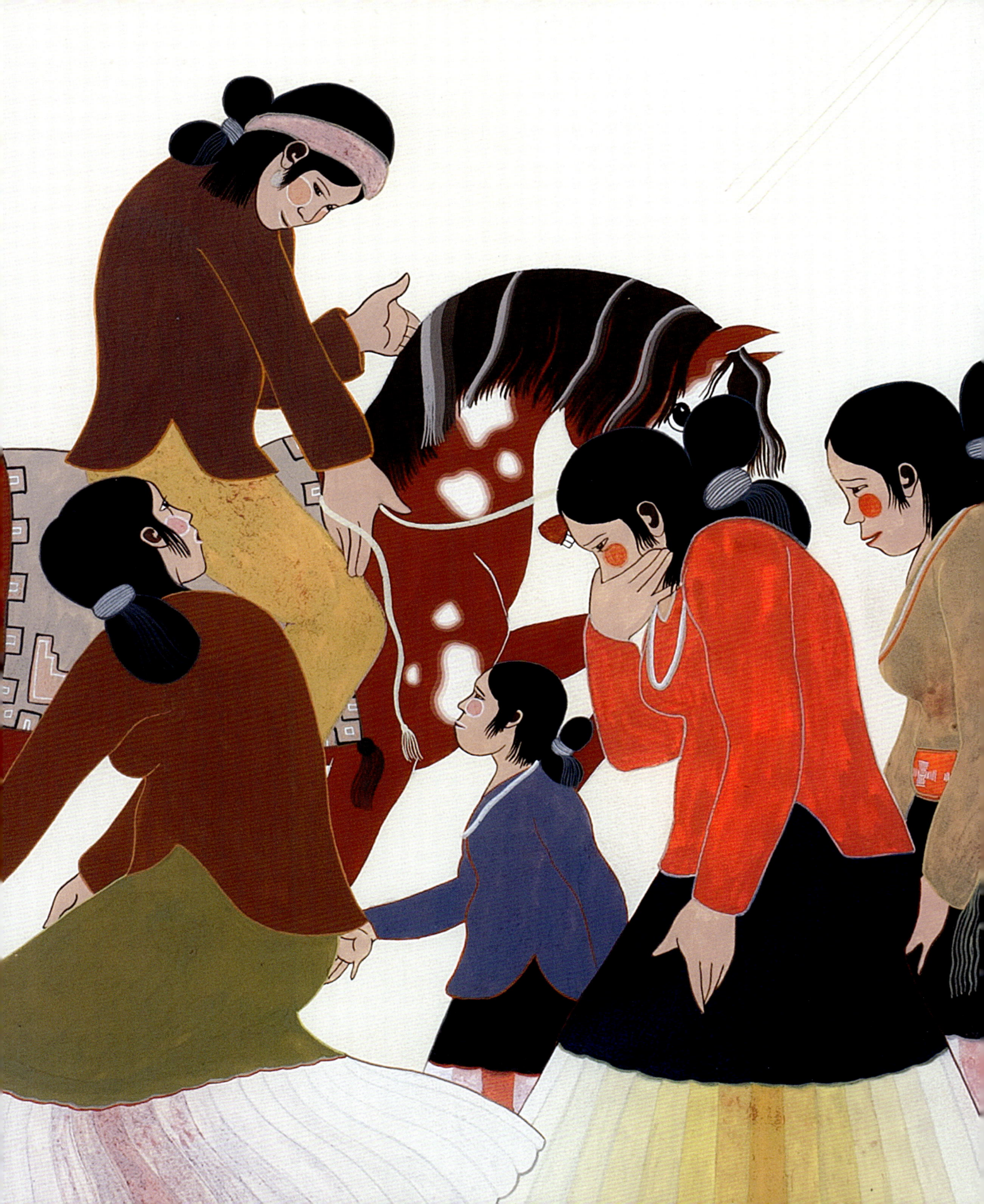

world famous. As a result, many Native artists gravitated to the university's art school, and in the 1950s Cheyenne artist Dick West and Nakota painter Oscar Howe received master's degrees in fine arts from the University of Oklahoma.

Although interest in Native arts waned somewhat after Jacobson's retirement from the School of Art in 1945, the University of Oklahoma saw a revival of interest in the 1980s. An expanding art history curriculum began to embrace the many epochs and genres of Native art, including precontact mounds cultures, art of the Northwest Coast, nineteenth-century Plains art, and, increasingly, contemporary Indian art. These new classes coincided with a strong national Indian art movement that emerged from the Bacone School of Art in Muskogee, Oklahoma, under the direction of Dick West. Also influential were the establishment in the 1960s of the Institute of American Indian Arts in Santa Fe, and the monumental 1977 exhibition *Sacred Circles: Two Thousand Years of North American Indian Art* at the Nelson-Atkins Museum of Fine Arts in Kansas City, Missouri. The University of Oklahoma began to proudly exhibit the works of the Kiowa artists during this period, and many serious art collectors donated Native artworks to the university's Fred Jones Jr. Museum of Art.

During the twentieth and early twenty-first centuries, the importance of Indian cultures and respective arts has been affirmed by the gifting to the university of many remarkable donations, including the William H. and Roxanne Thams, Richard H. and Adeline S. Fleischaker, Rennard Strickland, and Eugene B. Adkins collections, the latter shared with the Philbrook Art Museum. The collection recently given by James T. Bialac, showcased in this volume, significantly enhances the museum's offerings in the field of Native American art.

Jim Bialac's generous gift not only furthers popular understanding and fascination related to Native art, it enhances the university's century-long support of Native artists and their work. This commitment is especially apparent in the School of Art and Art History's well-established master's program and the recent addition of a Ph.D. program for the study of Native American art history and art of the American West. The James T. Bialac Collection will broaden the university's ability to foster Native American art studies and learning for years to come.

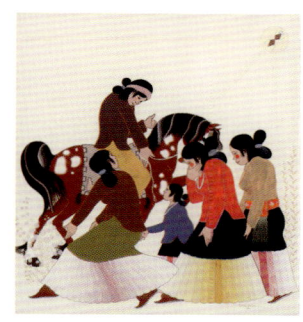

PLATE 2

GERALD NAILOR

U.S., Navajo, 1917–1952

Navajo Debutante, 1938

Watercolor on paper,

13½ x 12½ in.

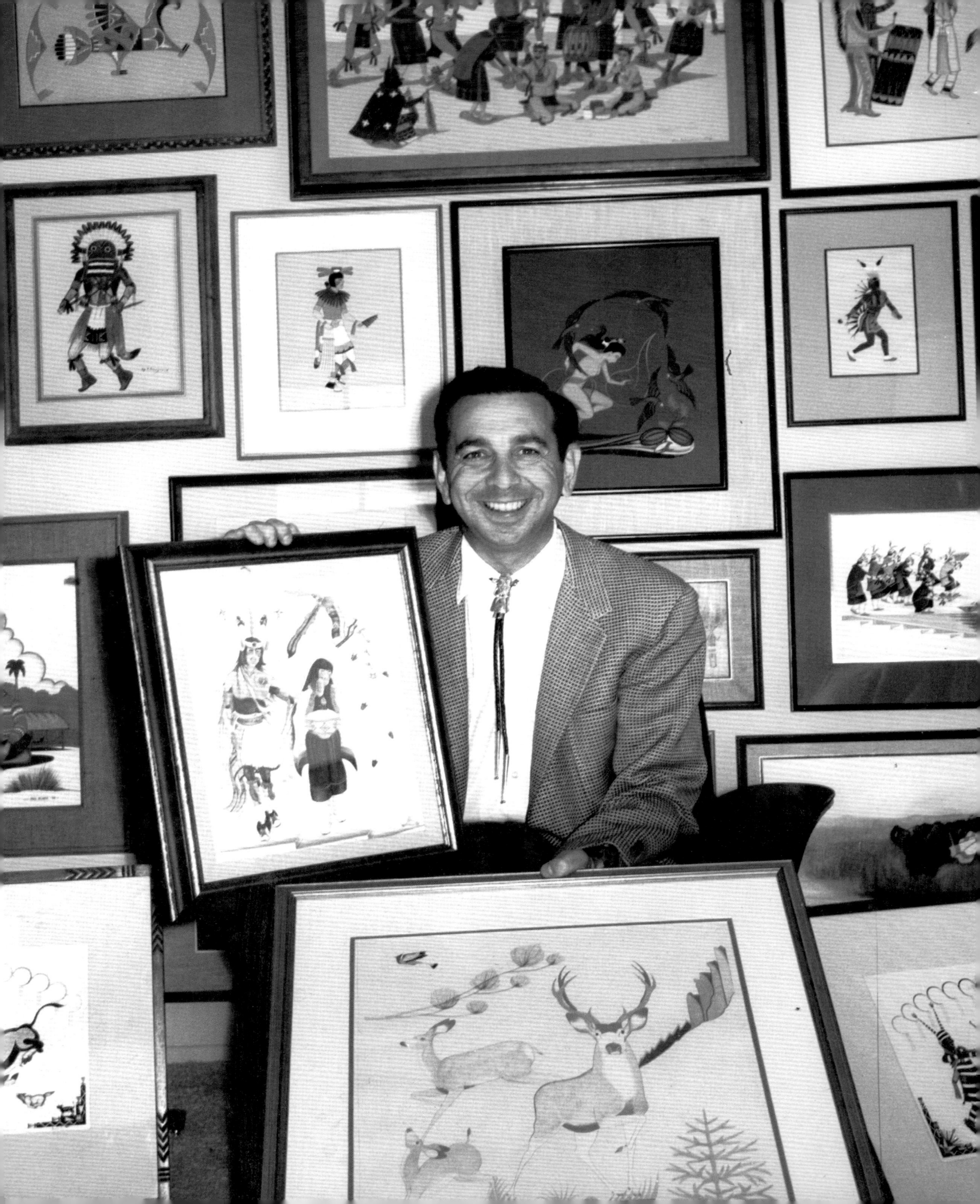

1 | James T. Bialac A LASTING LEGACY

Christy Vezolles

THE JAMES T. BIALAC COLLECTION of Native American Art is an encyclopedic compilation of American Indian easel paintings, augmented by an equally impressive collection of kachina dolls and various other three-dimensional works.[1]

The story of how this important body of approximately four thousand works came to be is itself remarkable. It is tale of a Midwest-born child of Jewish immigrants, who took a long circuitous journey to becoming a well-regarded attorney and renowned collector of American Indian paintings. A love of art was his prime motivator—and still is.

James T. Bialac, better known as Jim, was born to Samuel G. and Lee (Liebo) Bialac in 1928. His mother's parents had come from Russia in the late nineteenth century and settled in St. Paul, Minnesota, where she was later born and raised. His father, as a young boy, had immigrated with his family to Nebraska from Poland at the turn of the century. The young couple started their family in Omaha, Nebraska—the oldest son, Jerry, was followed by Jim and younger sister Alice.

James T. Bialac with his collection, c. 1967.

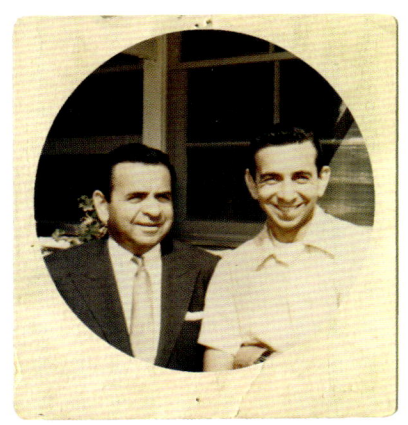

Samuel G. and James T.
Bialac, Phoenix,
Arizona, 1957.
Photograph courtesy of
James T. Bialac.

Among other things, the entrepreneurial Samuel G. Bialac made early cinema commercials. The family moved to New York, then to St. Paul, and westward to Los Angeles and Beverly Hills. There, the senior Bialac applied his savvy business skills as a developer and contractor. In 1945, Jim graduated from Beverly Hills High School and studied at Santa Monica City College. After transferring to the University of California at Berkeley, he earned his undergraduate degree in 1949 and worked in the family business.

About that time, he was drafted into the U.S. Army, where he was reportedly an excellent shot with a carbine. But he soon received an honorable discharge; he was highly allergic to the wool used in the uniforms and blankets. "I was in the service for six months and seventeen days," Bialac recalls. "From what I was told, I was the only U.S. soldier at that time that had a medical prescription permitting me to wear pajamas under my uniform and a third sheet on my bed."[2]

Although brief, Bialac's time in the military played an unexpected role in putting him on his future path as an art collector. While at Fort Lee, in Virginia, he saw an exhibition of eighteenth-century Italian art at the National Gallery of Art in Washington, D.C. "I fell in love with painting when I saw work by Francesco Guardi on exhibit," Bialac remembers. "I had never seen anything like it."

Returning home to California, he resumed working for the family business. Then, in the early 1950s, the Bialacs—including the three grown children—relocated to Arizona, where they built a 523-unit brick apartment complex on the west side of Phoenix. The largest in the state at the time, it was named Park Lee Alice, after Jim's mother and sister. Bialac managed the apartments for several years before deciding to become a lawyer, moving to Tucson to pursue studies at the University of Arizona College of Law.

One day, Jim wandered into Tom Bahti's Indian Arts near campus, where he discovered an array of jewelry, weaving, pottery, and something especially intriguing—kachina dolls (katsina tihu), small painted figures with an otherworldly quality. Fascinated, Bialac bought his first kachina doll from Bahti and was hooked. This purchase would lead to friendships not only with Tom and his son, Mark, but ultimately with dozens of the greatest Hopi carvers—as well as to the acquisition of approximately one thousand kachina dolls.

Upon graduation in 1959, Bialac passed the bar exam and opened a general practice office in Phoenix, representing clients in civil and criminal cases. In the early 1960s he visited the Heard Museum at the suggestion of Edward "Bud" Jacobson, a friend and fellow attorney. "I was told there was a big exhibit of a private collection of Indian Art—primarily painting. Works by many of the all-time masters were on display—Harrison Begay, Allan Houser, Oscar Howe," he recounts.

As with the Guardi paintings a decade prior, he was smitten. But this time, he was determined to learn more about the genre and the artists.

Hoping to gain further insight into collecting American Indian art, he called the collector, Byron Butler, and offered to treat him to lunch. "The collector—a prominent doctor—said he was too busy and hung up. Just like that! That lit a fire under me, and I set out to learn as much about Indian painting as I could." He began reading anything he could get his hands on as well as attending shows. He met Paul F. Huldermann, organizer of the *Scottsdale National Indian Arts Exhibition,* one of the premier venues of the time.

Huldermann owned the House of Six Directions, the gallery where in 1964, Bialac fell in love with and purchased a Robert Chee gouache entitled *Moccasin Game* (1961, plate 11), which depicts a traditional Navajo game played on long winter evenings. "Everything about it drove me wild, and it still does," he explains.[3] With the purchase of his first painting, he decided to collect American Indian art of the Southwest, which he did voraciously from the very beginning. Soon he befriended prominent collectors Henry Galbraith, Byron Harvey III, Clay Lockett, and Read Mullen, among others. As Bialac's personal taste developed, he was influenced not only by a growing cadre of local collectors but by others in California as well.

Early on, he became aware of two prominent San Franciscans, William and Leslie Van Ness Denman. Although they had passed away in 1959, they nonetheless left a mark on him. The Denmans had been dedicated to helping American Indian artists by purchasing and promoting Indian art, and to do so, they had traveled to the Southwest since before the reservations had roads.

Bialac admired their commitment and was intrigued to learn that for thirteen years, the Denmans had published elaborate Christmas cards featuring the paintings of artists such as Fred Kabotie and Otis Polelonema, in an effort to promote Indian art and culture. (Some forty years later, he was able purchase a set of the Denman cards, which he donated to the Fred Jones Jr. Museum of Art [FJJMA].) Inspired by the Denmans's tradition, he began creating holiday cards of his own, selecting one of his paintings and writing rhymed verse to accompany the image. It is a custom he has continued for decades.

The Denmans's most important allies in supporting southwestern Indian art were Charles deYoung Elkus and his wife, Ruth. They amassed a stunning collection of some 1,700 works—paintings, pottery, jewelry, kachina dolls, and textiles. Their son, Benjamin A. Elkus, had studied anthropology in college, and after retiring from a successful career as an insurance executive, he dedicated himself to organizing his parents' papers and collections, which he donated to the California Academy of Sciences. During one of Bialac's early trips to San Francisco, Ben

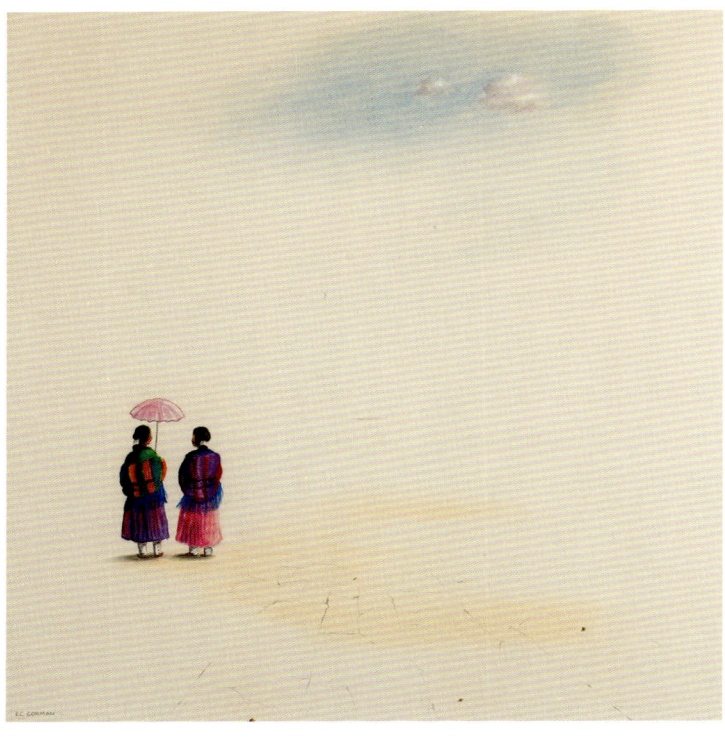

and Jim struck up a friendship. The importance of documenting and cataloging artworks was impressed on the nascent collector's mind—a process he has meticulously adhered to throughout decades of acquiring new works.

He also met Patrick Swazo Hinds and his family, as well as R. C. Gorman, Native artists who at the time were living in San Francisco. "I purchased a number of paintings and became friends with all of them. I still have a letter from R. C. saying, 'Come back and buy more paintings—I'm starving!'" Bialac recalls. "I purchased a painting at that time that I feel is one of his most outstanding—*The Parasol and the Cloud.*"

Soon, the collector who had spurned him— Byron Butler—became convinced of his sincere interest in the genre. Butler and his wife, Marilyn, would become Bialac's dear friends. Bialac served as legal counsel for Marilyn Butler Fine Art and the Elaine Horwitch Galleries, as well as for many of the artists they represented, including Fritz Scholder and Emmi Whitehorse. It was not uncommon for him to start a case for an artist and end up with a good friend and a new painting. "I did a lot of legal work for many of the dealers and artists in the state. I mainly collected locally, and at the time felt most comfortable with the art from the tribes of the Southwest. Painting was my main interest and still is," he says.

As Bialac's expertise and collection rapidly grew, Bud Jacobson convinced him to accept a position on the board of trustees for the Heard Museum, where he continues to serve as a life trustee. In 1967 the museum mounted an exhibit of about one hundred of his paintings—the first of several such showings—which connected him with more collectors, artists, and scholars of American Indian art, such as Clara Lee Tanner, who later curated and wrote the catalogue for an exhibit of his works at the Arizona State Museum.

Tanner was an anthropology professor at the University of Arizona, and her husband, John Tanner, owned the Desert House Crafts in Tucson. Sharing a mutual love of Indian art, the three became great friends. "Clara Lee and John were lovely people and extremely knowledgeable," he recalls. "She wrote several books on Native American Indian art. When we met, she was working on her painting book." In 1972, she included about thirty of Bialac's works in *Southwest Indian Painting: A Changing Art* (the expanded second edition to her 1957 publication).

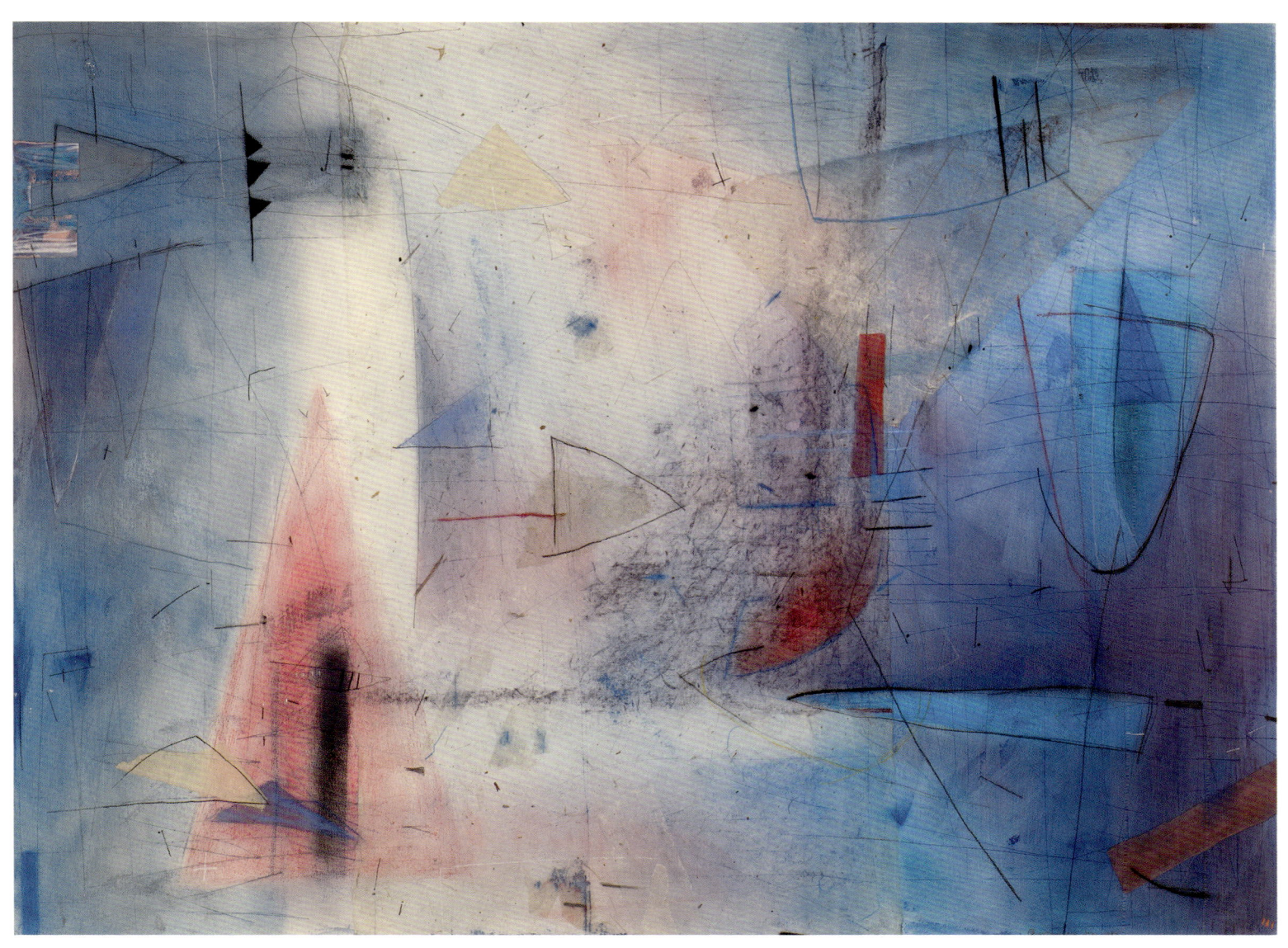

PLATE 4

EMMI WHITEHORSE

U.S. Navajo, b. 1956

Kin'nah'zin #413, 1984

Mixed media, 32 x 48 in.

Over the years, scores of Bialac's paintings and kachina dolls have been featured in books on American Indian art that—like Tanner's—have become classic tomes. Patricia Janis Broder's *Hopi Painting* and *Earth Songs, Moon Dreams* feature pieces from his collection, as do Lois and Jerry Jacka's *Art of the Hopi: Contemporary Journeys on Ancient Pathways* and *Enduring Traditions: Art of the Navajo,* Tom and Mark Bahti's *Southwestern Indian Ceremonials,* and others. In some of his many books on kachina dolls, Barton Wright included images of several dolls Bialac had collected. Bialac's artworks can even be found in the German book *Indianische Kunst,* edited by Gerhard Hoffman.[4]

Examples from Bialac's extensive eclectic collection can also be seen in publications by the Smithsonian's National Museum of the American Indian, *National Geographic, American Indian Art Magazine, Arizona Highways,* and *Western Art Collector. Native Peoples* featured a two-part article on the collection, written by Bialac's close friend Joel Harnett, a retired vice-president of *Look* magazine.

In addition, Bialac has been extremely generous in loaning his artworks to museums throughout the United States and Germany, as well as donating major gifts to various museums, particularly the Heard Museum. For Bialac, the end game is not simply the acquisition of art. It is the ability to share the genre, to inform and excite people about the works and the cultures from which they sprang.

As a result, artists, dealers, museum officials, academics, and collectors throughout the country are familiar with the man and his collection. "Some people have told me over the years, 'You're crazy to have your name published with your paintings! What if someone steals them?' But the truth is, there's little risk involved," Bialac explains. "The community of collectors is fairly small, and there is little opportunity for a thief to sell a work that is recognized as belonging to a known collector." In fact, there has never been a single attempted theft from his collection. On the contrary—Bialac's reputation as a collector, enhanced by the publication and exhibition of his holdings, has actually resulted in remarkable paintings being offered to him from various sources.

For example, a museum director (whom Bialac prefers not to name) was offered a spectacular early Fred Kabotie painting of a Hopi Snake Dance (*Snake Dance,* c. 1918, plate 80). It had been passed from writer Edward Larouque Tinker to Don Antonio Santamarina, a Buenos Aires collector of Impressionist paintings, then on to his son, Juan Carlos Santamarina. Eventually, the painting made its way back to Arizona, when the younger Santamarina died. Familiar with Bialac's collecting appetite and association with Kabotie, the director phoned Bialac. "The museum already had three or four paintings on the same subject, and the director felt that if he

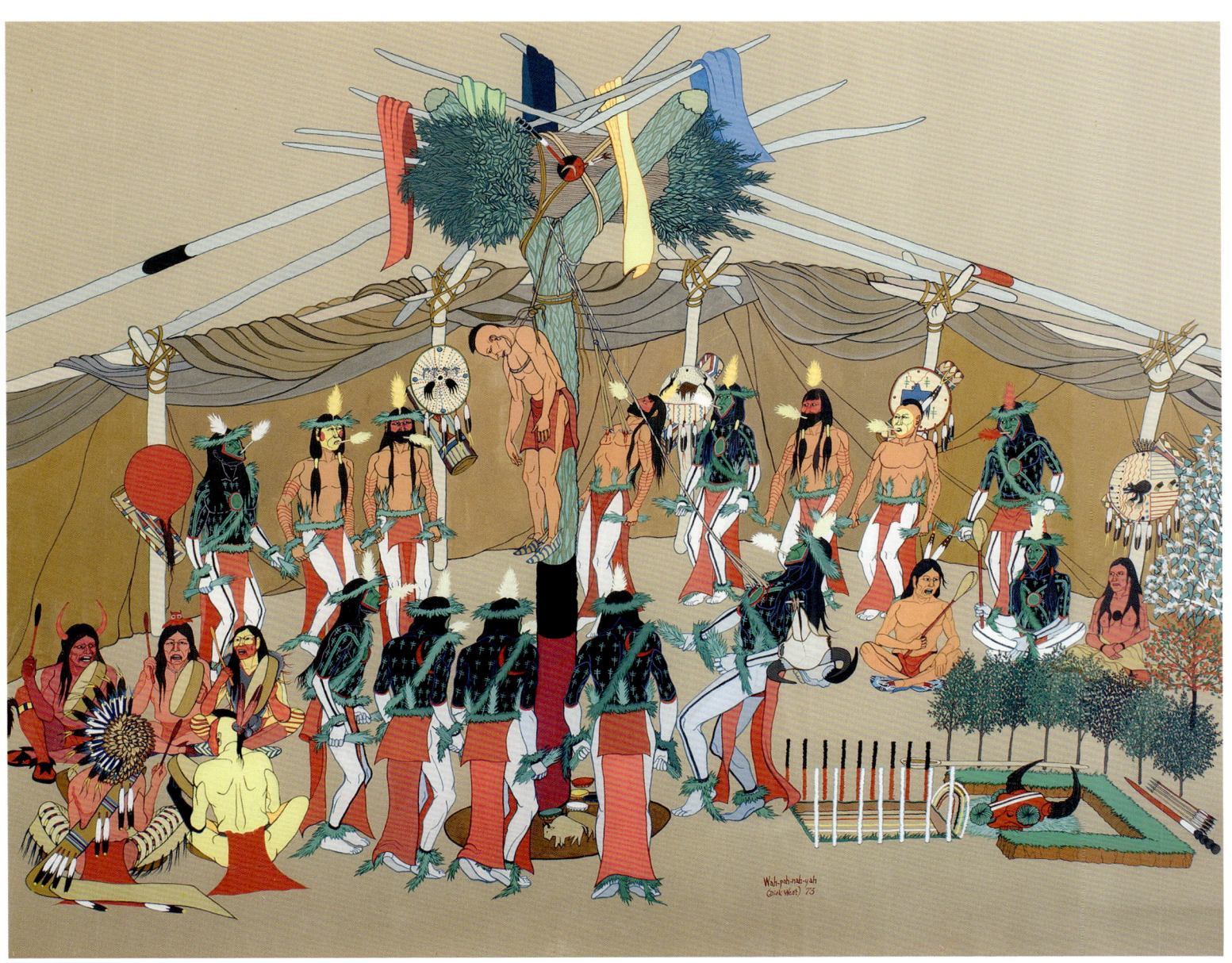

PLATE 5

WALTER RICHARD "DICK" WEST, SR.

(**WAH-PAH-NAH-YAH**)

U.S., Cheyenne, 1912–1996

Southern Cheyenne Sun Dance, or

"The Great Medicine Lodge Ceremony," 1973

Watercolor on paper, 31½ x 40 in.

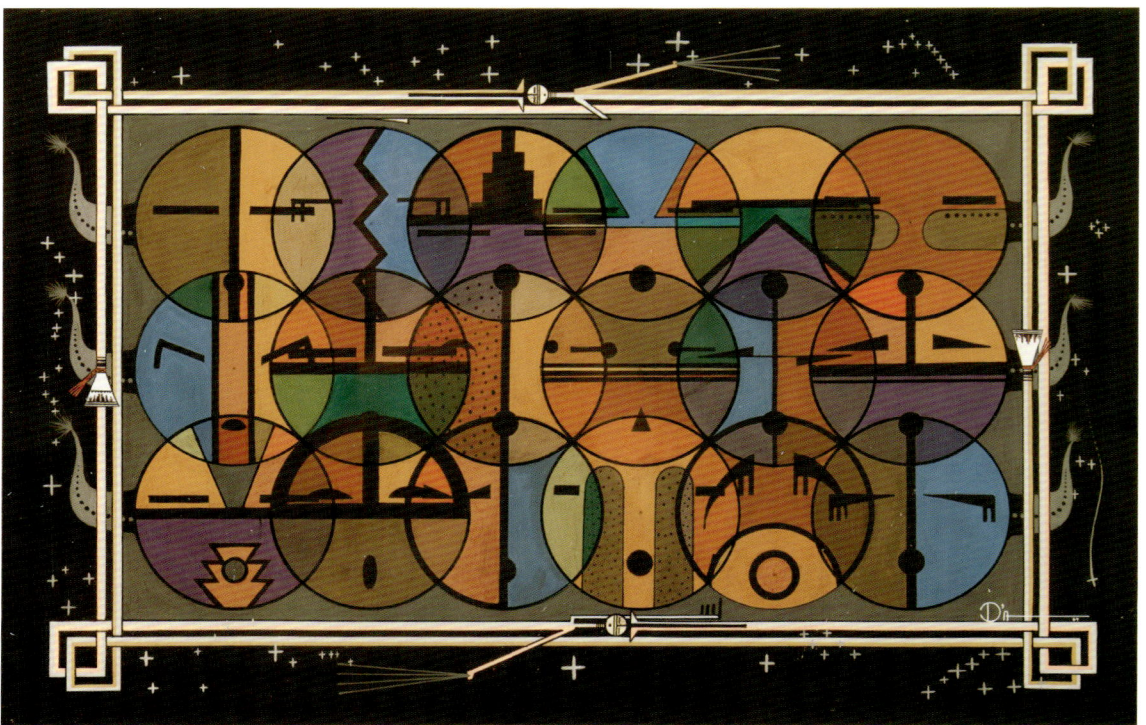

bought another one, his board of trustees might be a little skeptical about his purchases," Bialac recalls. "Having known Fred for so many years, and as his lawyer, I was very pleased. I, of course, bought it. As you can see, it's a very beautiful painting, showing the members of the Snake Clan and the Antelope Clan, who take part in the ceremony, as well as the place where the snakes are kept during the dance. Fred saw the painting at my house one night when we were having dinner here. He remembered it vividly and stated he completed it in Santa Fe in 1918."

Bialac developed enduring friendships with renowned artists who now figure prominently in his collection: Pablita Velarde, Gilbert Atencio, Dick West, Patrick DesJarlait, Helen Hardin, George Morrison, Harrison Begay, Allan Houser, Tony Da, and Fritz Scholder, to name a few. "Part of the fun of collecting is meeting the artists in their own villages or reservation homes and seeing, along with them, the ceremonies they'll later paint," he says.

Although he has rubbed shoulders with the most influential American Indian artists of the twentieth century, he is by no means stuck in the past. Bialac has befriended both preeminent and emerging artists of each decade and continues to do so, including Tony Abeyta, Marla Allison, America Meredith, Mateo Romero, Norma Howard, Shonto Begay, Jeffery Gibson, and so on. The current crop of artists who have captured his interest and won his respect and friendship often employ new media, techniques, and concepts.

Much attention has been focused on the nearly 2,500 paintings Bialac donated to the FJJMA. An assemblage of more than 1,500 three-dimensional items was also a large part of the generous gift, two-thirds of which are kachina dolls and other related items. Represented are esteemed carvers such as Alvin "Makya" James, Sr.; Peter, Henry, and Mary Shelton; Arthur Holmes; Neil David; Alfred "Bo" Lomahquahu; and many others. In a show of affection by the carvers, some of the Koshares display a striking resemblance to Bialac. "I did a lot of legal work up on the Hopi Reservation," he explains. "I represented four of the tribal chairmen, as well as many carvers and jeweler Charles Loloma in personal matters. Artist Hopid, the Hopi Cultural Center, and Hopi Arts & Crafts were also clients of mine." He made many friends among the Hopis and was particularly attracted to their depictions of the katsinam.

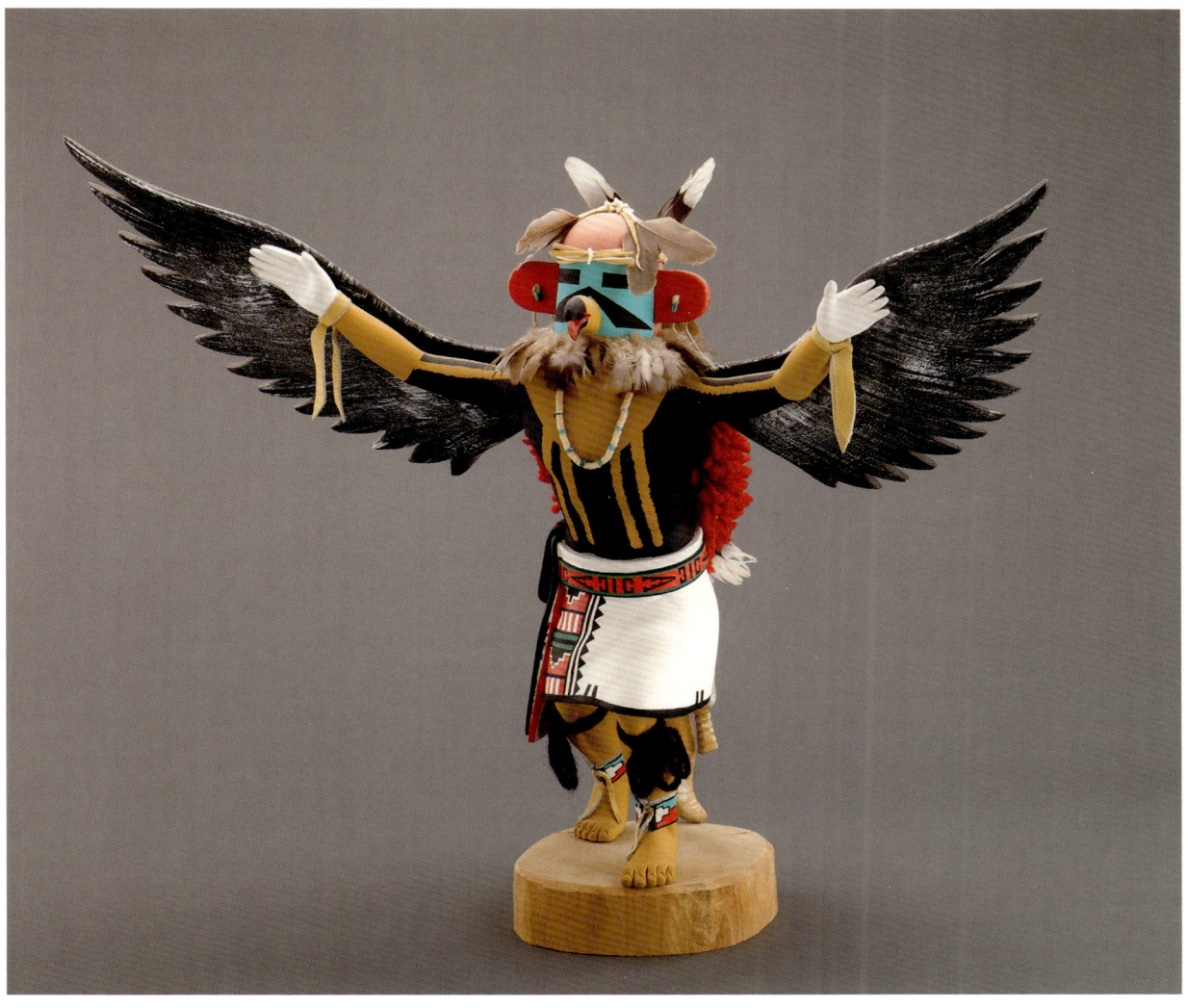

PLATE 8

ALVIN "MAKYA" JAMES, SR.

U.S., Hopi Pueblo,

1936–c. 2003

Mr. Bialac Koshare, 2003

Cottonwood root,

paint, stain, 15 1/16 in.

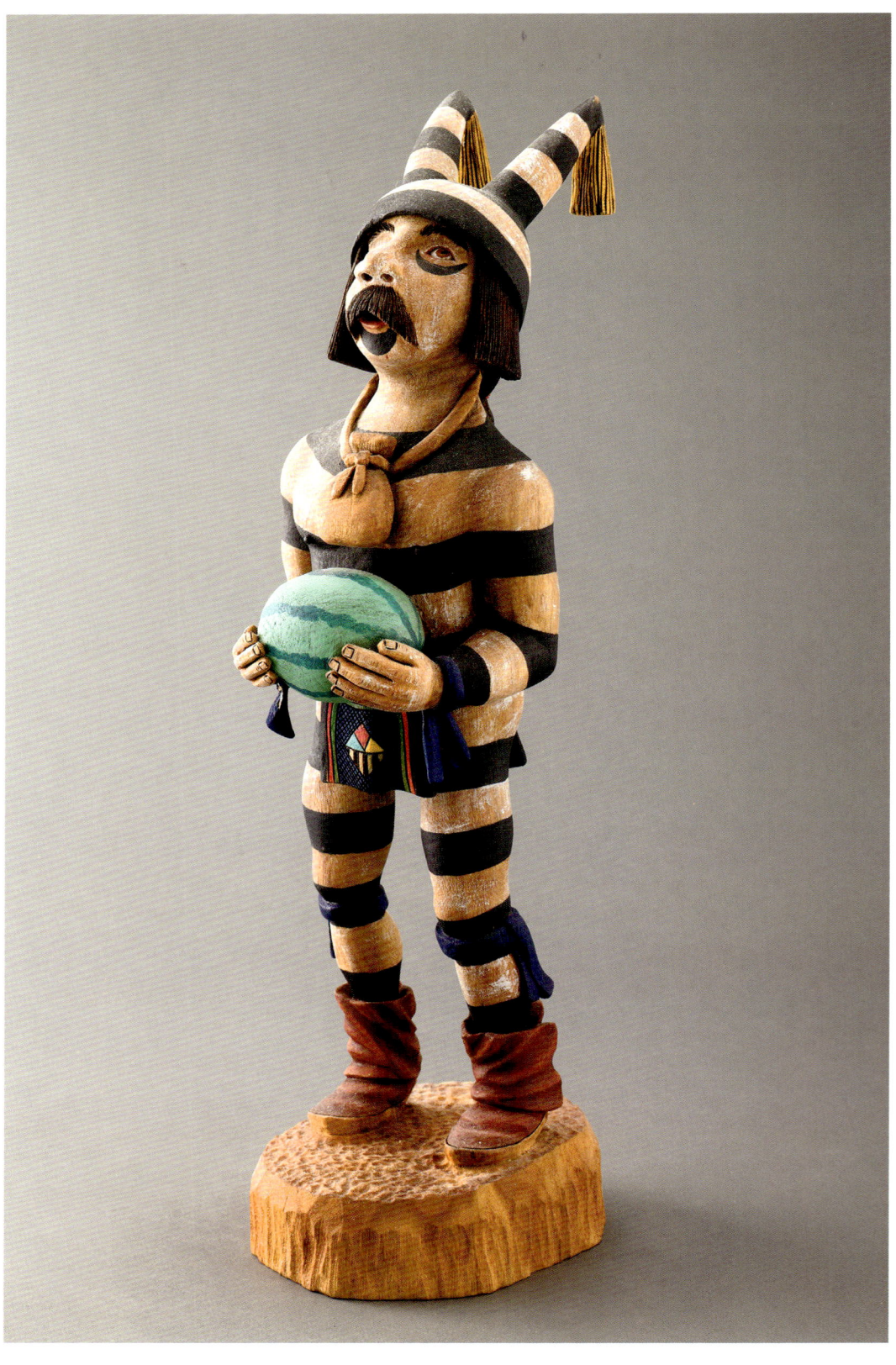

Also counted as friends are sculptors John Hoover and Roxanne Swentzell, whose works join that of Allan Houser; potters Camilio "Sunflower" Tafoya and Tammy Garcia; as well as jewelers Charles Lovato, Jesse Monongya, and Denise Wallace. Bialac collected the artists' work not just to acquire more things, but because he was genuinely interested in the artists themselves and what they wanted to express through their art. "Most of the artists I have met were such lovely people to talk with, to be with, to collect from, that it was a complete pleasure. I can say that from the earliest times, when I started collecting, clear up to now, with the new generation of artists," Bialac says. "I tried my best to bring in who I considered to be the best in the field."

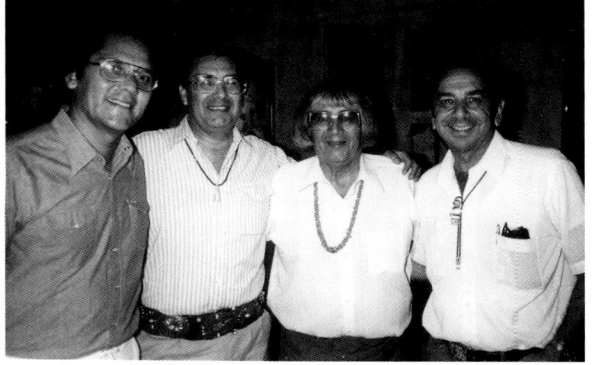

Al Qöyawayma (potter), Robert Piestewa Ames (judge), Charles Loloma (jeweler) and Jim Bialac, Santa Fe, New Mexico, 1984. Photograph courtesy of James T. Bialac.

The collection is especially strong in works by Arizona Navajos and Hopis from the pueblos of New Mexico. As he became more familiar with work from other areas, the collection became more diverse. Native peoples from regions across North America are represented, from the Arctic, to the Northeast Woodlands, the Southeast, the Plains, and into Mexico. The collections spans from about 1900 to present day.

In 1996, noted author and former Philbrook Art Center curator Jeanne Snodgrass King (Cherokee) guest curated *Drawn from Memory,* an exhibit of Bialac's finest paintings, at the Heard Museum. In the exhibition catalogue, she quotes Bialac saying, "I collect them for their beauty and honesty." She adds, "Jim Bialac's collection can tell pretty much the history of Indian painting. . . . Not too many collections can show this. . . . That's what I found exciting. Jim collected with a very open mind."[5]

Bialac believes strongly in trusting his own instincts rather than relying on the opinions of others: "If I liked it and could afford it at the time, I bought it. It was never important to me whether it was a known artist or not, or if it won a ribbon or not. I did not ever purchase a painting just to have a particular artist in the collection. Any competent collector collects for his own vision, and not that of another." This approach has resulted in a world-class collection befitting an institution of higher learning.

The University of Oklahoma's doctoral program in Native American art makes the gift all the more meaningful and valuable, as it will advance the scholarship of the subject. But Bialac is perhaps most pleased that the work will be continually displayed—on a rotating basis—not only in the James T. Bialac Native American Art Gallery, but also throughout the campus. "This way, many people will have access to the works on a continuing basis. The last thing any collector wants is to have his collection sitting in the basement of a museum."

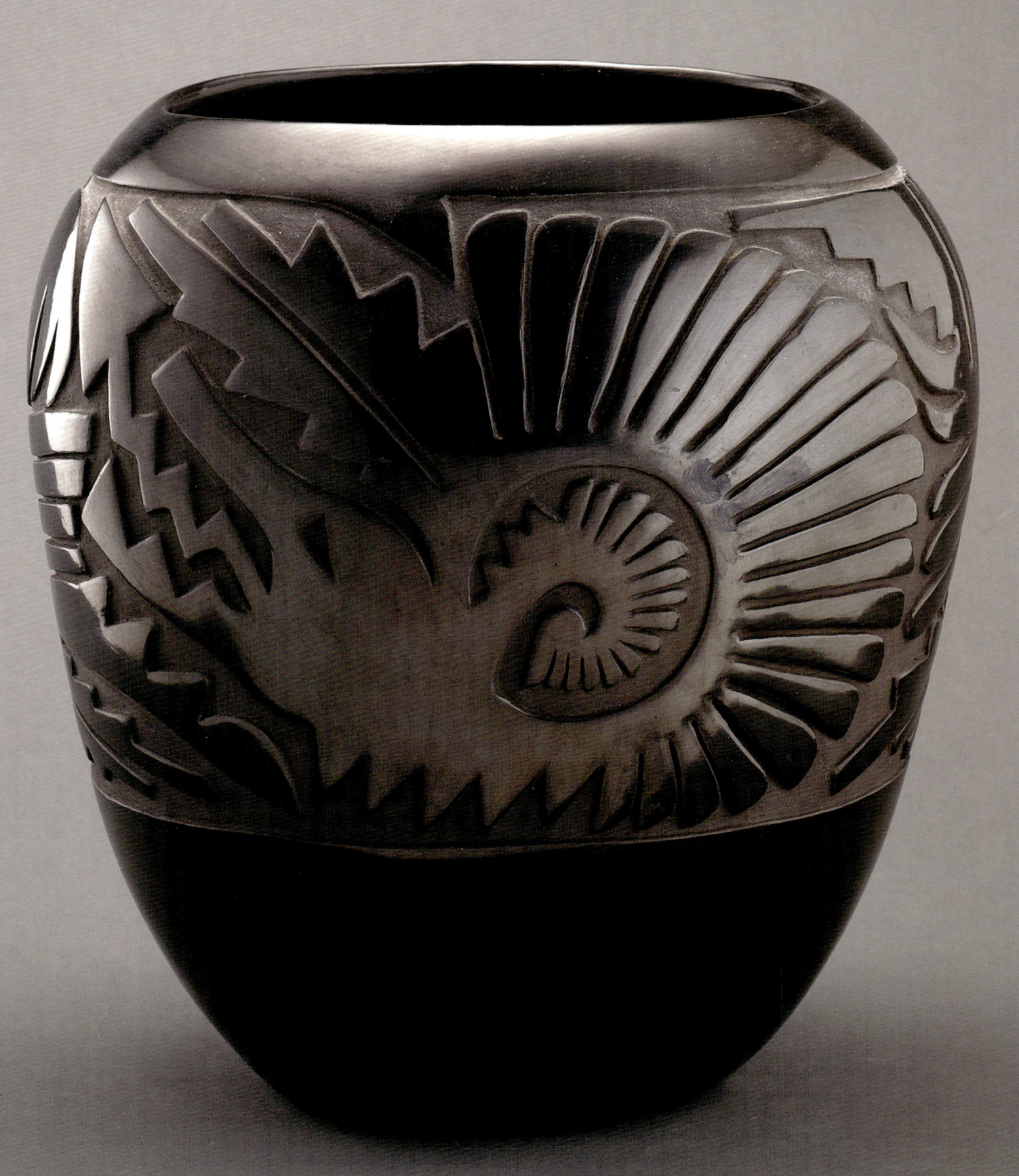

Bialac's enthusiasm for sharing his collection is nothing new. For decades, hundreds of his paintings have been on loan to his alma mater, the University of Arizona, and to Arizona State University—primarily the law schools. "When I visit the campuses, it excites me to hear how much the students, faculty, and administration love the paintings," he explains. "They seem to really enjoy them, and it enhances their understanding of art and Native cultures as well." Additional paintings are on display within the Arizona court system.

The paintings currently on loan from the Bialac Collection will remain in Arizona for as long as the institutions wish to retain them. "I believe this may be the very first time an agreement of this type has been forged between institutions in two different states," Bialac notes. "It's a win-win situation, and I'm very pleased with the outcome."

Ever mindful that the work is worth preserving for posterity, Bialac has a keen interest in its conservation. In his earlier days of collecting, he visited a California museum that had fallen on hard times. Although they had one of the finest basket collections in the world, he was shocked by the conditions in which he found the artworks.

"One of the paintings they had was a watercolor by Gerald Nailor," he recalls. "It had no glass to protect it and was covered with dust, as well as having acid mats. The baskets were treated in the same way—covered with dust and dirt. This convinced me that I must, in my collection, do my best to conserve things and see that they are properly cared for so that they would not deteriorate. Works on paper are particularly fragile. Over 90 percent of the paintings I have given to the Fred Jones Jr. Museum are conservatively protected. They have been deacidified, have acid-free archival mats and frames and UV blocking glass—particularly the watercolors. I feel that is very important, because as a result of that, the museum will not have to have a conservator do a lot of work on the collection, and it will be valid for the next 150 years or so."

James T. Bialac's foresight will ensure that the generous gift of his cherished collection of American Indian art to the Fred Jones Jr. Museum of Art at the University of Oklahoma will remain a lasting legacy for the education and enjoyment of generations to come.

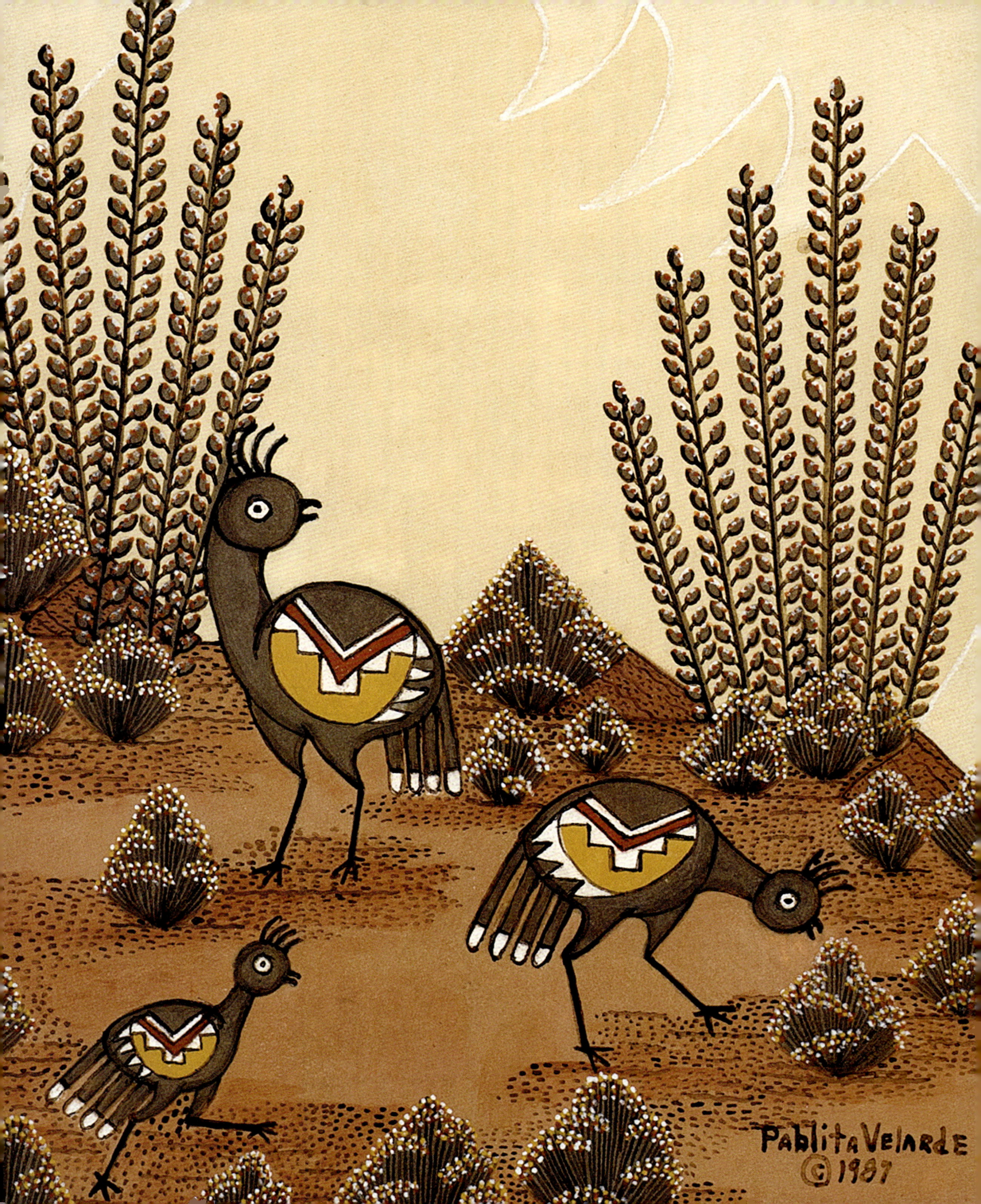

2 | James T. Bialac

AND THE PATRONAGE OF AMERICAN INDIAN ART

Mark Andrew White

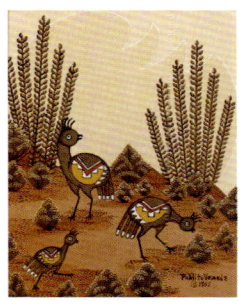

SCOTTSDALE attorney James T. Bialac began collecting American Indian painting and sculpture in 1964, during a pivotal decade for the field. Although a small number of museums and private collectors had helped to establish a system of patronage for American Indian fine art in the 1920s and 1930s, a younger generation of patrons entered the market in the late 1950s, attracted by both established exhibition annuals, such as the Philbrook Art Center's *American Indian Artists Exhibition* and the *Intertribal Ceremonial* in Gallup, and by newer exhibitions, such as the *Scottsdale National Indian Arts Exhibition,* held in Bialac's hometown. As Clara Lee Tanner observed in 1973, "Although both private and public collections existed prior to 1950, certainly the trend toward collecting took a new vigor during the late 1950s and was accelerated throughout 1960–70. Literally hundreds of paintings found their way into collections during these years. A feverish attendance at preview exhibits and equally feverish buying of paintings encouraged a healthy revival of painting and undoubtedly contributed to the making of full-time artists out of some young Indians who might otherwise have been forced to follow other endeavors."[1]

PLATE 10

PABLITA VELARDE

U.S., Santa Clara Pueblo, 1918–2006

Mimbres Quails, 1987

Natural pigments on board,

9½ x 7½ in.

This influx of new patronage also encouraged the diversification of American Indian fine arts in the 1960s. Younger patrons like Bialac developed interests in the contemporary styles introduced by artists trained at the Institute of American Indian Arts (IAIA) or institutions of higher education. This prompted annuals to create categories for the classification and award of painting and sculpture that followed established, or "traditional," styles of painting and "modern," or contemporary styles.[2] Bialac frequented these annuals, purchasing works by artists as diverse as Helen Hardin and Fred Beaver, and his increasing renown as a collector eventually resulted in the public exhibition of his collection on multiple occasions as well as the inclusion of works from his collection in academic publications. His regular attendance at annuals and exhibitions also afforded him the opportunity to meet many contemporary artists, which led not only to the formation of close friendships with artists such as Fritz Scholder, Michael Kabotie, and John Hoover but later to an interest in developing talents such as Tony Abeyta and America Meredith.

Concomitant with the changes occurring in the field, the 1960s also witnessed significant advances in the scholarship of American Indian art. Important histories were published by Clara Lee Tanner, Dorothy Dunn, and J. J. Brody. These histories often informed Bialac's patronage of American Indian art, and he sometimes purchased works that had been published in important surveys and exhibition catalogues. In turn, his collection informed scholarship through its illustration in canonical texts, such as Tanner's 1973 edition of *Southwest Indian Painting: A Changing Art* and numerous others. Over subsequent decades, Bialac would develop personal relationships with many scholars in the field, including Tanner, Brody, Edwin Wade, and Dorothy Jean Ray.

These professional and personal relationships, when considered with Bialac's regular attendance at exhibitions and his interest in the history and criticism of the field, placed him in a relatively unique position to influence the development of American Indian fine art and art history over the past fifty years. In many ways, his collection may be regarded as a time capsule of the important trends in American Indian art since the early 1960s. An examination of the history of Bialac as a collector provides intriguing insights into the vicissitudes of American Indian art and art history during the latter half of the twentieth century and helps to demonstrate the role that the market has played in those developments. Although Bialac's collection is notable for its breadth and diversity, an examination of it also reveals his consistent interest in encouraging and acquiring innovative and experimental contemporary works that challenged prevailing notions of American Indian art.

The formation of Bialac's taste and interests as a collector may be credited in part to the cultural environment of Scottsdale and Phoenix in the 1960s. When Bialac began collecting in 1964, the area had become a hothouse for the exhibition and patronage of American Indian art.

The Heard Museum had supported and exhibited Native arts and crafts since its founding in 1929, but in 1958, it launched both its shop and its Indian Market and Fair, creating further opportunities for contemporary arts and crafts. During the 1960s, the Heard often featured selected works from prominent collectors in Phoenix and Scottsdale, such as Byron and JoAnn Butler, Henry and Alma Galbraith, Byron Harvey III and Joy Harvey, Dean and Mareen Allen Nichols, Oscar and Dorothy Thoeny, and Read and Fran Mullan. An exhibition drawn from the Butlers' collection in 1963 first sparked Bialac's interest in American Indian painting, and he began a passionate study of the subject thereafter.

Bialac's self-education eventually led to the purchase of his first painting in January the following year, Robert Chee's *Moccasin Game* (1961). By the nomenclature of the time, Chee's watercolor would have been considered "traditional" in medium, subject, and style. Chee's use of a simple contour and unmodulated color as well as his focus on the pertinent action, to the exclusion of superfluous detail and background, were widely accepted as hallmarks of Indian painting. His subject, an age-old game among the Navajos, would also have been considered traditional, not only for its centuries of practice but also for its ethnographic specificity and its origin in tribal mythology.

PLATE 11

ROBERT CHEE

U.S., Navajo, 1938–1972

Moccasin Game, 1961

Watercolor on paper

22½ × 33 in.

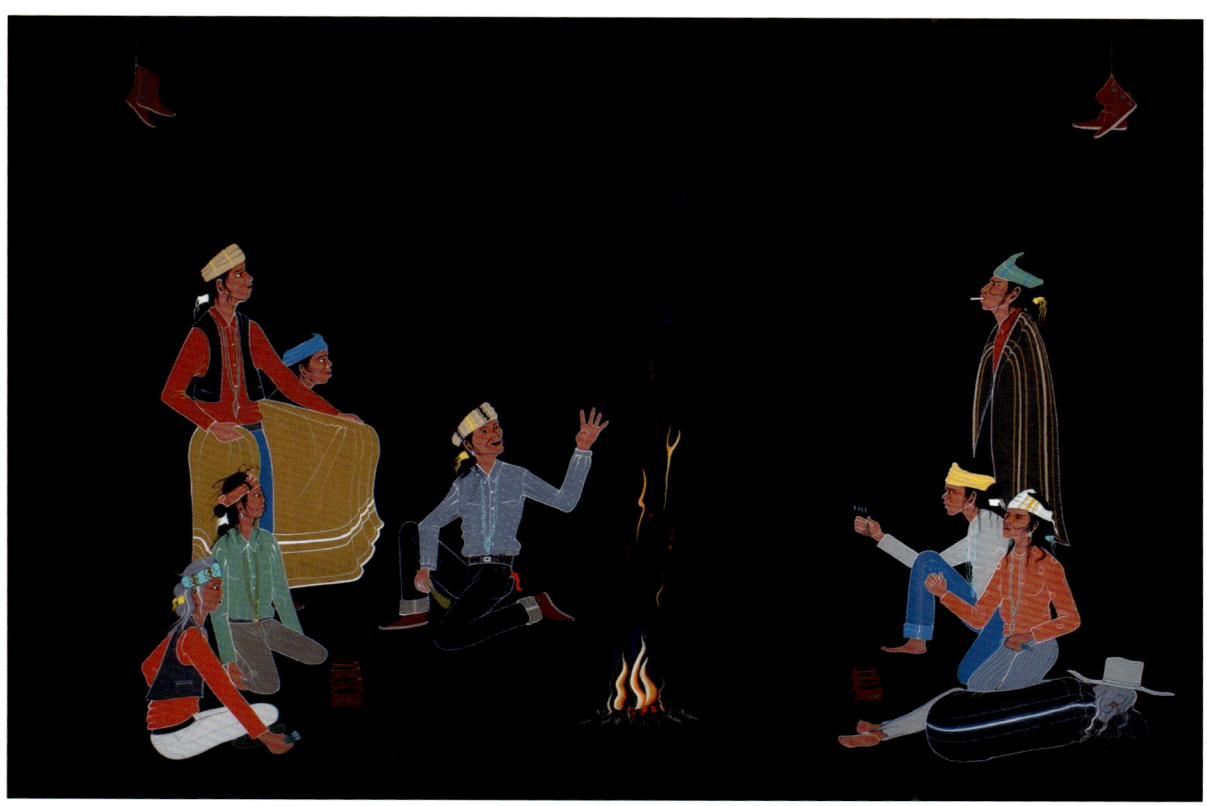

Bialac purchased *Moccasin Game* from the notable Scottsdale gallery the House of Six Directions, owned by Paul F. Huldermann.[3] Huldermann offered historical objects in the gallery, but he also supported contemporary artists who were experimenting with new media and techniques. Over the next thirty years, Bialac purchased nineteen works from Huldermann, many abstract in character, including R. C. Gorman's *The Parasol and the Cloud* (1965, plate 3), David Paladin's *Ancient Ones* (1966), and Pablita Velarde's *Mimbres Quails* (1987, plate 10). None of these would have been considered traditional by the aesthetic criteria applied to Chee's *Moccasin Game.* Huldermann's promotion of styles that would have been considered modern, contemporary, or experimental spoke to his involvement with the *Scottsdale National Indian Arts Exhibition,* which also had a strong influence on the early development of Bialac's collection.

Created in 1962, the *Scottsdale National* became "one of the most influential of all the competitive exhibits" by the end of the decade and helped to create a thriving market for modern and contemporary American Indian painting.[4] Much of the credit for this emphasis lay with Lloyd Kiva New, who had helped to establish a market for Indian arts and crafts in Scottsdale. In 1955, New completed construction on a business complex on 5th Avenue, later known as the Kiva Center, where several artists' studios and galleries, like the House of Six Directions, specialized in contemporary arts and crafts. New's success encouraged the Scottsdale Chamber of Commerce to develop plans for an arts and crafts exhibition, and they approached the Philbrook Art Center for organizational advice.[5] This led to the establishment of the Scottsdale National Indian Arts Council in 1961 and the exhibition the following year.

The first exhibition was relatively small, with approximately 170 entries, although the ambition for the annual grew rapidly.[6] Veteran artist Andrew Tsihnahjinnie won first prize for his *Slayer of Enemy Gods—Nayeinezani* (1962), a painting that was initially purchased by John Tanner, owner of Desert House Crafts in Tucson and husband of anthropologist Clara Lee Tanner. Bialac acquired the painting from John in 1966, and Clara Lee would later feature it in her second edition of *Southwest Indian Painting.* Tsihnahjinnie had long been identified with traditional painting but began to experiment with abstraction in the 1950s, partly out of his association with New. Although the painting's subject derives from Navajo mythology, its abstract style placed it within the context of modern American Indian painting and signaled the direction in which the *Scottsdale National* intended to proceed in future exhibitions.

Despite the relatively small size of the first *Scottsdale National,* the favorable response ensured a second in 1963. The success of the subsequent exhibition led Huldermann to boast that the *Scottsdale National* had become "the nation's leading annual for Indian painting," and he and New began to use the National to encourage more experimental American Indian arts

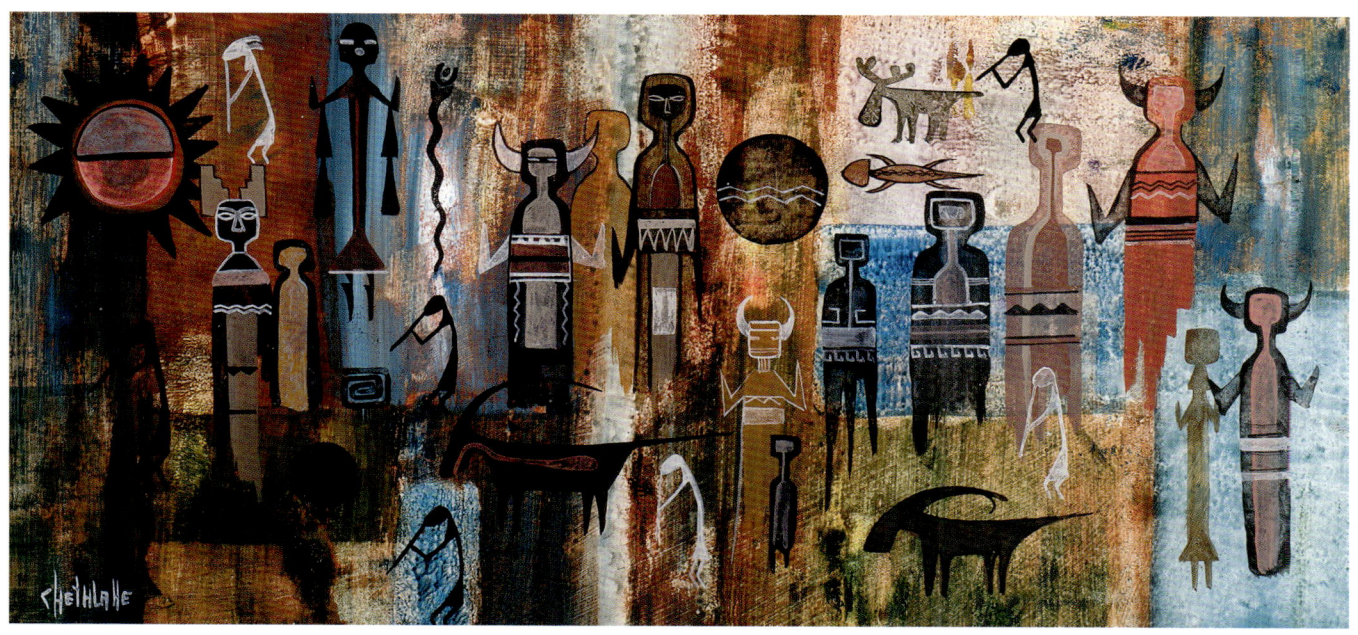

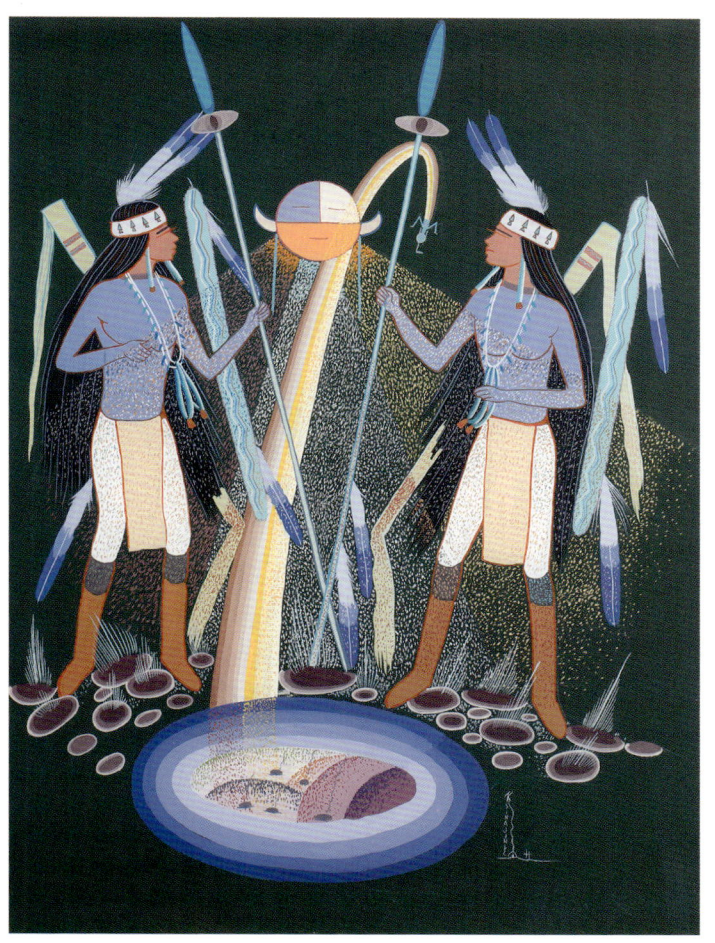

PLATE 12

DAVID "CHETHLAHE" PALADIN

U.S., Navajo, 1926–1984

Ancient Ones, 1966

Acrylic on canvas, 7½ x 15 in.

Courtesy of the artist's estate

PLATE 13

ANDREW TSIHNAHJINNIE

U.S., Navajo, 1918–2000

Slayer of Enemy Gods—Nayeinezani, 1962

Watercolor on paper, 26½ x 19½ in.

Courtesy of Minnie Tsihnahjinnie

and crafts. New had recently co-founded the IAIA in Santa Fe in 1962, where he hoped to introduce modern art and design to a younger generation of American Indian students. That philosophy informed the direction of the *Scottsdale National,* which began to classify entries based on medium as opposed to the geographic locations, such as Southwest or Woodlands, that had characterized the Philbrook's annual. New, Huldermann, and other organizers hoped the new classifications would encourage creative freedom and integrate younger artists into a broader discourse of American art. New delivered an address at the opening in which he "made a strong plea for the Indian artist to be freed from 'traditional' bounds, contending there is no such thing as what is popularly conceived as 'traditional' in Indian art."[7] As Huldermann further explained: "There was realization that the Indian must be removed from the mental and spiritual 'Reservation' on which he had been placed and that he must be allowed to participate in all areas of American artistic endeavors, rather than simply the traditional ones common to most Indian exhibitions. The organizing committee also recognized that, if an Indian contribution to the whole field of American arts and crafts is to be made, tribal barriers would have to be removed."[8] The approach apparently unnerved some older artists, who feared "the modern trend will force Indian art into the general art world without identity," and an unidentified artist reportedly asked, "If an Indian painted a contemporary painting, who would know?" Pablita Velarde, who won an award in the experimental classification that year for one of her abstract earth paintings, disparaged some of the contemporary work that "looked like the artist spilled his can of paint."[9]

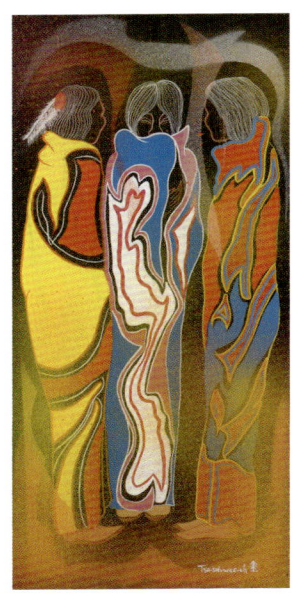

This ideological disagreement over the future of American Indian art largely derived from concern about erasing or softening tribal identity in favor of the individuality integral to modernist thought and practice. New employed the pedagogical approach he had taken at IAIA as a paradigm for the *Scottsdale National,* and that model emphasized what Joy Gritton has described as "a Western, modern aesthetic dominated by individualism and commercial success in the non-Indian art market over indigenous aesthetics distinguished by concern for communal welfare, social mores, and religious proscriptions and practices."[10] Although the *Scottsdale National* continued to encourage traditional painting with its water-based paintings classification, the comments of New and Huldermann make clear that modernist individualism and the expansion of market opportunities were important objectives for the exhibition.

Bialac had not yet begun to collect in the early days of the *Scottsdale National,* but he attended the fourth annual in 1965, where he purchased an honorable mention, Helen Hardin's *Medicine Talk* (1964). Hardin had entered the watercolor in the water-based classification, where it competed against traditional paintings, but the style and subject of *Medicine Talk* exemplified the type of contemporary Indian painting that New and Huldermann had hoped to encourage.

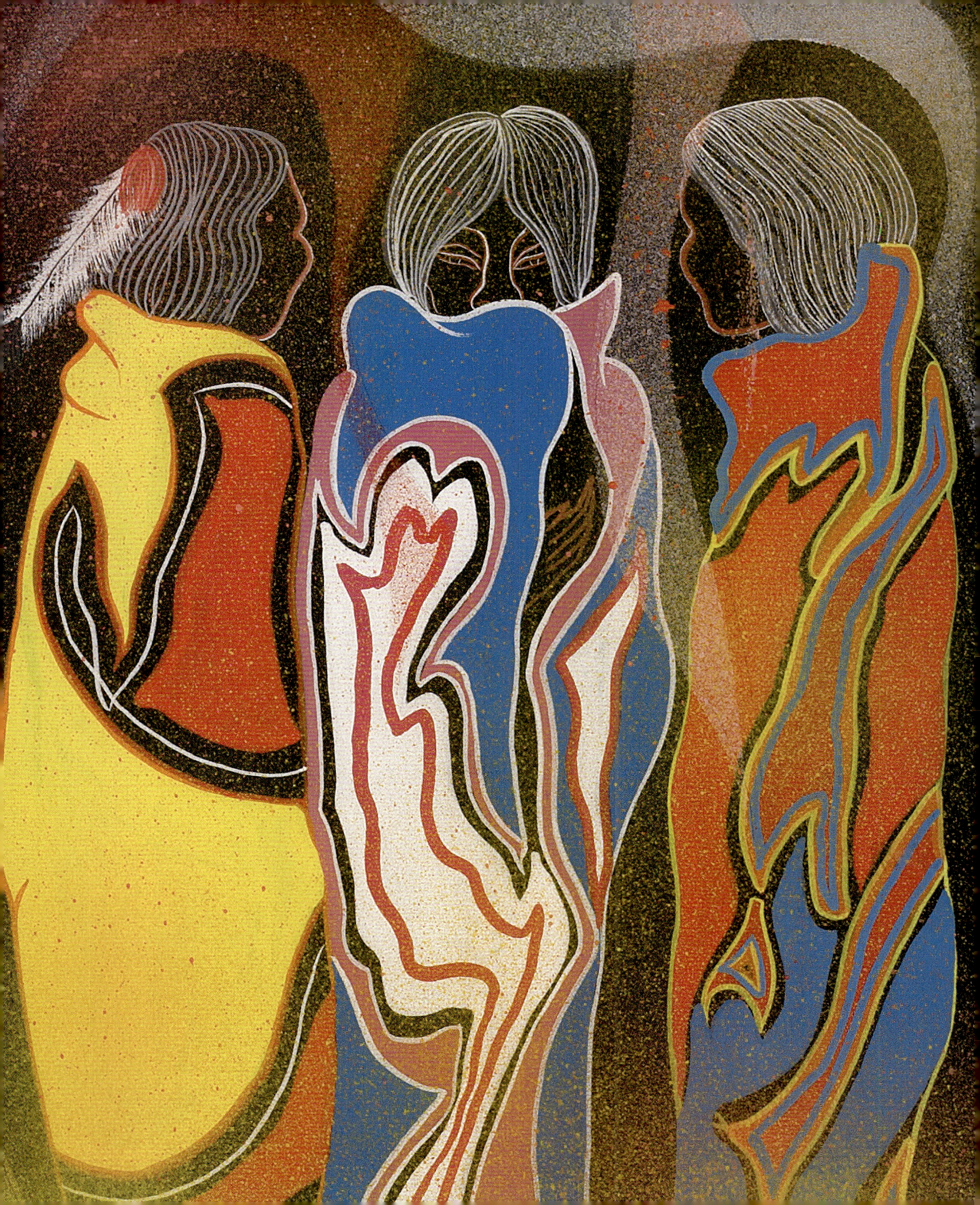

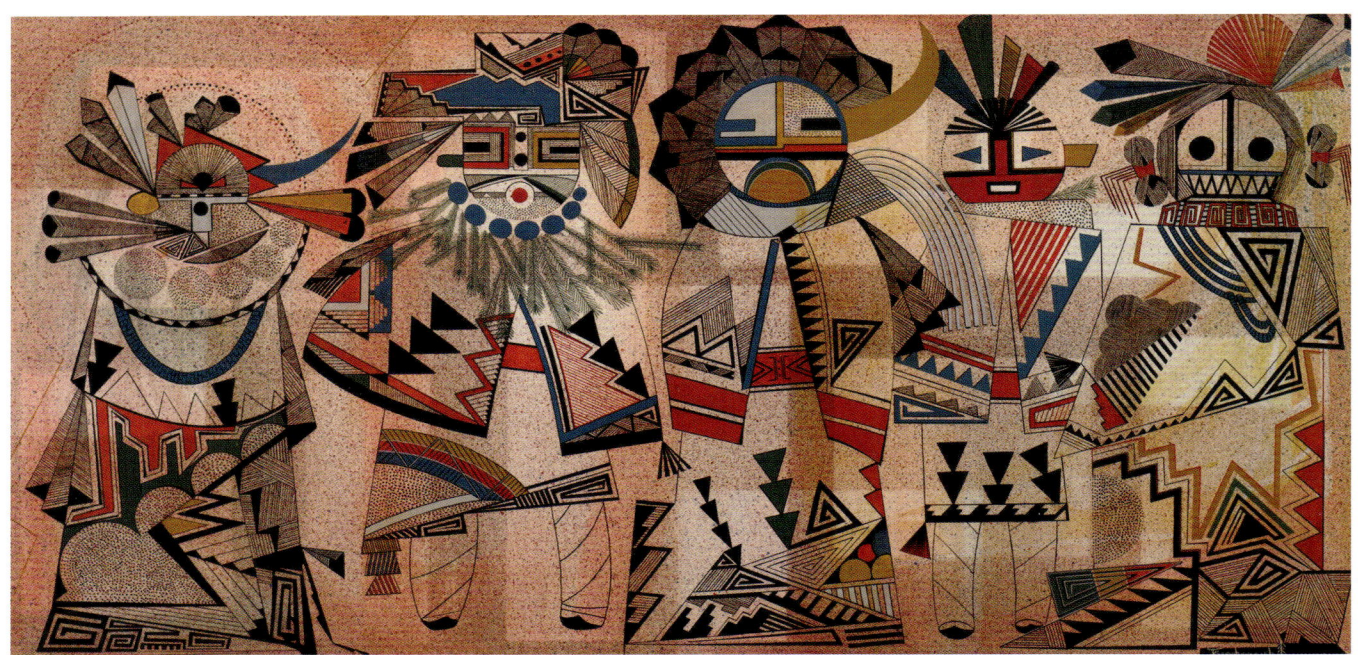

The abstract patterning of the blankets, when combined with the technique of sprayed paint, indicates a modernist sensibility similar to that of her mother, Pablita Velarde, who had won in the experimental classification two years earlier. *Medicine Talk* also conveys ambivalence toward ethnographic specificity, since the tribal origin of the figures is unclear, and their abstracted, prismatic attire could identify them as belonging to a Great Lakes, Plains, or Southwest tribe. Her depiction of American Indian spirituality, as opposed to an explicitly tribal subject, was likely informed by her own artistic approach, which emphasized an introspective search for identity and spiritual contemplation distinct from tribal concerns. She admitted in 1973, "While you are painting, you think of your life and your place in it. The painting itself is almost an automatic reflex."[11]

Bialac certainly appreciated Hardin's modern approach to painting and would acquire five more of her works in coming years, but his subsequent purchases from the *Scottsdale National* included more traditional works, such as Stephen Mopope's *Fancy War Dancer,* which was entered in the fifth annual in 1966. Mopope was among the first generation of American Indian painters in Oklahoma and helped to create the style that was commonly regarded as traditional. Although his style had matured over the decades, he maintained his earlier interest in Kiowa dance, the grace of the figure, and the details of dress to the exclusion of background and extraneous elements. Bialac, in purchasing Mopope's painting, supported the continuation of older styles, and for the sixth annual in 1967, the former donated award money in the water-based classification.

Bialac's support for older styles notwithstanding, most of his purchases from the *Scottsdale National* were more experimental. He began acquiring oils and polymers, media that had come into vogue among American Indian artists after the creation of the IAIA. The *Scottsdale National* changed their classifications in 1968 to include categories for oil and polymer, and in 1969, the James T. Bialac Award switched from the water-based classification to the polymer. Significant purchases in later years included Joan Hill's oil *Evening at the Pueblo* (1967), which won third prize at the sixth annual in 1967; Patrick Swazo Hinds's oil *Council of the Corn Maidens* (1969), which won the first award at the ninth annual in 1970; and Patrick DesJarlait's watercolor *Cleaning of the Wild Rice* (1972, plate 96), which appeared at the eleventh annual in 1972.[12] Bialac's most important acquisition at the eleventh annual, however, was Helen Hardin's acrylic *Winter Awakening of the O-khoo-wah* (1972). That year, the painting won awards for best in show, first prize in painting and sculpture, and a special juror's award for acrylics. Bialac had met both Hardin and Velarde at the *Intertribal Ceremonial* in Gallup in a previous year, and he accompanied Hardin to the opening of the *Scottsdale National*. Hardin confided that *Winter Awakening of the O-khoo-wah* was her best effort thus far and urged Bialac to buy it. As it was reported in the press, "Bialac purchased the triple award winning painting by Helen Hardin by running faster and signing a sales slip quicker than anyone else when the doors opened for the preview showing."[13] *Winter Awakening of the O-khoo-wah* eventually became one of Hardin's most reproduced and celebrated paintings, and it represented Bialac's last major purchase at the *Scottsdale National,* although he continued to buy works from the exhibition until it closed in 1976.

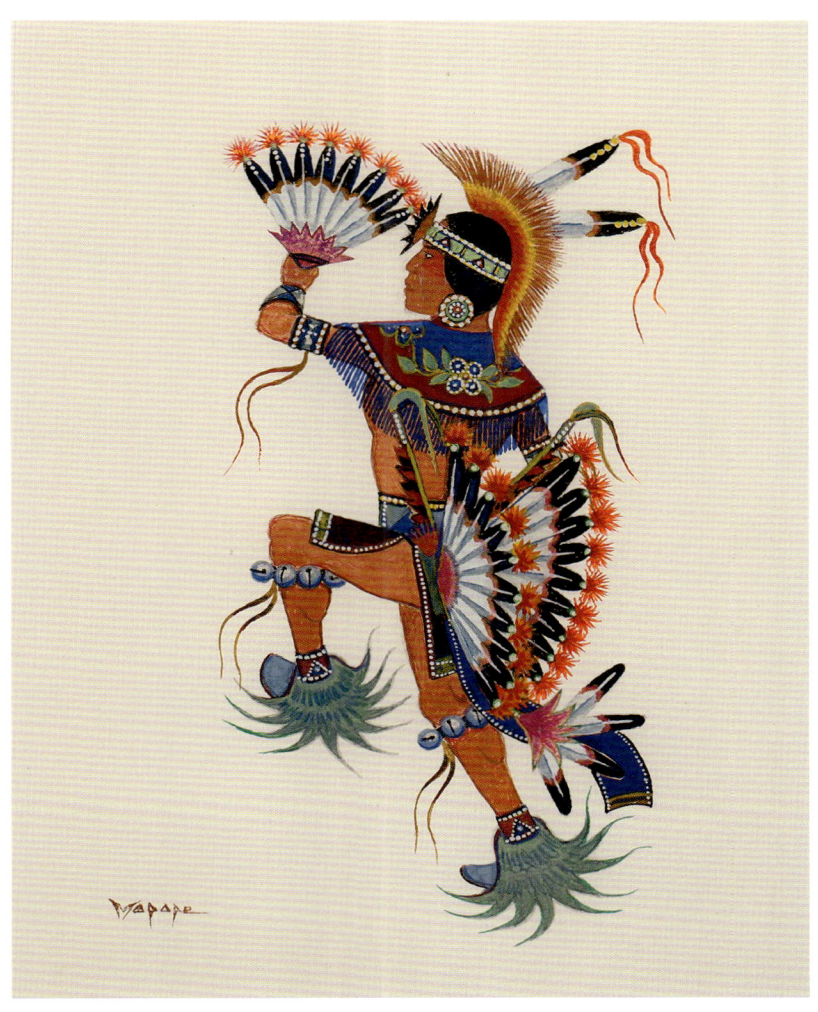

PLATE 16

STEPHEN MOPOPE

U.S., Kiowa, 1898–1974

Fancy War Dancer, c. 1966

Watercolor on paper,

11¼ × 8¾ in.

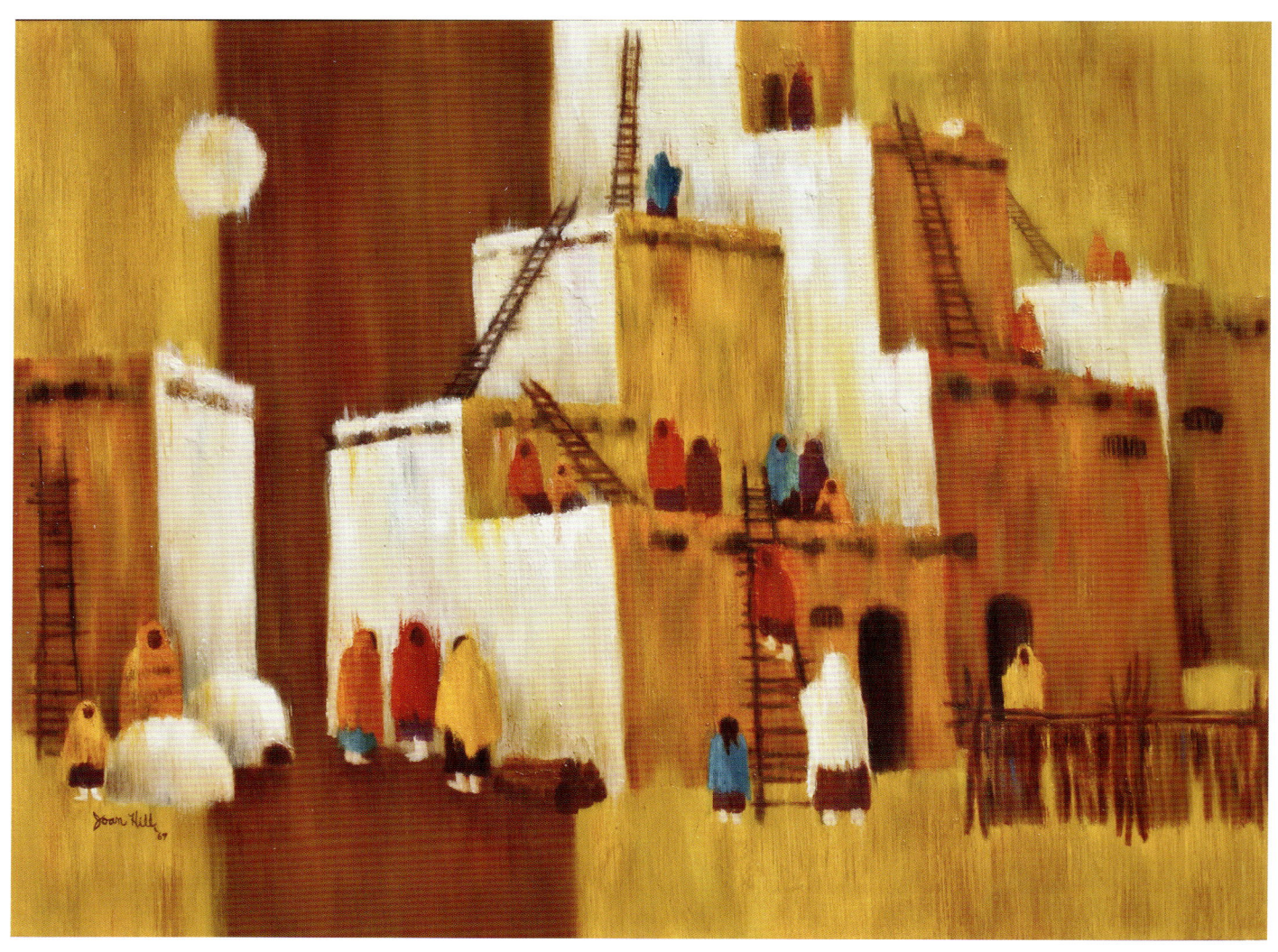

PLATE 17

JOAN HILL

U.S., Creek/Cherokee, b. 1930

Evening at the Pueblo, 1967

Oil on canvas, 30 x 24 in.

PLATE 18

PATRICK SWAZO HINDS

U.S., Tesuque Pueblo, 1929–1974

Council of the Corn Maidens, 1969

Oil on canvas, 30 x 24 in.

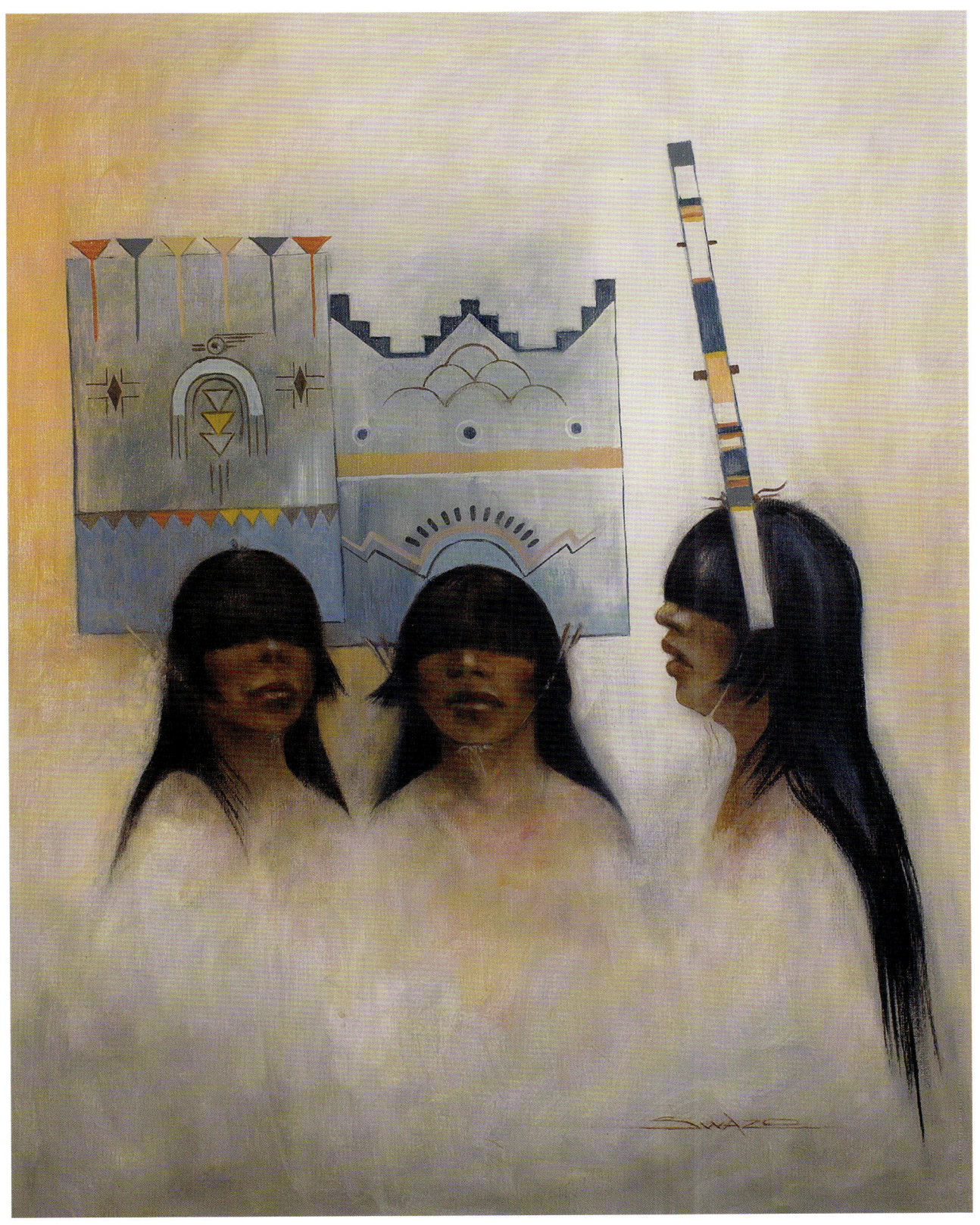

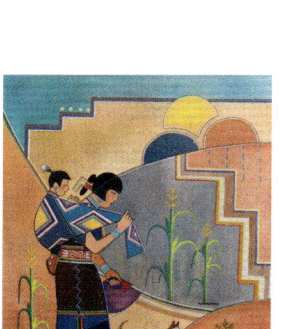

The purchase of Hardin's painting strengthened Bialac's established reputation as a serious collector, but by 1972, his collection had already received scholarly attention from museums and art historians in the Southwest. His notable purchases in the 1960s resulted in the organization of two separate exhibitions of his collection in 1967: one by the Heard Museum, and the other by the Arizona State Museum, the latter organized by Clara Lee Tanner.

The Heard's exhibition, *The James T. Bialac Collection: Amerindian Paintings and Graphics,* celebrated his connoisseurship of contemporary American Indian painting. Bialac would be asked to join their board of trustees in 1968, and the exhibition may have helped to initiate that relationship. Curator of Indian Art Joan Hale praised Bialac as "among the few discriminating art collectors with the foresight to recognize contemporary American Indian paintings and graphics as a facet that is to become a highly significant chapter in the history of American art." Even though his collection numbered little more than one hundred works at the time, she considered it "unsurpassed in aesthetic quality and ethnological value" and positioned him alongside established collectors such as Butler and Harvey.[14]

The exhibition included aforementioned paintings by Chee, Gorman, Mopope, Paladin, and Tsihnahjinnie, as well as other recent acquisitions. He had purchased a number of important paintings the previous year that were part of the exhibition: for example, Gilbert Atencio's *Mother and Child* (1962), a second-prize winner at the 1963 *Intertribal Ceremonial* in Gallup, and Fred Beaver's *Young Florida Seminoles* (1966), a second-prize winner at the Philbrook's twenty-first annual *American Indian Artists Exhibition.*[15] Beaver's work was one of many traditional paintings included in the Heard exhibition that Bialac had purchased in an effort to broaden the scope of his collection.

That year he also acquired Gerónima Montoya's *Santo Domingo Bird* (1959), Velino Herrera's *Calf Roping* (c. 1940), and Woody Crumbo's *Rainbow Mother* (c. 1949), purchased from Taos dealer Tony Reyna. In addition, the exhibition included paintings acquired as a result of Bialac's budding friendships with a number of artists, such as Otis Polelonema's *Clowns Between the Dances* (1966) and Michael Kabotie's *Coming of the Shalako* (n.d., plate 71).

Like the Heard exhibition, Arizona State Museum's *The James T. Bialac Collection of Southwest Indian Paintings* included most of the major purchases Bialac had made since 1964. Tanner emphasized the growing stylistic diversity of the collection, but its strong focus on modern and contemporary work reinforced her perception that "today Indian art is going through one of the most dramatic changes in its history." With the growing influence of IAIA and the *Scottsdale National,* she believed that American Indian art was in the midst of a transitional period from a largely craft-based production to that of the fine arts.[16]

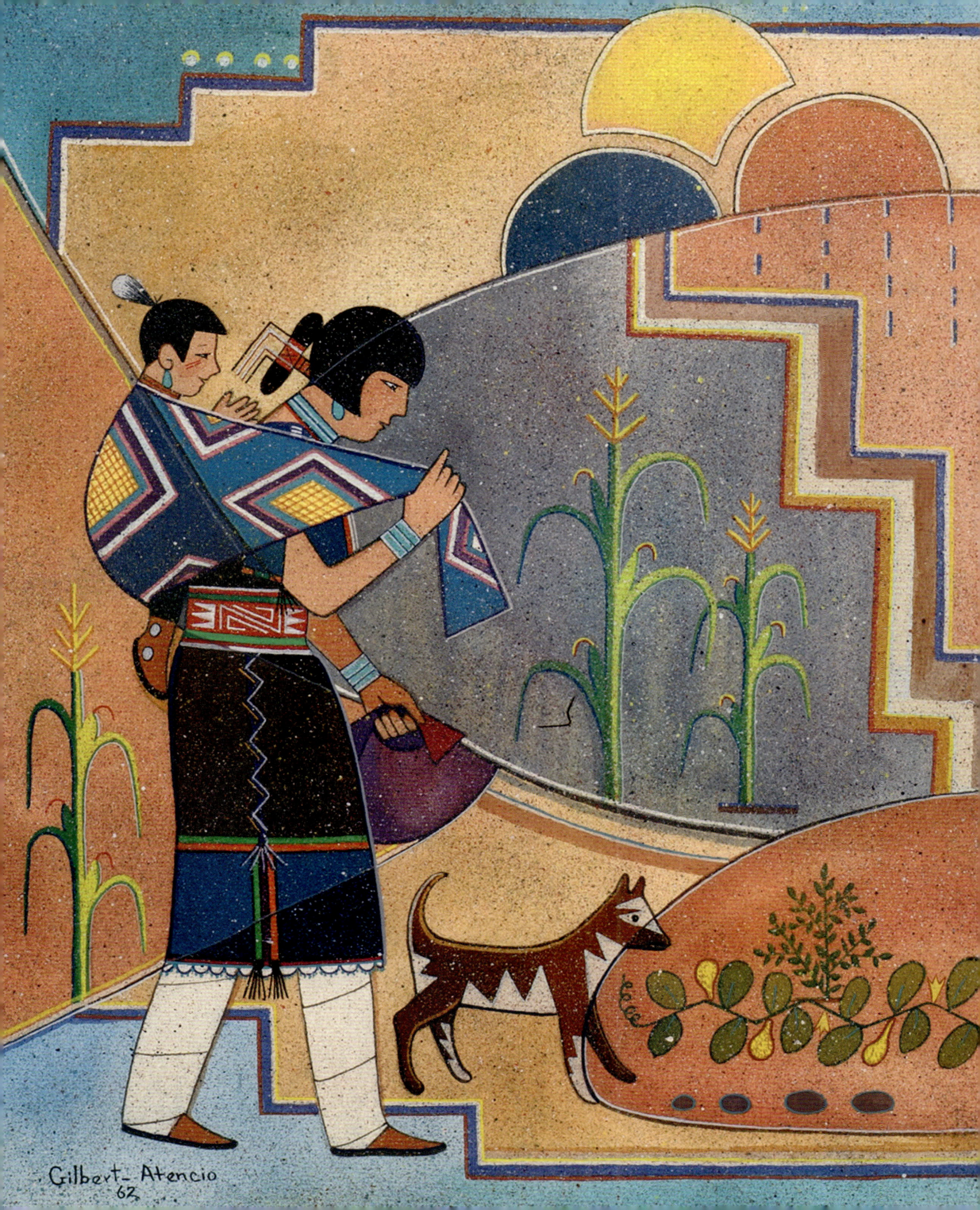

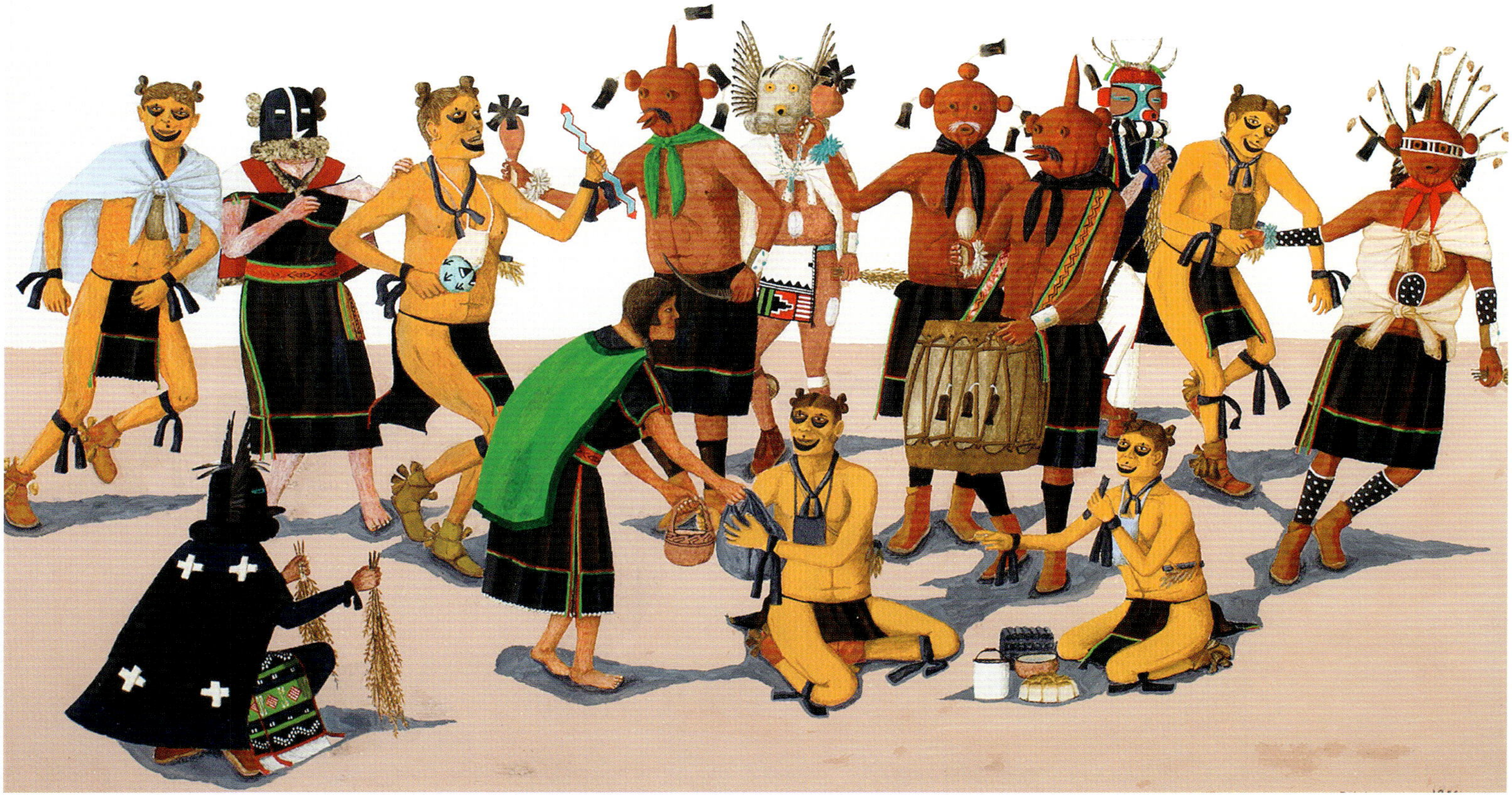

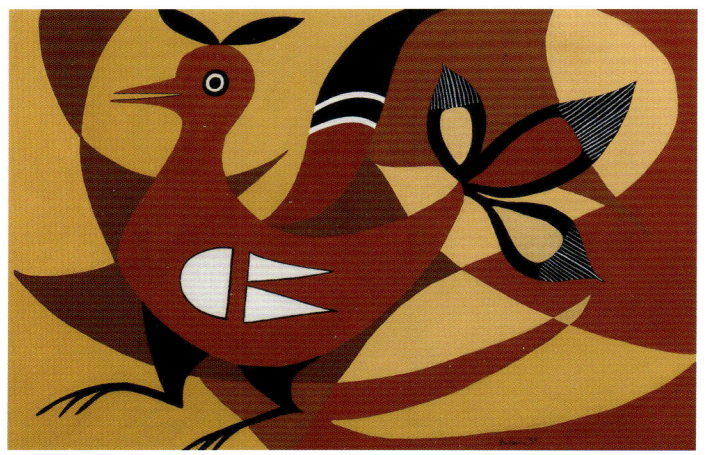

PLATE 20 (ABOVE)

OTIS POLELONEMA

U.S., Hopi Pueblo, 1902–1981

Clowns Between the Dances, 1966

Watercolor on paper, 17⅜ x 29½ in.

PLATE 21 (LEFT)

GERÓNIMA MONTOYA (P'OTSÚNÚ)

U.S., Okhay Owingeh, b. 1915

Santo Domingo Bird, 1959

Watercolor on paper, 11½ x 17 in.

PLATE 22

WOODROW WILSON
"WOODY" CRUMBO

U.S., Creek/Potawatomi, 1912–1989

Rainbow Mother, c. 1949

Watercolor on paper, 17 x 13¾ in.

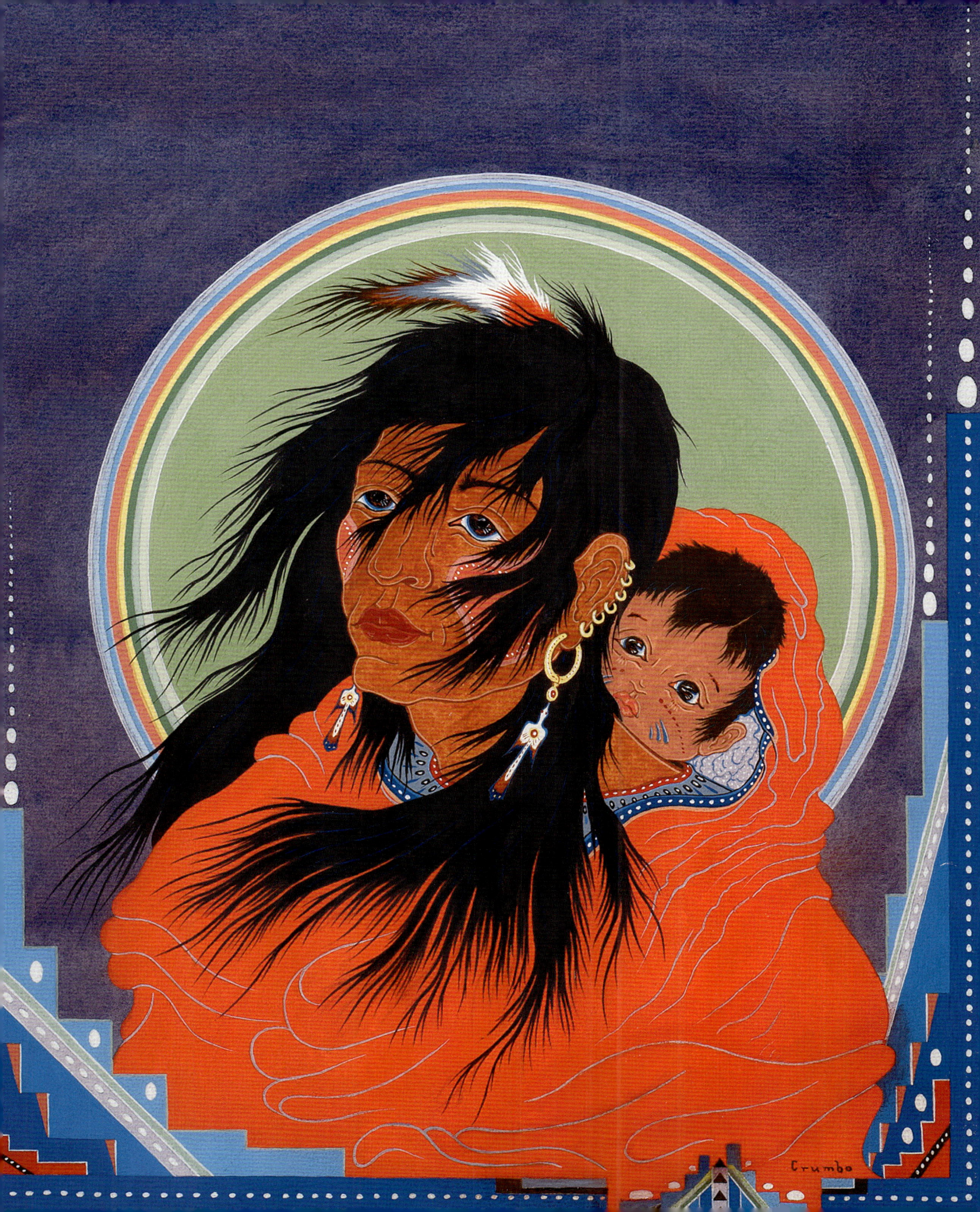

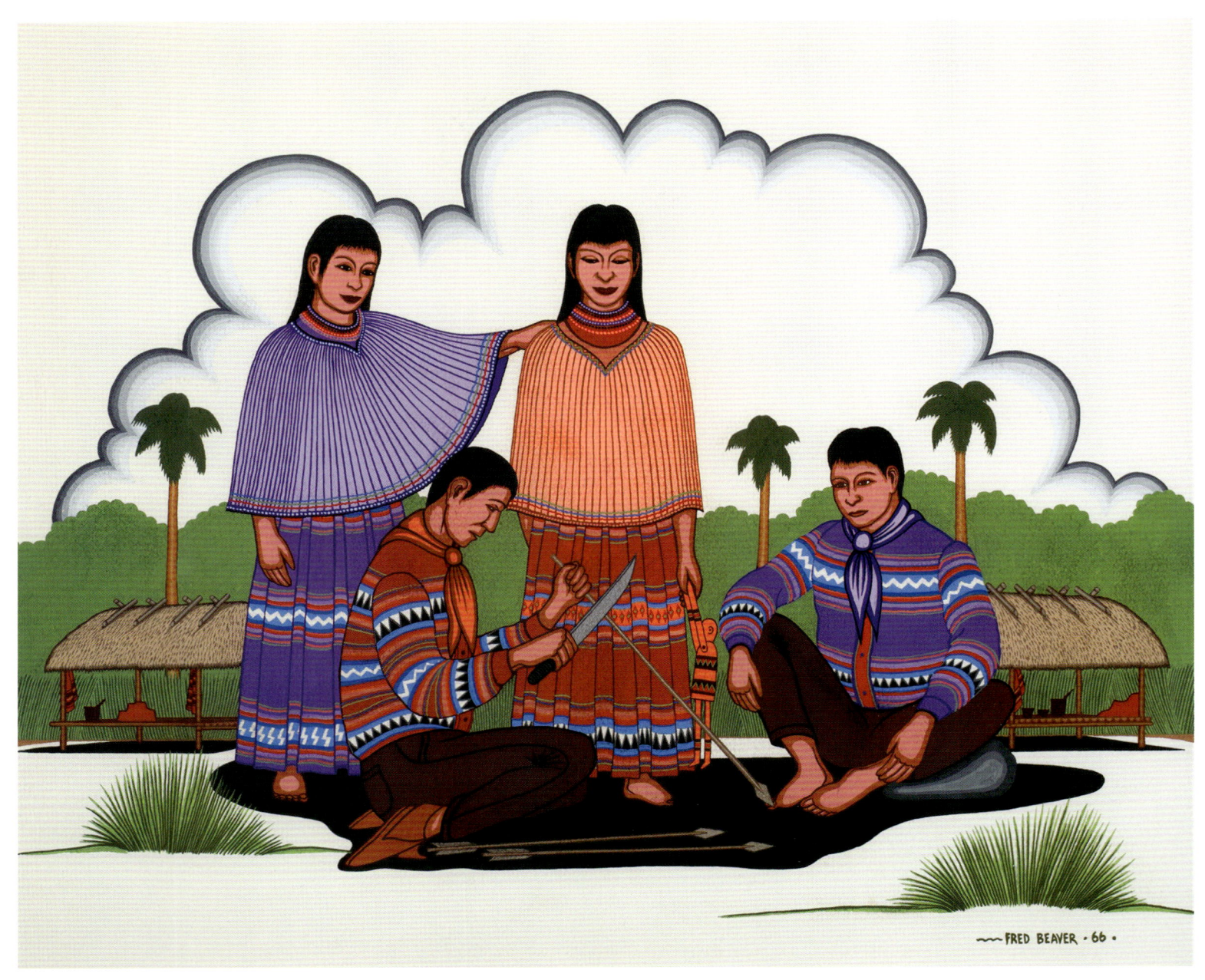

PLATE 23

FRED BEAVER

U.S., Muskogee/Creek, 1911–1980

Young Florida Seminoles, 1966

Casein on paper, 18¼ x 21¾ in.

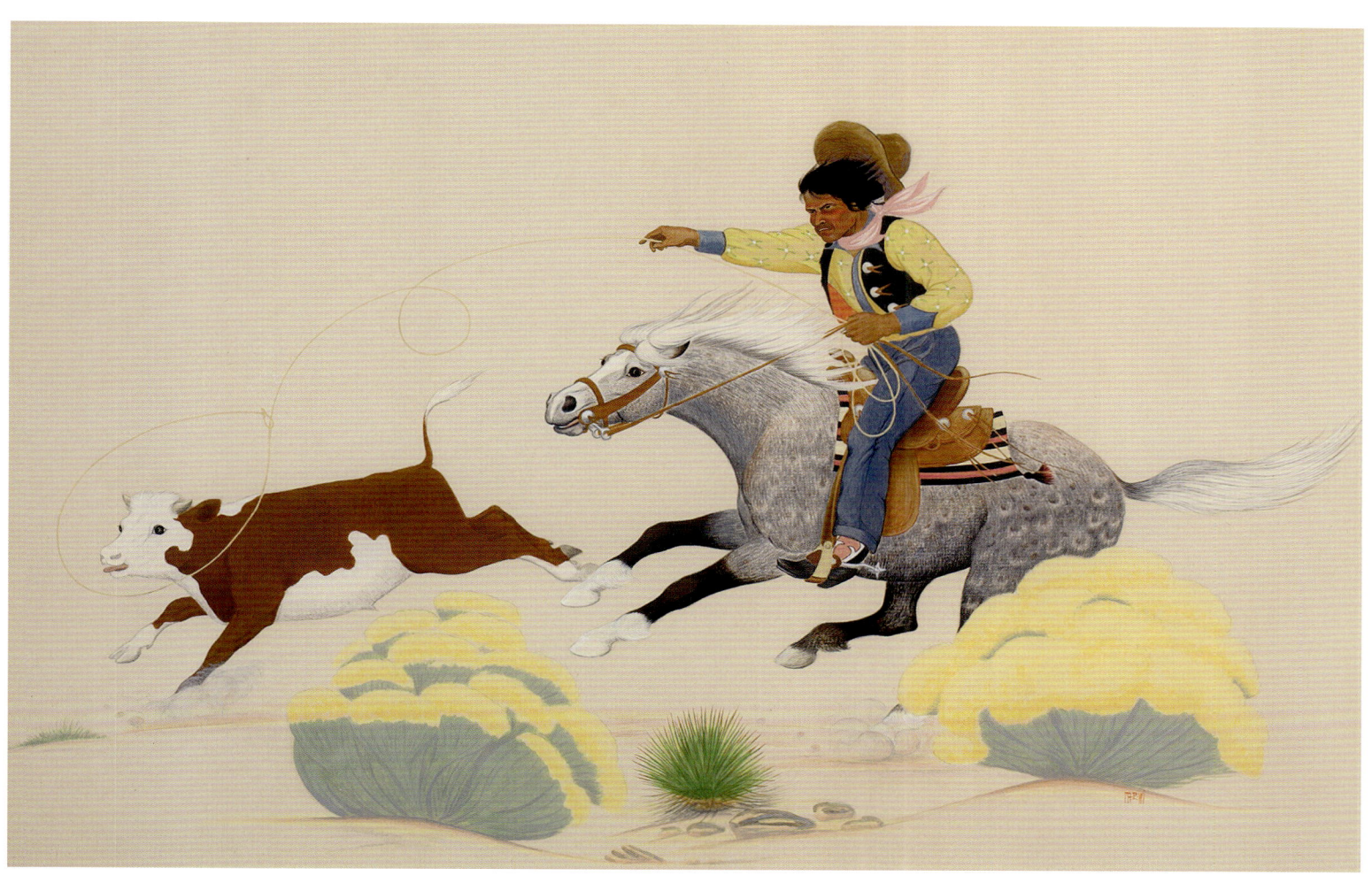

PLATE 24

VELINO SHIJE HERRERA (MA-PE-WI)

U.S. Zia Pueblo, 1902–1973

Calf Roping, c. 1940

Watercolor on paper, 14 x 21½ in.

PLATE 25

HARRISON BEGAY

(HASKAY YAHNE YAH)

U.S., Navajo, b. 1917

Navajo Yei'bichai

Dancers, n.d.

Watercolor on paper,

13 x 26½ in.

PLATE 26

WALDO MOOTZKA

U.S., Hopi Pueblo,

1910–1940

Mythical Bird, n.d.

Watercolor on paper,

11¾ x 15¼ in.

Tanner's catalogue, in many ways, was a primer for her forthcoming second edition of *Southwest Indian Painting: A Changing Art.* She included over forty paintings from Bialac's collection in the book, and although she did illustrate traditional works such as the Chee, many of the works were contemporary. Hardin's *Medicine Talk,* Hinds' *Council of the Corn Maidens,* and Tsihnahjinnie's *Slayer of Enemy Gods* received special attention for their modernist sympathies.[17] Tanner devoted significant attention to the changes in American Indian art introduced in the 1960s and its rise in popularity in recent years: "In the 1970s, Southwestern Indian easel art had reached the highest peak it had ever known. There were more outstanding individual painters, more tribes producing art, and more highly developed styles of painting than at any other point in the history of this unique expression. Too, within the preceding decade, there were more experiments with new media, more refinement in the traditional styles as well as experimentation with new ones, and more self-expression than ever before."[18] The illustrations she used from Bialac's collection offered tangible proof of this thesis. Bialac held Tanner's work in high esteem, and in 2009, he purchased a painting partly because it had been featured in her book: Harrison Begay's *Navajo Yei'bichai Dancers* (n.d.), which had been previously owned by the magazine *Arizona Highways.*

Tanner credited the strength of Bialac's collection to his practice of befriending artists and dealers in search of new acquisitions: "He frequents reservations and homes of the artists, becoming acquainted with many of them. He also makes personal contact with traders on and off the reservations, assuring direct sources of paintings."[19] As she rightly observed, Bialac increased the breadth and diversity of his collection in the late 1960s and early 1970s through close affiliation with important dealers such as Tom Bahti, E. P. Hunt, Pat Patania, Tony Reyna, and John Tanner, not to mention Huldermann. These dealers helped Bialac develop his collection of pre–World War II artists. For instance, Bialac purchased Waldo Mootzka's *Mythical Bird* (n.d.) from Patania in 1966, Percy Sandy's *Grinding Ceremony* (n.d.) from the Albuquerque gallery Price's All Indian Shop in 1967, and Oqwa Pi's *Harvest Dancers* from Hunt in 1967. Tom Bahti gave Bialac Jose Rey Toledo's *Antelope* (1936) as a gift in 1968. When Bialac met Kiowa artist Al Momaday in 1966, he acquired not only one of his paintings but also those of earlier artists that Momaday offered for sale: James Auchiah's *Peyote Bird* (1937, plate 89), Acee Blue Eagle's *Indian Maiden* (n.d.), and Tonita Peña's *Basket Dance* (c. 1919, plate 88). Henry Balink, Santa Fe dealer and son of the Taos artist, also offered Bialac several paintings by the early Kiowa artists, including Monroe Tsatoke's *Contemplation* (1929, plate 1).

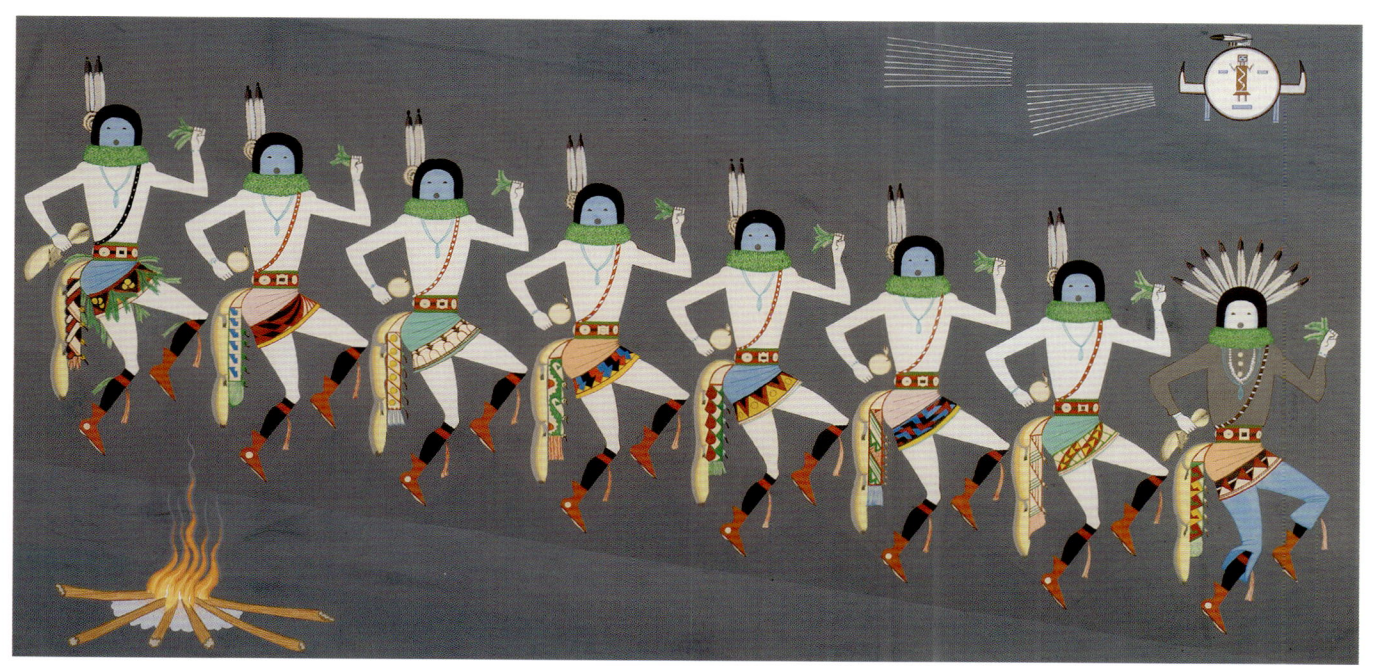

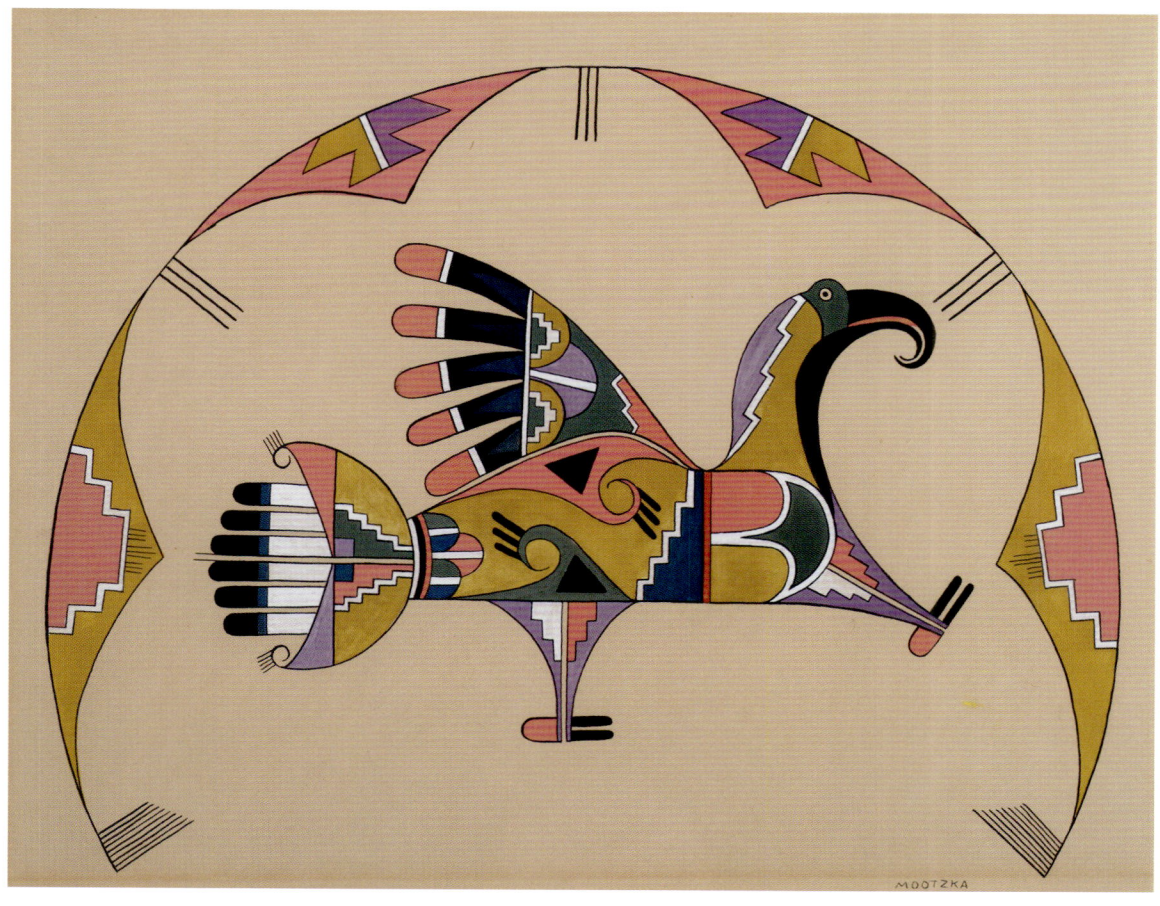

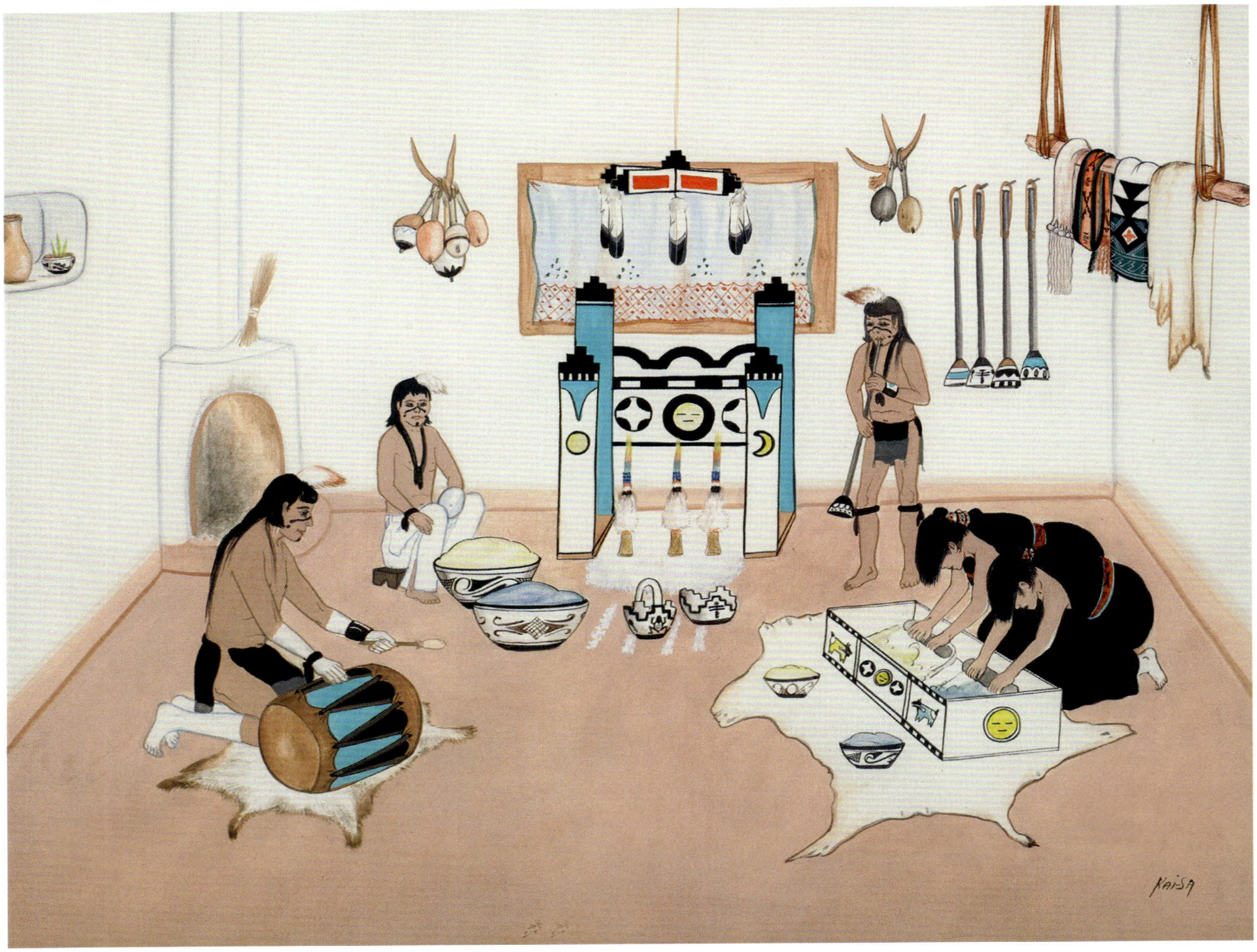

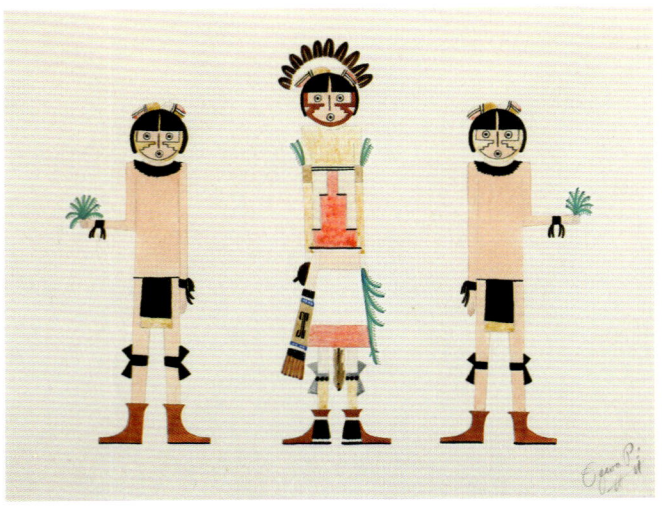

PLATE 27

PERCY SANDY (KAI-SA)

U.S., Zuni Pueblo, 1918–1974

Grinding Ceremony, n.d.

Watercolor on paper, 12¾ x 16½ in.

PLATE 28

ABEL SANCHEZ (OQWA PI)

U.S., San Ildefonso Pueblo, 1899–1971

Harvest Dancers, n.d.

Watercolor on paper, 10⅜ x 13½ in.

PLATE 29

ACEE BLUE EAGLE

U.S., Creek, 1907–1959

Indian Maiden, n.d.

Watercolor on paper, 13½ x 11 in.

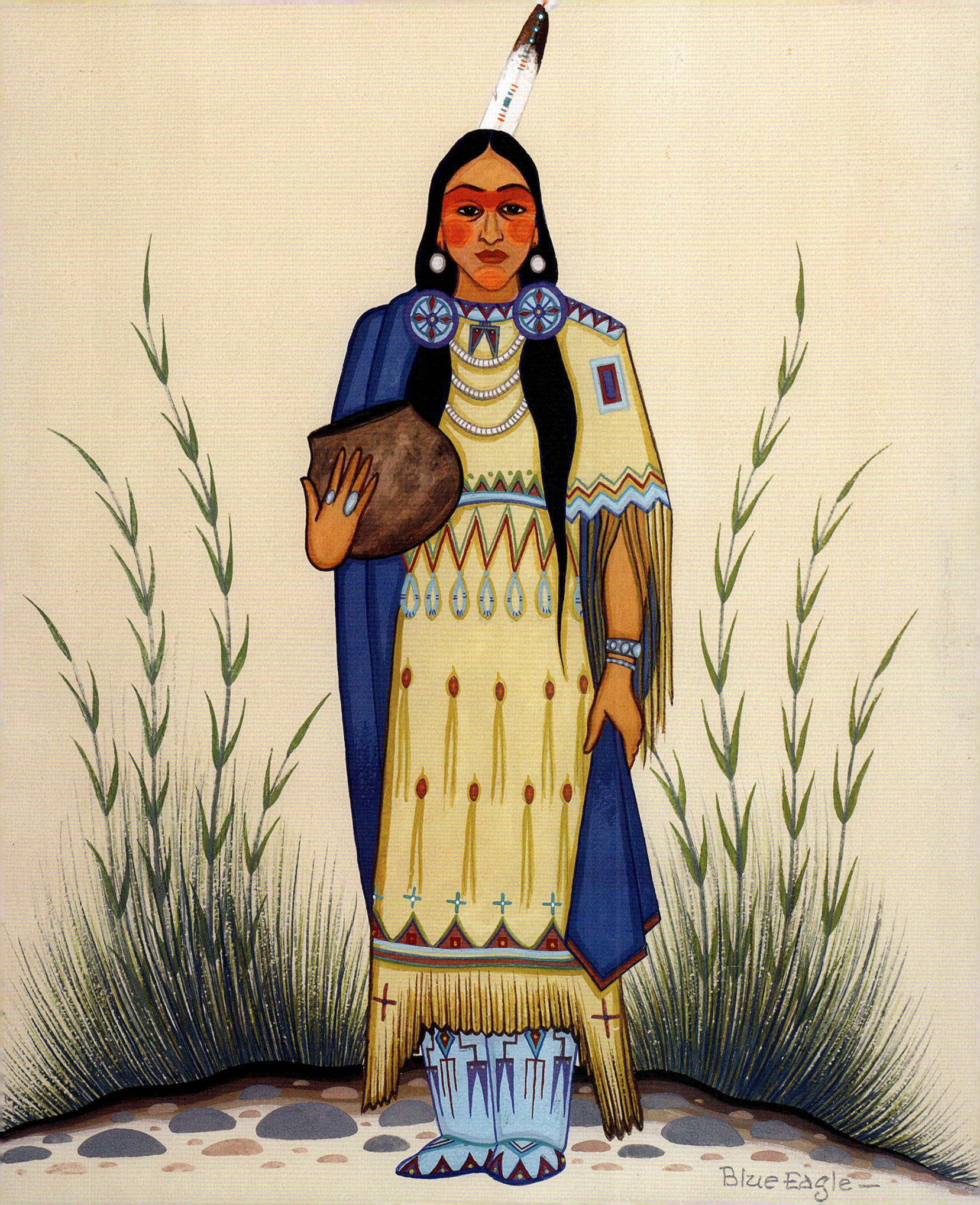

Blue Eagle

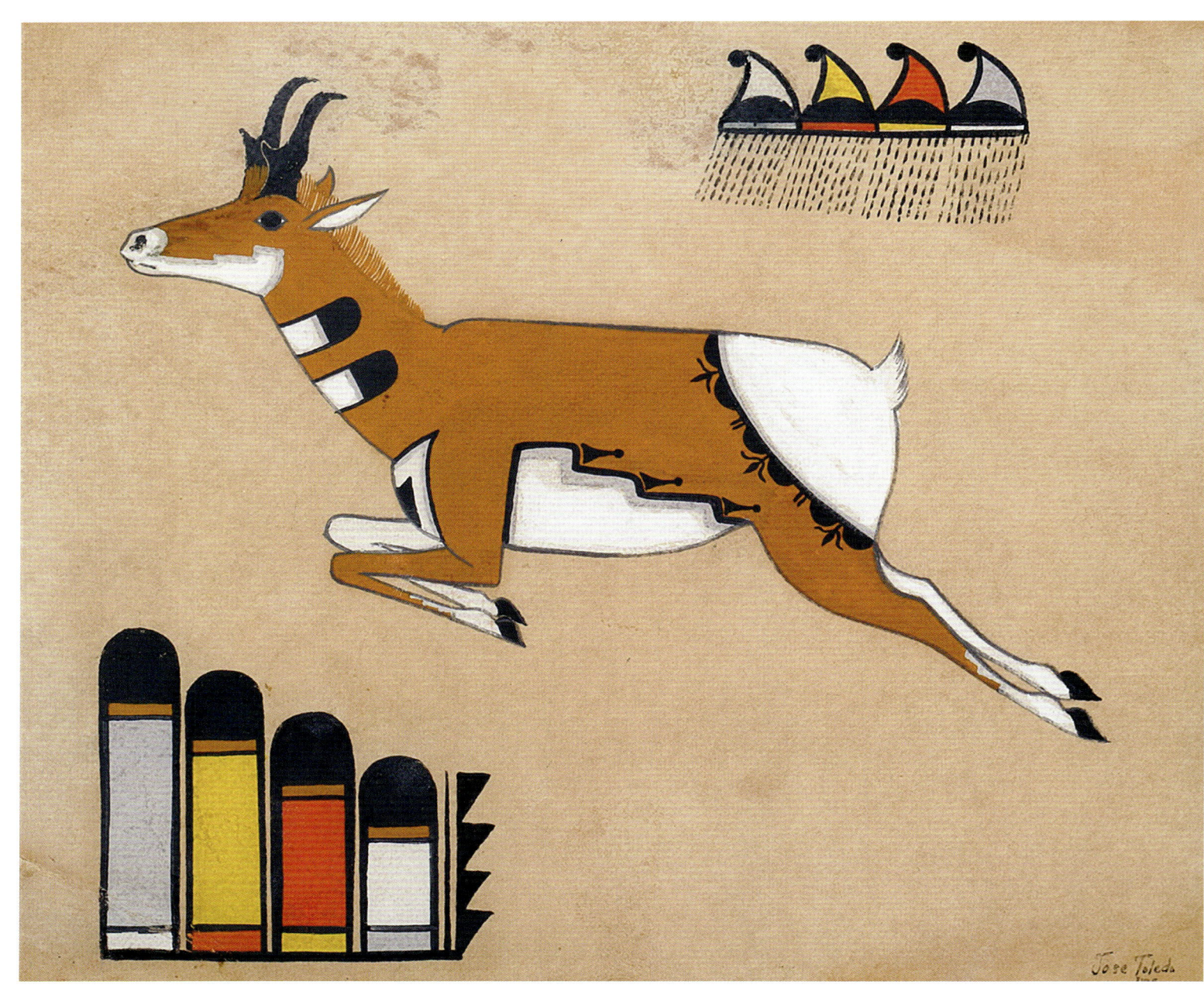

PLATE 30

JOSE REY TOLEDO

U.S., Jemez, 1915–1994

Antelope, 1936

Watercolor on paper, 6½ x 7¾ in.

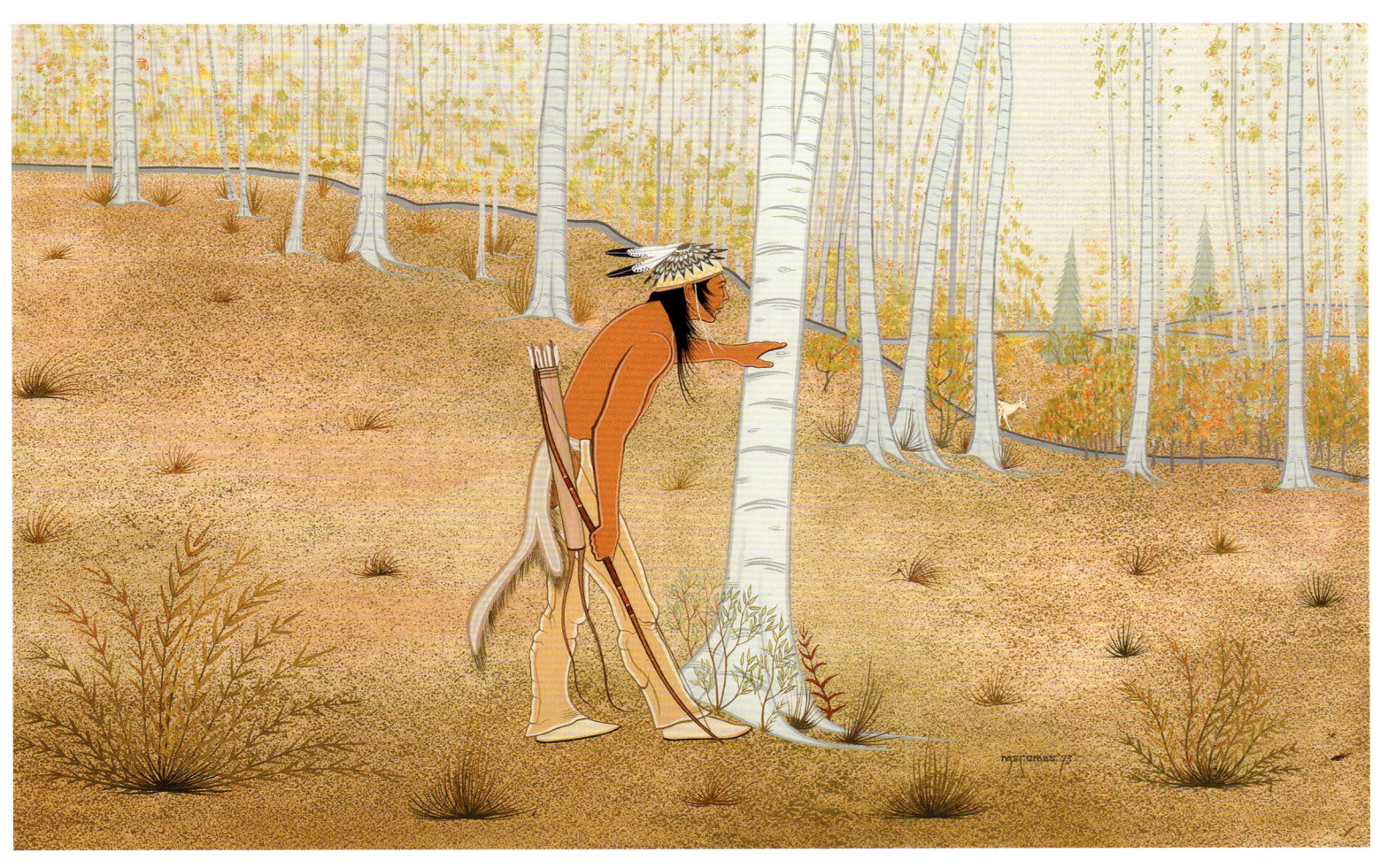

PLATE 31

SOLOMON McCOMBS

U.S., Creek, 1913–1980

Stalking Deer, 1973

Acrylic on paper, 17¾ x 28 in.

The acquisition of historical works not only broadened Bialac's collection but also coincided with the publication of important surveys of American Indian art history. Few comprehensive surveys of twentieth-century American Indian painting existed before the late 1960s, save for Tanner's 1957 edition of *Southwest Indian Painting,* but the turn of the decade saw the publication of Dorothy Dunn's *American Indian Painting of the Southwest and Plains Areas* (1968) and J. J. Brody's *Indian Painters and White Patrons* (1971). Although the theses of the two books differed dramatically, both provided an important analysis of the development of American Indian painting in the Plains and the Southwest from the early twentieth century to the contemporary period. Dunn did not illustrate any paintings from Bialac's collection, and Brody included only one, although Tanner's 1973 edition compensated for this neglect.[20] Regardless, Bialac's collection broadened significantly in the late 1960s and began to take on the character of a survey of Southwest and Plains Indian art.

Despite Bialac's growing interest in historical works, he continued to establish friendships with artists and to purchase contemporary art, which only strengthened his national reputation as a serious and discriminating collector. These friendships gave him an intimate appreciation for the works of art, and he later affirmed, "I not only enjoyed collecting but I enjoyed those people who prepared the items which I collected."[21] For example, he purchased Narciso Abeyta's *Werewolf* (1959, plate 95) and Michael Kabotie's *Guardian of the Water* (1966, plate 70) directly from the artists in 1967. In 1973, Bialac traded a work of art to Fritz Scholder in exchange for the latter's *Indian, Dog and Teepee* (1973, plate 99). The following year, he purchased several pieces directly from the artists: Solomon McCombs' *Stalking Deer* (1973), Oscar Howe's *Waci (He is Dancing)* (1973), and Allan Houser's *Heading for the Squaw Dance* (1957). Of the aforementioned artists, both Kabotie and Scholder would become close personal friends of Bialac's, as well as influential figures in the development of contemporary American Indian art. In this regard, Bialac continued to encourage innovation and experimentation, and his relationship with the two artists deserves further attention.

Bialac met the Kabotie family in the mid-1960s. Patriarch Fred Kabotie had become one of the most celebrated Hopi artists of his generation, and his son Michael was just beginning his career. Bialac made an attempt to acquire important early works by the elder Kabotie, including *Snake Dance* (c. 1918, plate 80), but Michael's *Coming of the Shalako* (n.d., plate 71) was the first painting by a Kabotie to enter Bialac's collection. Michael became a close friend and later a client in 1973, when he asked Bialac to draft legal documents for the new artists' collective, the Artist Hopid. In addition to Kabotie, the group included Neil David, Sr., Delbridge Honanie, Milland Lomakema, and Terrance Talaswaima. They set as their mission the promotion of Hopi

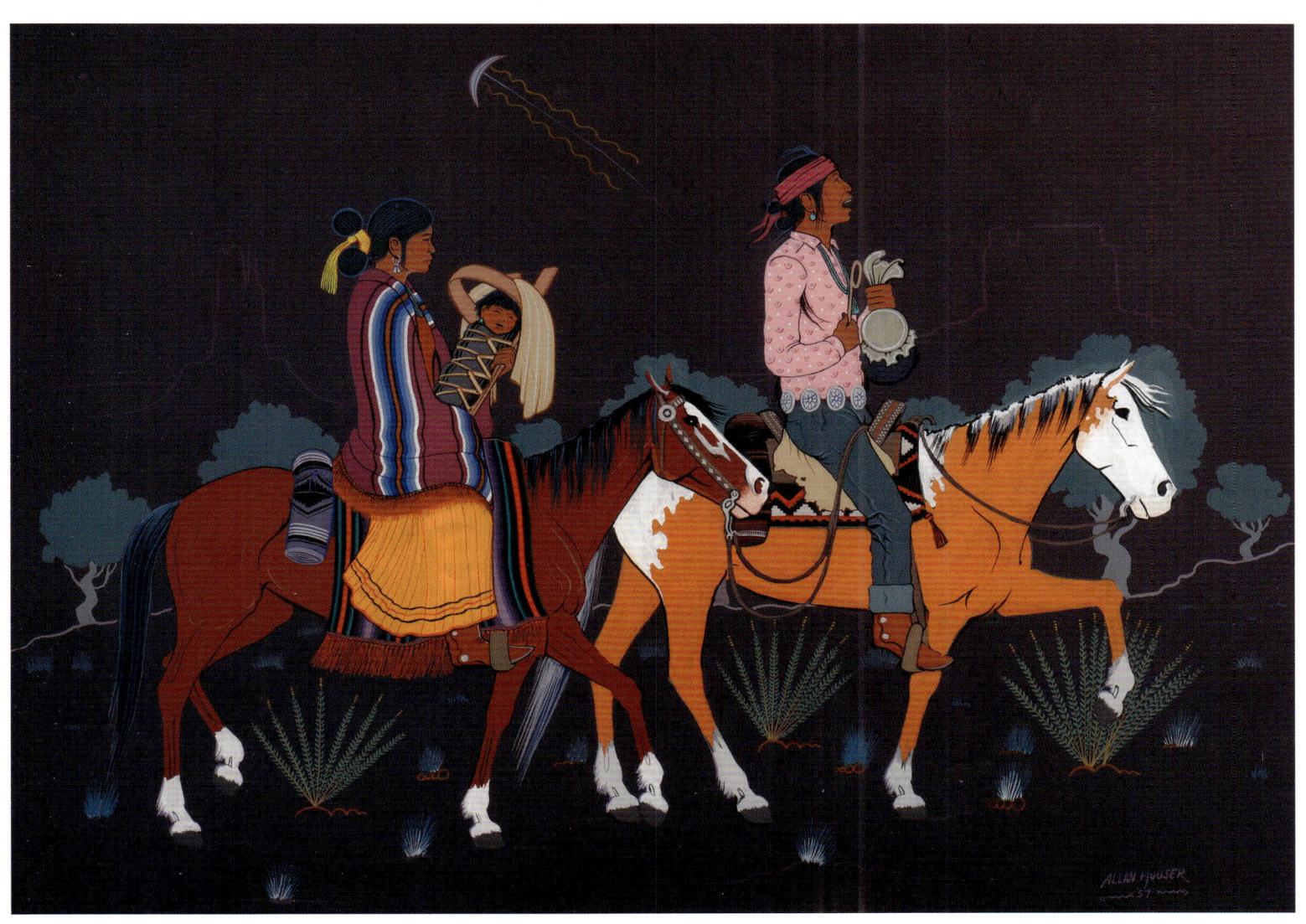

PLATE 32

ALLAN HOUSER

U.S., Chiricahua Apache, 1919–1994

Heading for the Squaw Dance, 1957

Watercolor on paper, 21 x 30 in.

© Chiinde LLC

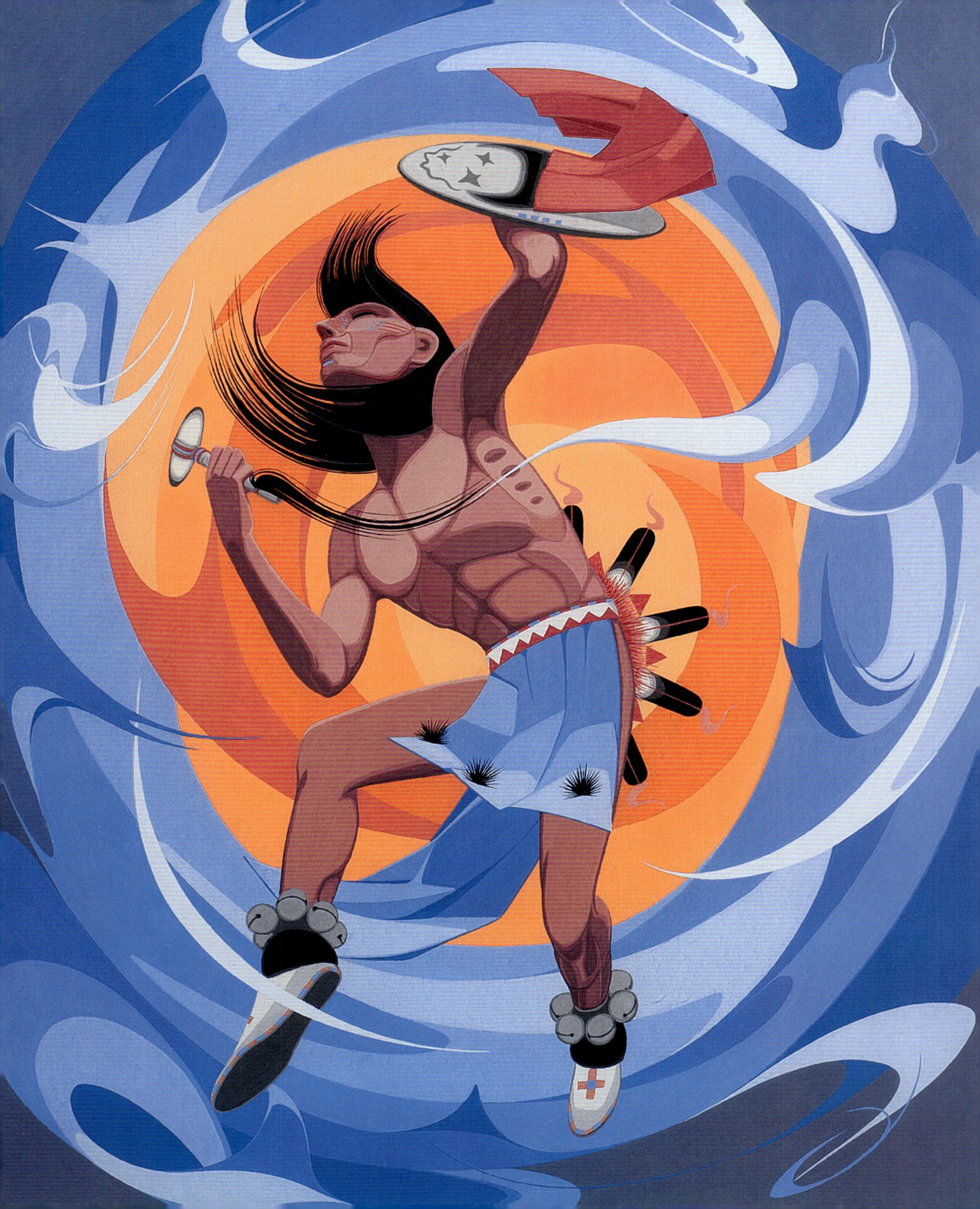

art, culture, and history and produced a manifesto enumerating their concerns, including the intent "to experiment and test new ideas and techniques in art, using traditional Hopi designs and concepts" and "to control their artistic talents and markets." The Artist Hopid felt that the established market for American Indian art had stifled creativity among the Hopis, "leaving confusion and cultural chaos," and they believed a synthesis of modernist experimentation and traditional Hopi design offered a means of artistic revival.[22]

Because the group had sought Bialac's legal counsel, he frequently sat in on meetings when they discussed their work and objectives.[23] He developed a deep admiration for the group and acquired works from all its members. Bialac's friendship with Scholder developed slightly later than that with Kabotie but was no less important. They met sometime between 1966, when Scholder won first prize in the experimental category at the fifth annual *Scottsdale National,* and 1971, during the artist's one-man exhibition at the Heard. Scholder, unlike Kabotie and the Artist Hopid, was less concerned with cultural revival than an interrogation of the popular clichés of American Indians that were ubiquitous in American culture and still present in the legacy of the Santa Fe and Taos art colonies. A quarter Luiseño, he often refuted the label of Indian artist and initially vowed never to paint American Indian subjects when he joined the faculty of IAIA in 1964. He reversed his decision in 1967 and began the Indian series to which *Indian, Dog and Tepee* (plate 99) belongs. The painting typifies Scholder's stylistic and thematic direction, derived from a mixture of Bay Area abstraction, Pop Art, and the postwar abstraction of Francis Bacon. Scholder probably based *Indian, Dog and Teepee* on a historical photograph, but he has distorted the central figure as a "deconstruction of a historically constructed, but now-fixed, fictional identity," as W. Jackson Rushing III has argued.[24] The series met with controversy from some American Indian communities, as Scholder remembered: "I was surprised by the uproar that came about because I had realized that the subject needed to be brought into a contemporary mode. . . . The older Indians felt that I, in some way, was against Indians."[25] Although he denied an Indian identity, he was consistently characterized as an American Indian artist in exhibitions from the 1960s and 1970s, and by authors such as J. J. Brody and Jamake Highwater, whose *Song of the Earth* (1976) positioned Scholder as "one of the few Indian painters who has a major reputation in the leading cities."[26] Bialac collected numerous works from Scholder in a variety of media, and it was not uncommon for the latter to give a gift to the former, such as the 1976 print *Indian in Paris* (plate 100). Their friendship also led to experiments in Scholder's career, namely the creation of his only stained glass window, *Pottery Motifs,* which was fabricated for Bialac's Scottsdale residence around 1980.

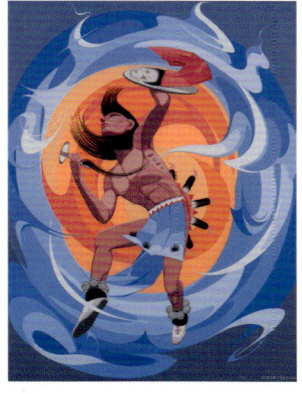

PLATE 33

OSCAR HOWE

U.S., Yanktonai Nakota, 1915–1983

Waci (He is Dancing), 1973

Watercolor on paper, 22½ x 17 in.

Courtesy of Oscar Howe Estate

Friendships with artists such as Scholder and Kabotie firmly linked Bialac and his collection to some of the more important developments in contemporary American Indian art. In the 1980s, he acquired works by innovative artists that had helped to change perceptions about American Indian art. For example, he purchased Emmi Whitehorse's *Kin'nah'zin #122* (1981, plate 109) from Marilyn Butler Fine Art in 1982 and Jaune Quick-to-See Smith's *Summer Journey II* (1988, plate 108) from the gallery in 1990; Harry Fonseca's *Coyote Doin' a Rudolph Valentino* (1985, plate 105) from Elaine Horwitch Galleries in 1991; and T. C. Cannon's *Zuni (After S. Gordon Photo)* (1976, plate 50) from W. E. Channing Company in 1993. Bialac also developed a friendship with George Morrison in the 1980s and worked out a trade in 1991 for the latter's *Soft Light, Warm Violet Day, Red Rock Variation: Lake Superior Landscape* (1990, plate 97). In the 1980s, many of these artists were featured in exhibitions and books that offered historical surveys of American Indian art, but with the theoretical purpose of constructing an ideological continuity between the art of the past and present and between disparate tribal traditions. Authors such as Highwater, Arthur Silberman, Rennard Strickland, and Edwin L. Wade addressed how questions of "Indianness" informed the perception and criticism of American Indian art and art history, and each explored questions of identity irrespective, to some degree, of tribal affiliation.[27] Artists from the Southwest and Plains were examined next to those of the Eastern Woodlands, the Northwest Coast, and the Arctic, with the intent not only of introducing audiences to artists that had been previously unappreciated but also of examining how modernity had affected the art of different cultures. Only Silberman included works from Bialac's collection in his exhibition catalogue, *100 Years of Native American Painting*. These publications, and their investigation of multiple tribal traditions, coincided with the expansion of Bialac's collection into contemporary art of the 1980s and beyond the cultural groups of the Southwest and the Plains.[28]

PLATE 34

FRITZ SCHOLDER

U.S., German, French,
English, Luiseño, 1937–2005
Pottery Motifs, c. 1980
Mixed media, 65¼ x 96¼ in.

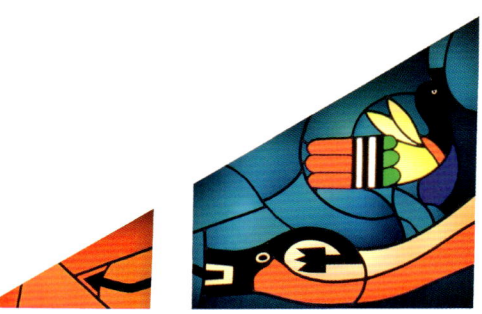
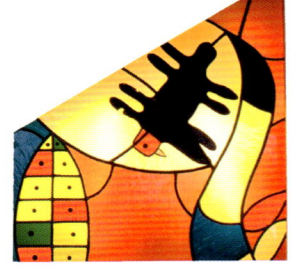
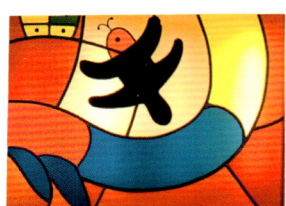

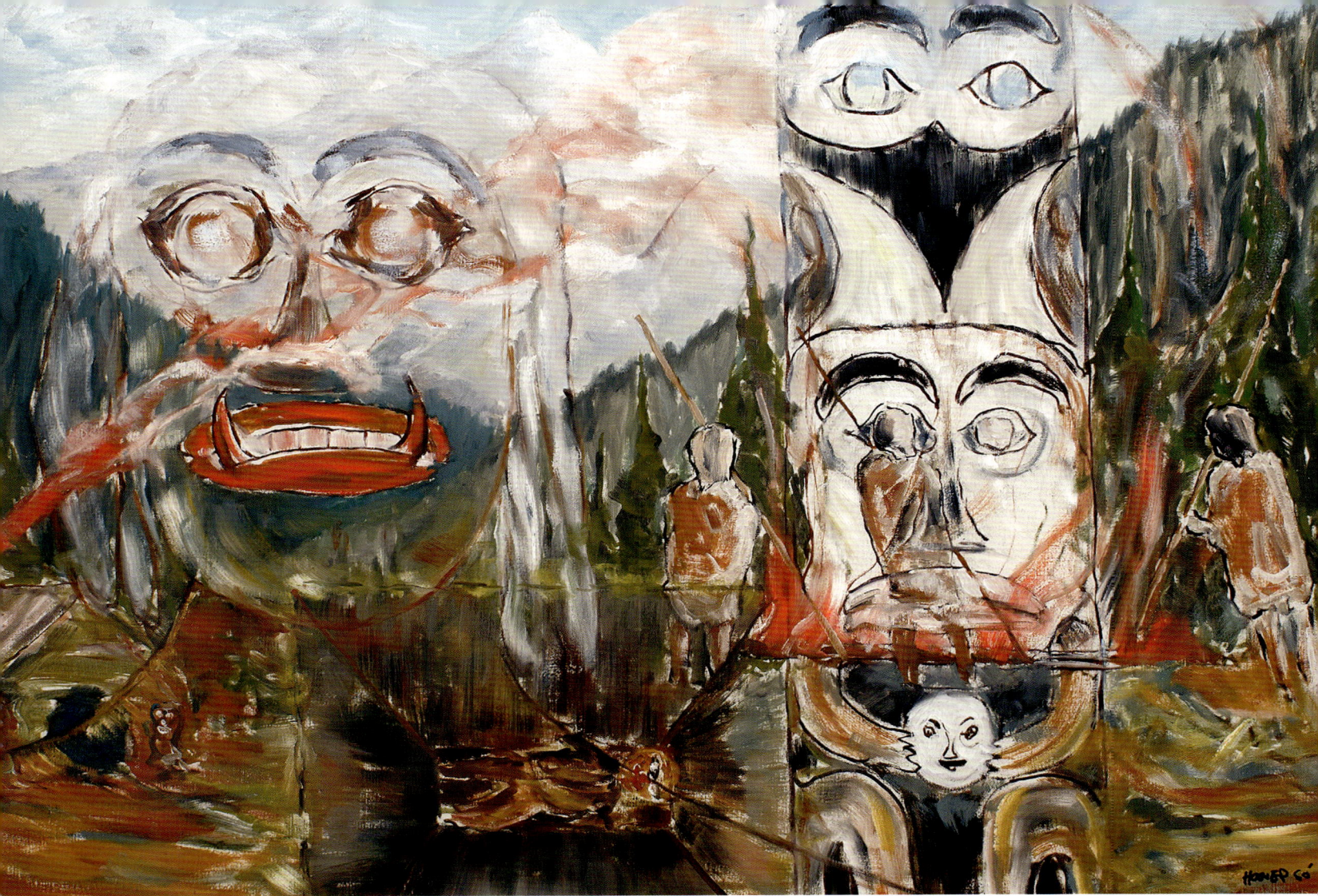

This expansion of the collection took various forms in the 1980s and 1990s. Arguably, Bialac's fascination with the artists of the Arctic in the late 1990s was most significant. Dan Albrecht, the former president of the Heard Board of Trustees, suggested that Bialac explore Alaskan material, and the latter purchased a few pieces in the late 1990s; however, Bialac's friendship with Aleut artist John Hoover facilitated a sizeable acquisition of Aleut, Inuit, Inupiat, and Yupik art.[29] The two likely met in 1973 at Hoover's exhibition at the Heard, and Bialac would become a friend and an important patron, purchasing mature sculpture such as *Shaman Catching a Soul* (1978, plate 166) as well as early paintings, such as *How the Mosquitos Were Formed* (1960).[30] In the 1980s, Hoover became one of the most respected contemporary artists from Alaska, and his work was featured in the publications of Highwater, Wade, and Strickland.

PLATE 35

JOHN HOOVER

U.S., Aleut, 1919–2011

How the Mosquitoes Were Formed, 1960

Oil on canvas,

23¼ x 34¼ in.

As Bialac's interest in the Arctic increased, Hoover offered to introduce him to Dorothy Jean Ray, one of the foremost scholars and collectors of Arctic art. Since the late 1940s, Ray had been influential in the critical support and promotion of numerous artists, including George Aden Ahgupuk, his brother-in-law James Kivetoruk Moses, Robert Mayokok, and Florence Nupok Chauncey-Malewotkuk. She had recently donated much of the collection she had amassed during her long career to the University of Alaska–Fairbanks; however, Ray retained pieces by most of the major artists, and in 2002, Bialac began to purchase many of those works. He initially acquired numerous pieces by Moses, including *Eskimo Igloo* (1964) and *Walrus Hunters* (1968), prompting Ray to speculate that his collection "must be one of the largest. At any rate, it's one of (no, I mean *the*) best preserved!"[31]

In 2003, he expanded the collection with pieces such as Ahgupuk's *Summer Camp Life* (2008) and Mayokok's *Polar Bear Hunting* (n.d.). Prints had been of particular interest to Ray, and she also offered Bialac Joseph Engasongwok Senungetuk's *Abstract Man and Birds* (1966) and Bernard Katexac's *Nomad's Scrimshaw* (1966), the latter of which had been included in Ray's 1969 publication for the Indian Arts and Crafts Board, *Graphic Arts of the Alaskan Eskimo*.[32] Ray also parted with a pair of prints by Milo Minock, *Spring Muskrat Hunting* (1976), and his son Patrick Minock, *Potlatch Dance (Lower Yukon, Alaska)* (c. 1978), both of which were illustrated in her 1981 *Aleut and Eskimo Art: Tradition and Innovation in South Alaska*.[33]

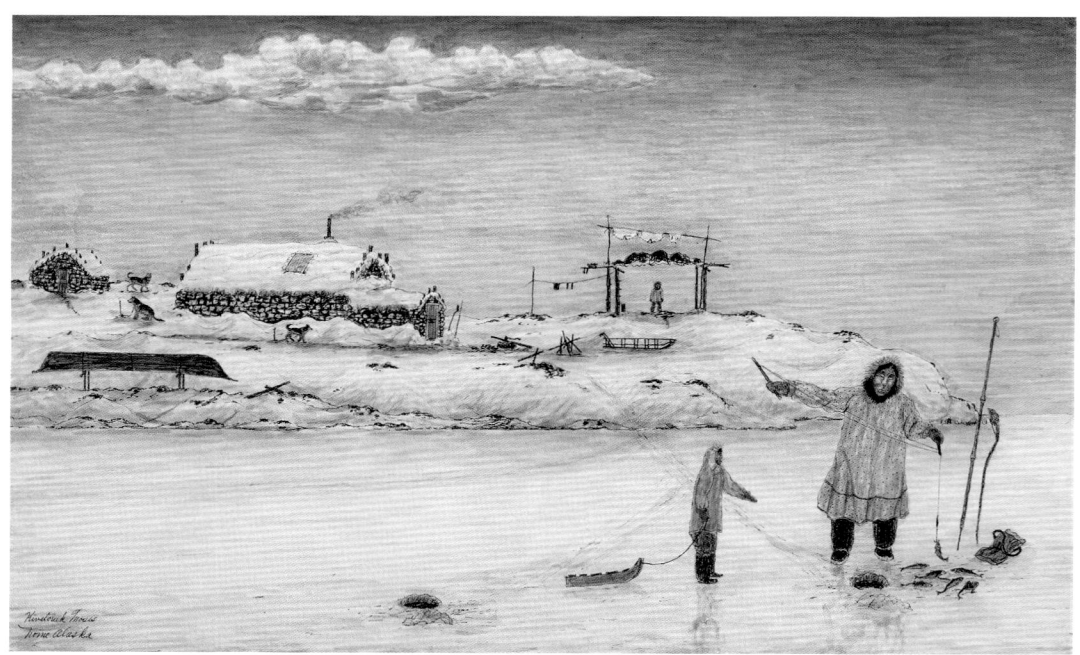

PLATE 36

JAMES KIVETORUK MOSES

U.S., Inupiat, 1900–1982

Eskimo Igloo, 1964

Ink and pencil on paper,

10 x 15¾ in.

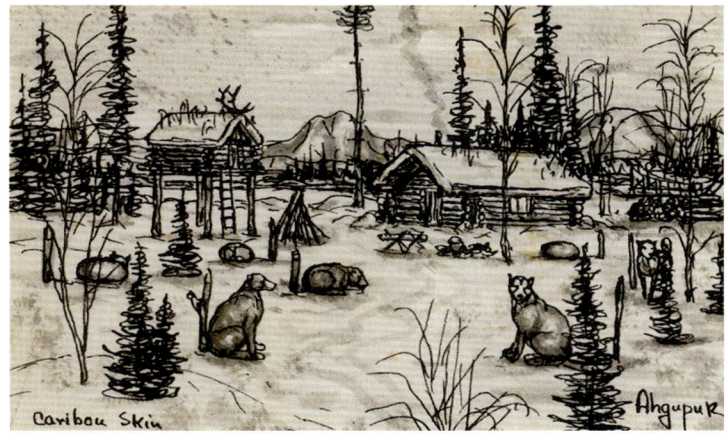

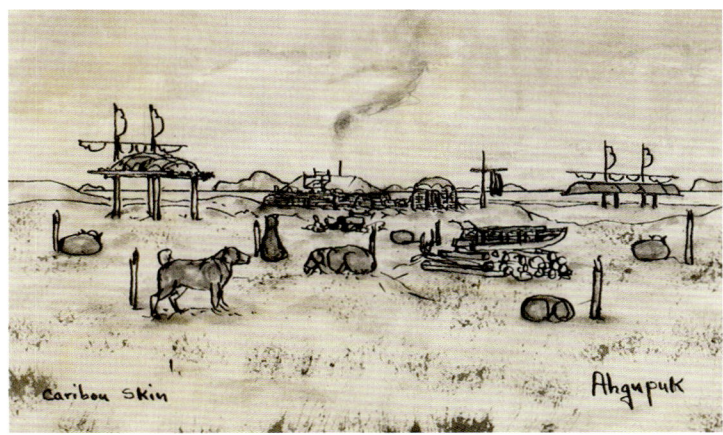

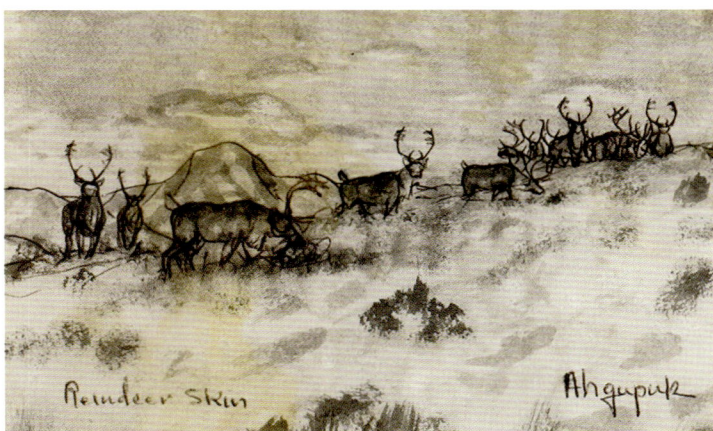

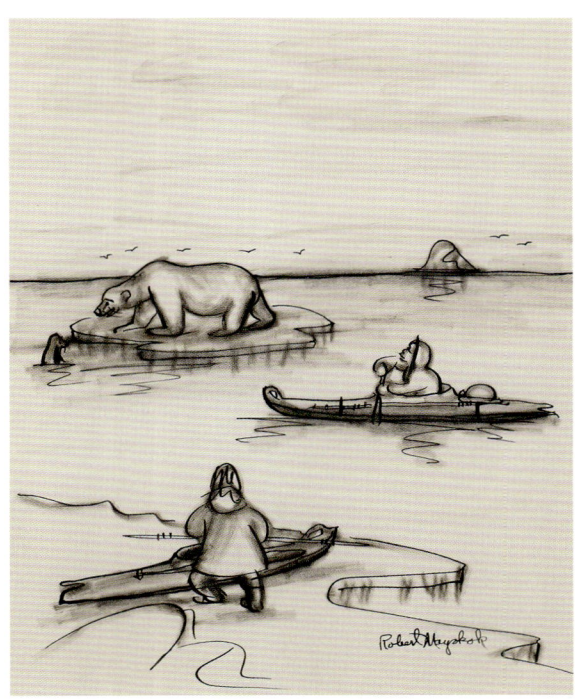

PLATE 37 (LEFT COLUMN)

GEORGE TWOK ADEN AHGUPUK

U.S., Inupiaq, 1911–2001

Summer Camp Life, 2008

Pen and ink on caribou skin, 3¾ x 5¾ in. each

PLATE 38 (ABOVE)

ROBERT MAYOKOK

U.S., Inupiat, 1903–1983

Polar Bear Hunting, n.d.

Pen and ink on paper, 9¾ x 7¾ in.

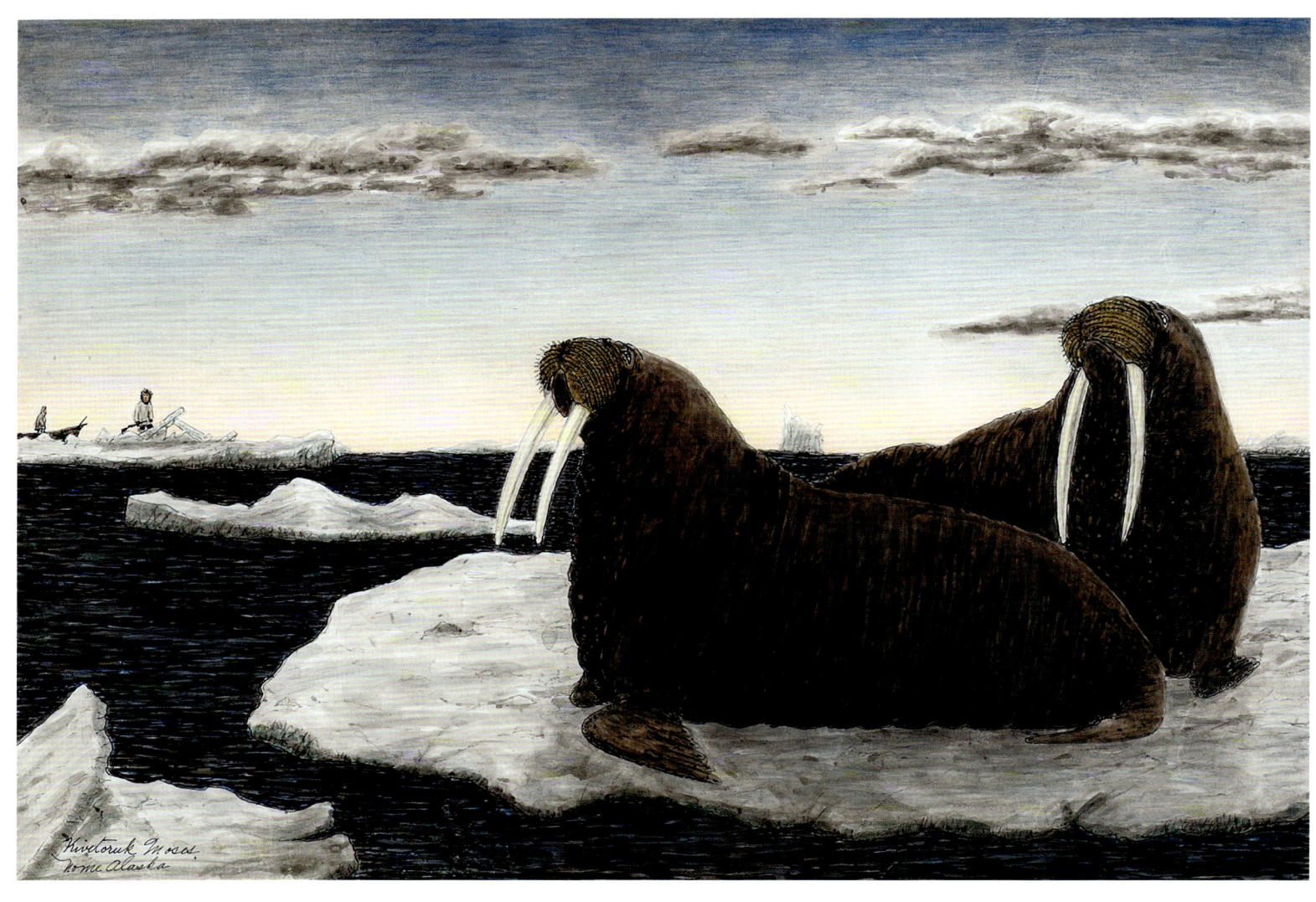

PLATE 39

JAMES KIVETORUK MOSES

U.S., Inupiat, 1900–1982

Walrus Hunters, 1968

India ink and colored pencil on paper, 8 x 11½ in.

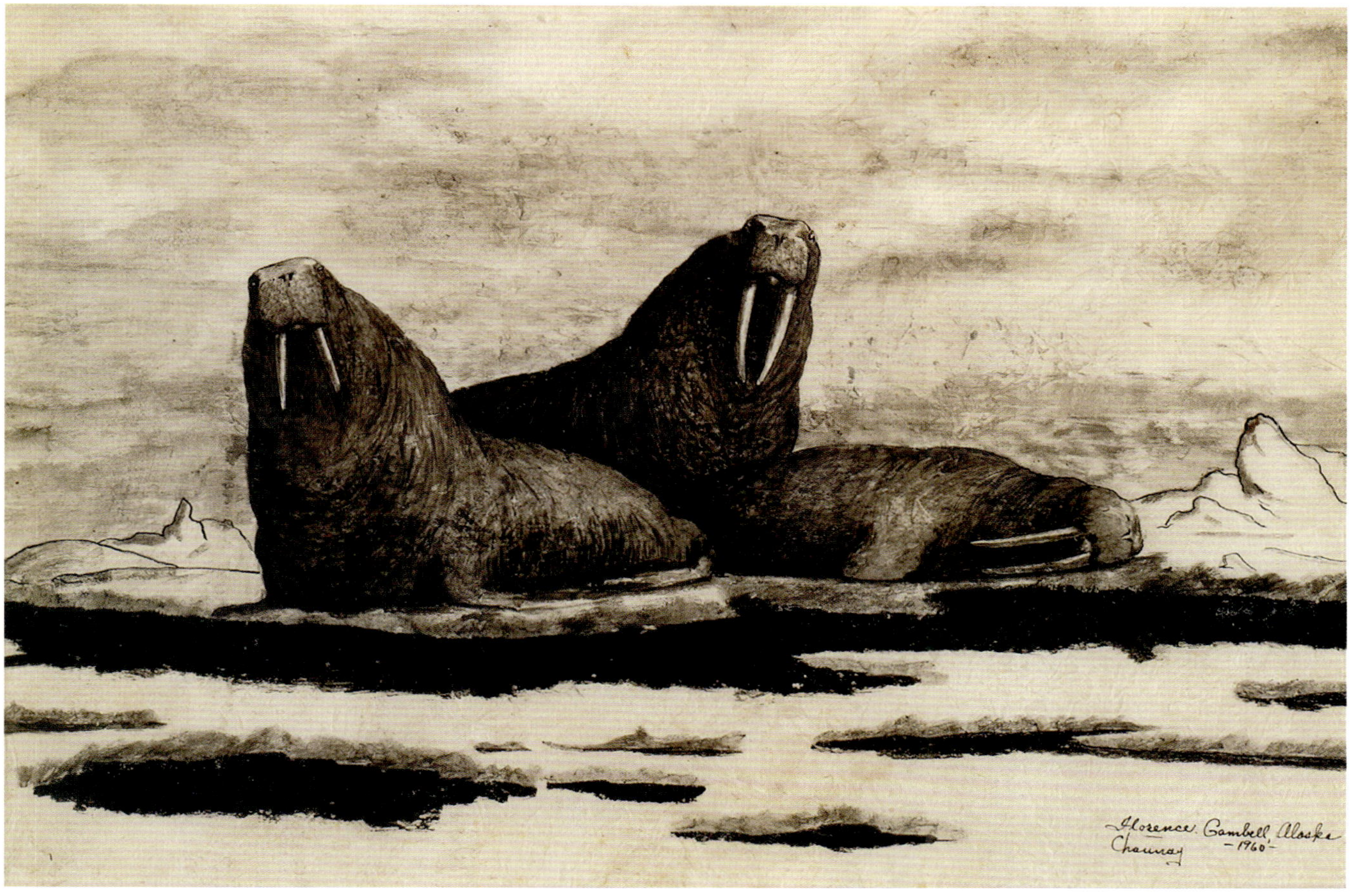

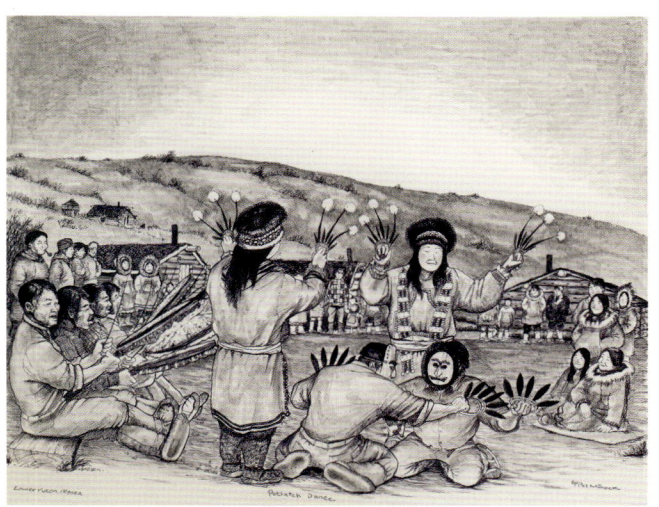

PLATE 40 (LEFT)

PATRICK MINOCK

U.S., Yupik, b. 1947

Potlatch Dance (Lower Yukon,

Alaska), c. 1978

Pen and ink on paper, 10¾ × 13¾ in.

PLATE 41 (ABOVE)

FLORENCE NUPOK

CHAUNCEY-MALEWOTKUK

U.S., St. Lawrence Yupik, 1905–1971

Walruses, 1960

Ink on reindeer skin, 6 × 8¾ in.

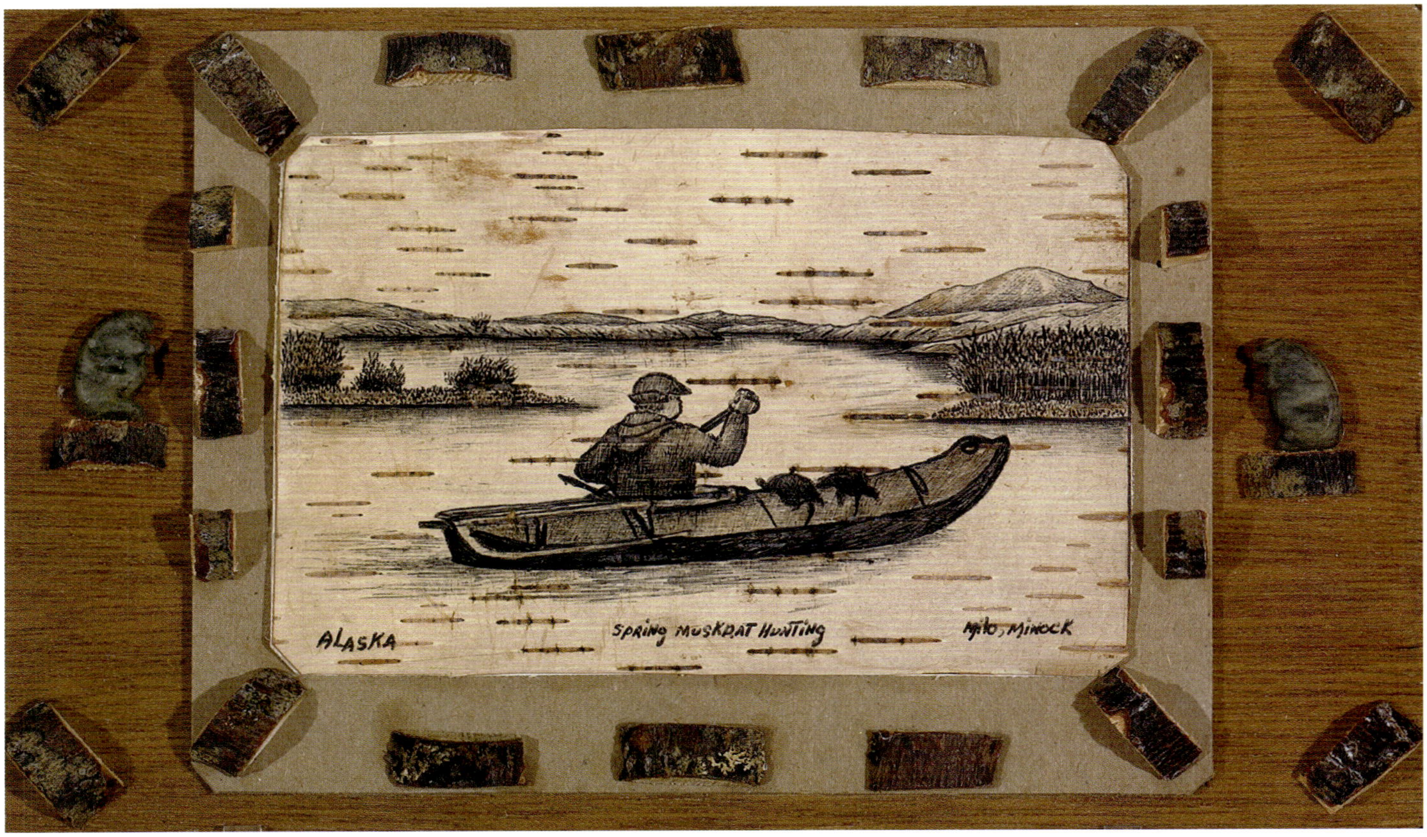

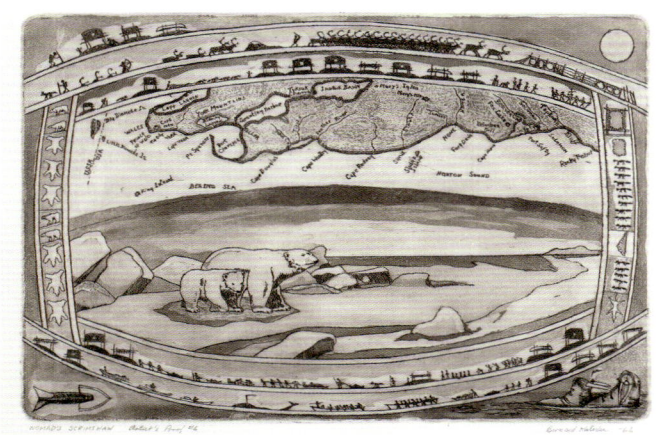

MILO MINOCK

Spring Muskrat Hunting, 1976

PLATE 42

MILO MINOCK

U.S., Yupik, 1912–1996

Spring Muskrat Hunting, 1976

Mixed media, 5½ x 9¼ in.

PLATE 43

BERNARD TUGLAMENA KATEXAC

U.S., Inupiat, 1922–1987

Nomad's Scrimshaw, 1966

Etching, 24 x 36½ in.

PLATE 44

JOSEPH ENGASONGWOK

SENUNGETUK

U.S., Inupiat, b. 1940

Abstract Man and Birds, 1966

Woodcut, 15 x 13¼ in.

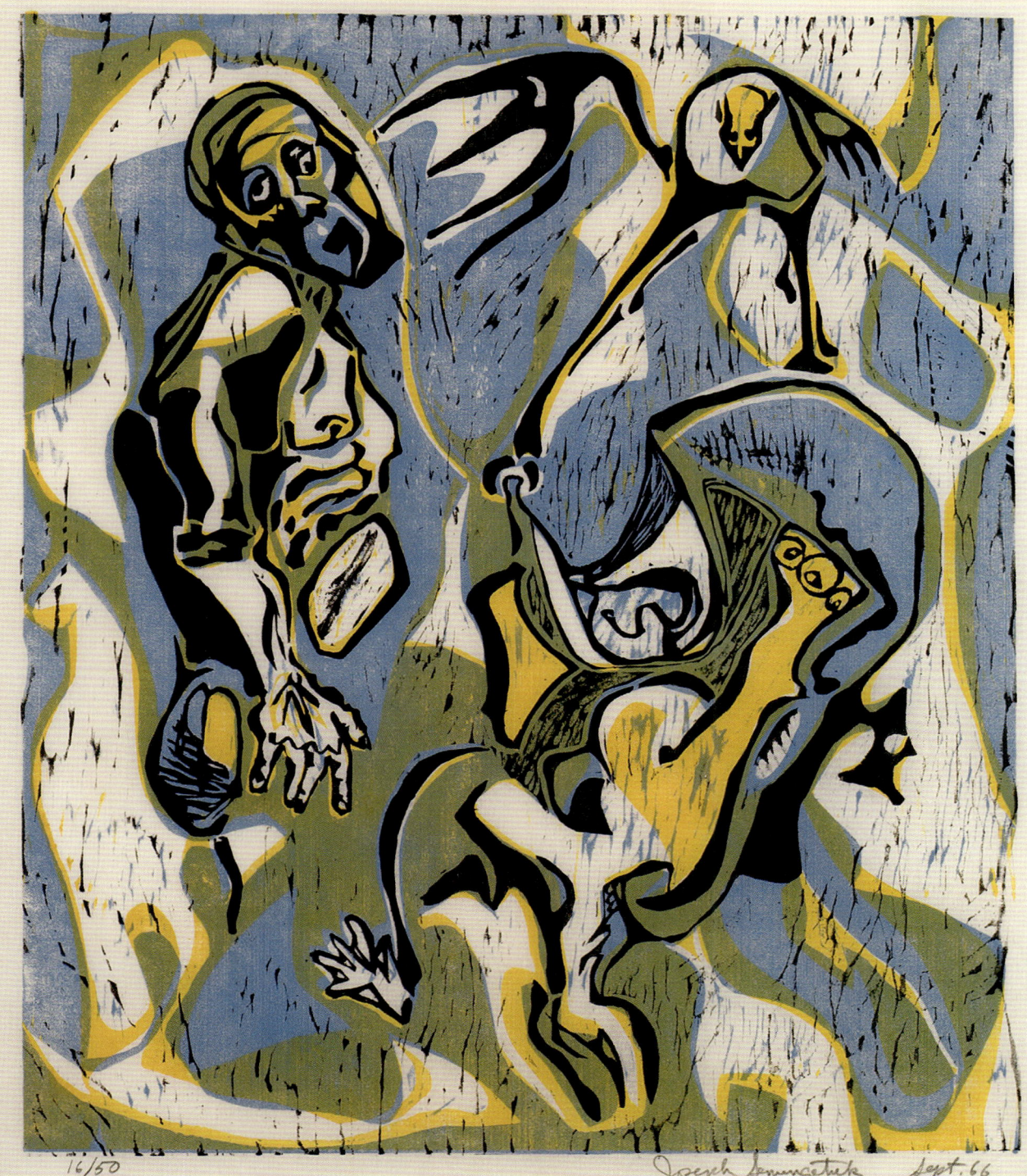

16/50   Joseph Senungetuk   Sept. 66

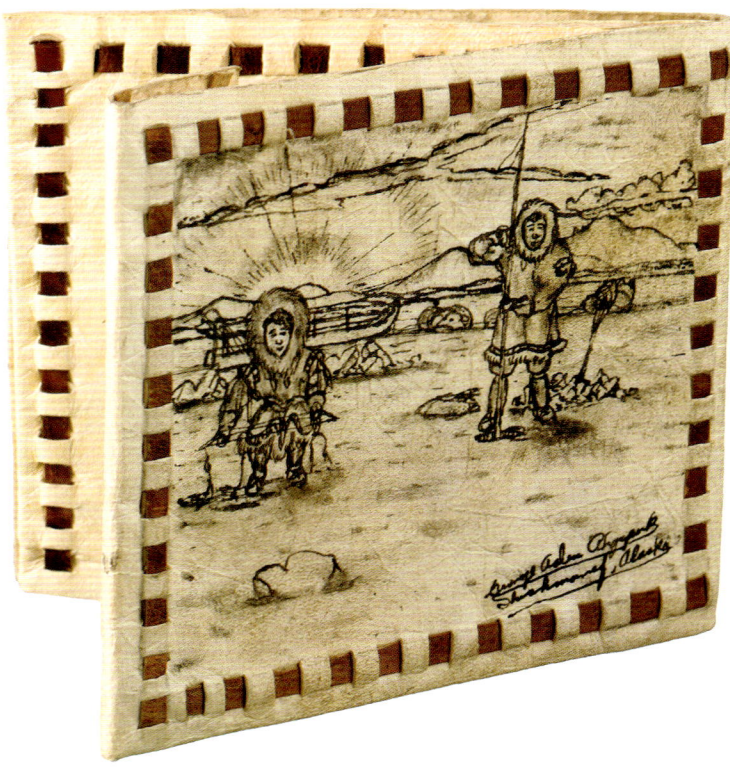

When Ray no longer had available pieces by important artists, Bialac sought out suitable examples elsewhere, as was the case with *Walruses* (1960), by Florence Nupok Chauncey-Malewotkuk. His interests in Arctic art expanded over the subsequent decade to include intriguing objects for the tourist market, like a wallet Ahgupuk created in the 1940s or '50s, and innovative contemporary constructions, such as Alvin Amason's *Arctic Sea Otter* (2007), with its gesturally painted otter complete with a sculptural nose.

With the acquisition of works by Arctic artists, Bialac's collection achieved a breadth and diversity unparalleled by any other private collector. The strength of his collection remained the Southwest and the Plains, but four decades of acquisitions had resulted in a rich survey of the major American Indian artists of the twentieth century from across the continent. Although he took a serious interest in historical artists beginning in the late 1960s, he remained consistently interested in contemporary art, and over the most recent decade, he purchased works by a younger generation of contemporary artists of varying stylistic and conceptual bents. Many of the works were acquired directly from the artists, a practice he has continued since the 1960s. Recent acquisitions have sometimes been representational, such as Norma Howard's *Little Brother of War* (2001), which had won first place at the eightieth annual Santa Fe Indian Market. Howard's painting owes a clear debt to the history of traditional American Indian painting, with its focus

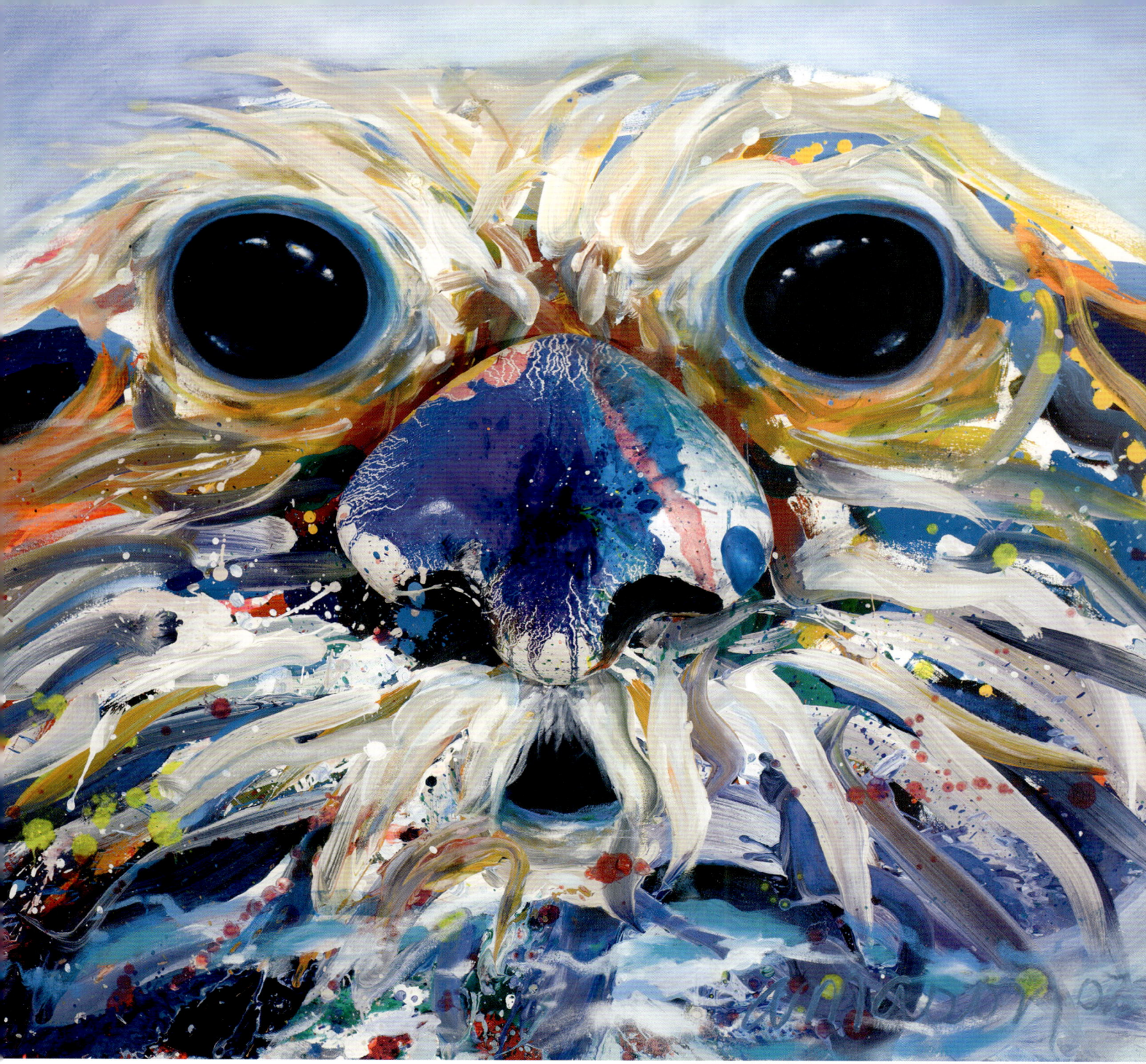

PLATE 46

ALVIN AMASON

U.S., Sugpiaq, b. 1948

Arctic Sea Otter, 2007

Mixed media, 31½ x 34½ in.

on the salient details of the figures. By contrast, Benjamin Harjo, Jr.'s *Imagine That* (2003), which won a first-place ribbon from the eighty-second Santa Fe Indian Market, seems to have little to do with the tradition of American Indian painting. Harjo's style references Cubism and mid-century abstraction, although his color and patterning demonstrate some influence from Seminole patchwork clothing.

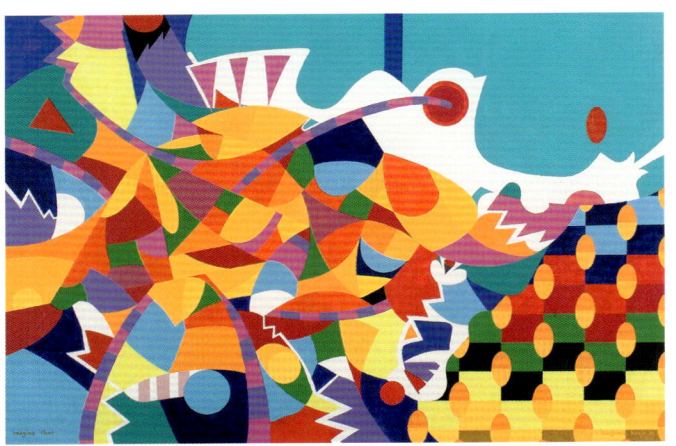

Similarly, Tony Abeyta's *Seed Simply Emerging* (2008, plate 115) is decidedly abstract and was purchased from the artist after it appeared in the Heard's 2008–2009 exhibition *Underworldness.* The painting depicts germinating seedlings, flanked by two panels containing pieces of black micaceous clay. Abeyta's interest was the mysterious world beneath the surface of the soil, among growing plants and the remnants of ancient pottery. While the Abeyta seems to have little in common with the Howard, both testify to Bialac's varied taste and his appreciation for tradition and innovation.

This aspect of Bialac's connoisseurship is epitomized, in many ways, by an acquisition from 2008, America Meredith's *Acee Blue Eagle and Echogee* (2008). The painting belongs to a series celebrating the achievements of important figures in the history of American Indian art. Blue Eagle stands before his painting of the blue deer, *Echogee,* that he immortalized in paint and in a children's book he wrote in 1932 (posthumously published in 1971). Meredith, in paying homage to Blue Eagle, also locates herself in a venerable tradition of American Indian painting that continues to inform contemporary art.

The acquisition of works by artists such as Meredith, Abeyta, and Howard demonstrate the important role Bialac has played as a patron of American Indian art in the present period. From his early purchases at the *Scottsdale National* to the recent decade, he has consistently supported contemporary American Indian art, whether "traditional" or experimental. His friendships with artists, dealers, and scholars placed him in a unique position to witness and influence important developments in the field, and his collection has achieved renown through exhibition and publication as one of the most important in the country, if not the world. In this regard, James T. Bialac's history as a patron and a collector offers important insights into the history of American Indian art in the latter half of the twentieth century.

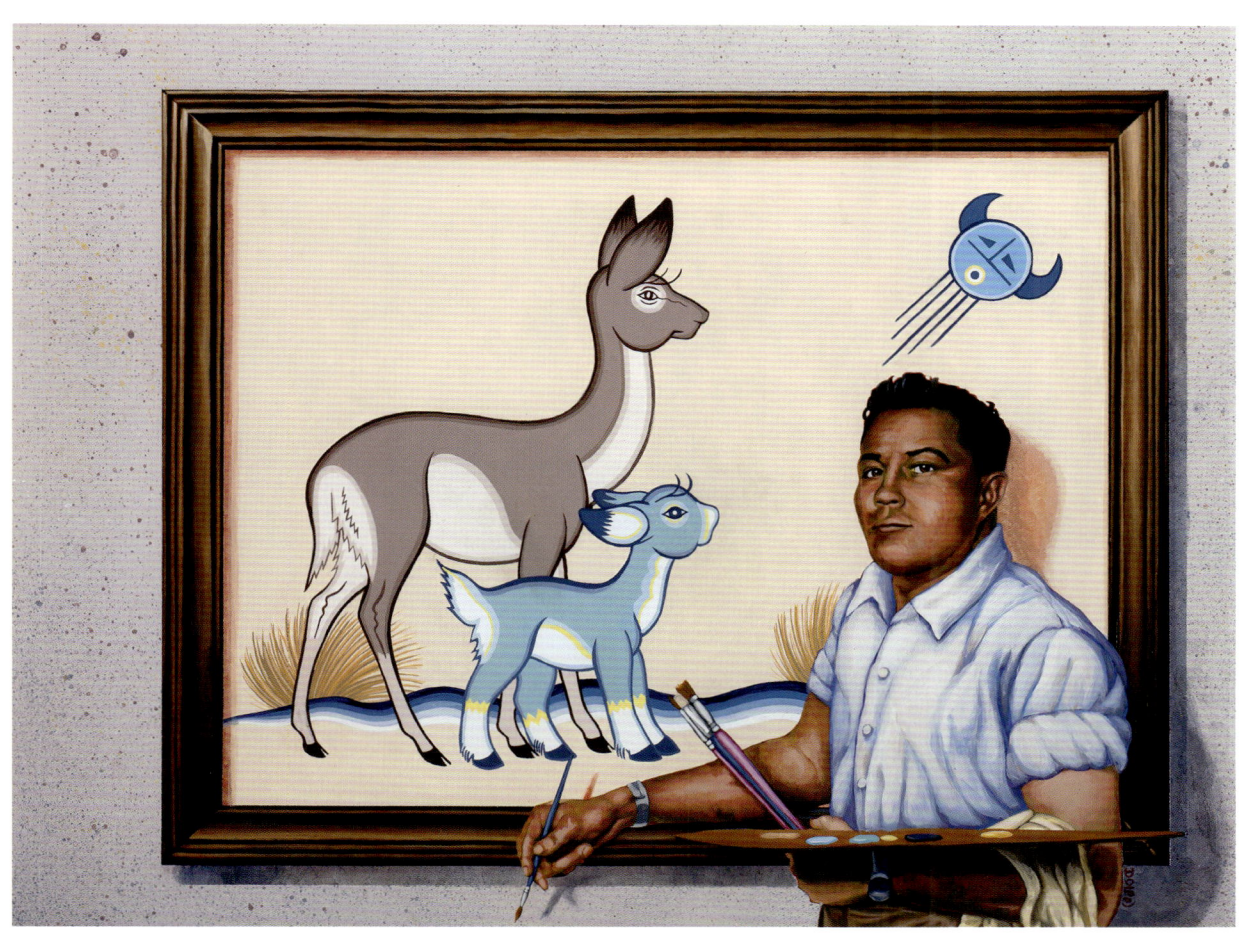

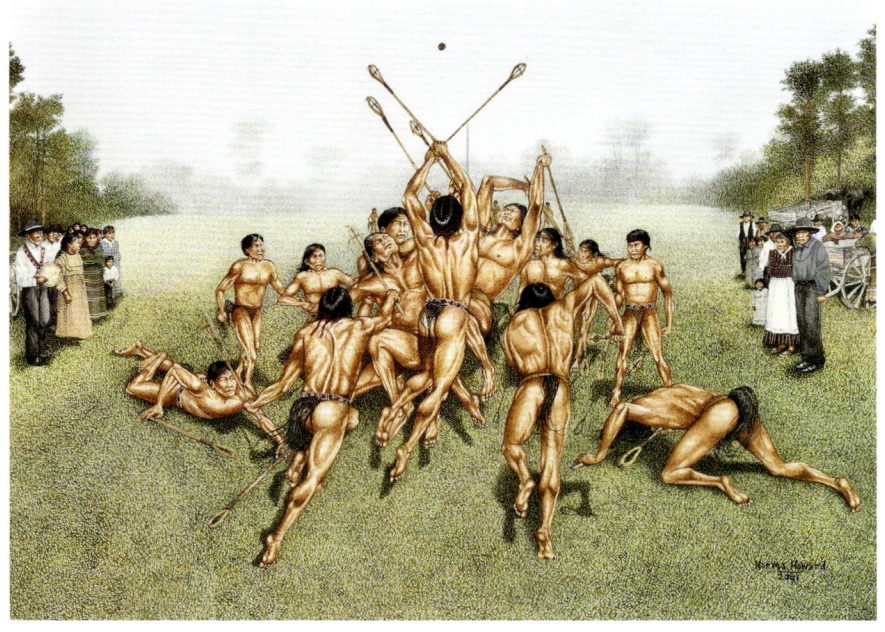

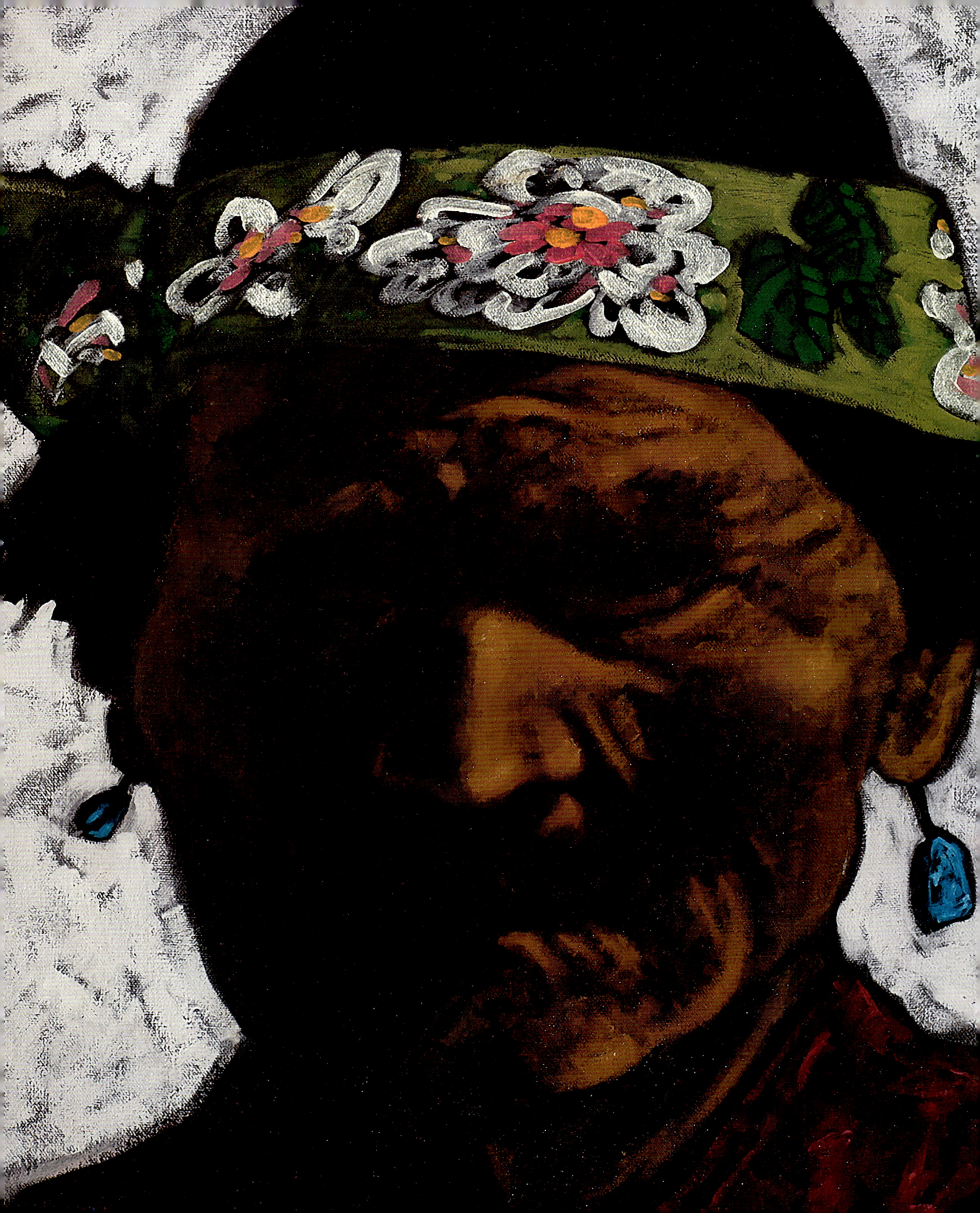

3 | Native American Painting

SCHOOLS, STYLES, AND MOVEMENTS

Edwin L. Wade and Rennard Strickland

EVERY MINUTE DETAIL of European-Indian relations has affected and shaped the image and character of Indian painting, from initial exploratory encounters, the ensuing trade relations, treaties made and broken, wars, the establishment of reservations, and turn-of-the-century punitive anti-Indian legislation to, finally, an overdue corrective legal overture to Native sovereignty during the last two decades of the past century. This tapestry of events is inextricably woven into the impetus to paint, communicate, and record the Native narrative, and, depending on the circumstances of place and time in Native America, various media have been employed to deliver the message. Over decades of thoughtful collecting, Jim Bialac has assembled a body of Native paintings that illuminates both the broad movements and subtler, less known corners of this history.

It is not the purpose of this chapter to document the history of Native North America; others have acquitted themselves admirably in tackling that task. Yet, the general historical record in the field of Native American art has perhaps too often given way to the recitation of "known"

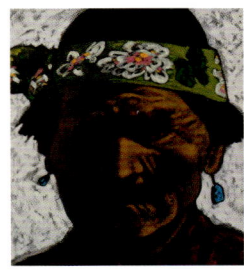

PLATE 50

T. C. CANNON

U.S., Kiowa/Caddo, 1946–1978

Zuni (After S. Gordon Photo), 1976

Oil on canvas, 19 x 17 in.

© Joyce Cannon Yi–Executor

of T. C. Cannon Estate

events and the depiction of convenient characters who populate a subjective drama. Until the 1970s the history of Native American painting was pronouncedly self-attentive, and Indian painters remained opaque, blurred within the collective dazzle of their Anglo patrons' wishes and desires. Much time has been spent on anecdotal resuscitation of art market cult figures. As indisputably important as were the legendary patrons Dorothy Dunn, Margretta Dietrich, Edgar Hewett, Alice Corbin Henderson, Kenneth Chapman, Mary Colton, Oscar Jacobson, Susie Peters, Dolly Sloan, Mary Austin, Elizabeth DeHuff, Katherine Harvey, and others, and the organizations and institutions they founded (the Santa Fe Indian School, Southwest Indian Arts Association, School of American Research, Museum of New Mexico, Museum of Northern Arizona, Gilcrease Museum, Bacone College, and University of Oklahoma), their contributions to nurturing a nascent art is a story that has been told, and with the finding of any new fact, unabashedly told again. In deference to the pursuit of the broader spirit of an art growing and flexing beyond the singular, though important, lifetime of any one individual, Anglo or Indian, we will refrain from retelling this patron tale.[1]

What caused this obsession with Anglo collecting history to eclipse an exploration of Native artistic voice on its own terms? One major factor is the charisma, glamour, and cohesive social and economic might of Santa Fe, New Mexico, as the first "cosmopolitan" Indian art market town in the United States. By the turn of the twentieth century, it was well on its way to positioning itself as the birthing place of commercial Native easel painting. J. J. Brody cites the event as occurring specifically in the year 1900 in the nearby pueblo of San Ildefonso, a view that overlooks considerable prior history, such as the commissioned work of several nineteenth-century Zuni, Navajo, and Apache illustrators for their scientific sponsors twenty years earlier.[2] In truth, an entire complex history of Native American painting, inclusive of distinctive tribal and regional "schools," predates the iconic marketplace phenomenon of Santa Fe. For all its charms, the cult of Santa Fe has resulted in (1) an overemphasis on the social activities of a regional Anglo patronage at the expense of recognizing a self-aware national Indian artistry; (2) a misrepresentation of commercial Indian painting as a purely twentieth-century phenomenon; (3) the assumption that Anglo patrons often dictated styles and subjects within the new art to the exclusion of Native creativity; and (4) an underappreciation of the cultural continuity that existed between nineteenth-century tribal traditions and later Indian painting on paper and the existence of particular long-evolving schools of Native American painting. Fortunately, with the acquisition of the extensive James T. Bialac collection of Native American paintings, the University of Oklahoma is now poised through future exhibitions and publications to take a fresh look at old assumptions and to advance a new perspective on the meaning and significance of Indian painting.

Within the past twenty years, scholarly interest has gradually but definitively shifted toward the Native pictorial traditions of the equestrian Plains, resulting in a radically revised understanding of the history of commercial Indian painting. As early as the mid-1870s, a flourishing national market had existed for Plains paintings, albeit sold by Indian prisoners of war through military internment centers such as Fort Marion, Florida, and Fort Sill, Oklahoma Territory. These included the narrative scenes that came to be called ledger drawings, for the paper taken from ledger books upon which they were drawn.

The Northern Cheyenne *Two Warriors on a Horse* exhibits hallmarks of the traditional Plains style of drawing. The warriors sharing a mount are rendered in a flat two-dimensional style. To a Cheyenne viewer, significant cultural and identity information is conveyed in the picture. The feathered shield would identify the owner, as would the coup stick carried in his hand. The second warrior with the flowing eagle feather headdress likely has lost his horse and been rescued from an otherwise deadly situation.

PLATE 51

NORTHERN CHEYENNE

Two Warriors on a Horse,

c. 1880

Crayon on paper, 8½ x 9½ in.

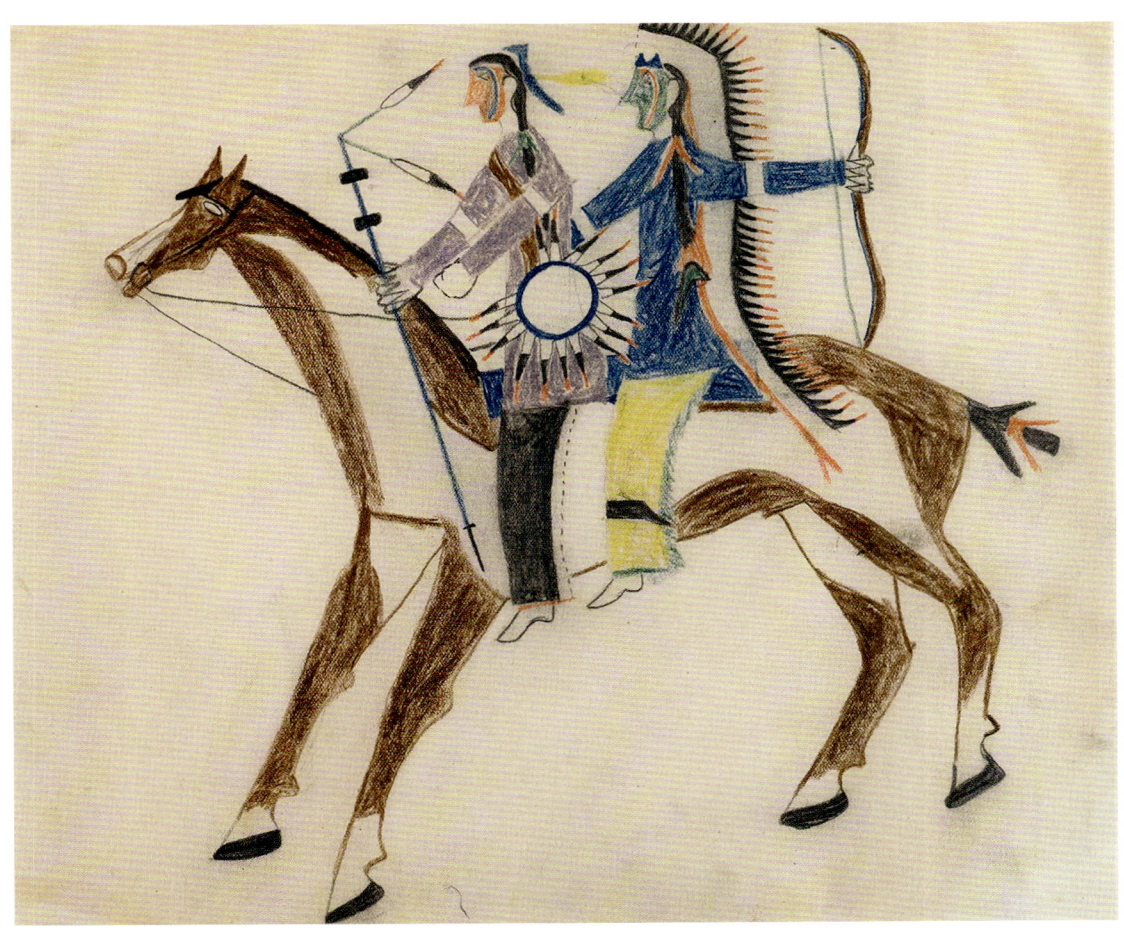

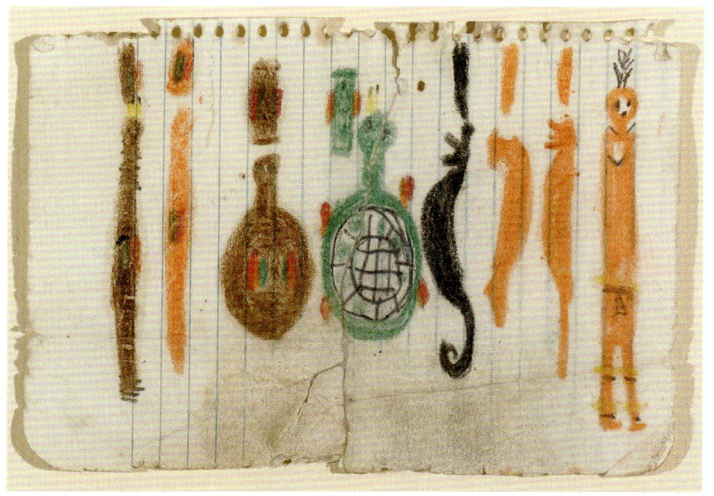

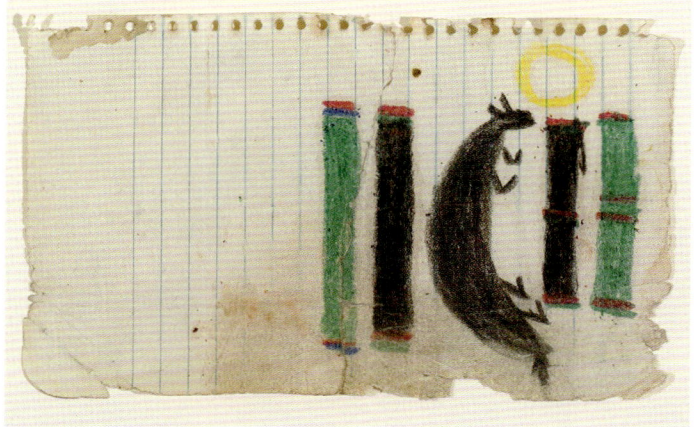

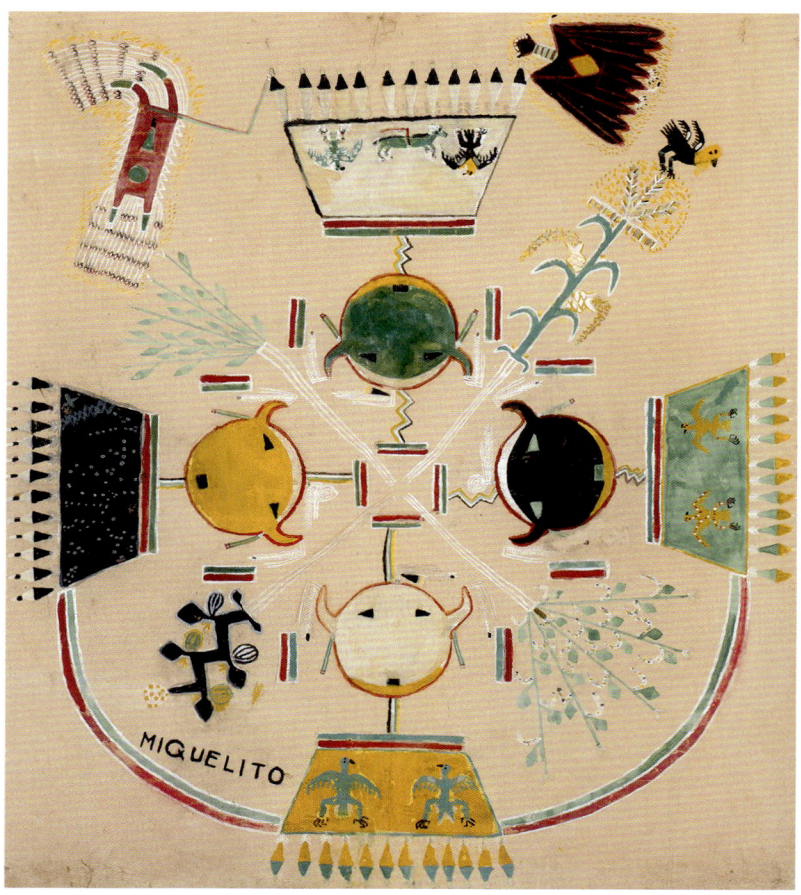

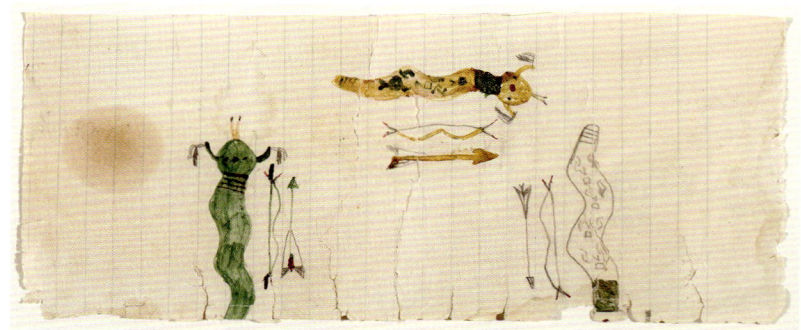

PLATE 52 (ABOVE)

UNKNOWN

U.S., possibly Navajo

Mnemonic Device #2, c. 1880–1890

Colored pencil on paper, 3¾ x 5¾ in.

PLATE 53 (BELOW)

UNKNOWN

U.S., possibly Navajo

Mnemonic Device #3, c. 1880–1890

Colored pencil on paper, 3¾ x 5¾ in.

PLATE 54 (ABOVE)

MIGUELITO

U.S., Navajo, dates unknown

Sand Painting (House of the Sun),

c. 1900–1910

Latex paint, 23½ x 20½ in.

PLATE 55 (BELOW)

UNKNOWN

U.S., possibly Navajo

Mnemonic Device #1, c. 1880–1890

Colored pencil on paper, 4¼ x 10¼ in.

Through the creative and malleable talents of nineteenth-century artists such as Making Medicine (Cheyenne), Bears Heart (Cheyenne), and Howling Wolf (Cheyenne), colored drawings built a fragile communicative bridge over the chasm of racial and cultural intolerance. And this new art, which spoke eloquently of a lost sovereignty and the encroachment of an uncertain future, was both stylistically and iconographically anchored in the visual and communicative traditions of tribal history.

Historically, strict compositional conventions prescribed the depiction of the human form in a two-thirds profile view. Equally important was an emphasis on material culture signifiers, such as hairstyles, painted shields and horses, and costuming, to denote a tribe or individuals, and physical attributes (humps, horns, and hooves) that characterized different animal species. All these traits were carried over into the prison art of the 1870s. They continued in the work of these same artists as they spoke to newer interests once they returned home. With the coming of the twentieth century, former Fort Marion prisoner Ohettoint (Charley Buffalo) would instruct his younger brother, Haungooah (Silverhorn), in the Kiowa way of drawing, as later Haungooah would teach his nephew Stephen Mopope, one of the founders of The Kiowa Five. In turn, Mopope would teach others both within and outside his tribe the evolving traditions of the past. This is what is meant by continuity between traditions, and it represents a codified Native American school of artistic expression.

Stories similar to those of the transitional Plains artists existed throughout Native North America, but none has been fully documented. Fortunately, the Bialac Collection is rich in turn-of-the-twentieth-century paintings that demonstrate the transmission of Native traditions across time and changing media. An example is a wonderful Navajo Chantway sand painting ('iikaah) on paper drawn from authentic nineteenth-century mnemonic drawings employed by Hataathli, or Medicine People.

Among the most important documents of such premarket Indian painting is *The Indian's Book*, published by Natalie Curtis Burlin (1875–1921) in 1907 and expanded and reissued in 1923. The Bialac Collection possesses the original portfolio of the two books acquired directly from Curtis's descendants. The importance of these publications is twofold. First, in the 1907 edition, all the illustrated paintings were obtained from named Native artists between 1903 and 1906. This is very early and reveals in the sophistication of the work a developed competency for painting on paper. Of particular significance is a painting by Ma-Pe-Wi (Velino Shije Herrera) titled *Lololomai's Prayer*, produced for the 1923 edition of *The Indian's Book* between 1915 and 1920. This remarkable painting incorporates elements of Hopi figurative art (the four warriors), Art Deco (the sky disk), and thirteenth-century Mimbres painting (the black creature to the right

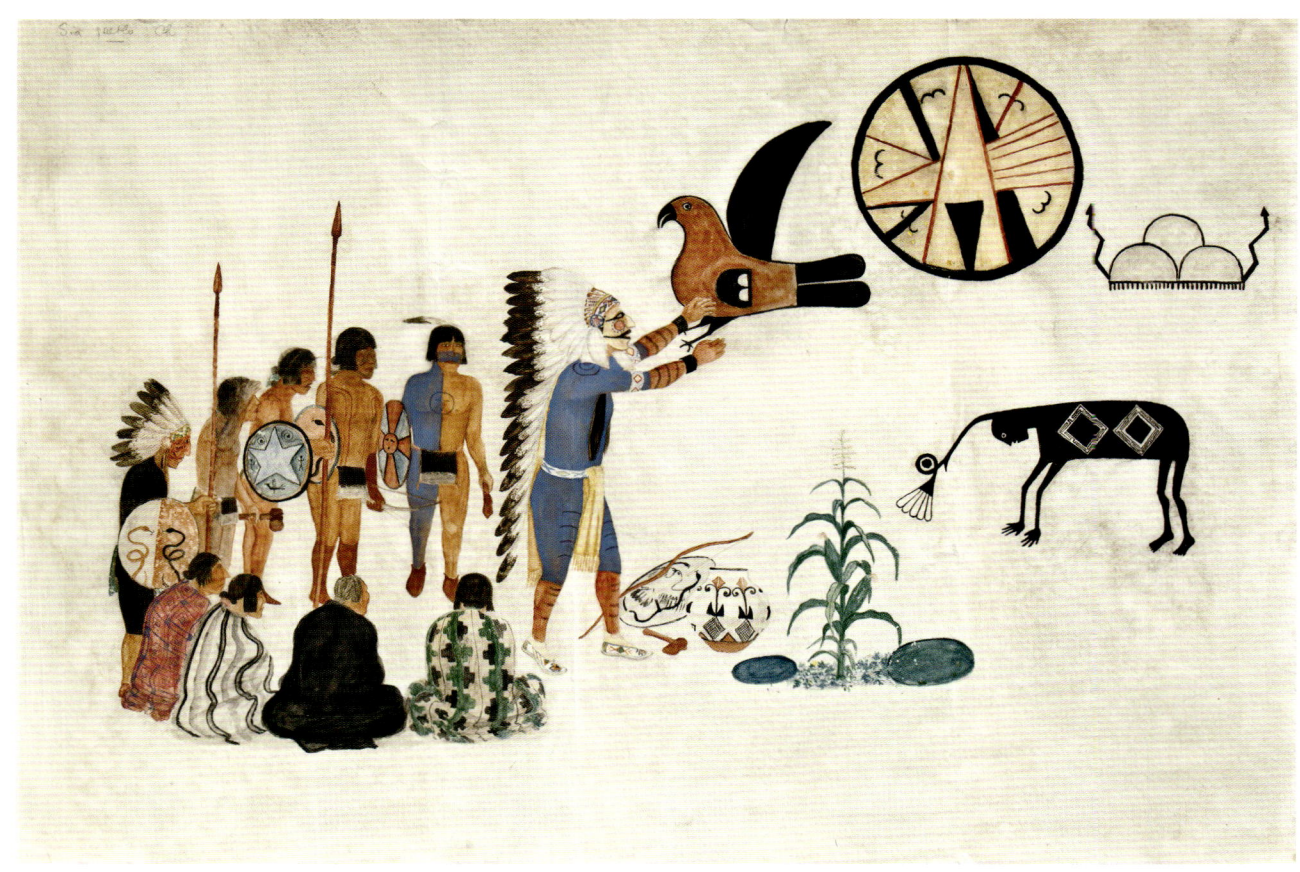

PLATE 56

VELINA SHIJE HERRERA

(MA-PE-WI)

U.S., Zia Pueblo, 1902–1973

Lololomai's Prayer, 1915–1920

Watercolor on paper, 14¾ x 22 in.

of the composition). Ma-Pe-Wi would have been at most eighteen when the work was created. Second, contrary to the common belief that painting was a man's art, a high percentage of the listed artists are women. Among the various women cited are the Cheyenne Wowesta, wife of the high chief Hiamovi; Hinook Mahiwi Kilinaka, a Winnebago; Ataloya, a Pima; and Ema-liya, a Zuni. The misconception that Native women did not paint may stem from the fact that most anthropologists of the time, unlike Natalie Curtis, were men, and tended to focus their attention on the activities of men.

Through the amalgam of former tribal territories into an emerging nation state, culturally bred traditions and aesthetics either merged into commercially viable regional "ethnic arts" or through neglect were eliminated from the expressive "gene pool." The Bialac Collection includes a range of representative regional works. Charles Nowell's drawing *Killer Whale,* for example, is executed in the southern Northwest Coast style using traditional Formline compositional conventions. Ovoids signify joints and eye sockets, with secondary faces inserted within them. From archaeological data we know that Formline extends back at least to the seventeenth century.

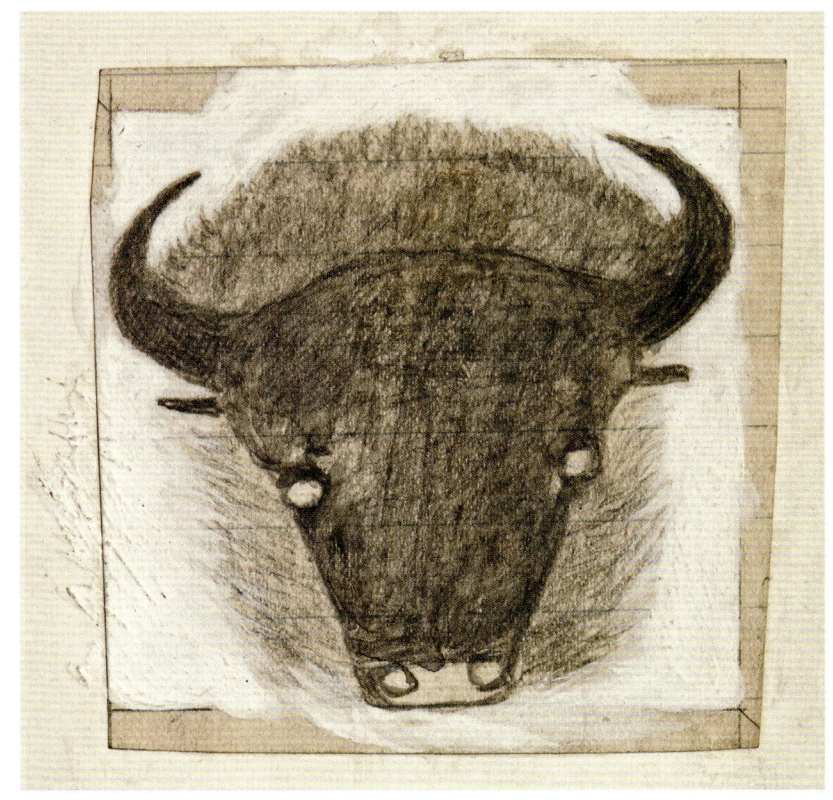

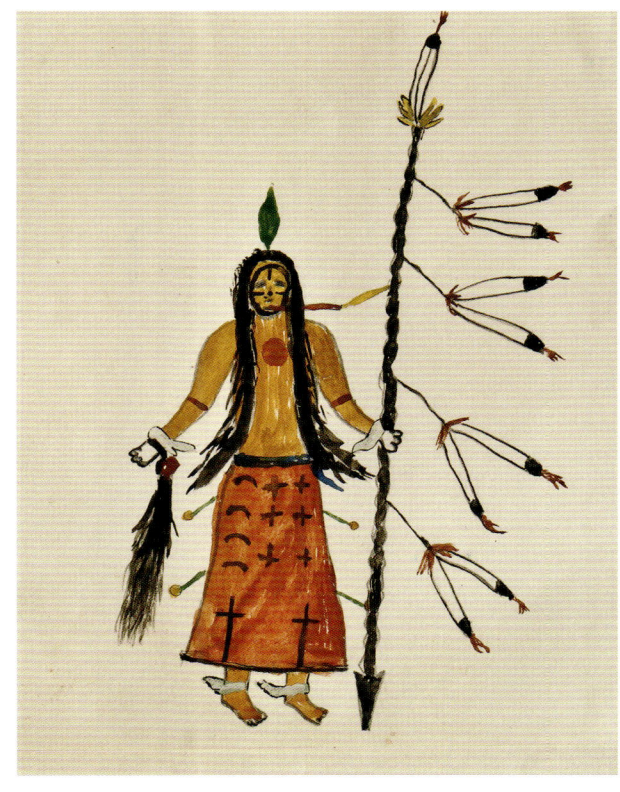

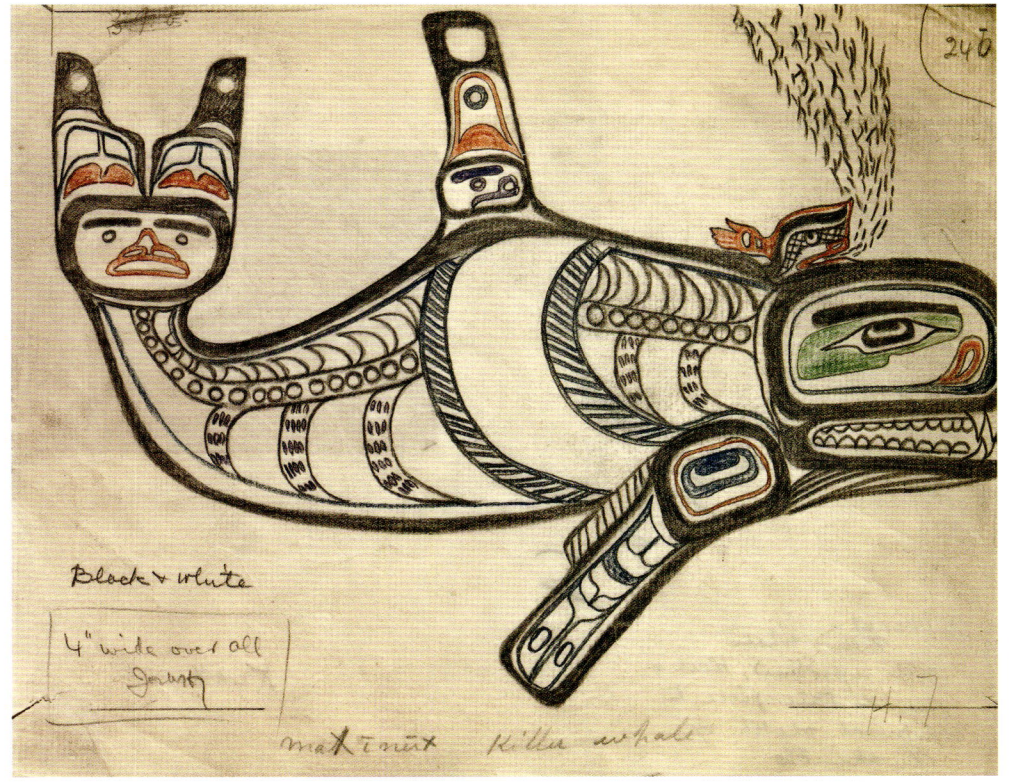

PLATE 57 (ABOVE LEFT)

HIAMOVI AND WOWESTA

U.S., Cheyenne, dates unknown

Buffalo Head, 1903–1906

Pencil and tempera on paper on cardstock, 3 x 2¾ in.

PLATE 58 (ABOVE RIGHT)

HIAMOVI AND WOWESTA

U.S., Cheyenne, dates unknown

A Dancer in the Cheyenne Sun Dance, 1903–1906

Ink and watercolor on paper, 5½ x 3½ in.

PLATE 59

KLALISH (CHARLES JAMES NOWELL)

U.S., Kwakwaka'wakw, dates unknown

Killer Whale, 1903–1906

Colored pencil on paper, 8 x 9¾ in.

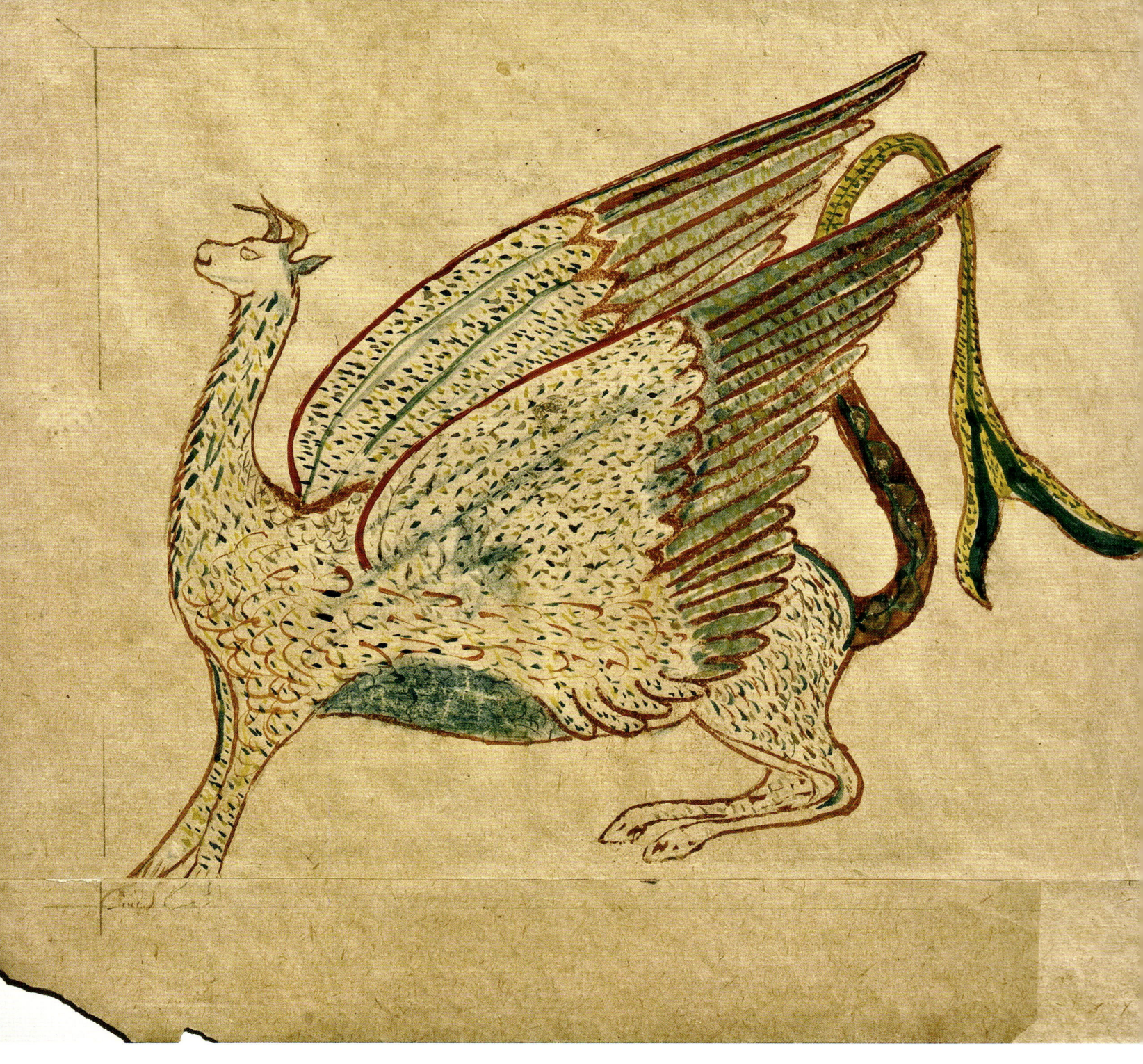

PLATE 60

IDIMA (JOHN CORN)

U.S., Laguna Pueblo, dates unknown

Dragon, 1903–1906

Watercolor on paper, 7½ x 8¼ in.

The first two decades of the twentieth century witnessed a solidification of individual and tribal styles into loosely defined schools of art. By the close of the nineteenth century, there were the southern and northern Plains schools, followed shortly, in the second decade of the twentieth century, by the Santa Fe movement of Pueblo and Navajo painting. Within Oklahoma, the southern Plains school segmented by the end of the 1920s into two traditions: The Kiowa Five–influenced western Plains tradition (Kiowa, Arapaho, Comanche, Cheyenne, and others), and that of the eastern Five Civilized Tribes (Cherokee, Choctaw, Chickasaw, Creek, and Seminole, with associated Shawnee, Delaware, Miami, Seneca, and others). Subject matter was initially the distinguishing characteristic between the two traditions. Eastern artists emphasized farming, fishing, forest hunting, stickball, and other tribal pastimes, while artists of the West focused on the nomadic Plains lifestyle, replete with buffalo hunts, sun dance rituals, and the warrior cult. Eventually, the two traditions resolved into their own separate schools, with Bacone College an anchor for the east and Jacobson's Studio at the University of Oklahoma for the west.

Further complicating matters was the explosive growth of the Peyote Cult, or Native American Church, during the 1930s and the cross-cutting of its popular imagery through both traditions. The evocative symbolism of cormorants, spectral primary colors, feathered fans, gourd rattles, beaded staffs, water pails, crosses, and the sacramental mother peyote bud would emerge at this formative time from the collective visions of Ernest Spybuck (Shawnee), Carl Sweezy (Arapaho), Woody Crumbo (Creek/Potawatomi), Cecil Murdock (Kickapoo), and Monroe Tsatoke (Kiowa), into the formal iconography of a still vital subschool of expression. Spybuck, in particular, as evident in his *Cornbread Dance,* stood out as a self-taught artist with a distinctively personal style of composition. Rather than the flat style of Plains drawing, he was more interested in attempting perspective and providing volume in his scenes. In many ways his art is more Folk than Native American.

PLATE 61

LORENZO BEARD

U.S., Cheyenne/Arapaho, 1914–1975

Peyote Prayers, n.d.

Watercolor on paper, 5½ × 10¾ in.

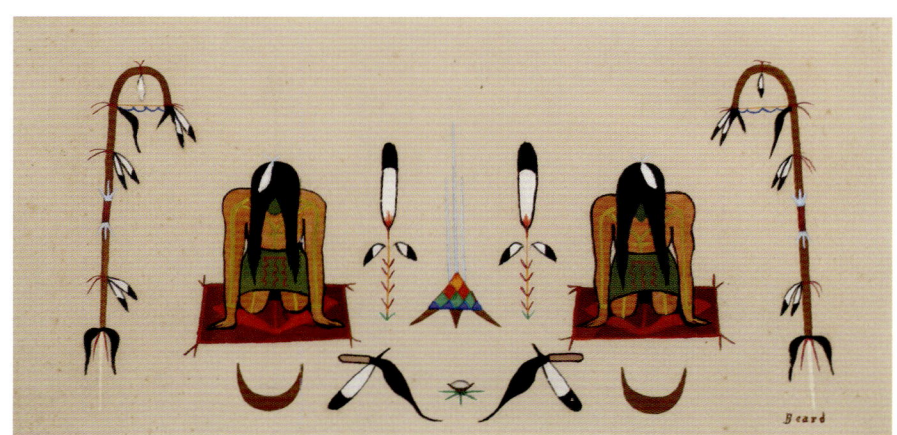

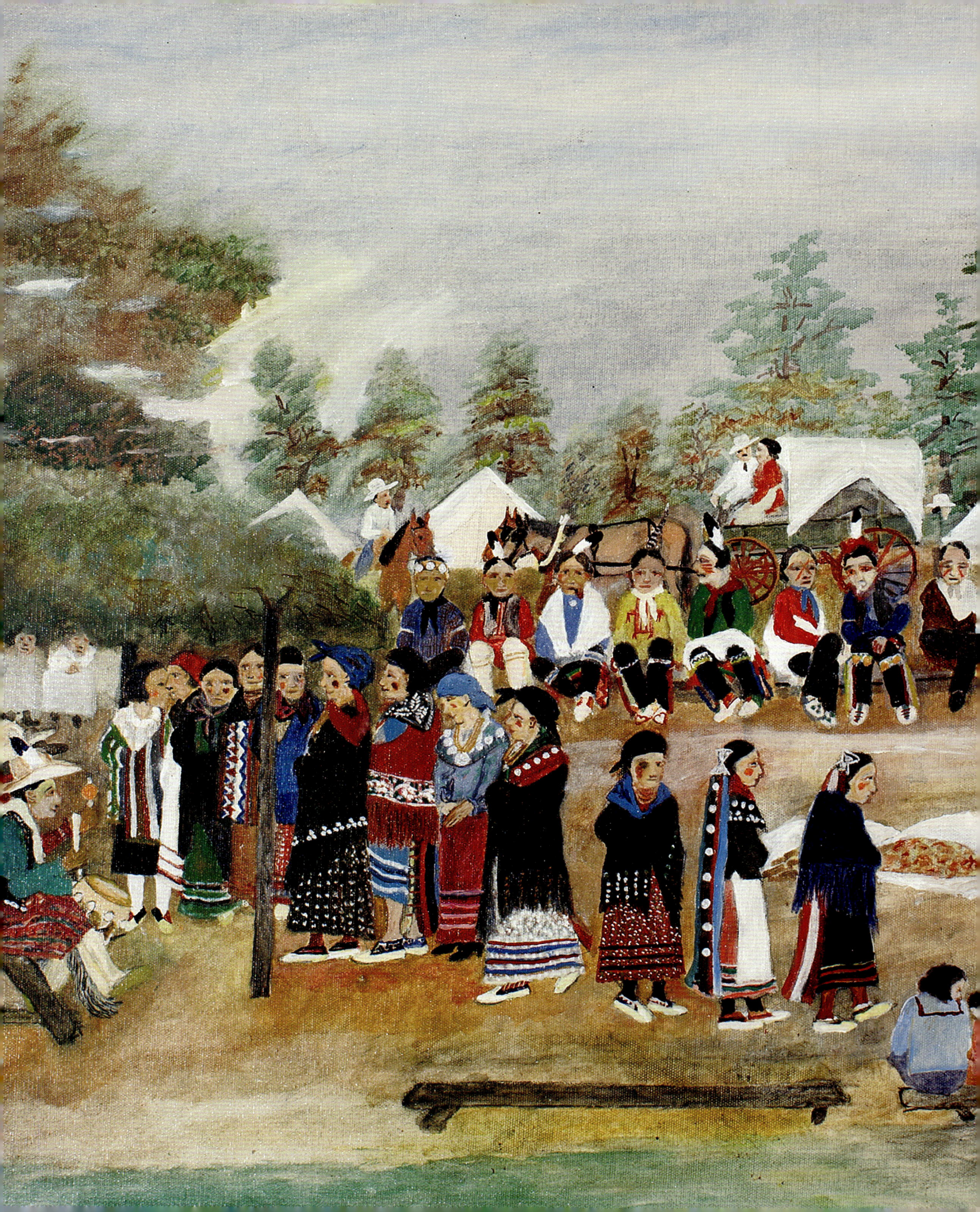

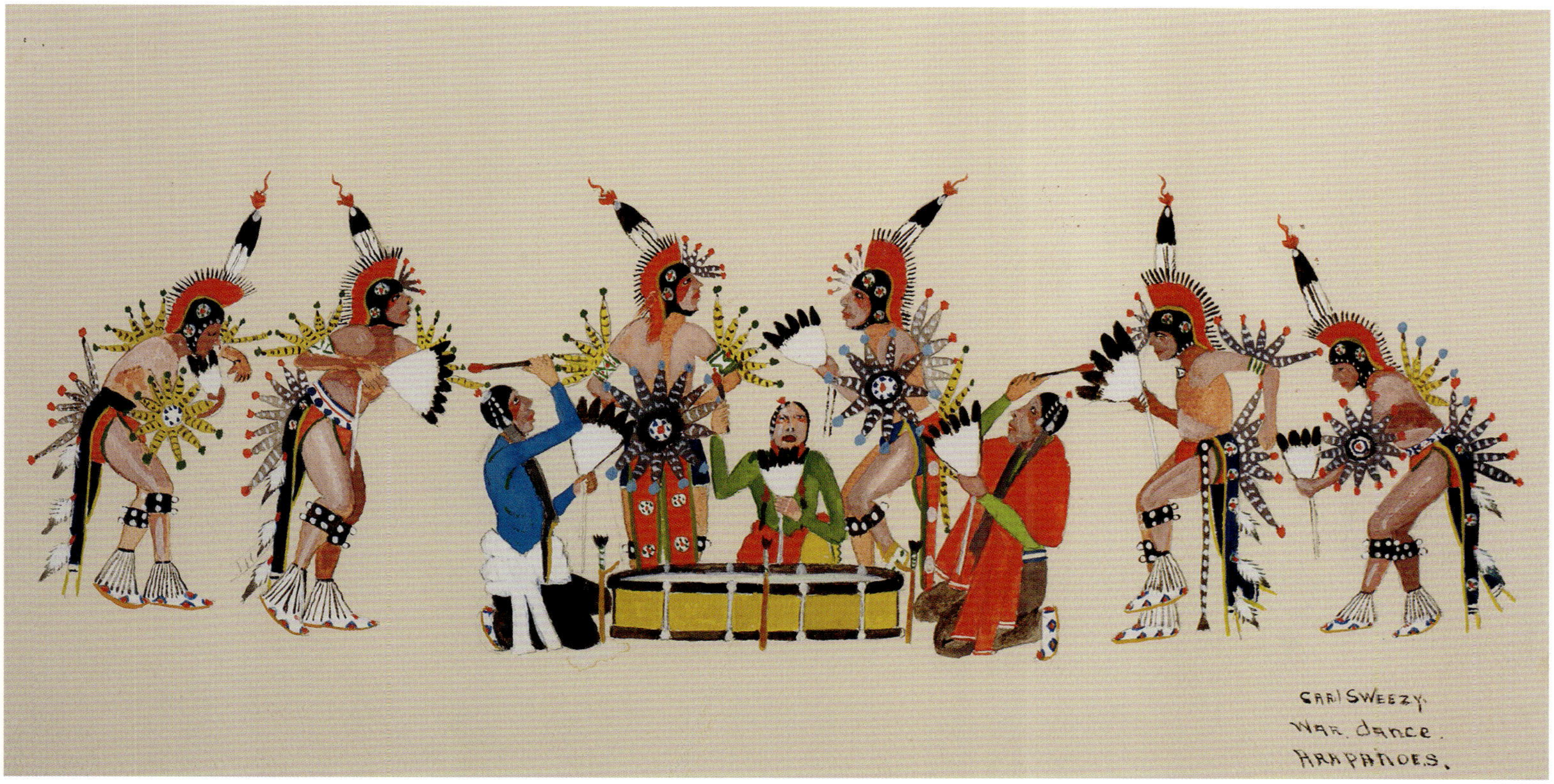

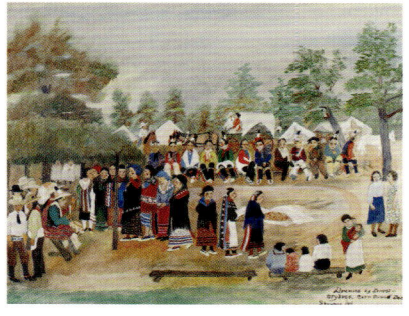

PLATE 63 (ABOVE)

CARL SWEEZY

U.S., Arapaho, 1879–1953

War Dance—Arapahoes, n.d.

Watercolor on paper, 11 x 21 in.

PLATE 64 (OVERLEAF)

WALTER RICHARD "DICK" WEST, SR. (WAH-PAH-NAH-YAH)

U.S., Cheyenne, 1912–1996

Buffalo Hunt, n.d.

Watercolor on paper, 17½ x 23½ in.

PLATE 62 (FACING)

ERNEST SPYBUCK

U.S., Absentee Shawnee, 1883–1949

Corn Bread Dance, n.d.

Oil on canvas, 22¾ x 29 in.

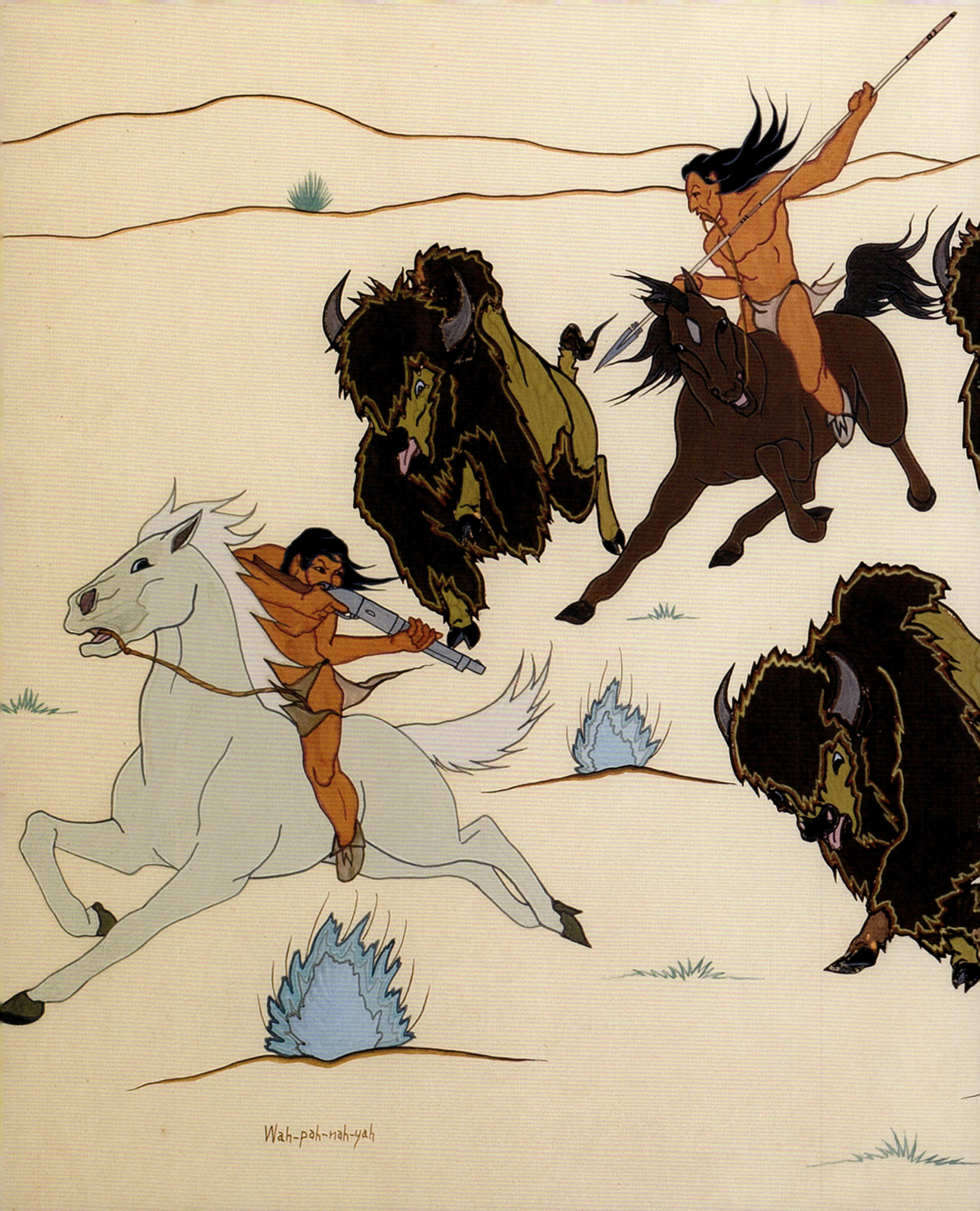

Wah-poh-nah-yah

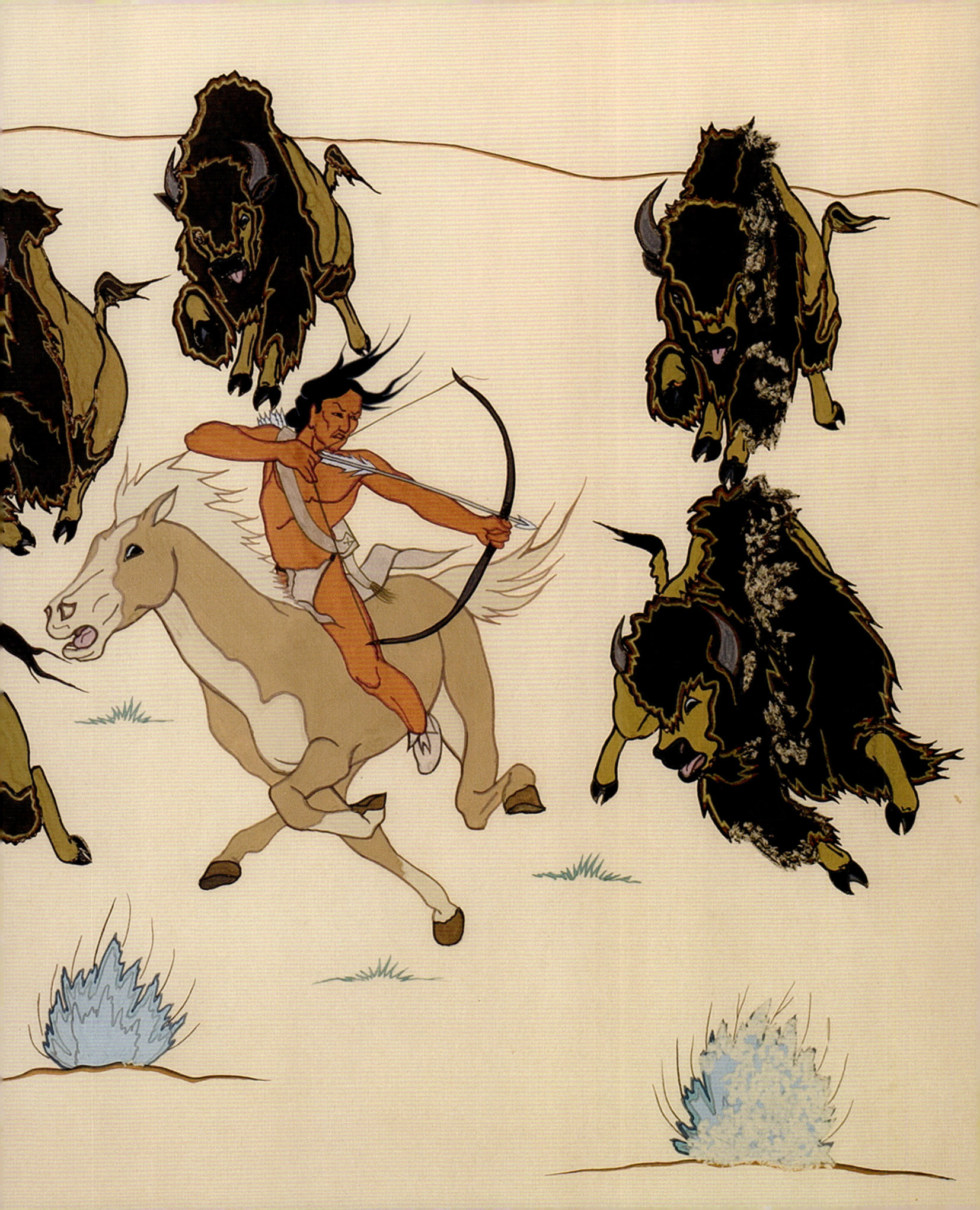

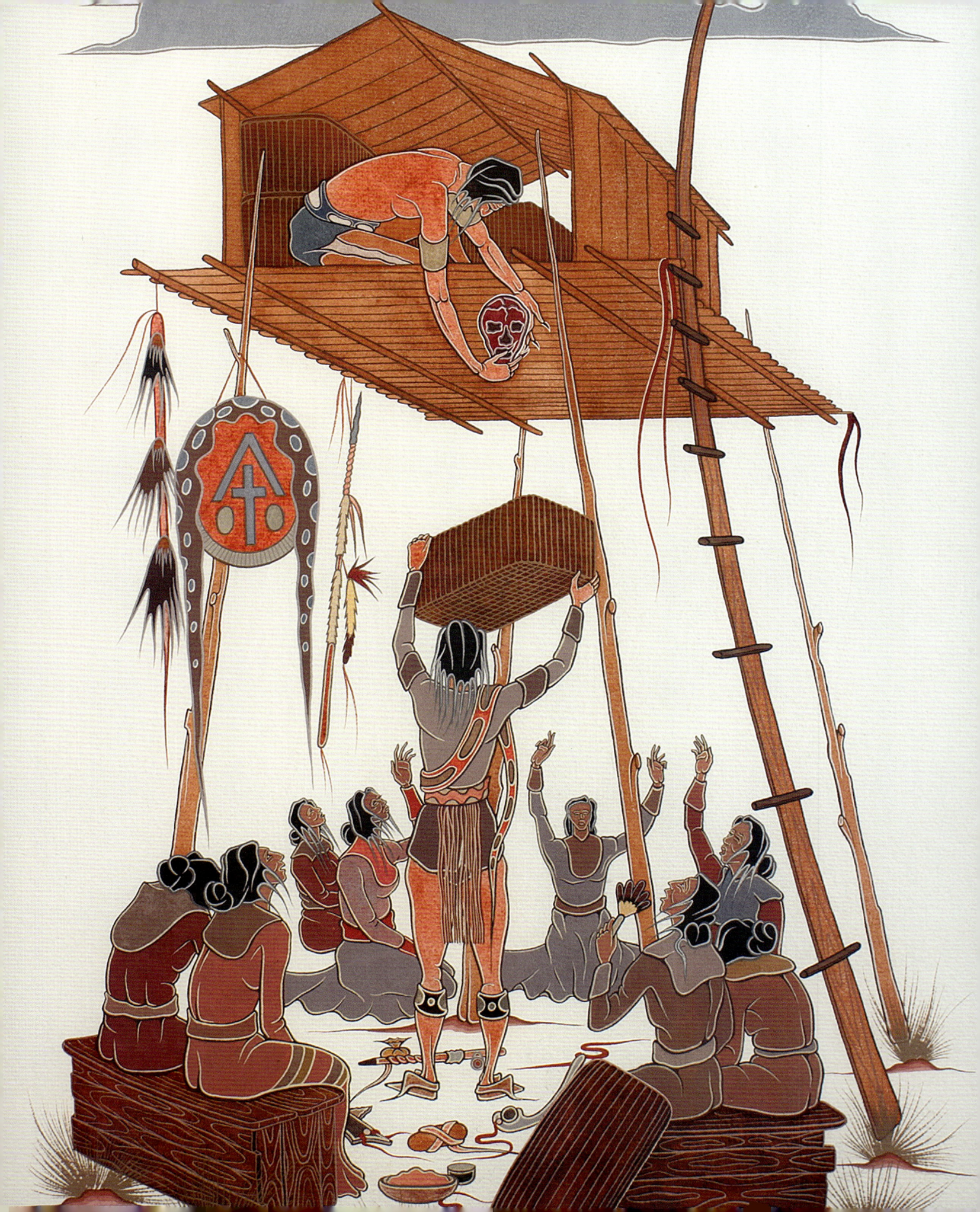

Since this new Indian art initially served limited seasonal marketplaces and fairs, most painters alternated between executing personal voice and creating more standardized compositions for cash-crop target audiences. Most collectors' tastes leaned toward ethnographic subjects, so an artist's legitimacy as a bona fide "of the blood" conveyor of ethnic authenticity proved strategically important to marketability. This had both positive and negative consequences for the emergence of regional and individual style. Fellow artists (the majority of well-known Indian painters up until the 1960s were male) more freely swapped compositional conventions, the visual delivery systems of subject, than might have been expected within a competitive market. Wherever Indian paintings were sold—at powwows; tribal fairs; university, museum, and gallery exhibitions; or the ubiquitous curio stores—painters tracked the market, attentive to prevailing selling trends. So what if you were Cherokee from the eastern forests of Oklahoma? This Flat Style of western Plains painting was hot, so adapt it to your particular ethnic subject matter.[3] This is why Calvin Tyndall (Um-Pah), an Omaha, painted his 1930s buffalo hunts in the popular Kiowa style. Similarly Charles Pushetonequa, a Sauk/Fox, adapted a Puebloan composition by Velino Shije Herrera (Ma-Pe-Wi), a Zia, for his *Woodlands Buffalo Dance.* San Ildefonsan Julian Martinez (c. 1930) reconfigured a Plains buffalo hunter into Pueblo garb and showed him confronting a horned water serpent vis à vis Saint George and his adversarial Romanesque dragon.

Within the profession, the more resourceful played with style as well as cultural subject to meet market demand, and no one felt tribally appropriated. At least from the 1920s to the 1950s, no one is recorded as complaining—suggesting a lack of contentiousness that would be welcome in the present. Acee Blue Eagle (Creek/Pawnee), Woody Crumbo (Creek/Potawatomi), and Wolf Robe Hunt (Acoma) were master style shifters, dancing in, out of, and between the emerging regional conventions coming to be known as Native American painting.

They also did not hesitate to make the occasional foray into the Anglo domain of commercial illustration, from buxom pinups to sports logos. It was here that the foundation was laid for a peaceful coexistence and comingling between what was old and what was new, what was traditional and what was modern, what was tribal and what was individual. This was at least true among Indian painters, if not within the larger Anglo collecting culture.

The result, until the 1960s, when the floodgates of individuality overflowed and the image of Indian painting fundamentally changed, was the emergence of an increasingly pan-Indian painting style, a style in which regional and more specifically tribal identification was distinguished by distinct tribally based ethnic subject matter rather than by differing compositional conventions. At the same time, though largely ignored by curators and collectors, strikingly original and personal compositions were created outside the acknowledged genre and market for Indian painting.

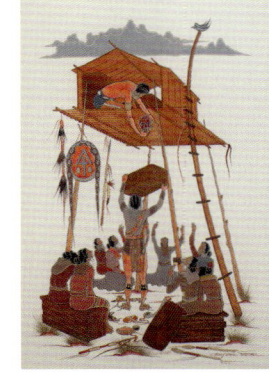

PLATE 65

CHIEF TERRY SAUL

U.S., Choctaw/Chickasaw,

1921–1976

Ancient Choctaw

Burial Custom, n.d.

Watercolor on paper,

29 x 19 in.

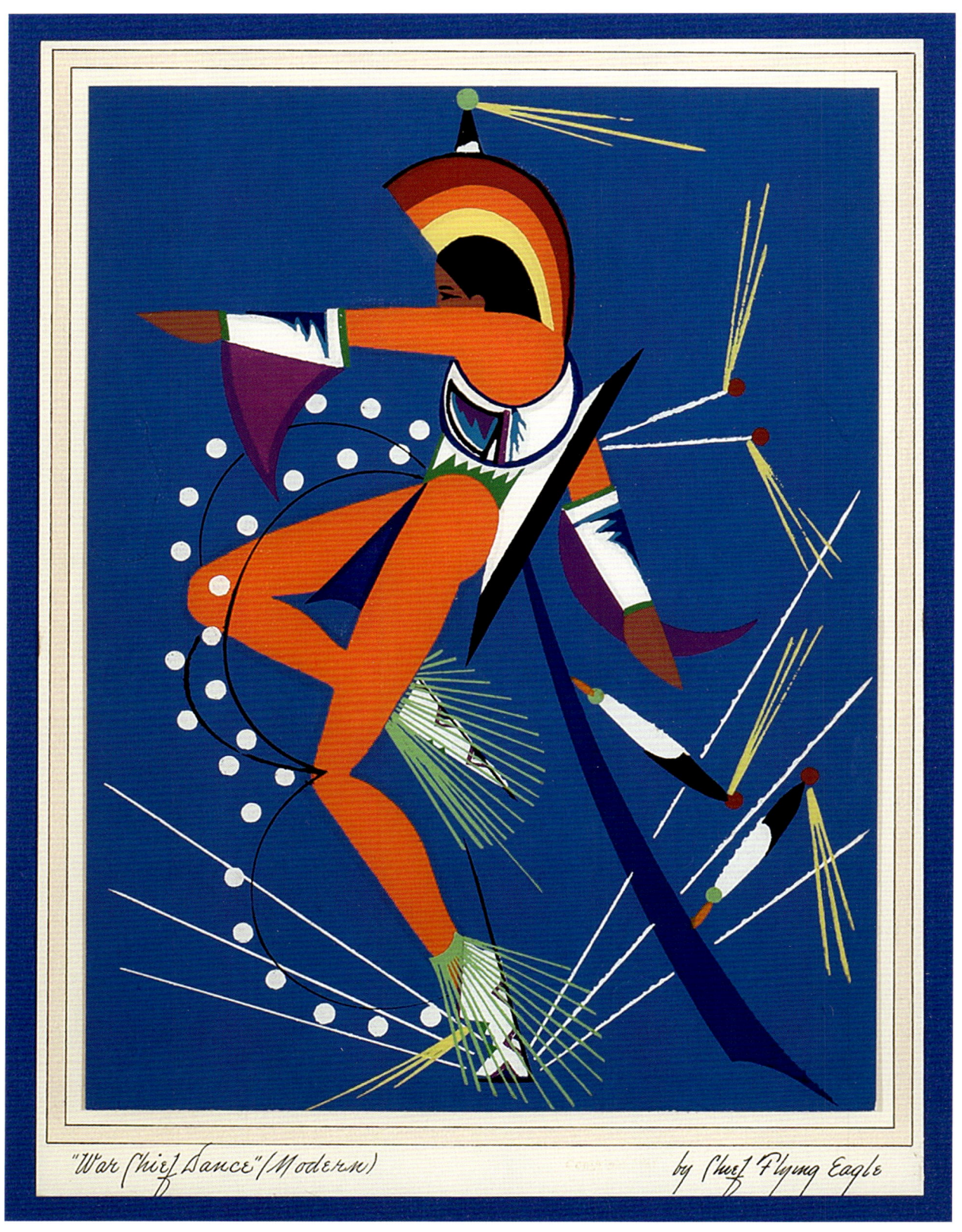

"War Chief Dance" (Modern)   by Chief Flying Eagle

The quirky Art Deco dancers of Paul Goodbear (Ahmehate, or Flying Eagle, Cheyenne) in his *War Chief Dance (Modern)* and the painfully self-introspective Expressionism of Princess Wa Wa Chaw (Benita Nunez, Luiseño) are cases in point.

The founding of the Institute of American Indian Arts (IAIA) in 1962 (with its purposeful adoption of the Modernist creed as the legitimate, noncolonized voice of liberated Native American expression) is the most pronounced instance within Indian art of a formal school of thought. Instantly, it separated the former "Res" artists, with their assimilated traditions and passive subject matter, from a new confrontationalism. Driven by a minority elite adhering to the philosophical embrace of social activism, this was the first time that Modernism as a codified organizational principle was appropriated into Indian painting. Earlier uses of Modernist conventions, such as abstraction during the late 1940s and '50s by Oscar Howe (Yanktonai Nakota), Joe Herrera (Cochiti), Dick West (Cheyenne), and others, were seen as appropriation of method, not of philosophy.

The IAIA, conditioned by its own empowerment rhetoric, wholeheartedly embraced the twentieth-century Western image of the alienated, socially corrective, spiritually seeking artist as warrior. Suddenly, owing to pictorial charm and idealism, a hundred previous years of artistic declaration and positive social advancement were abruptly swept aside, denigrated as "Uncle Tom," or "Apple," and subservient colonial decoration. Youth, though talented, can be truly arrogant.

Modernism allowed this urban intellectual minority an expression of the tension between what had gone before, what was accepted and respected, in contrast to a new art of righteous change and enlightenment. Twenty years earlier, American Abstract Expressionists had railed against academy Regionalism; their old manifestos were dusted off and innocently plagiarized during these heady days of Indian self-rediscovery.

Modernism allows the solace of an undemanding god—the spiritual. Whether in the hands of Jackson Pollock, through his proverbial demonic expunging, or Mark Rothko, adrift in the abyss of color, the spiritual has always been a valid, if convenient, justification for abstractionism. "If you don't get what I'm saying, well, after all, it's abstract; it's submerged below the delusion of surface representationalism." In other words, the message is in the seeking, the seeking is the message, and if we do not come to a common ground, well, that is okay too, since it is spiritual.

The referential responsibility of a former generation of Indian painters was now invalid. Worse yet for those "Res" brethren who persisted in such "submissive tokenism," it was embarrassing. Legitimacy of voice now required no more than legitimacy of heritage, even if that heritage and familiarity with its language and customs was completely estranged. And the skill to convey content could ride on the back of intention.

PLATE 66

PAUL GOODBEAR

(CHIEF FLYING EAGLE)

U.S., Northern Cheyenne,

1913–1954

War Chief Dance (Modern), 1941

Tempera monotype silkscreen,

8¾ × 6½ in.

During the turbulent 1960s Clement Greenberg declared that "in the long run there are only two kinds of art: the good and the bad. This difference cuts across all other differences in art. At the same time, it makes all art one. No matter how exotic." And he was assailed as Eurocentric and paternalistic.[4] He had suggested that, irrespective of context, a concept of quality existed in all aesthetic traditions, and that with a tuning of the eye and familiarity with a tradition, even outsiders could execute reasonable critical judgments. This idea was not tolerable to a Modernist Native minority whose causes were increasingly blurred with those of Black, African American, Chicano, feminist, gay, and Third and Fourth World representatives.[5] The assessment of quality, worth, and value by Westerners of non-Western expression was argued as the underpinning of racism and colonial appropriation. Building on the opinions of Thomas McEvilley and Michel Foucault, Gerald R. McMaster summed it up: "Colonizing the space of the Other and imposing 'transcultural criteria of universal quality,' for example, is part of Western domination whose assumption is that the Other is striving towards similar goals."[6]

PLATE 67

BILLY SOZA WAR SOLDIER

U.S., Cahuilla/Apache,

b. 1949

Clown, 1968

Mixed media, 11½ x 8¾ in.

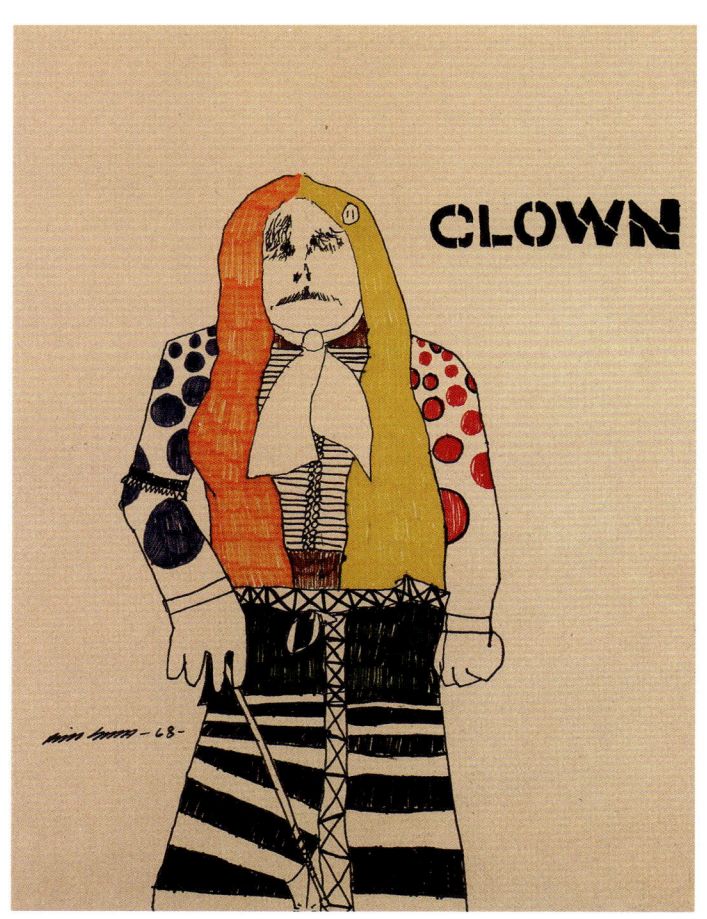

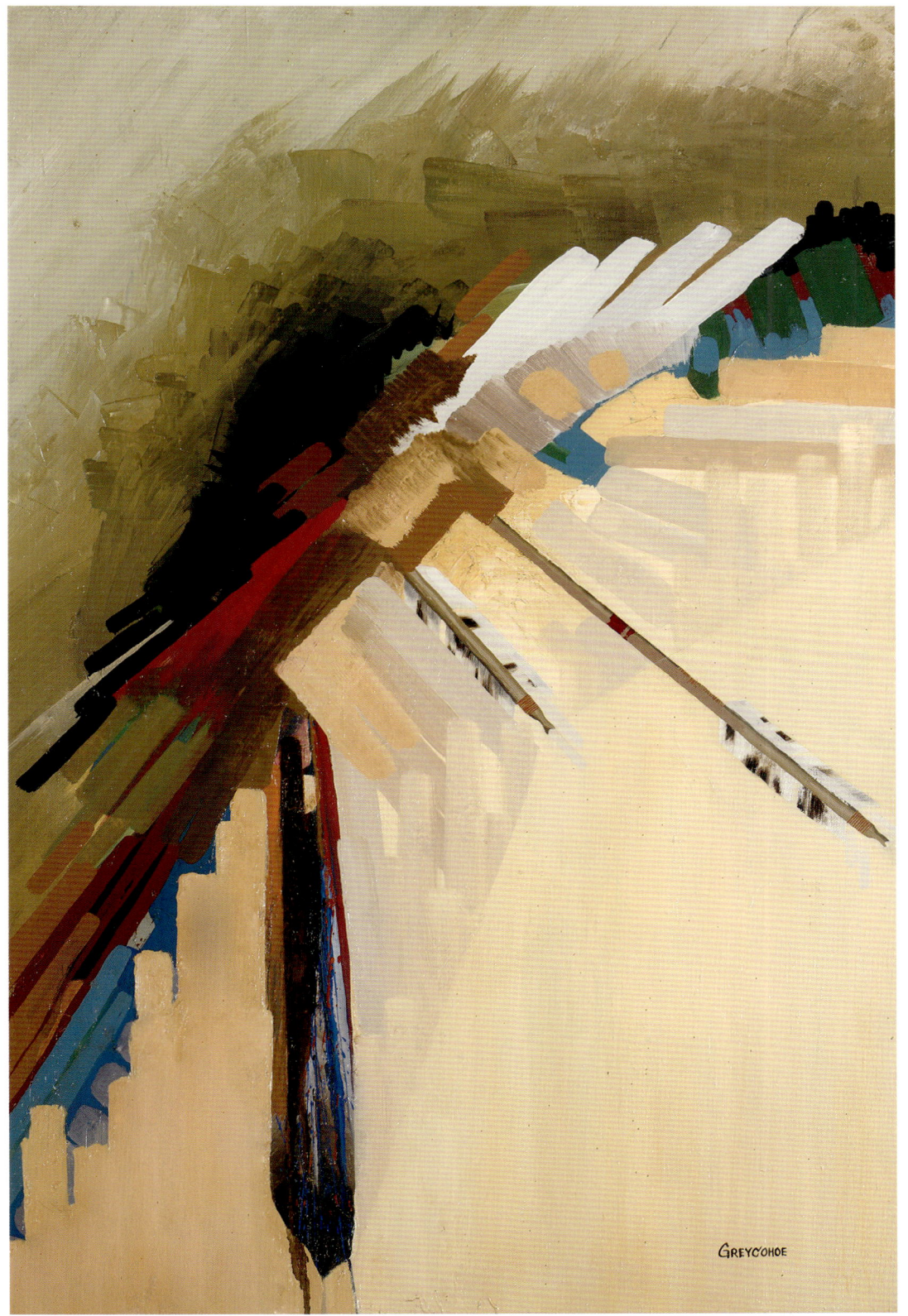

PLATE 69

DAN NAMINGHA

U.S., Hopi Pueblo, b. 1950

Untitled, c. 1970s

Oil and collage on canvas,

59½ x 41½ in.

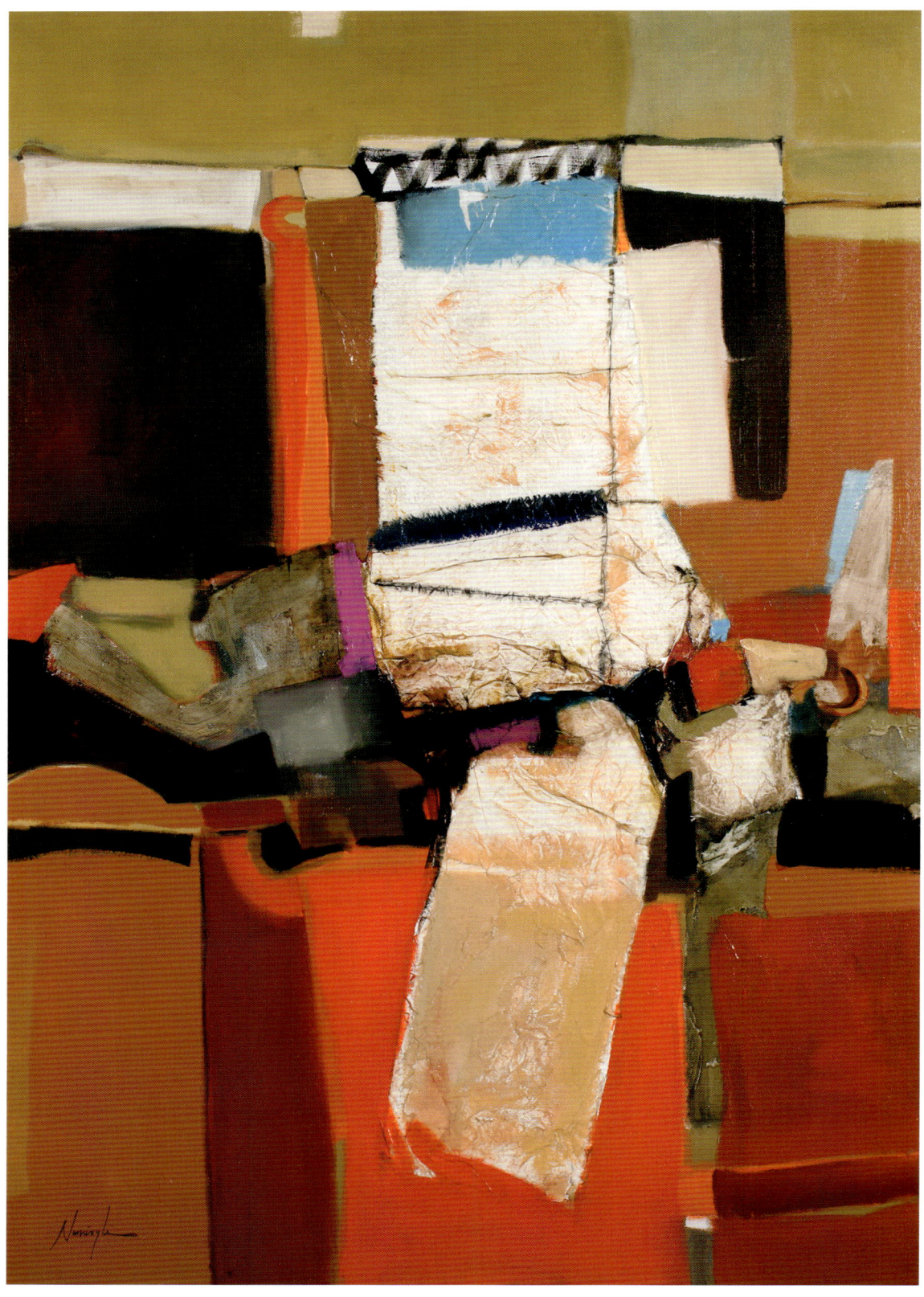

Quality was now subjective, both socially and culturally relativistic. There could be no judgment by anyone who had not lived the life, talked the talk, and walked the walk of the minority—or, as newly rephrased, the Native perspective. Only through corrective purging could the shackles of suppressive capitalism be loosened. Unintentionally, the university-bred Indian intelligentsia had now surrendered the political sovereignty of Native American expression to a moralistic Modernism of minority rights. The vitriol grew at the expense of both technical and communicative skill. The situation mirrored what Robert Hughes observed in his *Culture of Complaint:* "The self is now the sacred cow of American [minority] culture, self-esteem is sacrosanct, and so we labor to turn arts education into a system in which no one can fail. In the same spirit, tennis could be shorn of its elitist overtones: you just get rid of the net."[7] Such self-limiting would lead to decreased commercial viability and eventually to the transformation of institutional modernist Indian painting.

Within the first decade of the IAIA's operation, the creative and sometimes brilliant energy of these young artists splintered. Benny Buffalo (Cheyenne) adapted Photorealism to optical polarism, conveying the impression of a Peyotist view of the contemporary Indian world. However, the punch of his vision lies in the disquieting contrast between a phosphorescent palette used to capture a disembodied, ghost-like stasis, not his intentionally passive subject. Grey Cohoe (Navajo) and T. C. Cannon (Kiowa) vied for the playful nickname Gauguin, owing to their equally masterful decorative application of vibrant, verdant colors seductively masking acute social observation.[8] Kevin Red Star (Crow) mischievously adapted Western nineteenth-century art icons of the Plains genera—the warrior bust, the Indian maiden—into fashionable "mod" logos. Dan Namingha (Hopi) experimented with thick palette painting of abstracted pottery designs and architecture on circular canvas. Particularly in his paintings of the Hopi Pueblos of First Mesa, Namingha emphasized the cohesion of the rock-built dwellings with the sandstone terraces upon which they rest. The textured geology of his imagery reflects the unity of the Hopi people with their lands.

These were the bright spots, among others, as the initial swirl surrounding this new painting caught the attention of non-IAIA practitioners and ushered in what appeared to be a Modernist, soon followed by a Postmodernist, revolution.

Hopis Mike Kabotie (Lomawywesa), Neil David, Sr., Terrance Talaswaima, Milland Lomakema (Dawakema), all either self- or non-institute trained, founded a 1970s art cabal they called Artist Hopid. The stated goal of this fruitful collaborative was to foster tribal pride in their rich aesthetic and cultural heritage, as well as to project the voice and social consciousness of Hopis to the world. For a while it worked. Nevertheless, prior to and at times independent from

PLATE 70

MICHAEL KABOTIE

U.S., Hopi Pueblo, 1942–2010

Guardian of the Water, 1966

Watercolor on paper, 25 ½ x 15 ½ in.

the visual manifesto of Hopid, each artist experimented with various forms of graphic expression. Michael Kabotie was the most free ranging, comfortably shifting from Picasso-inspired eroticism to formal reinterpretation of ancient fifteenth-century Pueblo murals. Both interests, irrespective of their historical depth, were thrown into the modernist catchall.

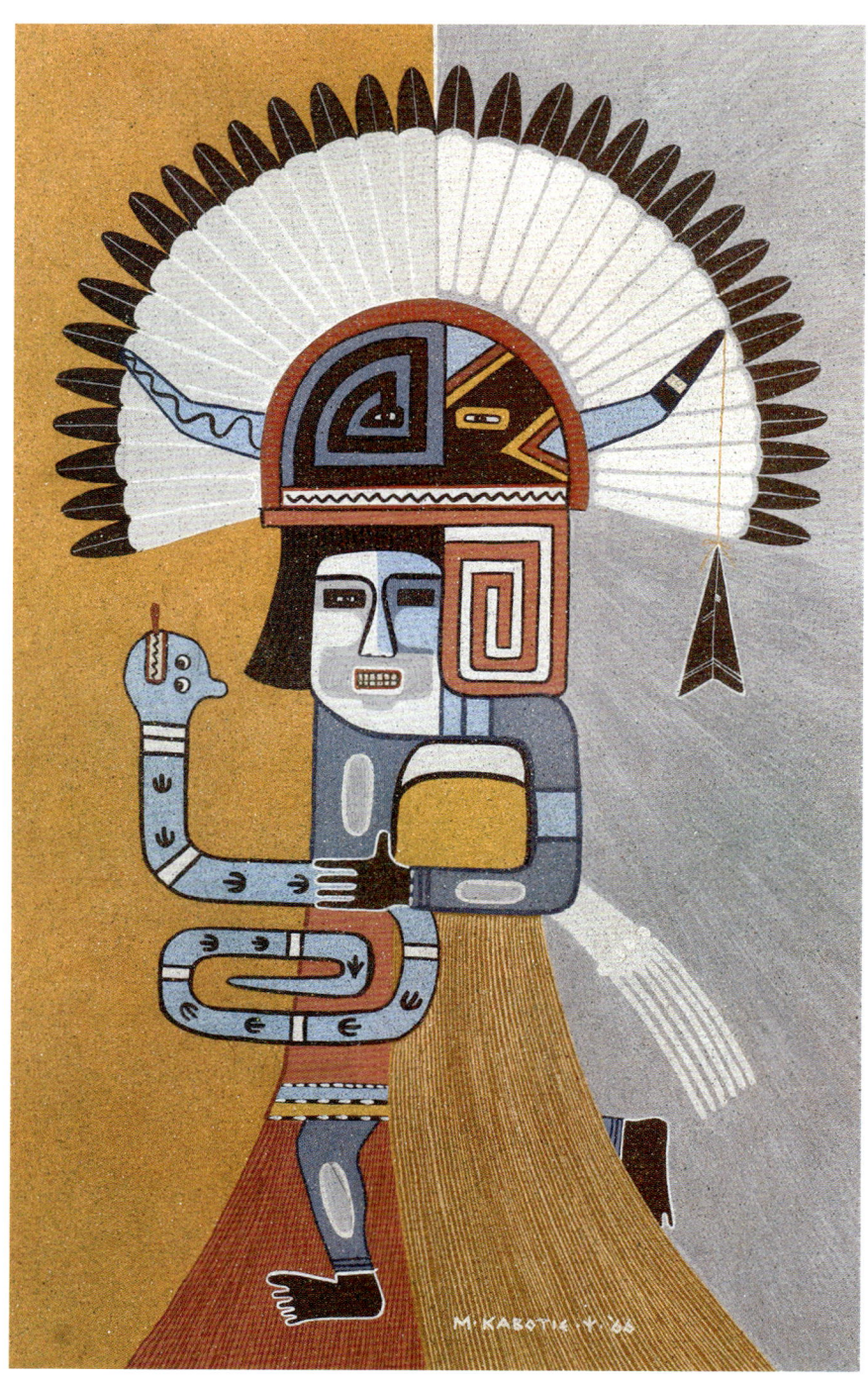

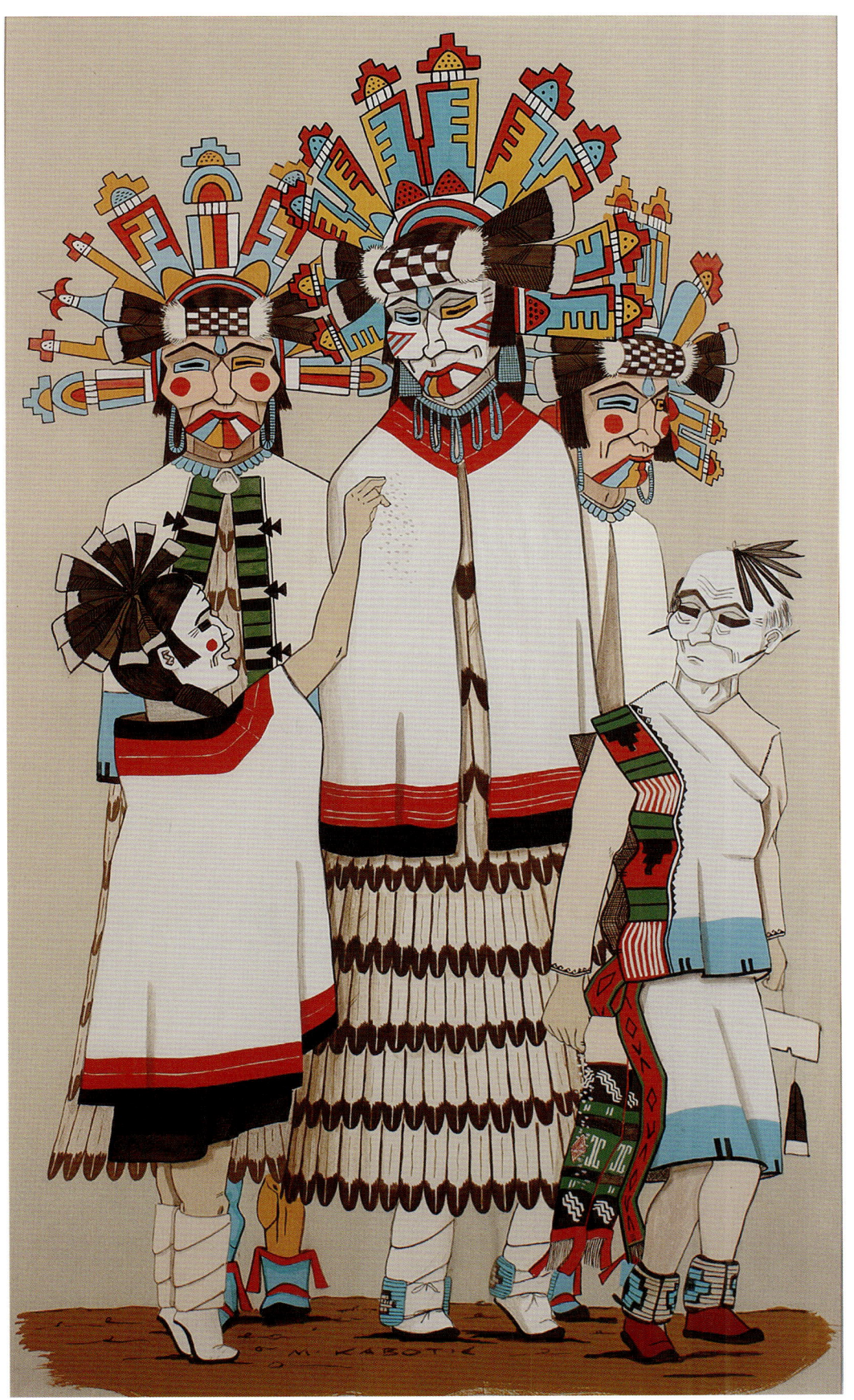

PLATE 71

MICHAEL KABOTIE

U.S., Hopi Pueblo, 1942–2010

Coming of the Shaiako, n.d.

Watercolor on paper,

28¾ x 16¾ in.

The IAIA, propelled by the growing notoriety and commercial success of teachers Fritz Scholder and Allan Houser, changed the previous perception of what was new and old in Indian art, just as it had over what was authentic versus colonially programmed. If a post-1960 composition was abstract or reductionist, it would be termed modern. Linda Lomahaftewa (Hopi) painted colorful renditions of centuries-old Hopi symbols (lightning, clouds, rainbows), petroglyphs, animals (mountain lions, parrots), and people (shamans, corn maidens), such as seen in the Bialac Collection work *Four Directions I.* In the early seventies her paintings were called visionary, breakthrough, and modern. Yet the original rock carvings and ancient Hopi motifs that inspired her work are still approached through the archaeological veneration of age and perceived as traditional, thus "primitive."

Stylistic labeling, including what we have employed to chart the course of Indian painting, is a device that conveniently clusters influences and trends characterizing the art of particular places and times. Such terms as "traditional" or "individualist" cannot define the complete body of an artist's work or a school's direction. But just as the academic and collecting community persisted in describing the strikingly asymmetric abstractions painted on fifteenth-century Hopi Sikyatki polychrome ceramics and the related kiva wall murals as either geometric or figurative (i.e., not modern), the IAIA Modernists ignored the visionary works of the 1920s and '30s artists. San Ildefonsans Julian Martinez and Awa Tsireh playfully experimented with inventive composi-

PLATE 72

LINDA LOMAHAFTEWA

U.S., Hopi Pueblo/Choctaw,

b. 1947

Four Directions I, 2004

Monotype, 13½ x 17½ in.

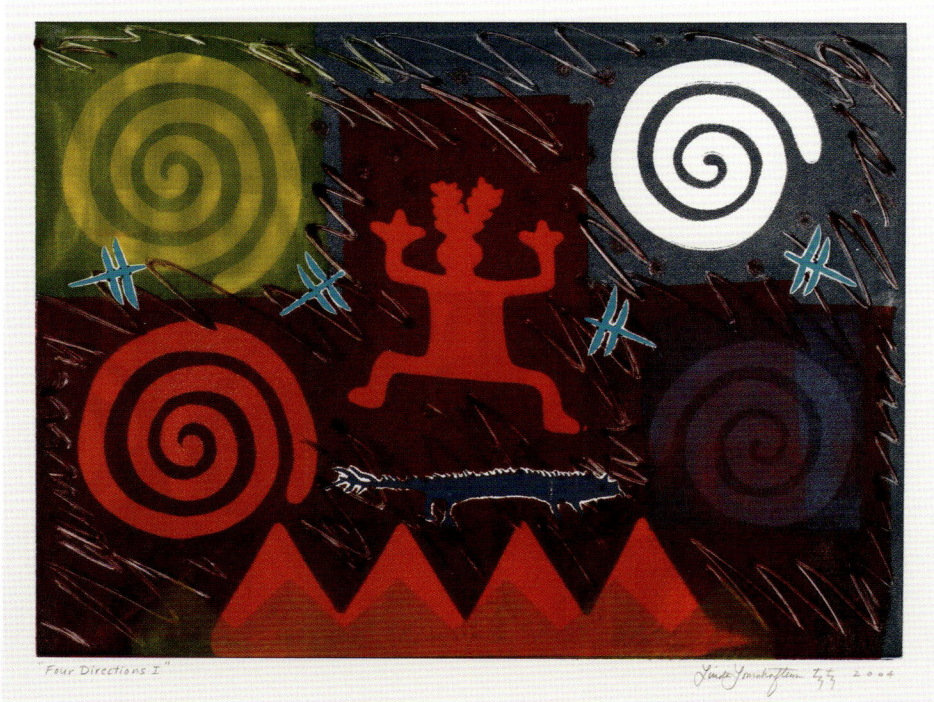

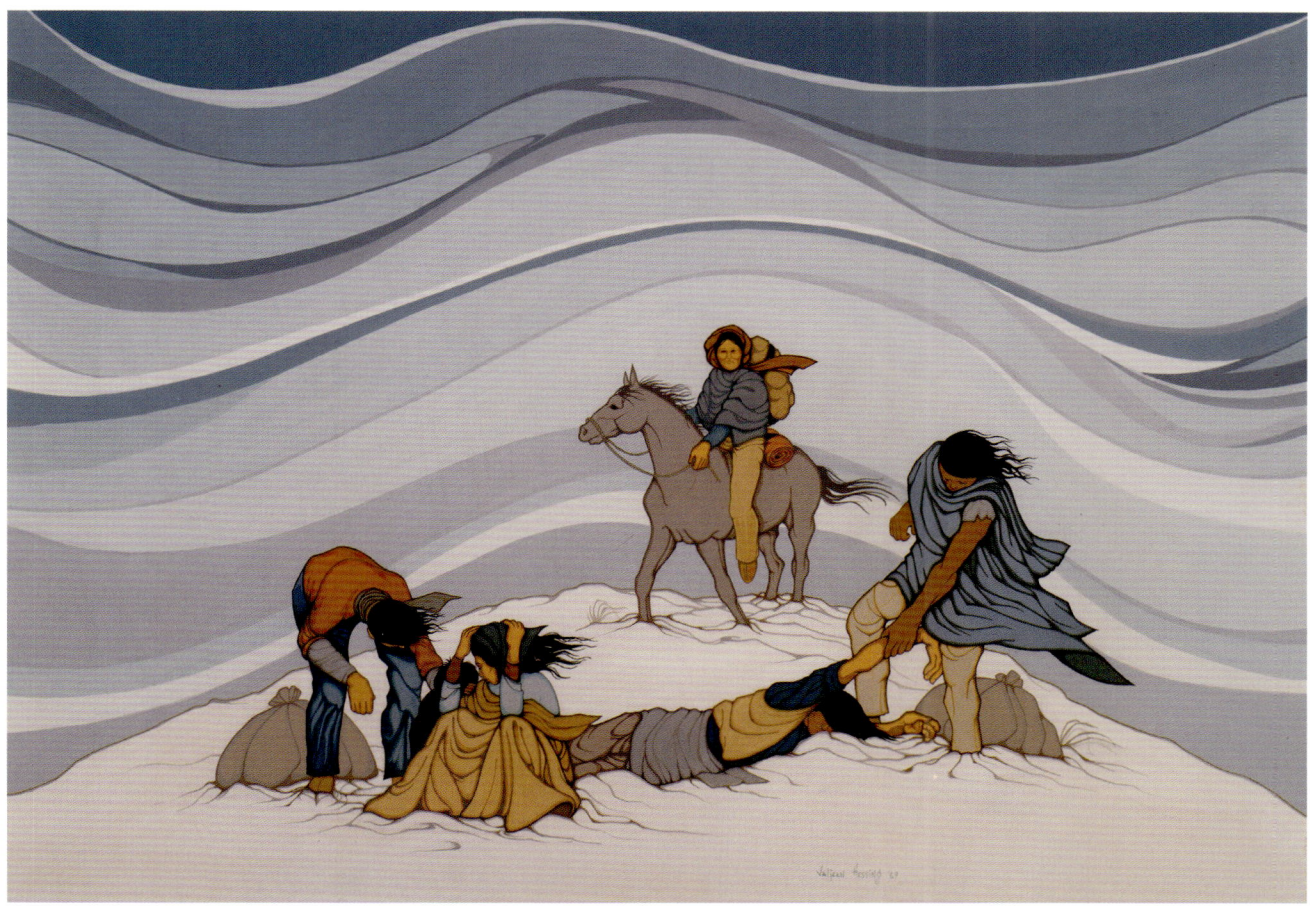

tions reminiscent of the process employed by Giuseppe Arcimboldo in his botanical surrealism. Replacing the carrots and figs for noses favored by the sixteenth-century Italian Renaissance fantasist, the Pueblo painters recombined pottery design, both ancient and contemporary, to form intricate birds, deer, and other familiar flora and fauna. Yet it is seldom that such pre-1950 compositions are noted for their modern qualities.

The institute and its aftermath effectively upended the usefulness of the historical schools as lenses through which to observe artistic development. The field became polarized between what was "old" style and what was "new." The commitment to a distinctive Kiowa, Hopi, Cherokee, or Sioux heritage of drawing was replaced with the vying for attention from a national market. Regionalism remains viable due to collecting interest in ethnic nostalgia and emotive interpretation. Entire art competitions within Oklahoma are still devoted to the topic of the 1830s deportation of the Five Civilized Tribes along the Trail of Tears, made artistically famous by Jerome Tiger (Creek/Seminole) in the 1960s. But nationally, the trend is Modern or Postmodern.

PLATE 73

VALJEAN McCARTY

HESSING

U.S., Choctaw, 1934–2006

Some Died Along

the Way, 1969

Watercolor on paper,

14¼ x 19¼ in.

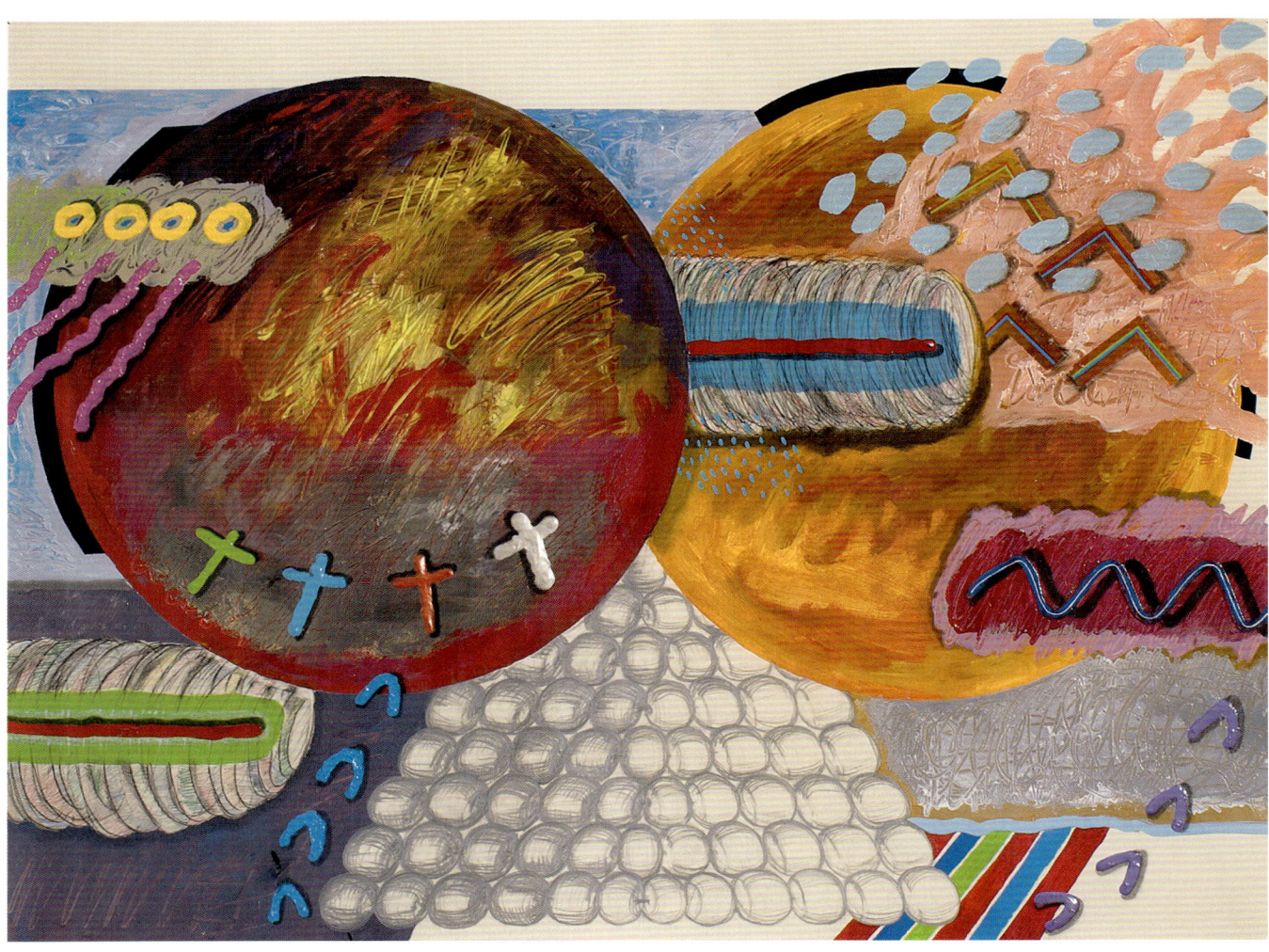

PLATE 74

GEORGE LONGFISH

U.S., Seneca/Tuscarora, b. 1942

Pooper and Beatie Receiving

Their Names, 1980

Oil and pencil on paper,

29½ x 39½ in.

Occasionally, circumstance favors a brief condensation of talent within a restricted locality, which gives the appearance of an institutional movement. Since the 1970s, largely owing to the hiring practices of the California university system, a number of artists have clustered in California, including Frank LaPena (Nomtipom Wintu), George Longfish (Seneca/Tuscarora), Ric Glazer Danay (Mohawk), Harry Fonseca (Maidu/Native Hawaiian/Portuguese), Frank Tuttle, Jr. (Yuki-Wailaki/Konkow Maidu), Brian Tripp (Karok), Karen Tripp (Chimariko/Hupa/Karok), and Jean LaMarr (Paiute/Pit River), among others. Over the decades attempts have been made, primarily by LePena, to organize—through joint exhibitions and publications—a cooperative, if not unified, Native artist presence. Nevertheless, the vagaries of the contemporary Native American exhibition and art market circuit impart a nomadicism of loyalty among its practitioners, who adapt composition to appeal to the few and far afield showing opportunities.

Special commemorative events, such as the Christopher Columbus Quincentennial Jubilee, allow for sporadic invigoration of both regional and national Native American expression. Yet, as evidenced by such exhibitions as the *Submuloc Show* (Columbus spelled backwards), organized by Jaune Quick-to-See Smith (1992), they can host objects representing a broad range of degrees of artistic consummation. Such exhibitions have attempted through visual irony, or even rage and shock, to evoke shame on the part of audiences for what their ancestors did to the indigenous peoples of the world. The passions at play can inspire works of intensity and deep message. However, the weight of the attempt to forge a belated historical justice for the displaced and misused through art can also become so heavy that it submerges artistry and skill beneath message.

Politics and art have long been bedfellows, but allegiances and alliances shift as movements swell and subside, develop and change, and individuals respond. No movement is static, and neither are artists. As Diane O'Leary told Jim Bialac in reference to her painting *Epitaph,* she was once a strong supporter of the American Indian Movement (AIM) but became disillusioned by what she saw as infighting within the organization and a tendency to marginalize reservation tribal communities. Her sense that the movement had turned its back on tribal heritage is powerfully communicated in the work.

PLATE 75

DIANE O'LEARY

U.S., Comanche, b. 1939

Epitaph, n.d.

Acrylic on paper, 30¾ x 38½ in.

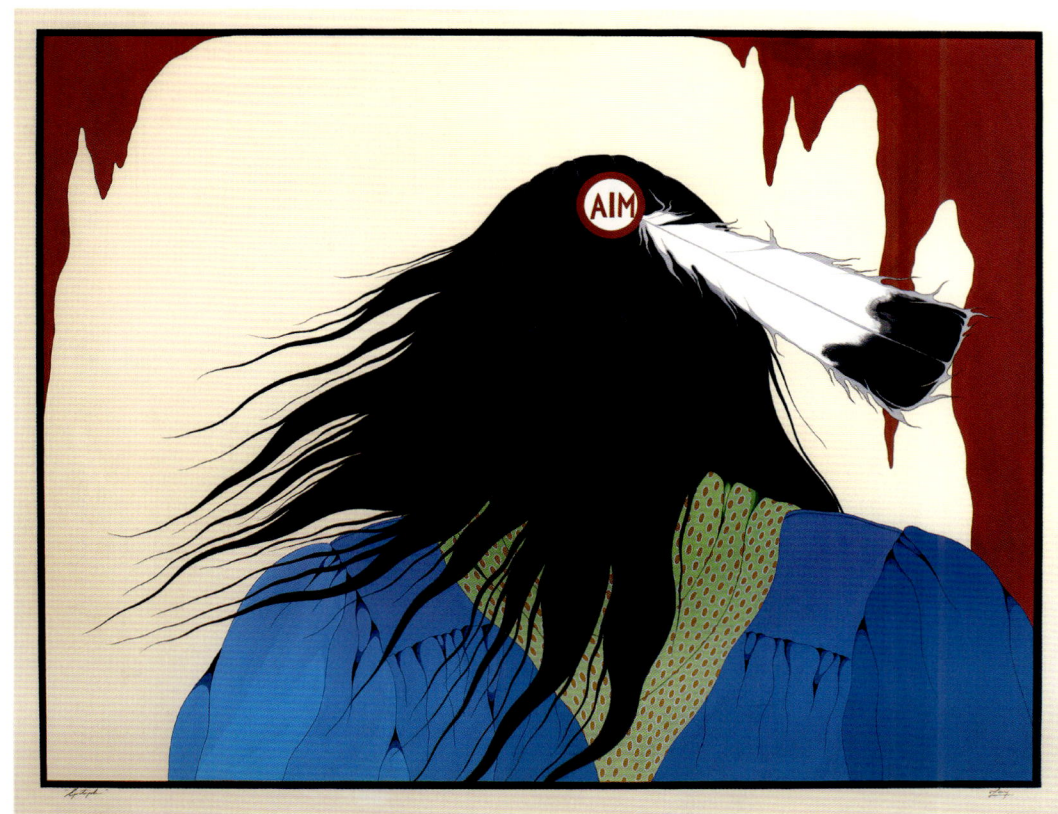

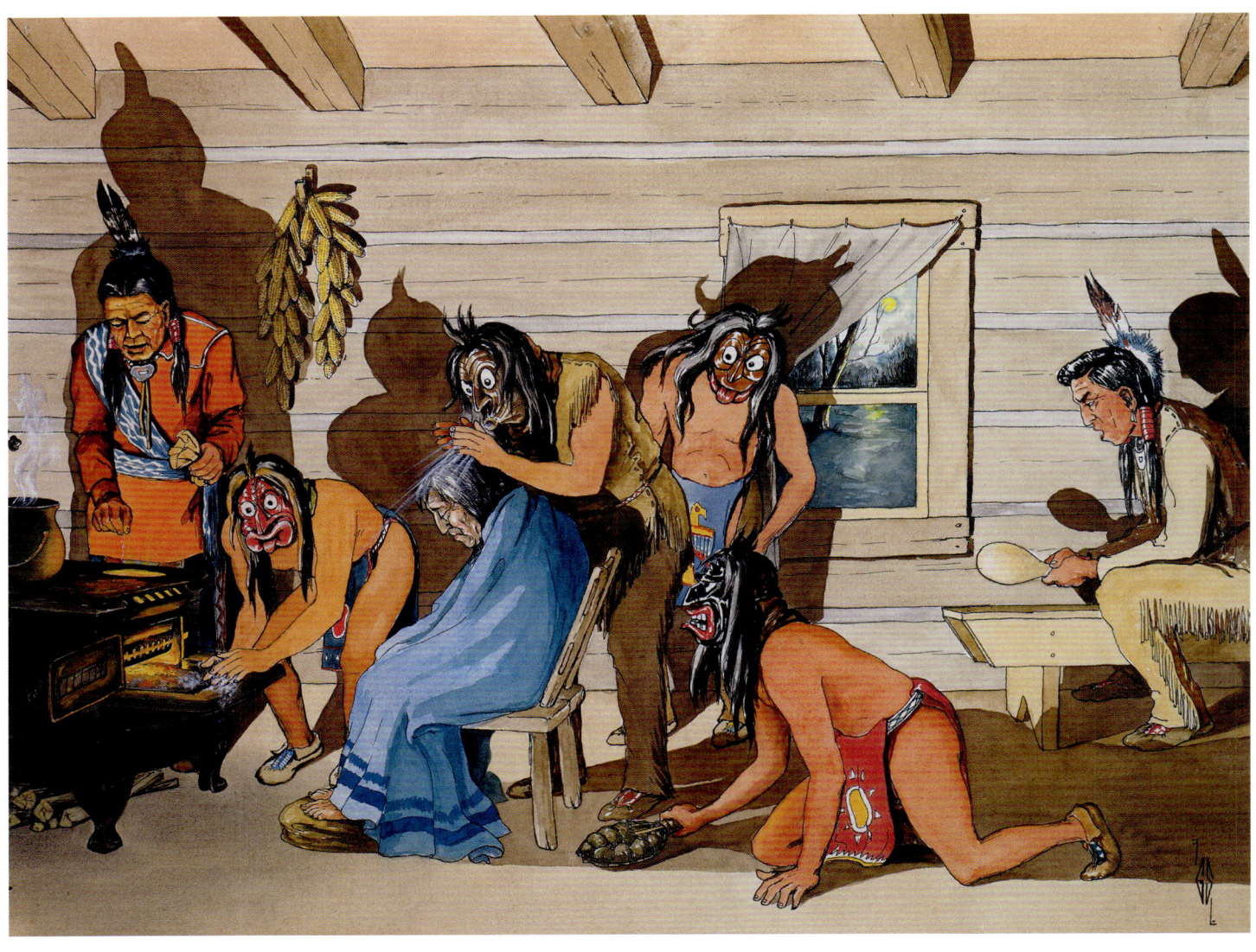

PLATE 76

ERNEST SMITH

U.S., Seneca, 1907–1975

False Face Healing Ceremony—

Breathing Health, n.d.

Watercolor on paper, 14¾ x 19½ in.

Finally, we direct some attention toward a loosely aligned group of contemporary artists drawn from the Eastern Iroquois Confederation.[9] As evidenced in the past through the artistry of the Cusick brothers (Tuscarora), Jesse Cornplanter (Seneca), Ernest Smith, and other nineteenth- and turn-of-the-twentieth-century painters, later inheritors descend from a stronghold of talent, although their vision can at times be romanticized in a way that softens the intensity of the earlier painters. Thomas J. "Two Arrows" Dorsey (Ga Hes Ka Lenni Lenape), Rick Hill (Tuscarora), and Joe David (Mohawk) carry forward this vein of expression. An image by Dorsey in the Bialac collection, for example, *Plains Ledger Drawing,* draws on the works on ledger paper by nineteenth-century Indian prisoners of war with which we began this chapter.

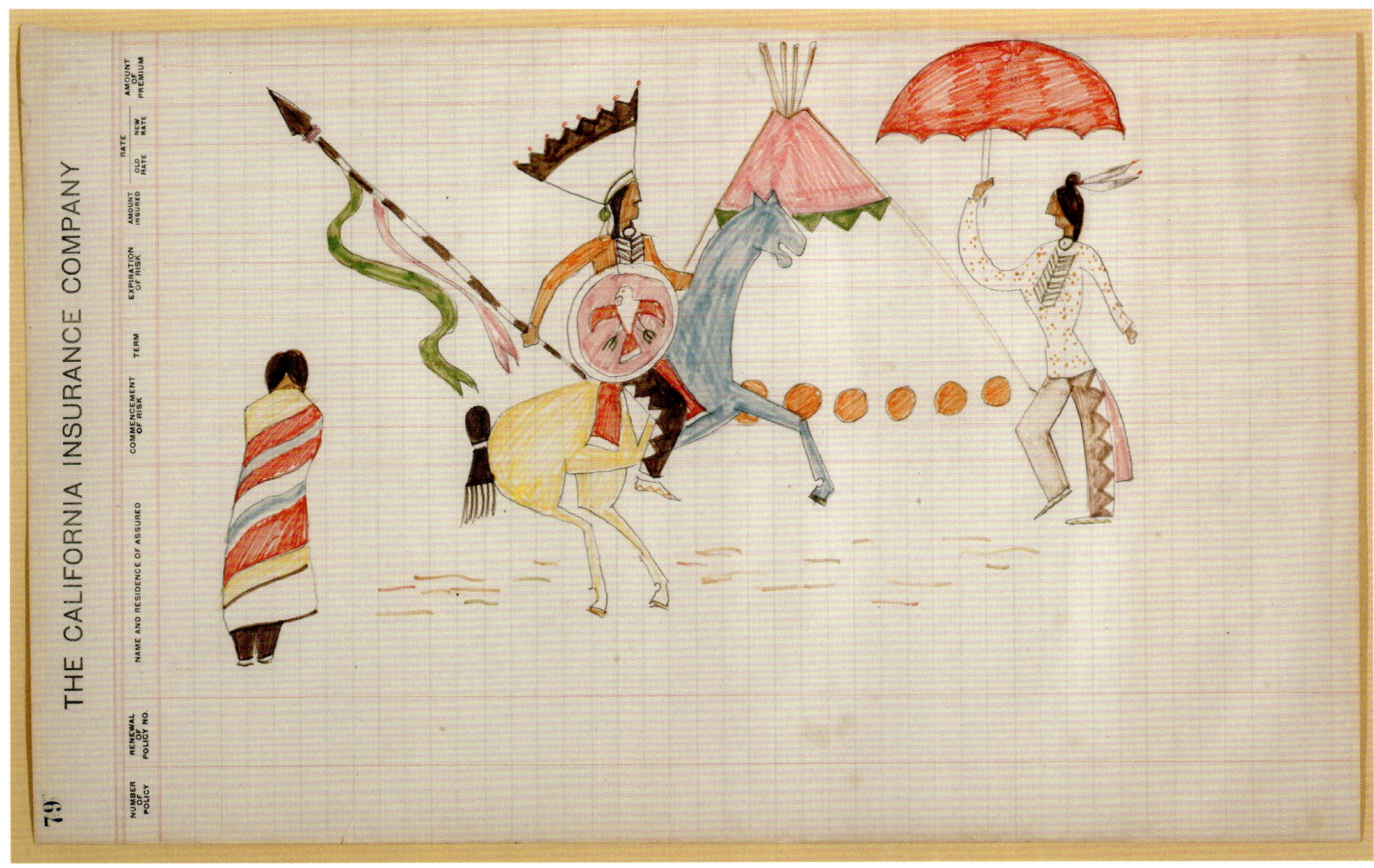

With the space allowed us here, neither the aesthetic impetus nor historical specifics of the various Native North American schools of painting can be fully explored. Fortunately, this is but the first of publications to be dedicated to the study of the James T. Bialac Native American Collection. Its breadth can support topics as diverse as the Canadian–American School of Northwest Coast graphics, First Nations, and Inuit art; postmodernism and the rise of Native artists the likes of David Bradley, Bob Haozous, Ric Glazer Danay, and Michael Kabotie, among others, as polemical tricksters; and multiculturalism and the ascendancy of so-called Fourth World ethnic artists together with their impact on formally autonomous Indian expression. Even the controversial issue of who in the twenty-first century is legitimately an Indian artist and what comprises authentic Indian expression may be sensitively explored. Owing to the generosity of James T. Bialac in gifting his unparalleled collection to the University of Oklahoma, the Fred Jones Jr. Museum of Art is uniquely poised to address the true complexity and brilliance of Native American painting.

PLATE 77

THOMAS J.

"TWO ARROWS" DORSEY

U.S., Lenni Lenape,

1920–1993

Plains Ledger Drawing, n.d.

Colored pencil on paper,

10¾ x 17 in.

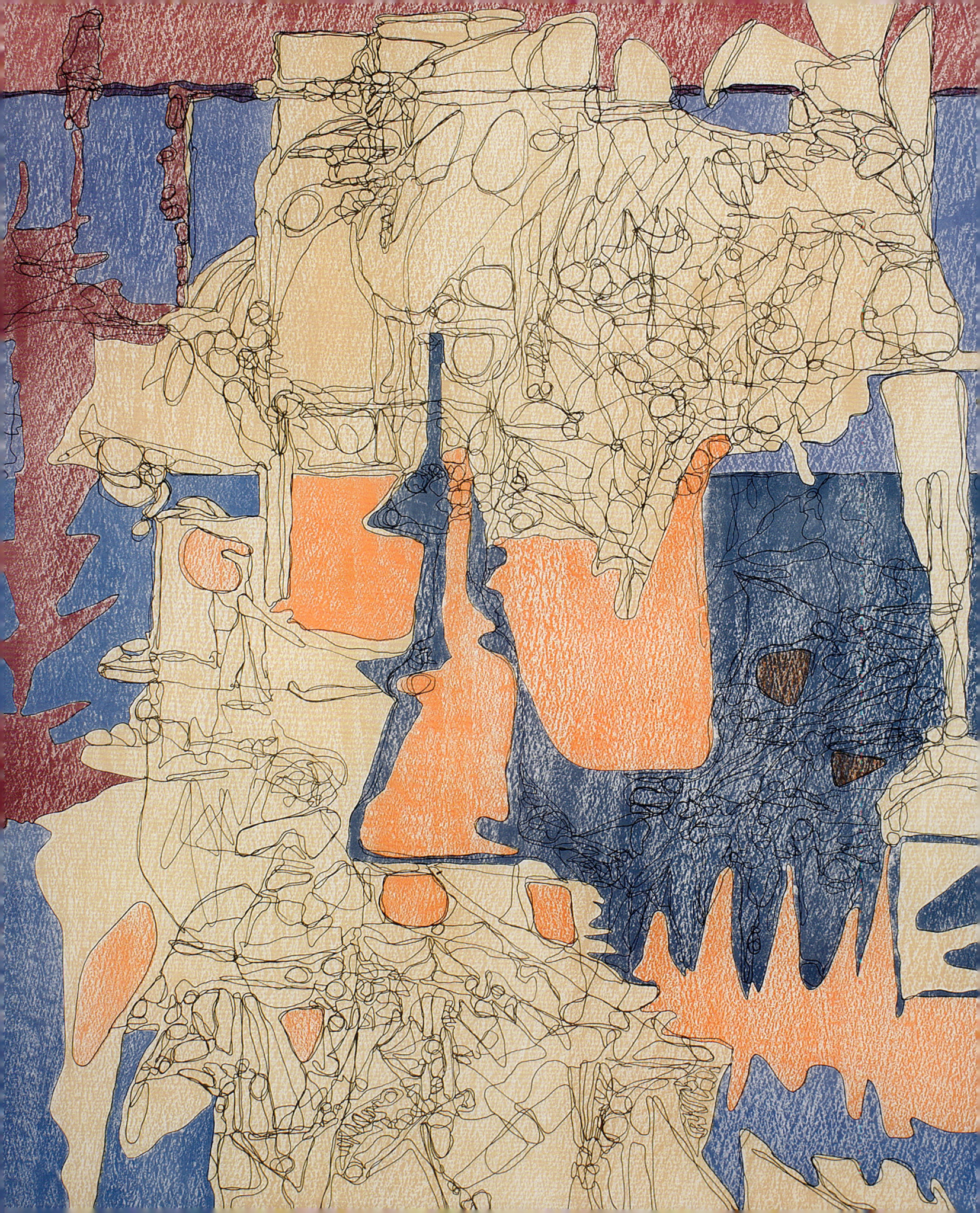

4 | Making Modern

SELECTED PAINTINGS, DRAWINGS, AND PRINTS

W. Jackson Rushing III

WHEN JAMES T. BIALAC DECIDED to gift his legendary Native American art collection to the Fred Jones Jr. Museum of Art (FJJMA) at the University of Oklahoma, both he and the university community at large recognized its tremendous educational potential. The 2,600 paintings and works on paper alone constitute a broad survey of key developments in twentieth- and twenty-first-century Native art. The cultural geography of the collection is similarly remarkable, ranging from visionary Huichol Indian yarn paintings (*arte en estambre*) from Nayarit in western Mexico to prints and drawings from the Arctic, including works by Kenoujak Ashevak (Inuit) and James Kivetoruk Moses (Inupiaq).

The Bialac Collection is especially strong in Southwest, Plains, and Southeast Indian painting, and many different styles, from ethnographic realism to abstraction and Pop Art, are included. Identifiable also is the influence of various schools and art centers, including the Santa Fe Indian School (SFIS); Bacone College in Muskogee, Oklahoma; the Institute of American Indian Arts in Santa Fe (IAIA); the Cape Dorset workshop; and certainly the School of Art and

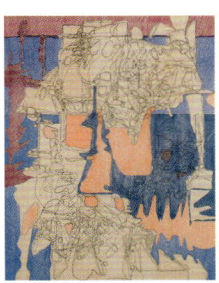

PLATE 78

GEORGE MORRISON

U.S., Ojibwe, 1919–2000

Untitled (Surrealist Landscape), 1997

Lithograph, 36⅜ x 28⅝ in.

Courtesy of Briand Morrison

Art History at the University of Oklahoma, where Oscar Howe (Yanktonai Nakota) Richard "Dick" West (Cheyenne), and others earned graduate degrees in fine arts. Mothers and daughters, fathers and sons, and teachers and students are likewise represented.

Clearly, the Bialac Collection, which is notable for both its breadth and its depth, will fuel numerous exhibitions, publications, symposia, and undergraduate and graduate seminars on such topics as the anthropology of art; masquerade and performance; human and animal relationships; cosmology and spirituality; the power of place; and aesthetic hybridity as a reflection of indigenous survival strategies. Indeed, the geographic sweep and aesthetic diversity of the collection mirrors the complexity of Native art in the modern period, especially painting, drawing, and printmaking. So even if a summary description only hints at the richness of the collection or its aesthetic and educational possibilities, this much can be stated with certainty: Jim Bialac's monumental collection is a modern one. For this introductory overview, I have selected works of art that embody and illustrate, in various ways, the notion of making modern.

We no longer speak of modernity, modern art, or modernism as singular phenomena, because to do so is both ahistorical and Eurocentric. Modernity did not develop or arrive everywhere simultaneously, so we should acknowledge that the "time" of modernity is irregular. Similarly, modernism is not a single style but multiple maneuvers in the arts that allow artists to negotiate modernity whenever and wherever they encounter it. In other words, modernities provoke modernisms. As the critic Kobena Mercer explains it, modernisms "took shape in different national and cultural environments." Noting that "crisis and innovation" are diagnostic characteristics of modernisms, Mercer identifies the "dynamic interplay between different cultures as a constant thread that weaves in and out of the story of Modern art as a whole."[1] Given the chronological parameters of the Bialac Collection—the earliest works, including Northern Cheyenne and Navajo ledger drawings, date from the 1880s—for the purpose of this essay, the "crisis" in a Native North American context was the "Indian wars" of the later nineteenth century and the subsequent beginning of the reservation period. The violent colonial subjugation of indigenous peoples is thus understood as an aspect of modernity.

In the American Southwest, the arrival of the railroad, various anthropological expeditions, the development of tourism, and an incipient cash economy, all of which stimulated arts and crafts revivals (the commoditization of culture), also signaled the arrival of modernity. The invention of new art forms or the repurposing of existing ones, usually supported by white patronage, is a hallmark of the earliest efforts to make what we understand in retrospect was modern Southwest Indian art. This transitional moment is represented in the Bialac Collection variously, but especially in the work of the Navajo artist Apie "Son of Milk" Begay, who was "discovered" in

1902 making drawings with rudimentary materials at Pueblo Bonito in western New Mexico by archaeologist and curator Kenneth Chapman, who provided him with good paper and the first colored pencils the artist had ever seen.[2] According to Chapman, "Before the afternoon was gone, Apie made three drawings for me [of ceremonial figures] that have been described and exhibited several times as the earliest known examples of Navajo art produced with white man's materials."[3] According to J. J. Brody, Apie Begay "consistently referred to traditional Navajo modes," but Clara Lee Tanner saw in the drawings Chapman collected a concerted effort to solve formal problems of figuration, including liberating himself from "the convention of unalterable rigidity and repetition of yei figures [holy people] in sandpaintings."[4] The Bialac picture is an undated watercolor, and the date of Begay's death is likewise unknown, although one source reports that he "died many years before 1936."[5] In any case, the Bialac picture was certainly made after 1902, for it shows firm draftsmanship and careful spacing of the forms. Although the figures are elongated, as in sandpaintings, relative to the drawings from 1902, the watercolor illustrated here is more stable and naturalistic, even as it employs (contra Tanner) the rhythmic repetition of "traditional Navajo modes." Someone, probably not the artist, has inscribed it at lower right: "yebichai dancers/

PLATE 79

APIE BEGAY

U.S., Navajo, late nineteenth century–c. 1920s

Yei'bichai Dancers, n.d.

Watercolor on paper, 9½ x 15 in.

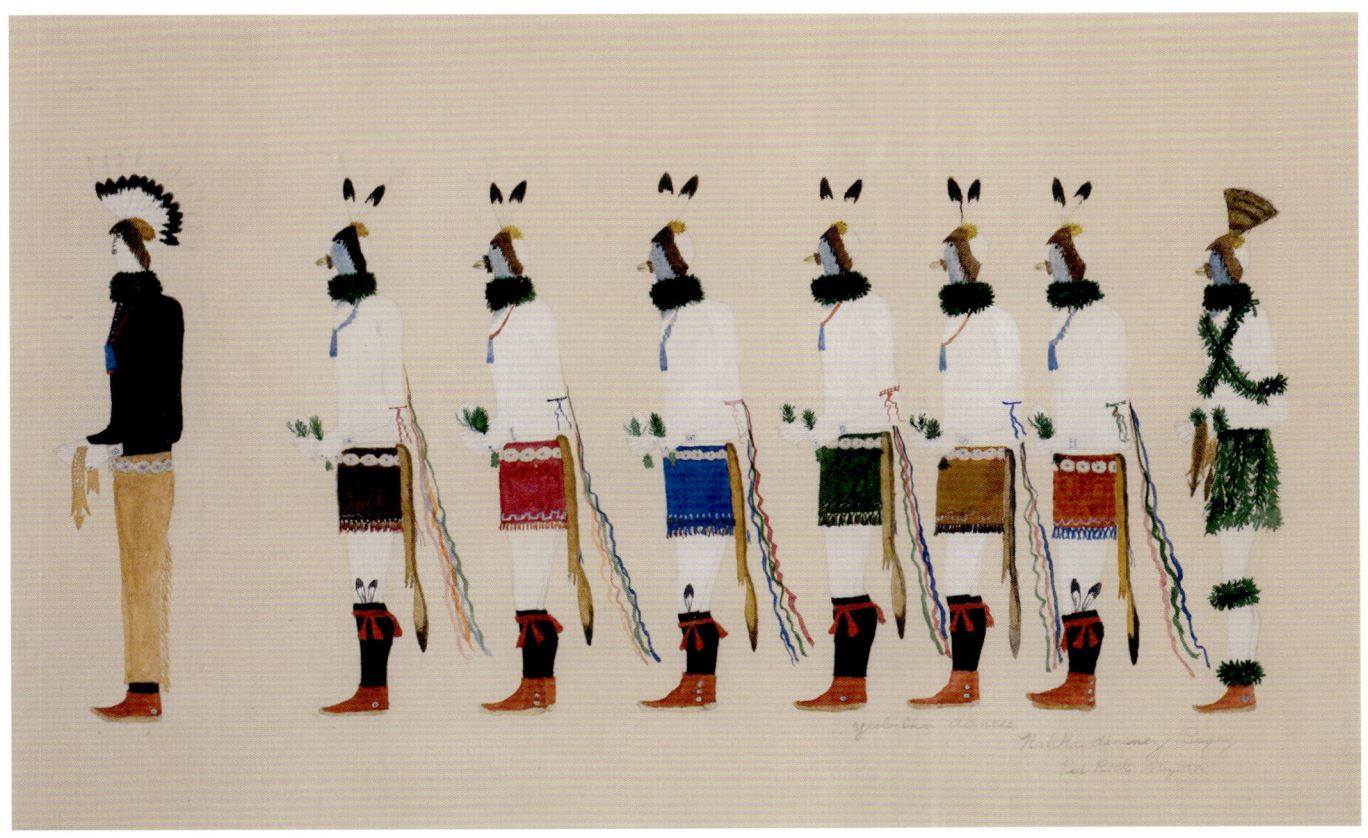

Nahkai dinenez Begay/Red Rock Arizona." According to Ann Hedlund, curator of ethnology at the Arizona State Museum, "one could interpret the name in modern spelling as Naakai Diné Nez Begay," which might translate roughly as "son of Tall Mexican-Navajo Man,"[6] a reading supported, perhaps, by the fact that the back of the picture is inscribed "Mexican Begay." Similarly, the distinguished Navajo weaver D. Y. Begay explains that the word "dinenez" in the inscription is a "direct physical description of a particular person—a tall man."[7]

Leland Wyman, who was a leading authority on Navajo religion and ceremony, wrote that Yei'bichai refers to "all the masked impersonators" of the "group of Holy People known as Yeis." These Yei'bichai dance in public performance the final night of the Night Chant ceremony, one of the Navajo ceremonials best known to outsiders, which Begay represents here.[8] Given the paucity of information about the artist and the scarcity of his work, the Bialac picture, with its informative inscription, must be seen as a rare document indeed, not just in the history of early modern art, but in Navajo-white relations, for like many indigenous images and objects created in the colonial contact zone, it served simultaneously as art and auto-ethnography.

Working for Edgar L. Hewett at the School of American Research (SAR), founded in 1907, Chapman was a key member of the Santa Fe culturati, whose patronage helped facilitate the emergence of modern Pueblo painting in the early years of the twentieth century. Inspired in part by pottery designs and murals painted on the walls of kivas (underground ritual chambers), the first generation of Pueblo watercolor painters was self-taught, and virtually all of them, including Velino Herrera (Zia), Fred Kabotie (Hopi), Julian Martinez (San Ildefonso), José Encarnacion Peña (San Ildefonso), Tonita Peña (San Ildefonso), Otis Polelonema (Hopi), Abel Sanchez (San Ildefonso), Awa Tsireh (San Ildefonso), and Romando Vigil (San Ildefonso), are represented in the Bialac Collection. Through a secular art form—nonceremonial paintings made for sale to collectors outside the community of origin—these artists sought to communicate Pueblo social and spiritual values as they participated in a cash economy. Painters and patrons were of one mind, although not necessarily for the same reasons, in their belief that Pueblo culture should be preserved and protected. Through trial and error, the artists quickly learned how to make modern: that is, to preserve their cultural and artistic integrity even as they met the romantic expectations of their patrons for authentic pictorial documents of supposedly unacculturated aboriginality.

The Hopi painter Fred Kabotie, who was born at Shungopovi at Second Mesa in Arizona, first began making and selling pictures at SFIS in 1916–1917 when he was about sixteen or seventeen years old.[9] Encouraged by Elizabeth DeHuff, wife of the school's superintendent, Kabotie soothed his homesickness by making images of Hopi ceremonies, or as he explained the situation many years later, "Loneliness moves you to express something of your home, your background."[10]

Kabotie's *Snake Dance* (c. 1918), one of his five works in the collection, is a fine example of his earliest watercolors, already notable for their naturalistic vignettes, lively composition, realistic modeling of figures, and sharp attention to detail (notice, for example, the dancer seen disappearing under a cottonwood bower at the back center of the picture). It is instructive to compare Kabotie's version of the Snake Dance with William Penhallow Henderson's *Walpi Snake Dance* (c. 1920) in the Eugene B. Adkins Collection at the FJJMA. A dramatic oil on canvas, Henderson's painting combines intense, high key color derived from Post-Impressionism and Fauvism with powerful scale (almost seven by nine feet) to make a grand if slightly fictive statement. In contrast, Kabotie's image is intimate, just 15 x 20½ inches, and emotionally reserved, seeking not rhetorical power but a sincere and direct communication of memory, idea, and feeling. Brody's thoughtful description of *Hopi Snake Dance* (c. 1920–1921), a remarkably similar Kabotie painting in the SAR collection in Santa Fe, is instructive here as well: "The view is panoramic, as though seen from a rooftop. The figures interact dynamically and are individualized by variations in posture, gesture, and facial expression. . . . All the figures are realistically modeled and, although they are in a void, the implication of spatial penetration is clear; the world portrayed is a three-dimensional one confined within the margins of the paper."[11] Auspicious beginnings indeed for a self-taught teenage artist, one who was later awarded a Guggenheim Fellowship (1945) to support production of his book, *Designs from the Ancient Mimbreños* (1949), and who supervised a team of artists that recreated murals from the ancient Hopi village of Awatovi for display at the Museum of Modern Art in New York, in 1941, at the historic exhibition *Indian Art of the United States.*[12]

The Bialac Collection reflects a key element in the emergence of early modern Pueblo painting: the productive relationship between a group of artists at San Ildefonso Pueblo and the social scientists at the SAR in Santa Fe, who often employed Pueblo men whose watercolors they collected to work at the museum or at archaeological excavations on the Pajarito plateau. One such artist was Awa Tsireh (also known as Alfonso Roybal), whose uncle, Crescencio Martinez, made a series of paintings commissioned by Hewett in 1917 that documented ceremonial life at San Ildefonso. According to Brody, "Awa Tsireh was the most prolific Pueblo artist of his generation and, with Fred Kabotie, the most innovative and widely admired by contemporaneous Euro-American critics and patrons."[13] Like his uncle before him, Awa Tsireh (or Cattail Bird) was commissioned by Hewett in 1920 to make pictures of Pueblo life for the SAR, where he worked (along with Kabotie) occasionally until 1924.[14] Bialac's Awa Tsireh pictures constitute a collection within a collection—almost fifty in all, iconic images of a wide range of subjects, including Kiowa butterfly dancers, harvest maidens, sandpainting figures, sacred clowns, women firing pottery, and buffalo hunters.

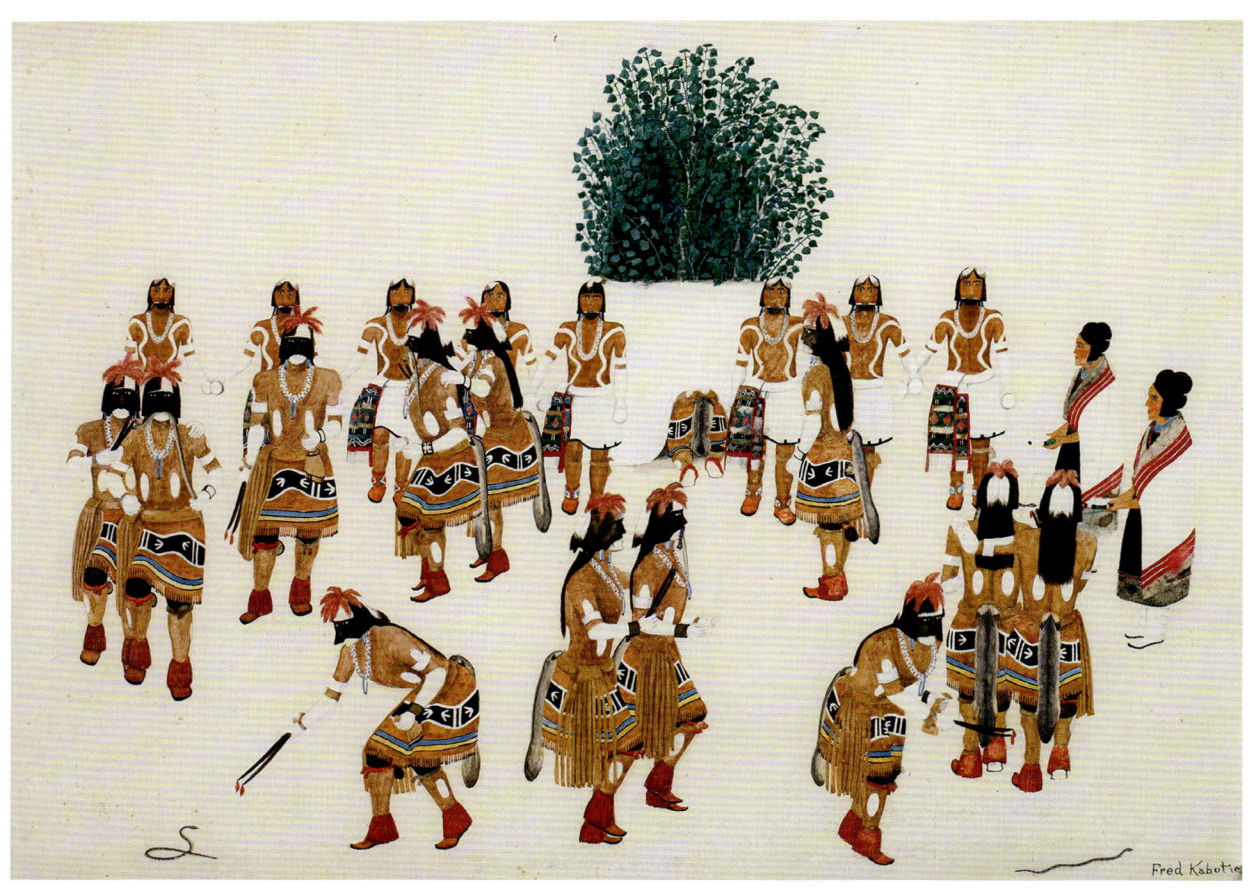

PLATE 80

FRED KABOTIE

U.S., Hopi Pueblo, 1900–1986

Snake Dance, c. 1918

Watercolor on paper, 15 x 20½ in.

PLATE 81

WILLIAM PENHALLOW HENDERSON

U.S., 1877–1943

Walpi Snake Dance, c. 1920

Oil on canvas, 42 x 55 in.
The Eugene B. Adkins Collection at the
Fred Jones Jr. Museum of Art,
University of Oklahoma, Norman, and
the Philbrook Museum of Art, Tulsa.

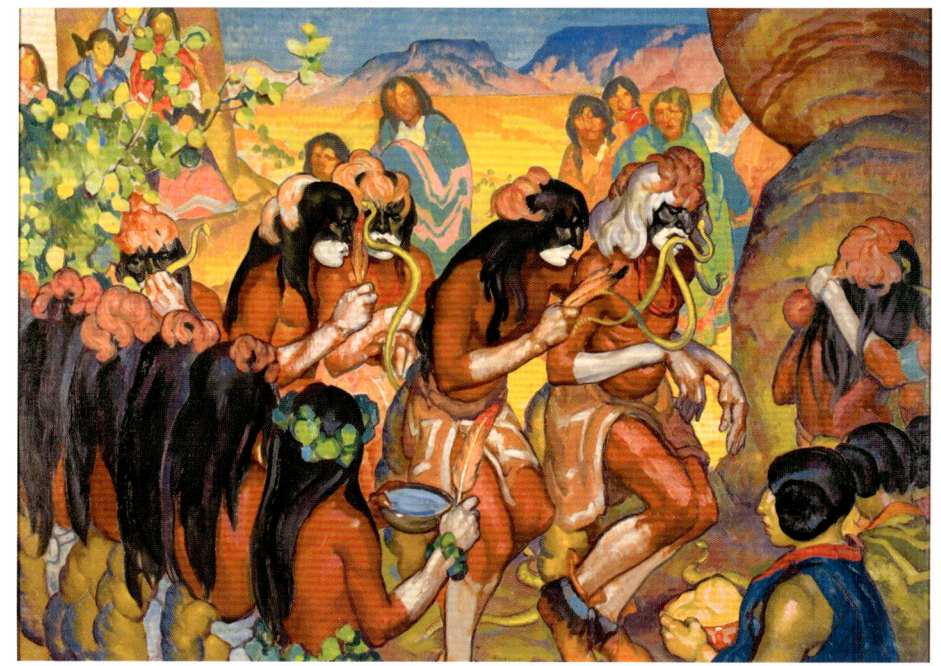

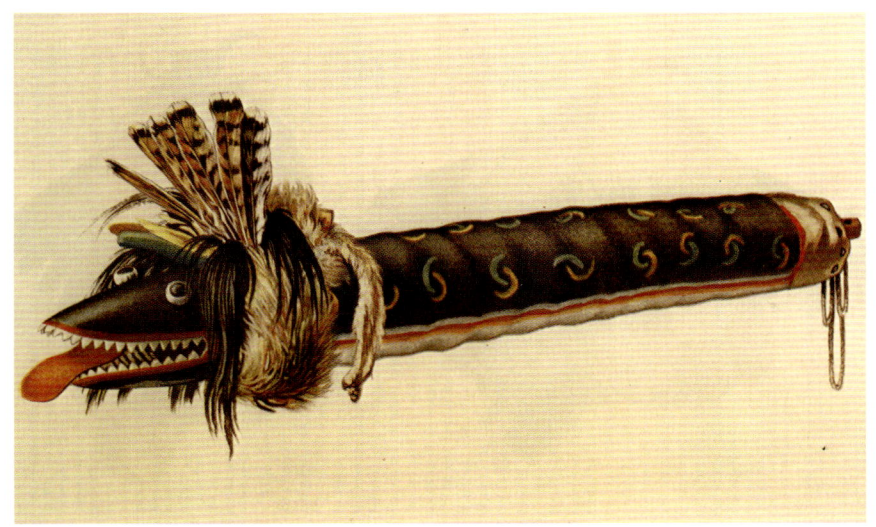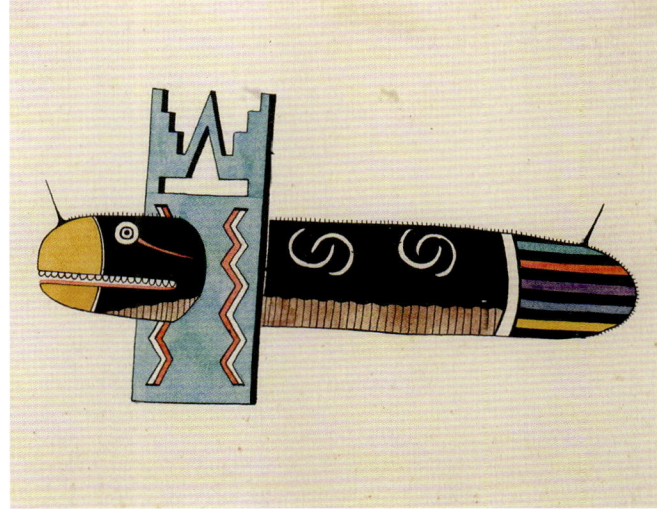

Two of the Awa Tsireh pictures in particular testify to the eclectic nature of Bialac's taste and to the differing styles employed by the artist. *Koloowisi with Tableta,* an undated mixed media work on paper, represents a sacred and powerful horned water serpent known to the Zuni, whose counterpart in Awa Tsireh's Tewa culture is the Avanyu, likewise a horned serpent whose image is often seen in pottery decoration and modern Pueblo paintings. In the Zuni worldview, Koloowisi protects the purity of spring water and may appear in the village, wearing a tableta (a geometric, wooden headdress), during long, elaborate boy's initiation ceremonies.[15] Awa Tsireh's image is strikingly similar to two illustrations of Koloowisi that accompanied Matilda Coxe Stevenson's monograph on the Zuni, which was published in the *23rd Annual Report of the Bureau of American Ethnology* (1904).[16] Like Hewett, Chapman, and the other scholars at the SAR, the artists who worked there, including Awa Tsireh, did research in the collection, which makes sense considering "ethnographic illustration was the goal, and the young artists were encouraged to portray arcane ceremonial dances and exotic or obsolete craft activities."[17] This may account for the highly stylized and "artifactual" quality of Awa Tsireh's serpent, which also resembles a *Kolowisi Water Serpent Puppet* collected by the Brooklyn Museum of Art in 1904.[18] We see a rather different aesthetic at work in his *Two Black Antelope Under Rainbow Jumping Over* (c. 1920s–1930s), which is less documentary, more imaginative. Hieratic and symmetrical, it uses quasi-abstract patterns derived from pottery decoration (and perhaps from Art Deco) to speak of balance, order, and the overarching presence of the sacred in the world.

PLATE 82 (ABOVE LEFT)

UNKNOWN (U.S., ZUNI)

Ko'loowisi (Plumed Serpent), n.d.

Mixed media

J. W. Powell, *23rd Annual Report of the Bureau of American Ethnology to the Secretary of the Smithsonian Institution,* 1901–1902, Washington, D.C.: Government Printing Office, 1904, plate 13.

PLATE 83 (ABOVE RIGHT)

AWA TSIREH

(ALFONSO ROYBAL)

U.S., San Ildefonso Pueblo, 1898–1955

Koloowisi with Tableta, n.d.

Ink and watercolor on paper, 4½ x 5½ in.

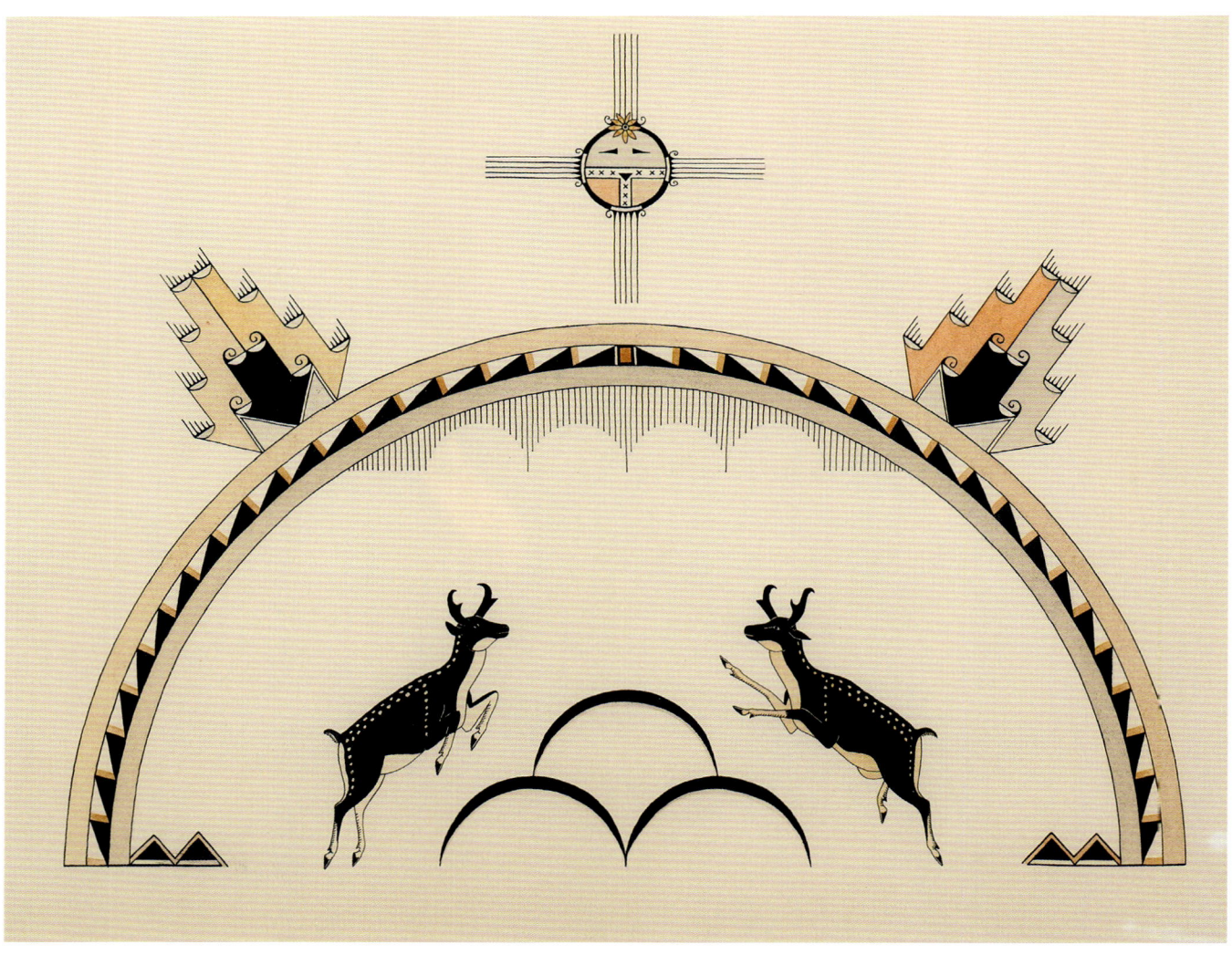

PLATE 84

AWA TSIREH

(ALFONSO ROYBAL)

U.S., San Ildefonso Pueblo,

1898–1955

Two Black Antelope Under

Rainbow Jumping Over,

c. 1920–1930

India ink and watercolor on

paper, 10⅜ x 13½ in.

Equally inventive is *Bird* (c. 1925), a watercolor made by Julian Martinez, whose wife and artistic partner was the world-renowned San Ildefonso potter Maria Poveka Martinez. Julian, who began decorating Maria's pottery in 1904, worked for Hewett at the Museum of New Mexico from 1909 to 1914, and as an artistic team, the Martinezes revolutionized Pueblo pottery in 1917, when they invented the now internationally acclaimed black-on-black style.[19] But Julian had also worked for Hewett, along with Crescencio Martinez, at the Pajarito excavations, perhaps as early as 1910 but certainly by 1912, and by 1927 he was so well established as a watercolorist that his works were selected to decorate the rooms at the La Fonda Hotel in Santa Fe, which had been recently acquired and renovated by the Fred Harvey Company.[20] *Bird* is a brilliant painting, stylistically comparable to works by Awa Tsireh that date from 1922 to 1925: a fantastic creature, inspired by pottery decoration and Pueblo architecture, and formed of organic and geo-

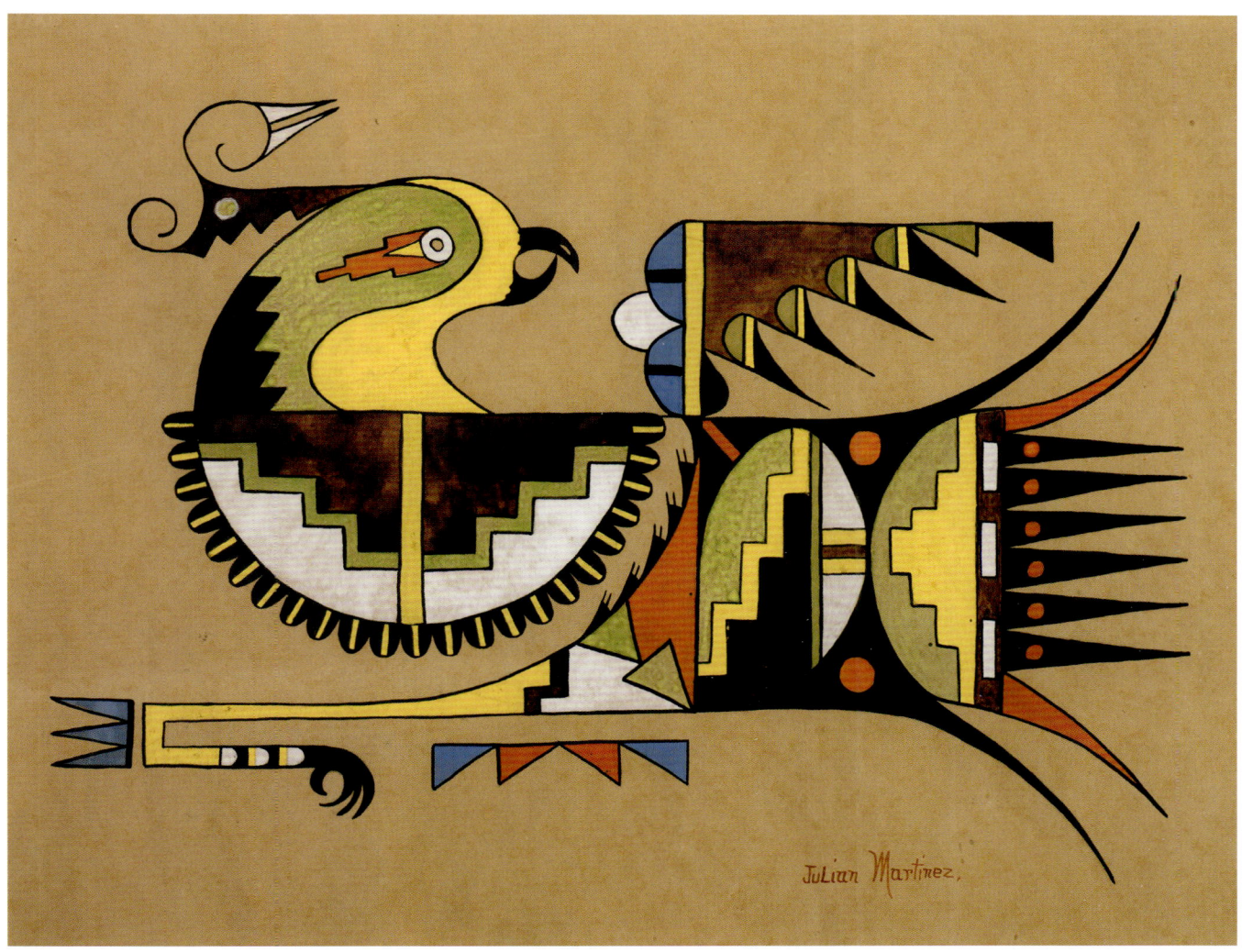

metric shapes interlocked in a taut, surface-oriented design.[21] Diagnostic of this first generation of Pueblo painting is its reliance on crisp linearity, discrete zones of color, and startling compositional complexity. Pleasing the eye and exciting the mind, *Bird* belongs to one of three broad style categories of early modern Pueblo painting identified by Brody: "flatly painted, abstract emblems based upon Pueblo pottery and ritual art, set within featureless backgrounds."[22] It is inarguably one of the finest examples extant of Julian's historic work.

The only female artist in the first generation of self-taught Pueblo painters was Tonita Peña (Quah Ah or White Coral Beads), whose *Comanche Dance* (1920–1921, plate 86) is but one of thirty-seven paintings by her in the Bialac Collection. Peña was born at San Ildefonso, but after her mother's death, she grew up at Cochiti Pueblo, where she married and raised a family. In the one-room school house at San Ildefonso, she and other young students were encouraged by their

PLATE 85

JULIAN MARTINEZ

U.S., San Ildefonso Pueblo,

1897–1943

Bird, n.d.

Watercolor on paper.

11¾ x 14¾ in.

teacher, Esther B. Hoyt, to make paintings based on how they felt while dancing in the plaza.[23] When Peña began painting as an adult, perhaps as early as 1919, but certainly by 1920, she was a twice-widowed mother of three children, and the income she realized from making pictures, most of which she sold in the first few years to Hewett at the SAR, was important for the well-being of her family. All the major scholarly sources agree that Peña's paintings are notable for their subtle refinement. In the first monograph published on the subject, *Southwest Indian Painting* (1957), Tanner offered a detailed and exacting analysis of Peña's ability to create convincing, naturalistic details, even though "a splendid dignity and peaceful feeling pervade her painting."[24] No less an authority than the teacher, curator, and proselytizer for Native painting Dorothy Dunn, who established The Studio for Indian arts at the SFIS in 1932, testified in 1968 to the significance of Peña's aesthetic achievement.

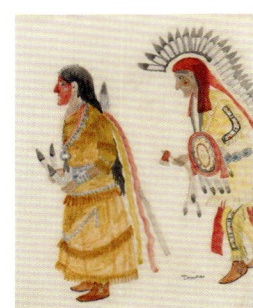

> Quah Ah's art is an art of radiance and tranquility. It is possessed of delicacy and grace, and much music. It is unequalled at conveying the dignity, the serenity, the great earnestness and wholehearted sincerity of the Pueblo ceremonial and the Pueblo people. Quah Ah's work is not ever spectacular or striking, but it is completely unpretentious and authentic. She might be called a conservative painter for she has set her own standards in keeping with tradition and has adhered to them through the years so consistently that, even beyond her death, she has never been superceded as the dean of Indian women painters.[25]

In terms of modernity, at least two aspects of Peña's art and career are important here: her incipient feminism and the latent political potential of her paintings. Among her many subjects are numerous quiet but ennobling images of women—working at traditional labors and participating in ritual life. That she conceived of herself as a painter at all was a radical turn, given the conservatism of Pueblo culture, and with her husband's support, she resisted efforts at Cochiti to censor or proscribe the content of her work.[26] The award-winning Santa Clara painter Pablita Velarde, who was a classmate of Peña's son, Joe Herrera, at The Studio and who is represented well in the Bialac Collection, always remembered Peña as her mentor and inspiring role model. According to Velarde, Peña "was the rebellion way back in the early 1920s. She gave me the inner strength that I needed to dare the men to put me in my own place or let me go."[27]

As for the covert political implications of Peña's work, we should observe that dance imagery was and is ubiquitous in Pueblo painting, for both internal and external reasons. For the Euro-American patrons who collected and celebrated paintings such as Peña's *Comanche Dance,*

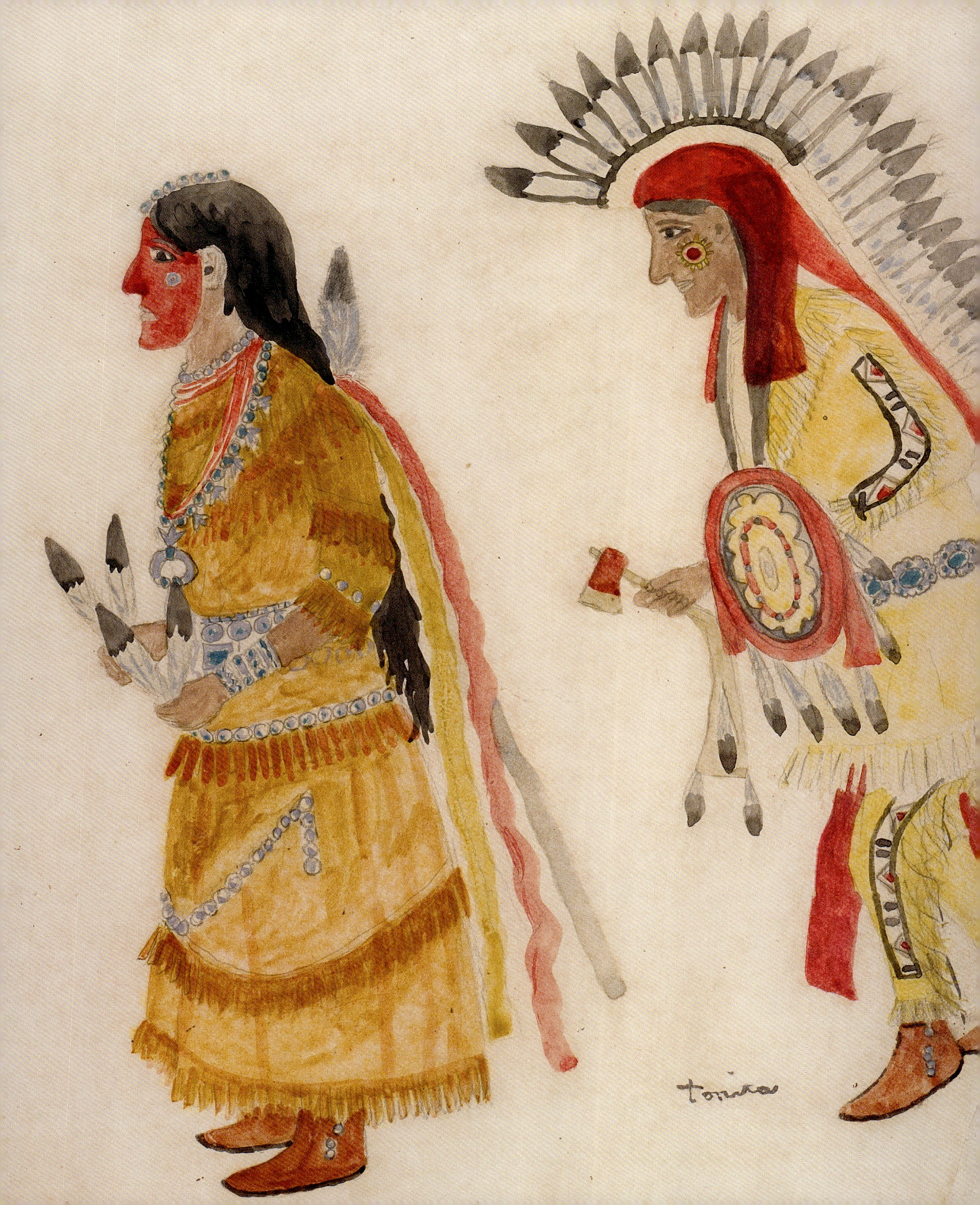

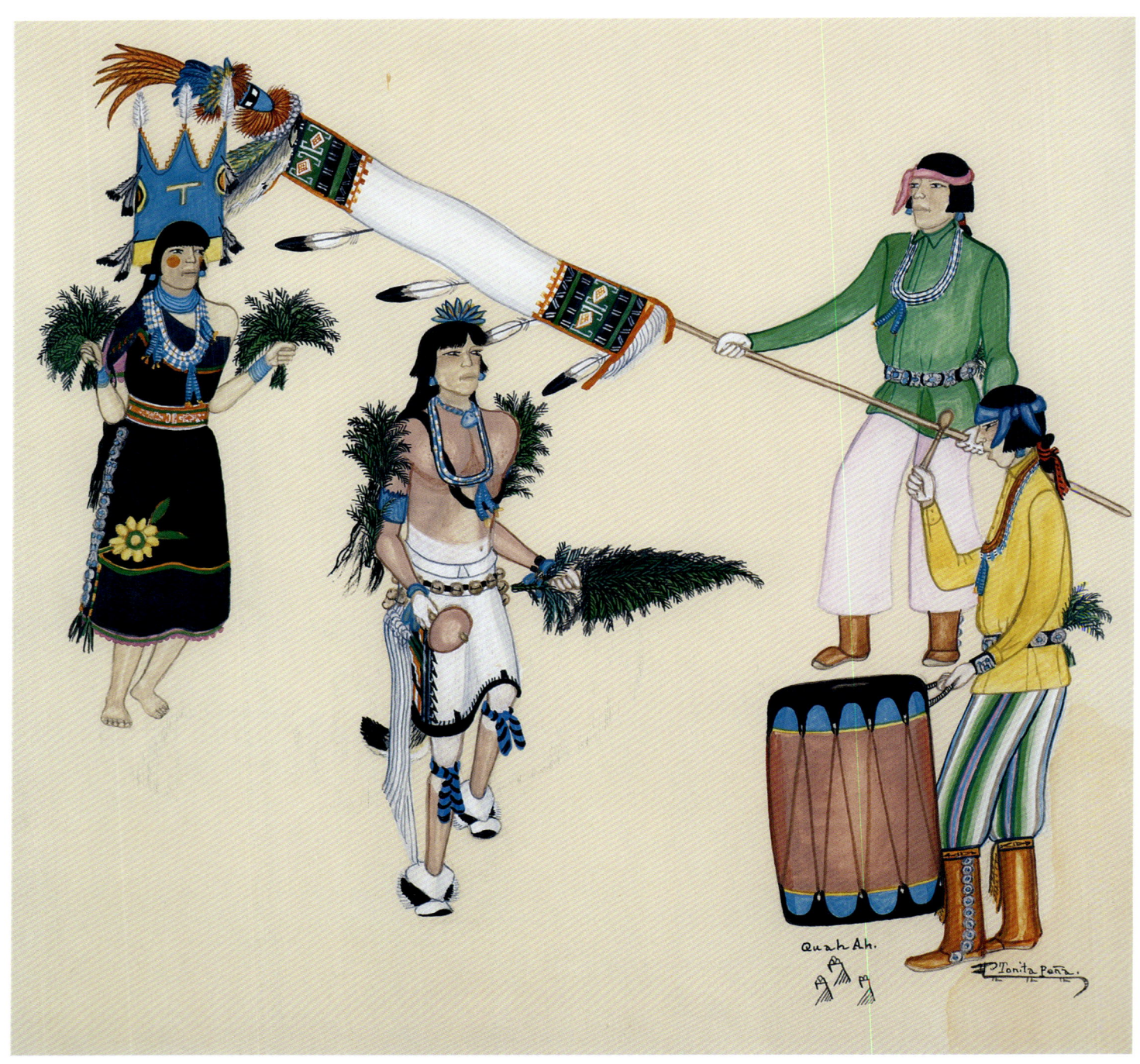

PLATE 87

TONITA PEÑA (QUAH AH)

U.S., San Ildefonso Pueblo, 1893–1949

Cochiti Corn Dance, n.d.

Watercolor on paper, 13¼ × 13½ in.

the dance was a manifestation of cultural and spiritual difference. And in their ardent attraction to paintings like the one illustrated here, which they collected eagerly, we can identify a wistful longing for unity with nature. For example, the modernist painter Marsden Hartley published an essay, "Tribal Esthetics," in 1918 in which he called Pueblo dances the unifying force of Indian culture. Speaking of their "precise beauty," Hartley described the dance "as an organized rhythmic conception and esthetic composition, spirit and body harmonized to symbolize . . . their so ardent desires."[28] Hartley and others were disappointed, naturally, that Pueblo dances had been characterized by some as barbaric. In fact, in the early 1920s there was pressure from New Mexico in Washington, D.C., to suppress Pueblo dances, which were criticized for debauchery and sexual excess, which strikes us today as ridiculous. In addition, the Bursum Bill (1921–1922) in Congress threatened to strip some Pueblos of most of their irrigated lands. Thus, the efforts in the early 1920s of the painter John Sloan and others to exhibit on the East Coast paintings like Peña's magnificent *Comanche Dance,* her *Cochiti Corn Dance* (n.d.), and her reverential *Basket Dance* (c. 1919)—all in the Bialac Collection—was about more than just art appreciation, although it was

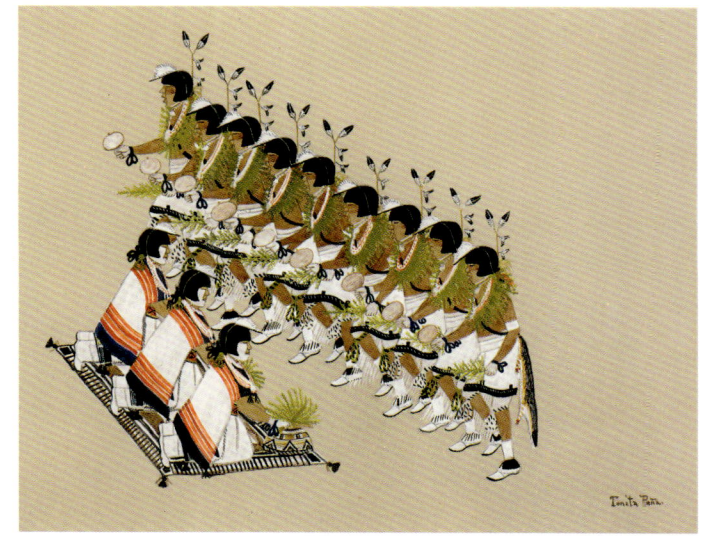

certainly that. Far more was at stake than just recognizing artistic quality. Most of us probably would not describe Peña's dance imagery as political art, but work like this was mobilized for political and educational purposes. For eastern audiences who had never visited a Pueblo, the dances were demystified by such pictures, and any imagined danger was ameliorated by recognition of their compelling beauty.[29] Just a decade later, Peña and other Pueblo (and southern Plains Indian) painters were exhibited in the historic *Exposition of Indian Tribal Arts,* which opened at the Grand Central Galleries in New York City, where it was viewed on the opening day by more than three thousand visitors, after which it toured the country for two years, closing at the Corcoran Gallery in 1933 as part of the Washington bicentennial.[30]

The inclusion of watercolors by The Kiowa Five in the 1931 exposition was facilitated by one of their primary mentors, Oscar B. Jacobson, director of the School of Art at the University of Oklahoma. The so-called flat style of modern Plains Indian painting associated with The Kiowa Five, which was indebted to nineteenth-century ledger book drawings (like those collected by Jim Bialac) and paintings on muslin, was "born" at St. Patrick's Mission School in Anadarko, Oklahoma, where Spenser Asah, James Auchiah, Jack Hokeah, and Stephen Mopope had their first art classes circa 1914 with Sister Olivia Taylor (Choctaw). All of them, plus Monroe

Tsatoke, had art lessons from Indian Service field matron Susan Ryan Peters in 1918, meaning that chronologically the emergence of modern Plains Indian painting was coincident with the so-called San Ildefonso movement. The "original" Kiowa Five—Asah, Hokeah, Mopope, Tsatoke, and Lois Smoky, the only female Plains painter in that first generation, began special classes at the university under Jacobson's supervision in 1926. Auchiah's arrival at the university in 1927 was paralleled by Smoky's departure. Jacobson arranged for an exhibition of their work at the First International Congress of Folk Arts in Prague in 1928, and with C. Szwedzicki, he published a historic portfolio of the show, *Kiowa Indian Art,* in Nice, France, in 1929.[31] Many accolades, exhibitions, and publications followed, and the legacy of The Kiowa Five is very much part of the University of Oklahoma's institutional memory and identity. All six of the Kiowa "five" are represented in the Bialac Collection, including Auchiah, whose *Peyote Bird* (1937) embodies multiple aspects of modernity.

According to Weston La Barre, in precontact Mexico, both the Aztecs and the Cora-Huichol practiced ritual consumption of peyote, a vision-inducing cactus found in south Texas and Mexico.[32] By the 1870s, as a result of intertribal contact, a new religion based on peyote consumption was established on the southern Plains, with Kiowa people playing a primary role in its diffusion. Peyote ritual is syncretic (and thus modern) in its fusion of aspects of Christianity with the Ghost Dance and other Aboriginal elements in an effort to help Native peoples adapt to, and survive in, radically new circumstances.[33] New ritual objects and new iconographies were necessary, and emblematic, quasi-abstract water birds, like the one illustrated here, were and are the primary symbol of peyote religion. According to the anthropologist Daniel C. Swan, Auchiah's bird is a scissor-tail flycatcher, whose feathers are used in peyote fans that symbolize morning or dawn in the ceremonial context.[34] Auchiah's ascendant bird is surrounded by symbolic patterns, like those he rehearsed in his decorative *Beadwork Designs* (1921), a watercolor in the Arthur and Shifra Silberman Native American Art Collection at the National Cowboy and Western Heritage Museum in Oklahoma City.[35] The designs may also reflect those seen in Kiowa "German silver" peyote jewelry, which, as Swan observed, was marked by great innovation between the 1920s and 1940s.[36] The design above the bird suggests, abstractly, the fire, altar, and fetish around which the practitioners are seated during an all-night ceremony of songs and prayers. The visionary quality of the image would seem to argue against a political reading of it, but attempts to suppress the peyote ritual and the Native American Church born of it (chartered in Oklahoma in 1918) had begun in the late nineteenth century and continue to this day. Thus Auchiah, a leader in the church, is giving form to both religious freedom and the uplifting and healing power of the "medicine" (ritual sacrament) consumed in the ceremony.

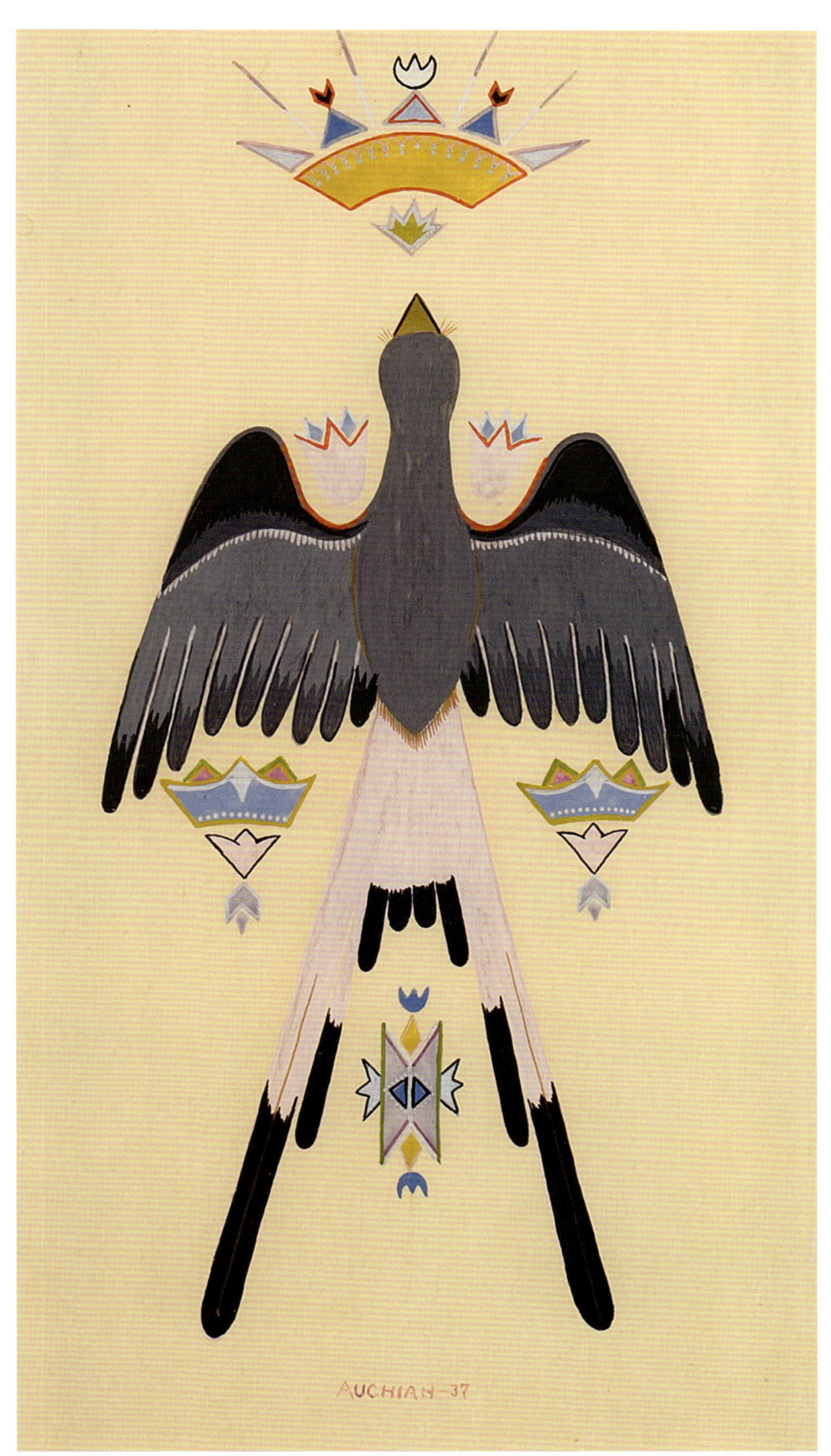

PLATE 89

JAMES AUCHIAH

U.S., Kiowa, 1906–1974

Peyote Bird, 1937

Watercolor on paper, 10¾ x 5½ in.

PLATE 90

JAMES AUCHIAH

U.S., Kiowa, 1906–1974

Beadwork Designs, 1921

Tempera on paper, 14 × 9½ in.
National Cowboy and Western
Heritage Museum, Arthur
and Shifra Silberman Native
American Art Collection,
1996.27.20.

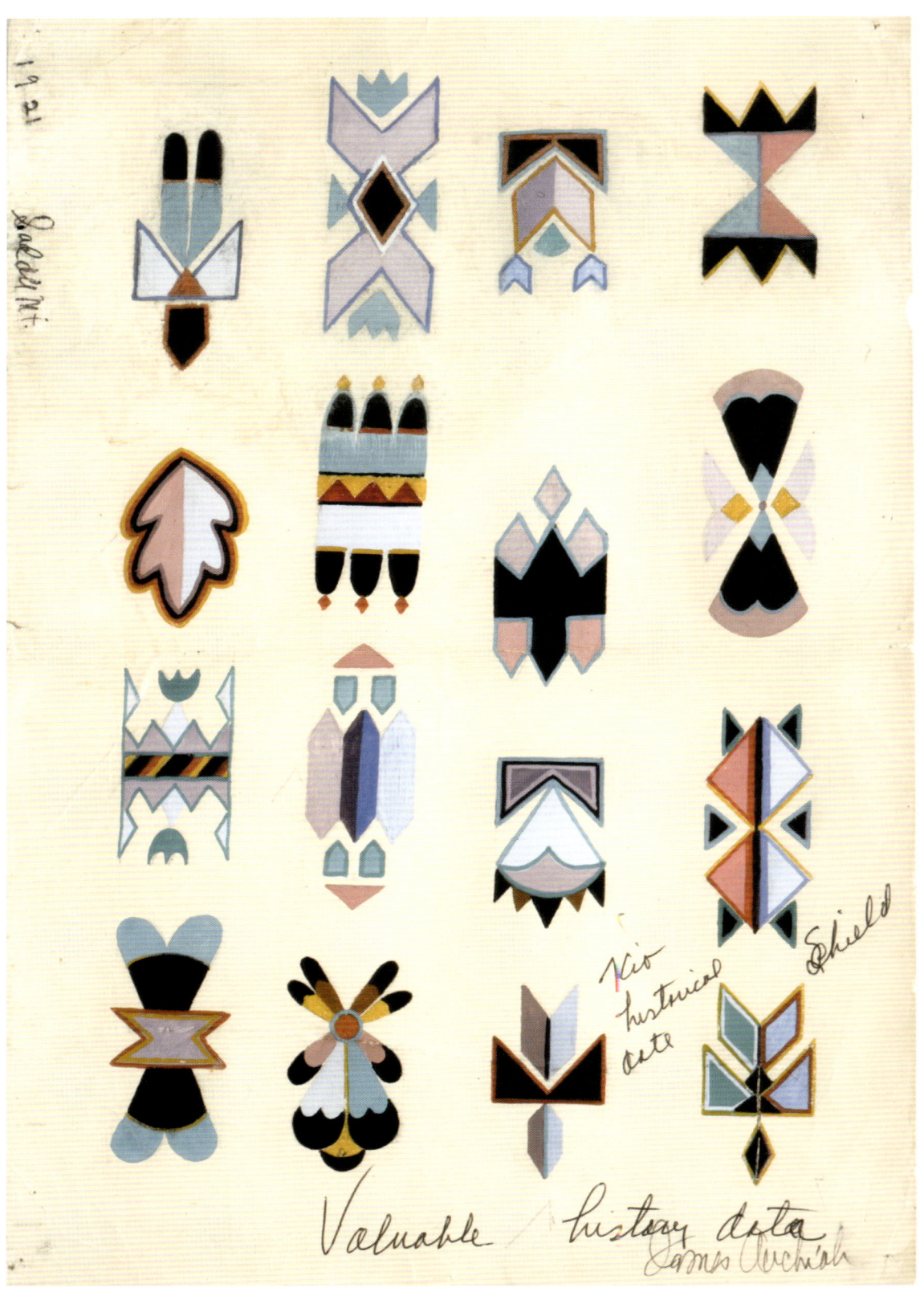

The stylistic elements of the new Pueblo and Plains Indian painting were synthesized and codified in the curriculum established by Dunn at The Studio in 1932, and the first Studio generation consisted of a stellar group of artists, whose names are legendary in Native American art history; many of them are featured in the Bialac Collection, including Narciso Abeyta (Navajo),

Harrison Begay (Navajo), Joe Herrera (Cochiti), Allan Houser (Chiricauha Apache), Oscar Howe (Yanktonai Nakota), Gerald Nailor (Navajo), Pablita Velarde (Santa Clara), and Andrew Tsihnahjinnie (Navajo). One of the gems from this period is a rare work by Hansen Twoitsie (Hopi), who painted "modern Indian frescos" (c. 1935) with "earth pigments extracted and ground in the Studio." According to Dunn, Twoitsie "worked in a scholarly manner, going to prehistoric sources for Hopi ceramic patterns and adapting them to easel paintings."[37] His *Parrot Sikyatki* (c. 1940) is a fine example of that approach. Sikyatki, an ancient Hopi village abandoned circa 1500, was partially excavated by Jesse Walter Fewkes (Smithsonian Institution) in 1895, revealing pots with a complex form language and abstract bird iconography that inspired subsequent generations of Hopi artists, including the

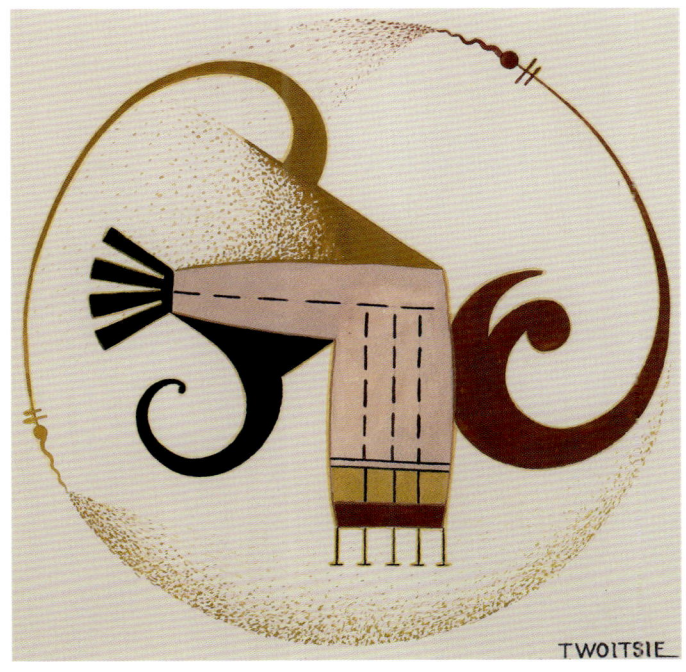

renowned potter Nampeyo and her great-great-grandson, Dan Namingha. Parrots were kept in the kivas for ritual purposes, and here Twoitsie has magnified a design element from ancient pottery, reaffirming its abstract and iconographic character. Dunn herself has inscribed the picture on the back, noting that it is a "pre-Columbian pottery motif." The importance of the work is underscored by Dunn's inclusion of it in a historic exhibition, *Contemporary American Indian Painting*, which she organized for the National Gallery of Art in Washington, D.C. (1953).

Like his mother, Tonita Peña, Joe Herrera was a major figure in modern Native painting, and the Bialac Collection of his art—twenty-one pictures, Studio and post-Studio work alike—is the finest one extant. Before World War II, Herrera made award-winning genre paintings of Pueblo life in The Studio style, predicated on the achievements of his mother's generation. After his wartime service, he worked for Chapman at the Laboratory of Anthropology, making studious copies of pottery designs, and in 1950 he enrolled at the University of New Mexico, where his mentor, the modernist painter Raymond Jonson, introduced him to various aspects of modernism. Both teacher and student shared an interest in Anasazi rock art—pictographs and petroglyphs—and

PLATE 91

HANSEN TWOITSIE

U.S., Hopi Pueblo, dates unknown

Parrot Sikyatki, c. 1940

Watercolor on paper, 9⅝ x 9⅝ in.

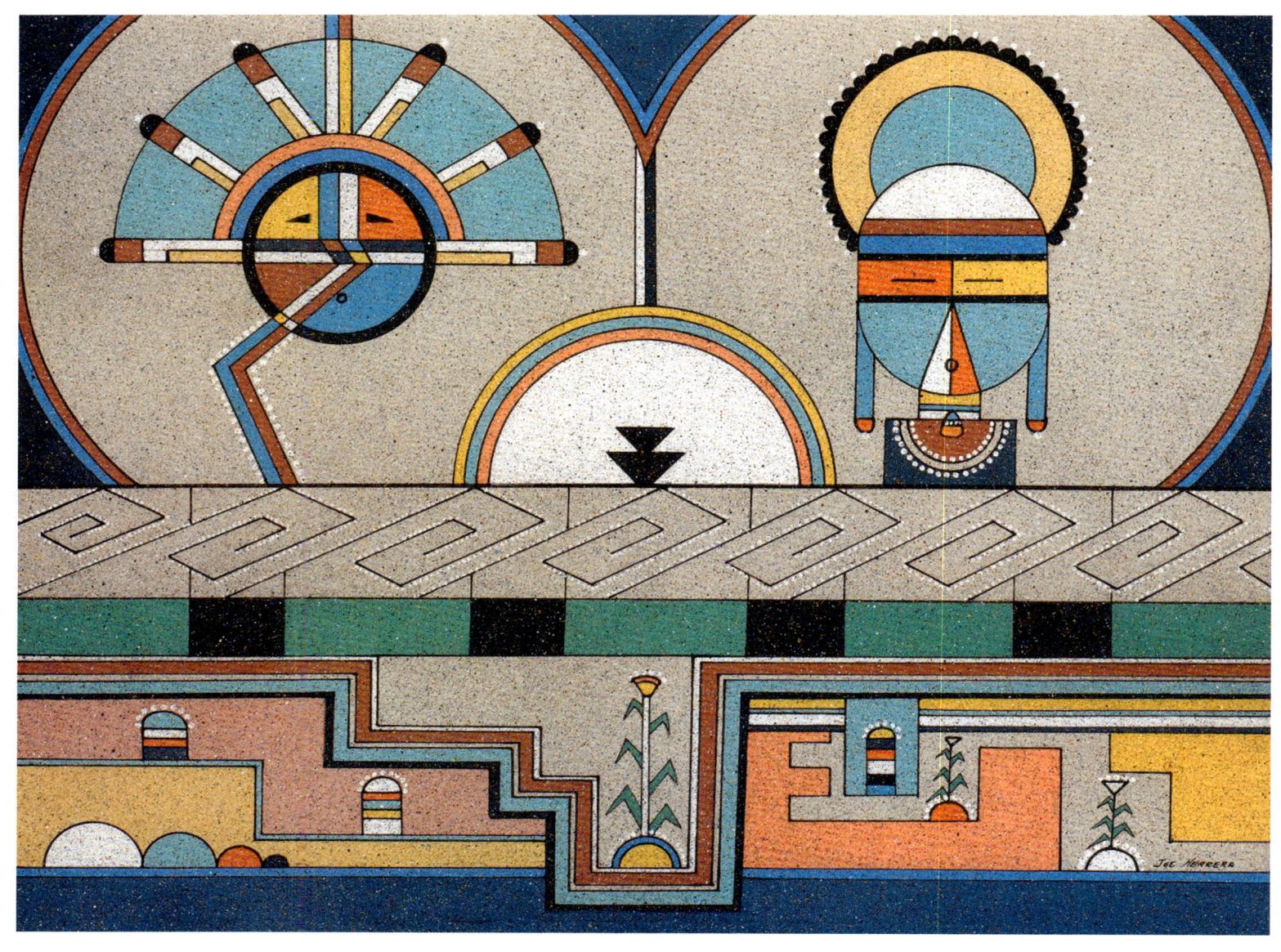

PLATE 92

JOE HILARIO HERRERA (SEE-RU)

U.S., Cochiti Pueblo, 1923–2001

Germination, 1982

Watercolor on paper, 16¾ x 21½ in.

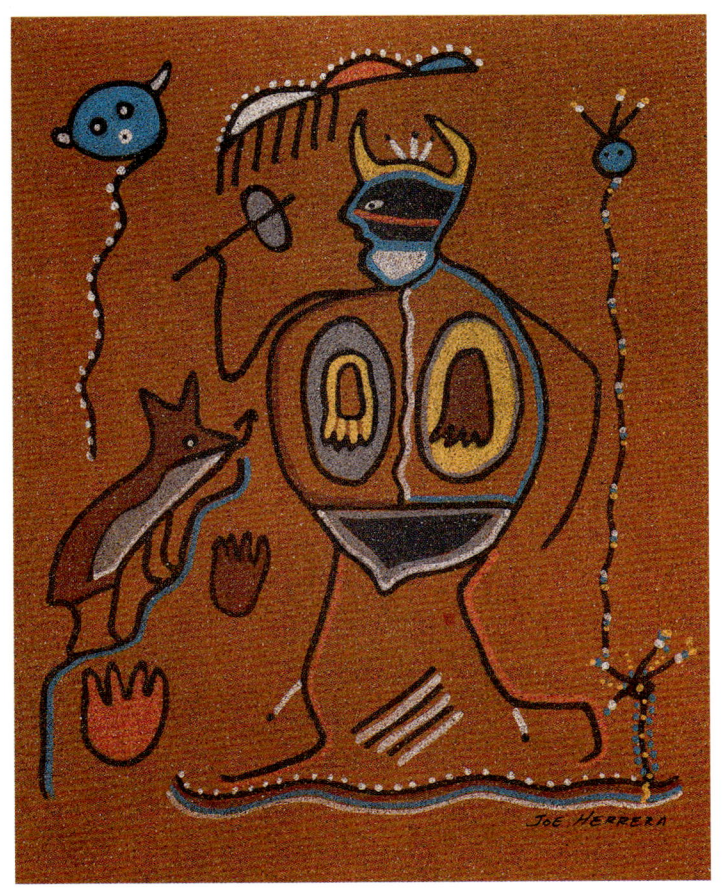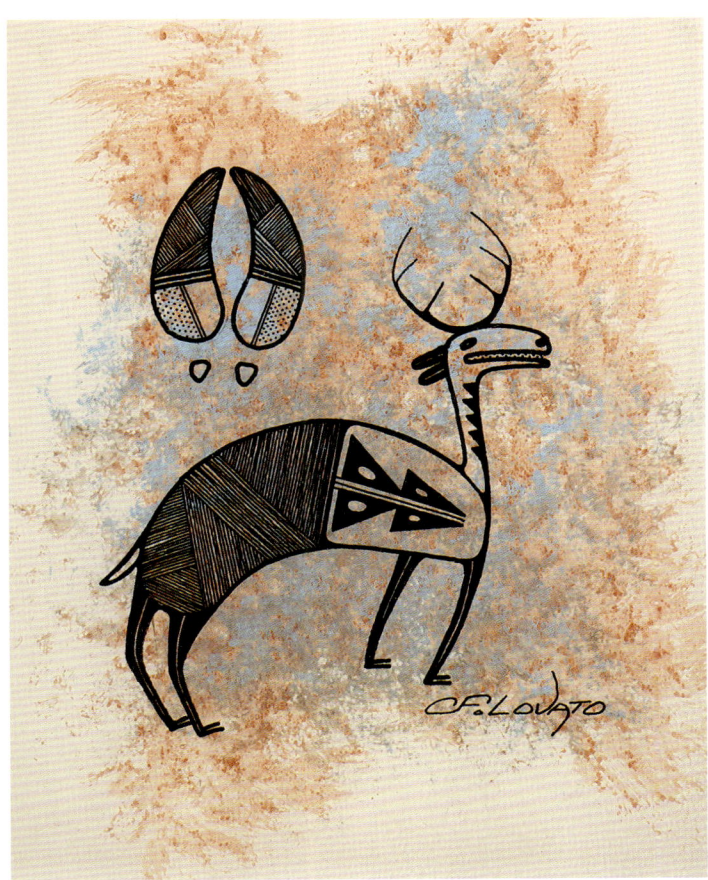

textile and pottery designs. Herrera traveled widely in the early 1950s, studying rock art sites and sketching excavated kiva murals. Using these sources, he rather quickly transformed Southwest Indian painting with such works as *Fox Hunter* (c. 1954), which draws inspiration from both ancient art and Joan Miro's primitivism more than it does the ethnographic realism of the Studio style. Using a telluric surface to suggest the painterly ground of antiquity, Herrera reactivates pictography (a diagnostic quality of American abstraction in the 1940s and early 1950s).[38]

Dunn greatly admired his post-Studio art, writing in *El Palacio* that Herrera "had convincingly demonstrated the fact that current American Indian painting which incorporates prehistoric designs and techniques can be entirely modern."[39] Indeed, as a result of works such as *Fox Hunter,* with its sharp linearity, abstract space, and symbolic forms and images, Herrera took all the top prizes at the Gallup *Intertribal Ceremonial* in 1954 and was awarded *Les Palmes Académique* from the French Academy.[40] Although Herrera painted sporadically in the 1960s, because of his mentoring, his work became increasingly important for a younger generation of artists. After occupying a series of leadership positions in Pueblo culture and state government,

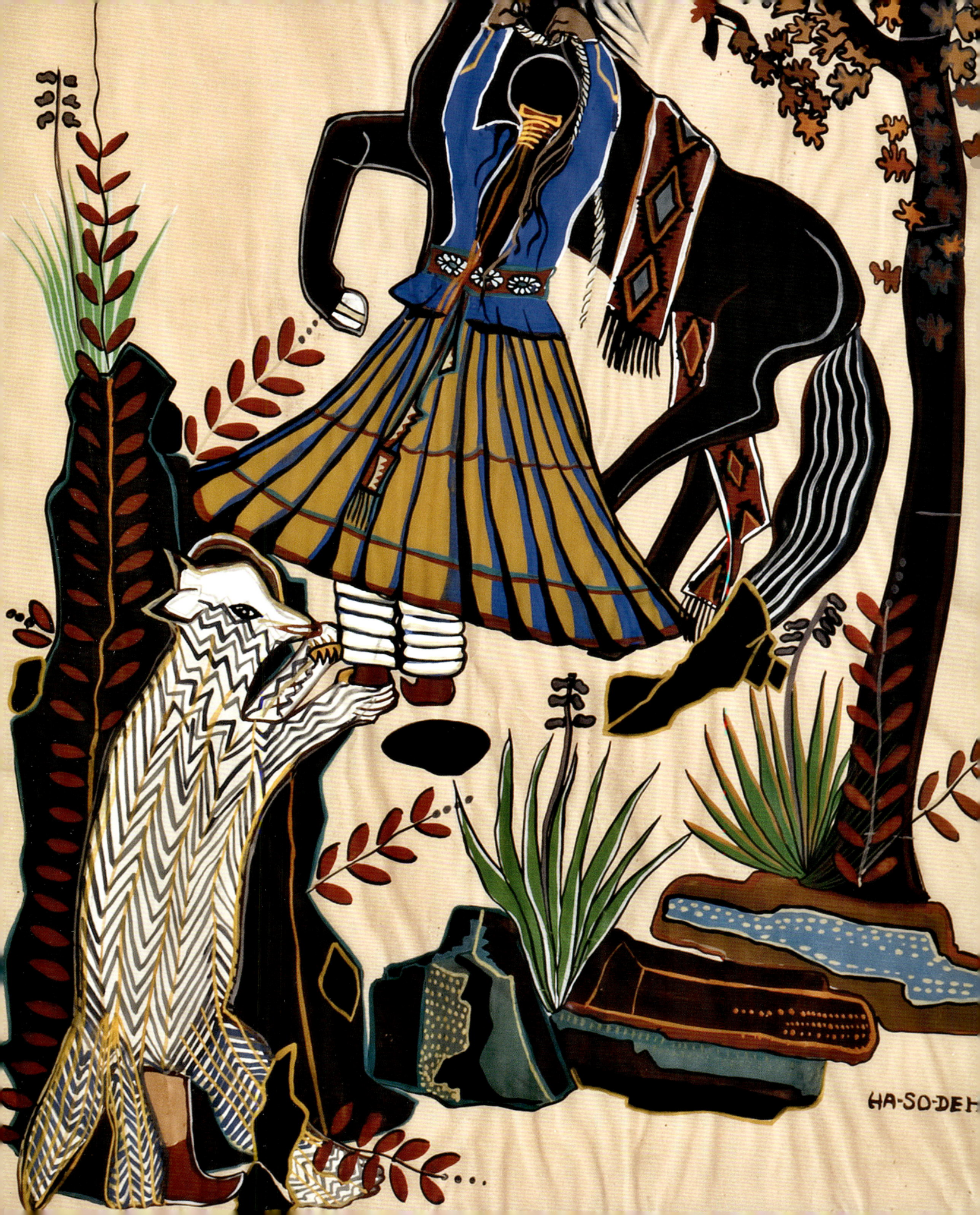

he returned to painting in the 1980s, producing a series of compelling images, many of which are based on kiva murals, such as *Germination* (1982). These later paintings, which are represented well in the collection and are notable for their compositional complexity, subtle orchestration of color, and admixture of abstract and pictorial languages, are master works of Native American art. We can easily track Herrera's influence in key works in the Bialac Collection: Michael Kabotie (Hopi), *Guardian of the Water* (1966, plate 70); David Paladin (Navajo), *Ancient Ones* (1966, plate 12); Helen Hardin (Santa Clara), *Winter Awakening of the O-khoo-wah* (1972, plate 15); and Charles Lovato (Kewa), *Deer and Track #1* (n.d., plate 94).

In addition to Herrera's work, Bialac collected other post-Studio modern expressions, including Oscar Howe's *Waci (He is Dancing)* (1973, plate 33) and *Werewolf* (1959) by Narciso Abeyta (Navajo), who also earned a BFA at the University of New Mexico after World War II, studying with Raymond Jonson and the Abstract Expressionist Lez Haas. And like Herrera, Abeyta (also known as Ha-So-De) painted sporadically in the middle years of his career, but he, too, developed a singular style, one that emphasized decorative pattern and a Gauguinesque perspective, in which the figurative drama of the picture is spread up or across a contiguous planar space. His paintings based on Navajo mythology, which he studied assiduously, such as *Werewolf*, are psychologically expressive, and their elemental blocks of color and linear striations—so pleasing to the eye—fail to mask the macabre undercurrent in the narrative. Abeyta was awarded prizes in various museum competitions and at art fairs (Santa Fe, Scottsdale, San Francisco, and Tulsa, among others), and his work found critical acclaim. Brody described him as an individualistic innovator, whose paintings were marked by "artistic intelligence" and "expressive unity."[41] Individuality and innovation, we should note, are hallmarks of modernism in the visual arts.

Not all Native modernisms were associated with a particular school or group style, however. The work of the "independent" Ojibwe artists Patrick DesJarlait and George Morrison is a case in point.[42] By the mid-1940s, DesJarlait was combining "the flatness of mural painting with cubism to create an abstract yet personal perspective on modernism."[43] Even though he refuted the influence of Diego Rivera on his work, which numerous critics identified in his humanistic images of traditional life on the Red Lake Reservation in Minnesota, his paintings do seem to reflect an awareness of Mexican mural paintings, as well as the machine-made figures of the French Cubist Fernand Léger. Even his earliest paintings use modern idioms to speak of the dignity of traditional Native (communal) labors.[44] DesJarlait won awards in several national art competitions in the 1960s (Minneapolis, Phoenix, Scottsdale, and Tulsa) and his *Cleaning of the Wild Rice,* made the year he died (1972), shows no decline in quality or in his insistence on visualizing Ojibwe emplacement.[45]

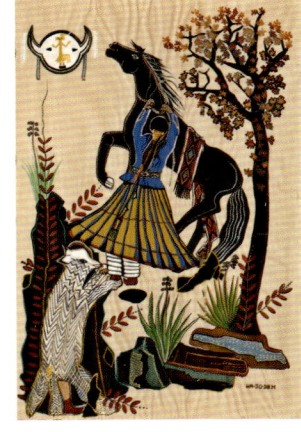

PLATE 95

NARCISO ABEYTA

(HA-SO-DE)

U.S., Navajo, 1918–1998

Werewolf, 1959

Watercolor on paper, 29 x 19 in.

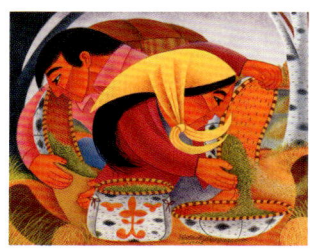

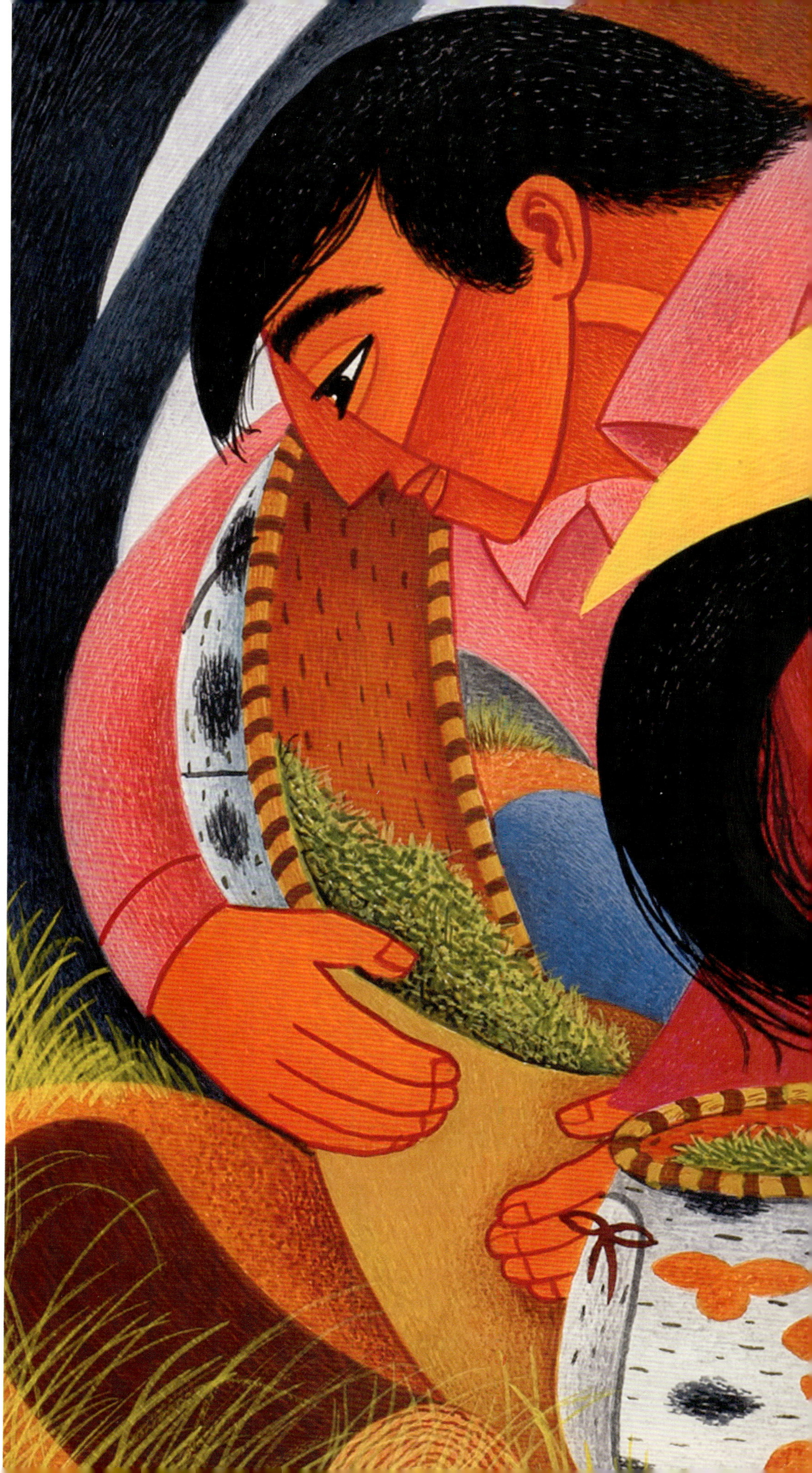

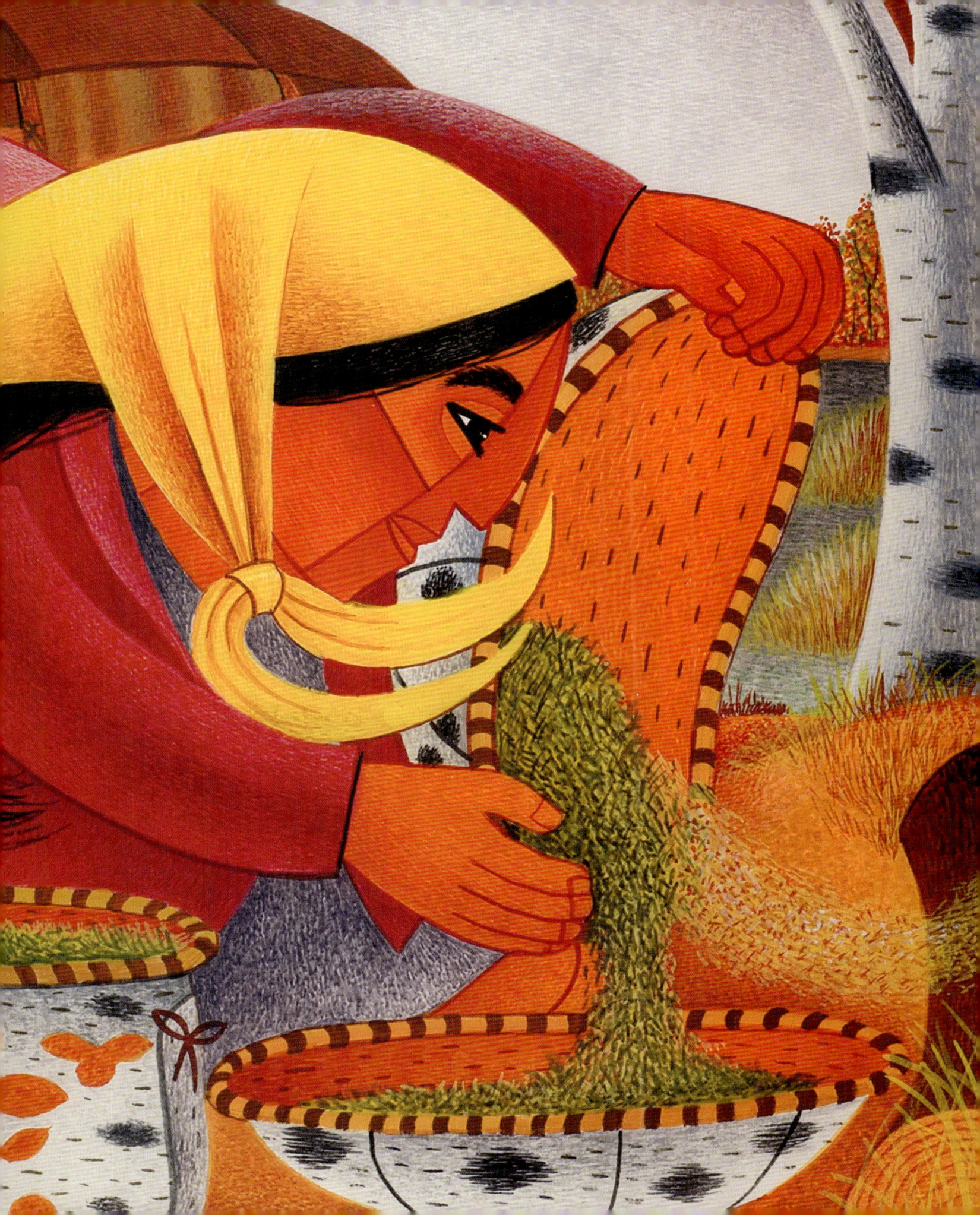

Unlike DesJarlait, Morrison was not a "preservationist," always insisting instead that he was an artist who happened to be Indian. Inarguably one of the preeminent artists of his generation, he graduated from the Art Students League in New York City in 1946, by which time he was already synthesizing Cubism, Expressionism, and Surrealism. The paintings in the first of his twelve solo exhibitions in Manhattan (1948) were described as mysterious, sensuous, and intellectual.[46] Over the course of a long and prolific career, Morrison made critically acclaimed biomorphic watercolors, gestural abstractions, collages in various media, and totemic sculptures, both large and small. His was an eclectic vision, nourished by many sources, including European and American modernism, pre-Columbian art and architecture, and Australian Aboriginal art. Morrison's work was widely exhibited, published, and collected, and in 1999 he was honored as the inaugural Master Artist in the Eiteljorg Fellowship for Native American Fine Art in Indianapolis. Despite ill health, he was very productive in the eighties and nineties, and his *Untitled* (*Surrealist Landscape*) (1997, plate 78), a lithograph, combines two of his long-standing interests: the rocky north shore of Lake Superior, alongside of which he was born and raised, and Surrealist "automatic writing," which generates the quirky, wiry lines that thread their way across the flat, Cubist-derived blocks of color that suggest patches of a map. *Soft Light, Warm Violet Day, Red Rock Variation: Lake Superior Landscape* (1990), an acrylic painting on paper, forms part of his celebrated Horizon series, Abstract Impressionist images with layers of lyrical color and delicate but tactile surfaces that bespeak a meditative encounter with the primordial power and natural beauty of the superior lake.[47] Partly because he was an independent Modernist, Morrison's impact on the world of Native art wasn't fully in effect until the early to mid-1970s, by which time Fritz Scholder had already shocked traditionalists with his Super Indian series—drunken, laughing, grimacing, wounded, patriotic Indians rendered in a Pop Expressionist idiom.

Like Morrison, Scholder was suspicious of being categorized as an Indian artist. His ancestry was German, English, French, and Luiseño (Southern California Mission Indian), so he self-described as "primarily a painter and printmaker."[48] He shared with Morrison (and to some degree DesJarlait) being trained not in an Indian art school but in a fine arts department that did not stress ethnic identity or Aboriginal content. On the contrary, Scholder's work might be described as anti-Studio in its determination to use Pop Art, Abstract Expressionism, and historical photographs to critique the romanticism of the "Noble Savage" imagery he encountered in 1960, when he participated in the Southwest Indian Art Project, which resulted in the demise of The Studio and the birth of the more progressive Institute of American Indian Arts (IAIA).[49] Simply put, the Indian art revolution of the 1960s was initiated at least in part by Scholder's commercial, if controversial, success and by his presence on the IAIA faculty in 1964–1969, where his ironic

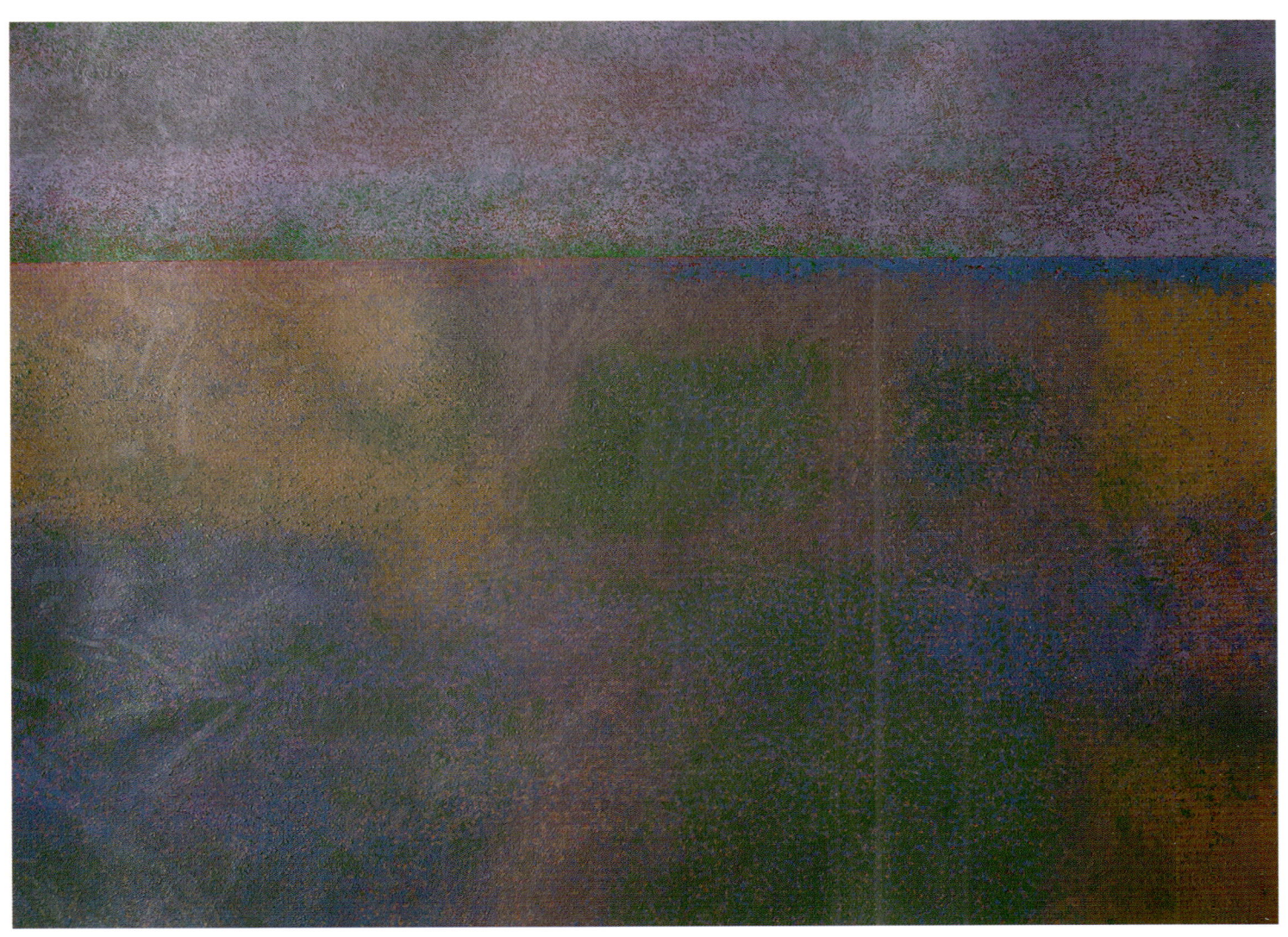

PLATE 97

GEORGE MORRISON

U.S., Ojibwe, 1919–2000

Soft Light, Warm Violet Day, Red Rock Variation:

Lake Superior Landscape, 1990

Acrylic on paper, 22⅝ x 30 1/16 in.

Courtesy of Briand Morrison

critique of stereotypical Indian images—triggered initially by the work of his students—became the order of the day.[50] Bialac, who knew Scholder well, collected fifty-three of his paintings, drawings, and prints, many of which are engaged with the history of art, such as *Noble Indian After Dixon* (lithograph, 1975). His *Indian, Dog and Teepee* (1973), a large (56- × 48-inch) acrylic painting from 1973, is a quintessential example of Scholder's ability to synthesize powerful design, bold color, and Expressionist paint handling with iconic imagery derived from the historical archive created by Euro-American ethnographers, painters, and photographers. The composition is both clear and elemental: the "ground," notable for its bilateral symmetry, is a flat red-green color field painting, on top of which sits a pyramidal form (teepee), notable for its inherent stability. The Indian's verticality and centrality implies vitality, which is slightly undercut by a gallows humor: he is positioned near "dead center." Formally speaking, the whole of it is a master class in orchestrating horizontals, verticals, and diagonals, and in resisting stasis with vectors (the teepee poles at top right center) and a pendant (the dog situated just off center). Reductive, like Minimalism, with shocking color contrast as in Pop Art and Expressionism, *Indian, Dog and Teepee*'s trifecta of form-color-image results in an arresting gestalt.

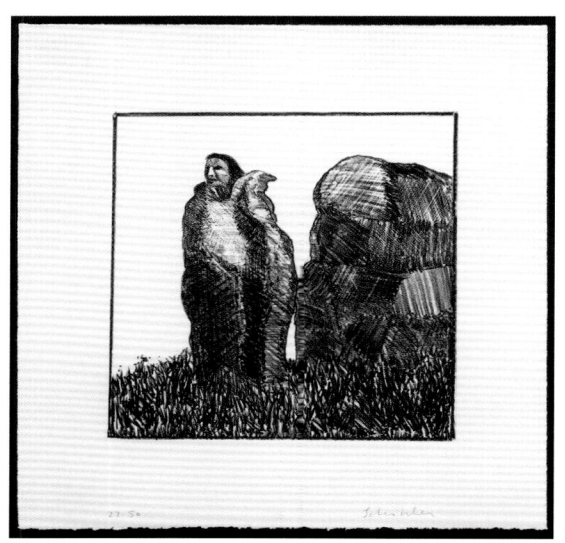

Scholder was a talented and prolific printmaker, and his striking lithograph *Indian in Paris* (1976) was made, naturally, in Paris at *Mourlot Imprimeurs,* a world-renowned studio founded in 1852, where numerous modern masters also worked, including Marc Chagall, Salvador Dali, Max Ernst, and Joan Miro.[51] A five-color print first exhibited at the *Centre Culturel Américain* in Paris, its subject matter—an Indian warrior in birthplace of modern art—refers simultaneously to Scholder's presence there and his conflicted feelings about artistic survival in the City of Lights.[52] It refers as well to the historical presence of other Indians in Paris, including Morrison, who made and exhibited work there in the early 1950s, and those who were brought there in the nineteenth century for primitivist spectacle by Buffalo Bill and his Wild West Show and by George Catlin, in conjunction with his Indian Gallery.[53] Scholder's Indian, regal and statuesque, is situated at the very front of the picture plane, establishing his dominance, while the Eiffel Tower is diminished in significance in the background.

The other major modernist painter and printmaker associated with the early years of the IAIA was T. C. Cannon (Caddo and Kiowa from Lawton, Oklahoma), who was Scholder's student (1965–1966) but quickly his teacher's equal in terms of aesthetic invention. Indeed, the

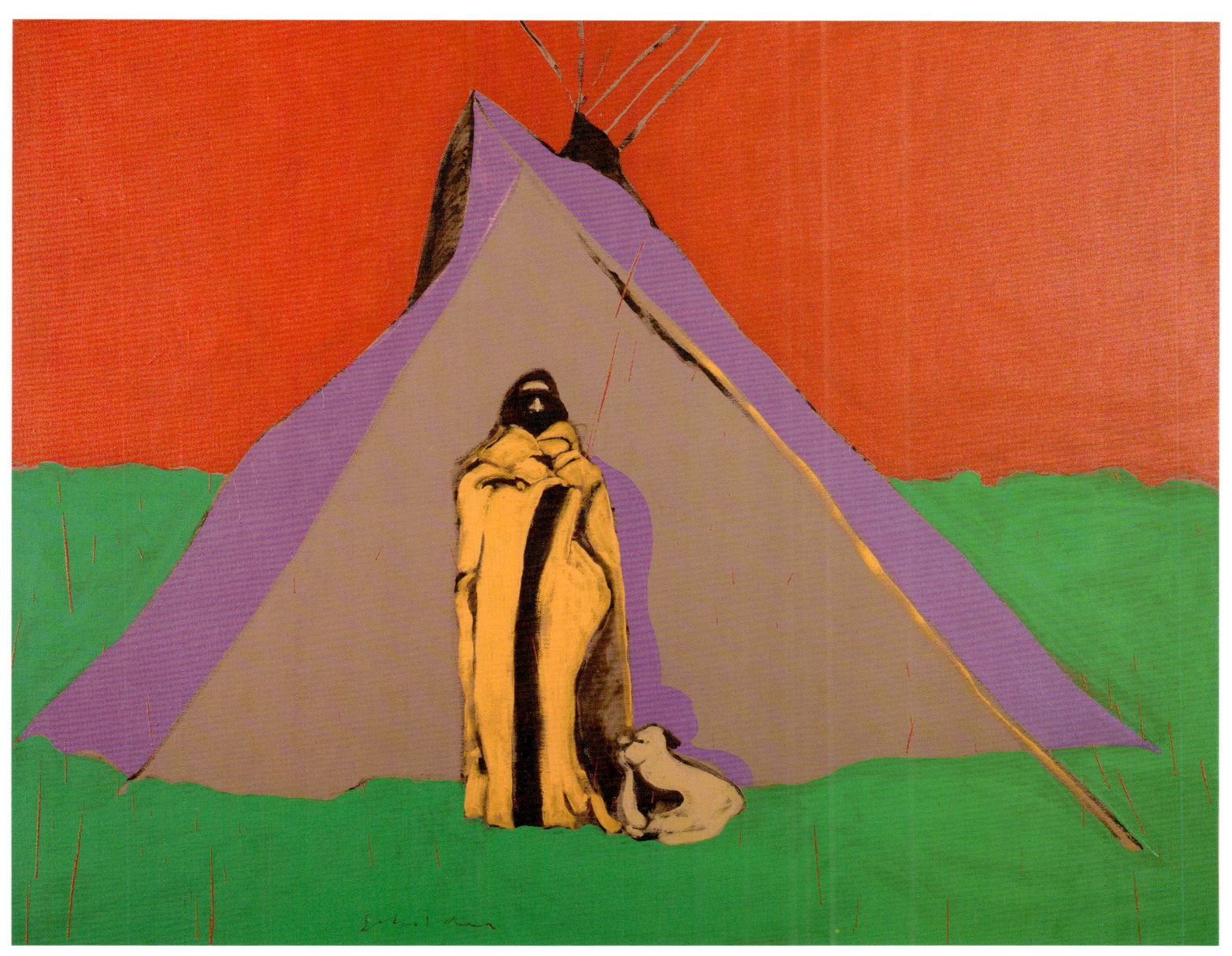

PLATE 99

FRITZ SCHOLDER

U.S., German, French,

English, Luiseño, 1937–2005

Indian, Dog and Teepee, 1973

Acrylic on canvas, 54 x 68 in.

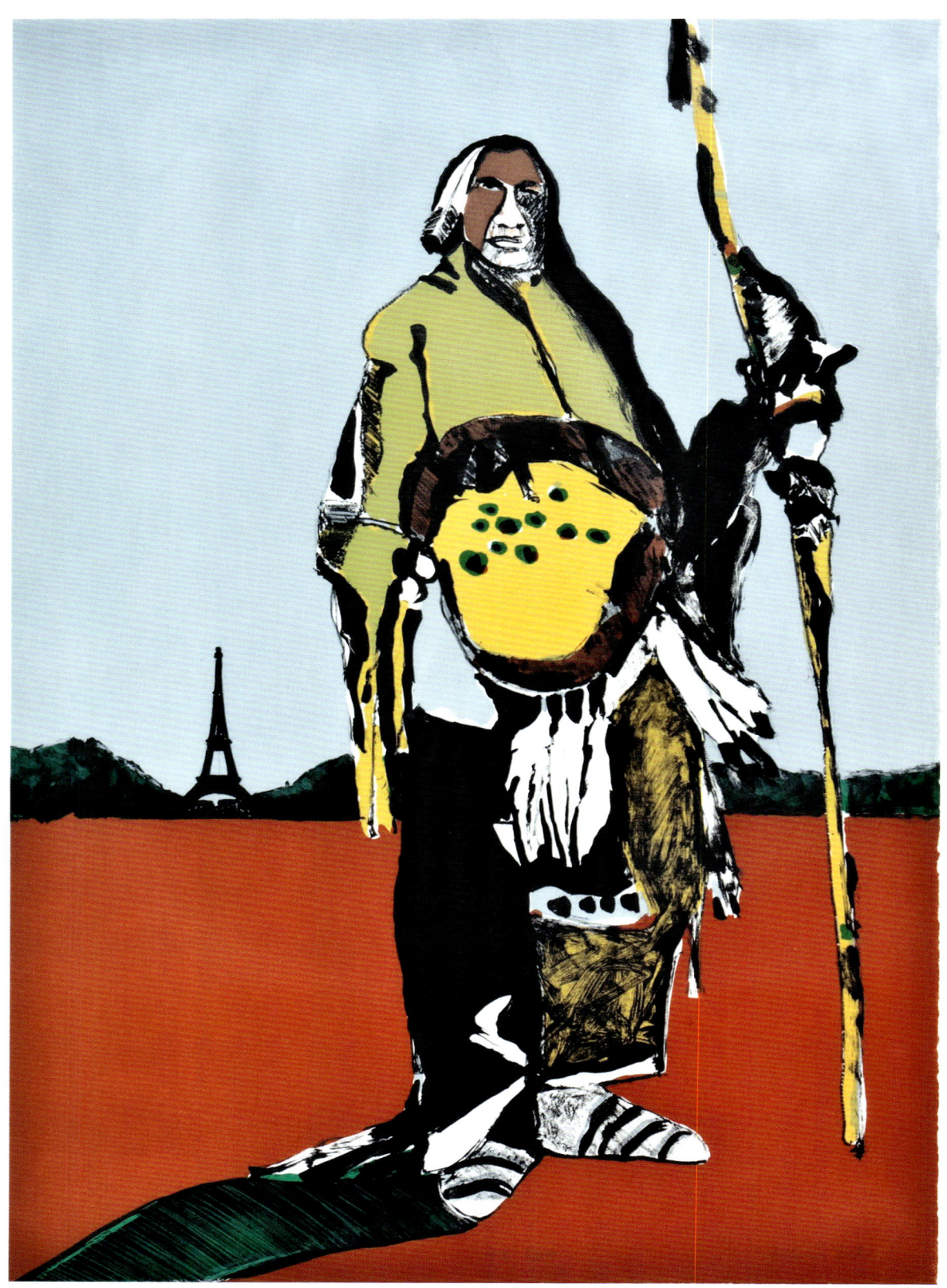

influence flowed both ways, and they were in a historic exhibition, *Two American Painters,* at the Smithsonian Institution in 1972. Cannon, whose work was born of extremely diverse stylistic sources (historical photographs, French and German modernism, Pop Art), was an artist-in-residence at Colorado State University (1974) and at Dartmouth College (1975). He interrupted his fine arts education to enlist in the U.S. Army (101st Air Cavalry, 1967–1969) and saw action in Vietnam, where he earned two Bronze Stars during the Tet Offensive.[54] Not surprisingly, the war changed Cannon as a person and as an artist, and his oeuvre is notable for numerous works whose subjects are warfare and historical and modern warriors, including selections in the Bialac Collection: *On Drinkin' Beer in Vietnam in 1967* (1971) and *Sioux-Soldier-Sold* (c. 1970s), an ink drawing that combines image and stenciled text. Warriors are honored in Kiowa society, and Cannon was both conflicted about and proud of his service in Vietnam. His bold black-and-white linocut print, *Big Soldier* (1973), based perhaps on an archival photograph and marked by a stenciled caption (like those seen in Cubism, neo-Dada, and Pop Art), reminds us that he was himself a big soldier. His tragic death in an automobile accident in 1978 at age thirty-two robbed the national Native arts community of one of its most accomplished and admired figures.[55]

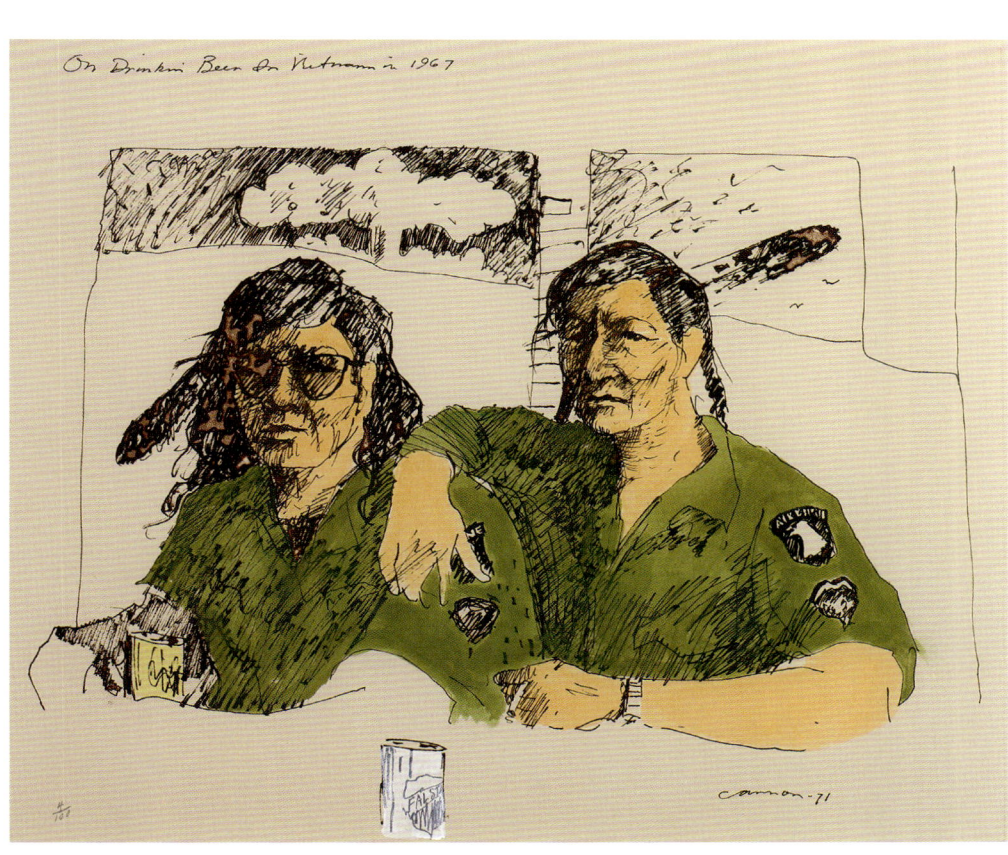

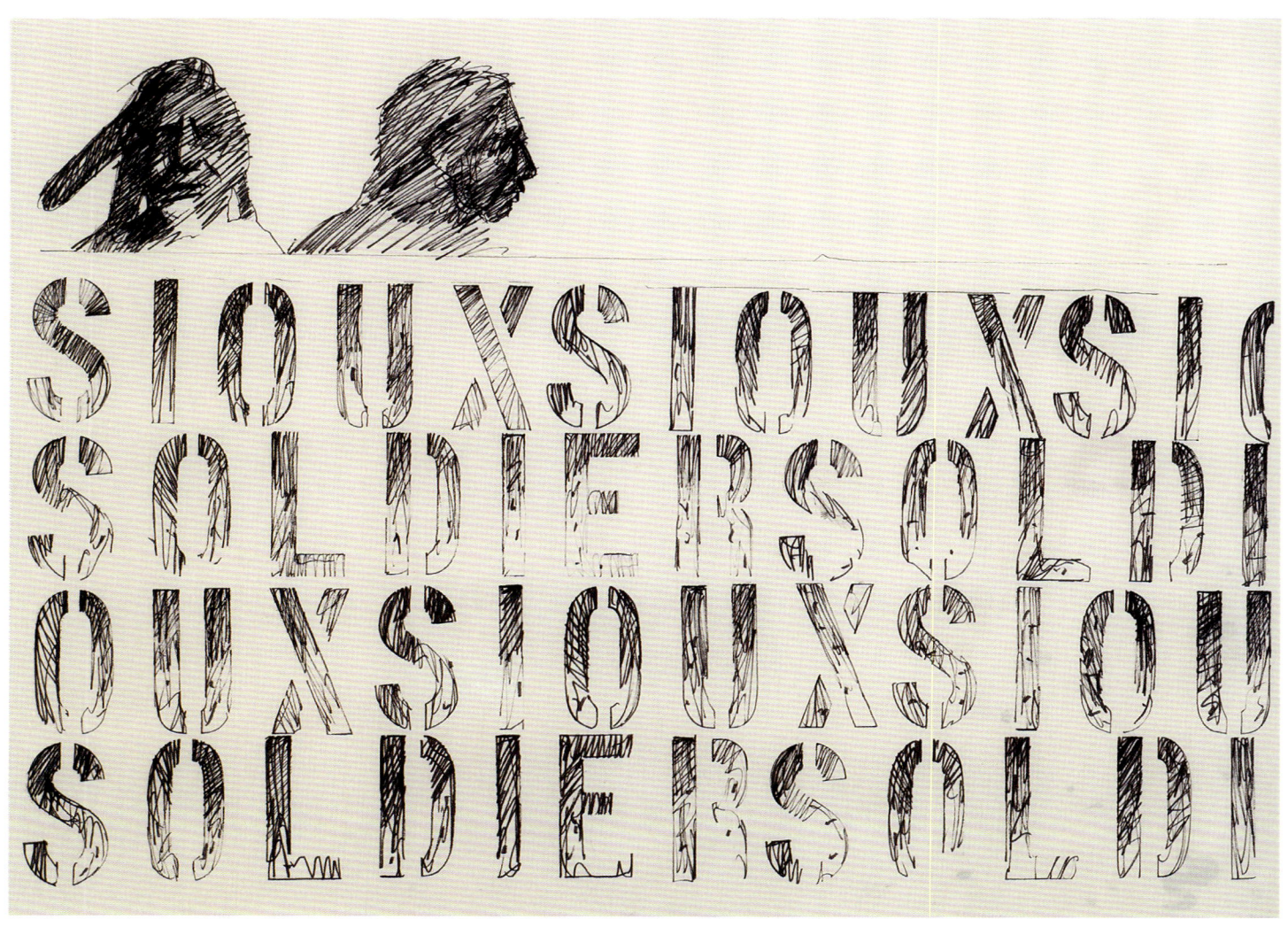

PLATE 102

T. C. CANNON

U.S., Kiowa/Caddo, 1946–1978

Sioux-Soldier-Sold, c. 1970s

Ink, 13½ × 16¾ in.

© Joyce Cannon Yi–Executor
of T. C. Cannon Estate

PLATE 103

T. C. CANNON

U.S., Kiowa/Caddo, 1946–1978

Big Soldier, 1973

Linocut, 26 × 22 in.

© Joyce Cannon Yi–Executor
of T. C. Cannon Estate

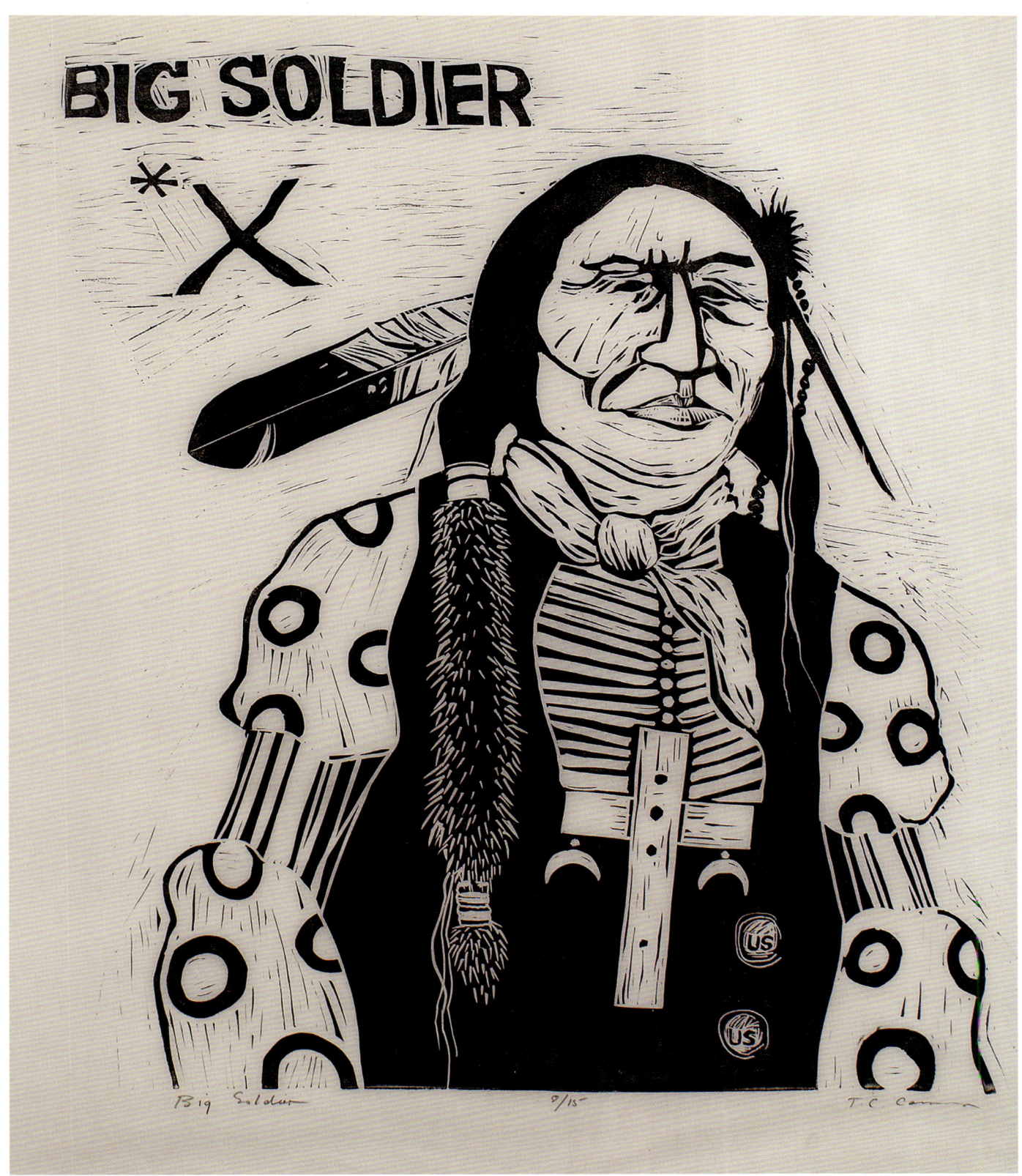

Big Soldier   9/15   T. C. Cannon

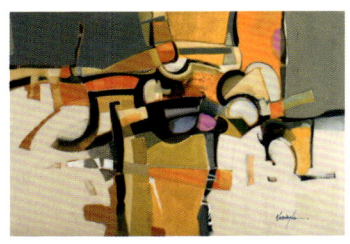

Like photo-based painting, collage is an artistic form that bespeaks modernity.[56] Although he is well known as a painter, sculptor, and printmaker, the Tewa-Hopi artist Dan Namingha, a central figure in the Nampeyo artistic dynasty, is one of the most accomplished collage artists active since the 1960s. By way of books and supportive teachers, Namingha was already aware of modern art when he graduated from the IAIA at age eighteen. However, while studying at the American Academy of Art in Chicago, he made an epiphanic visit to the Art Institute of Chicago, where he was confronted with Impressionism, Post-Impressionism, and Abstract Expressionism, and so began his journey as a Native modernist.[57] Namingha's Expressionist paintings of ceremonial dancers and southwestern landscapes have been exhibited internationally (at the Salon d'Automne in Paris, for example), and his contributions to fine arts were recognized by the Harvard Foundation in 1994. In the Bialac Collection, his large (59½- × 49½-inch) untitled abstract collage (c. 1970s, plate 69) is notable for its dynamic energy and a Hofmannesque "push and pull" of contrasting colors, which generates abstract pictorial space. Intentionally or otherwise, the collage is also curiously reminiscent of Richard Diebenkorn's Albuquerque abstractions from the early 1950s. In Namingha's collage, flat, fractured forms, some of them made with what appear to be rice paper and various fabrics, realize the shifting geometry and vivid color inherent in the primordial geology of Arizona's high desert country. Namingha's awareness of changeable light and weather conditions, natural processes, and the textures of unique landforms are presented here as abstract equivalents. No modern artist—and here I include Georgia O'Keeffe—has been any more sensitive to southwestern land, light, and color than Namingha, as evidenced by more than forty years of high quality work.

Despite their differences in style and geographic origin, Harry Fonseca (Maidu/Native Hawaiian/Portuguese), Jaune Quick-to-See Smith (U.S., Enrolled Salish, member of the Confederated Salish and Kootenai Nation, Montana), Emmi Whitehorse (Navajo), and Peter Jemison (Seneca) were all extremely active in an informal but energetic national network of contemporary Native American artists that emerged in the 1970s. In an early manifestation of DIY culture, they took it upon themselves to raise awareness about progressive Native art practices, especially by supporting and mentoring younger artists and by curating their own exhibitions. Jemison and Smith have been particularly tireless and inspiring advocates for Native artists across the United States and Canada.

A much-beloved "trickster" from Northern California, Fonseca was a painter, printmaker, and sculptor who spent most of his career in Santa Fe. Widely exhibited and collected, he was named an Eiteljorg Fellow in Native American Fine Art in 2005. In addition to charming book illustrations and monumental paintings based on Maidu rock art and origin stories, Fonseca is

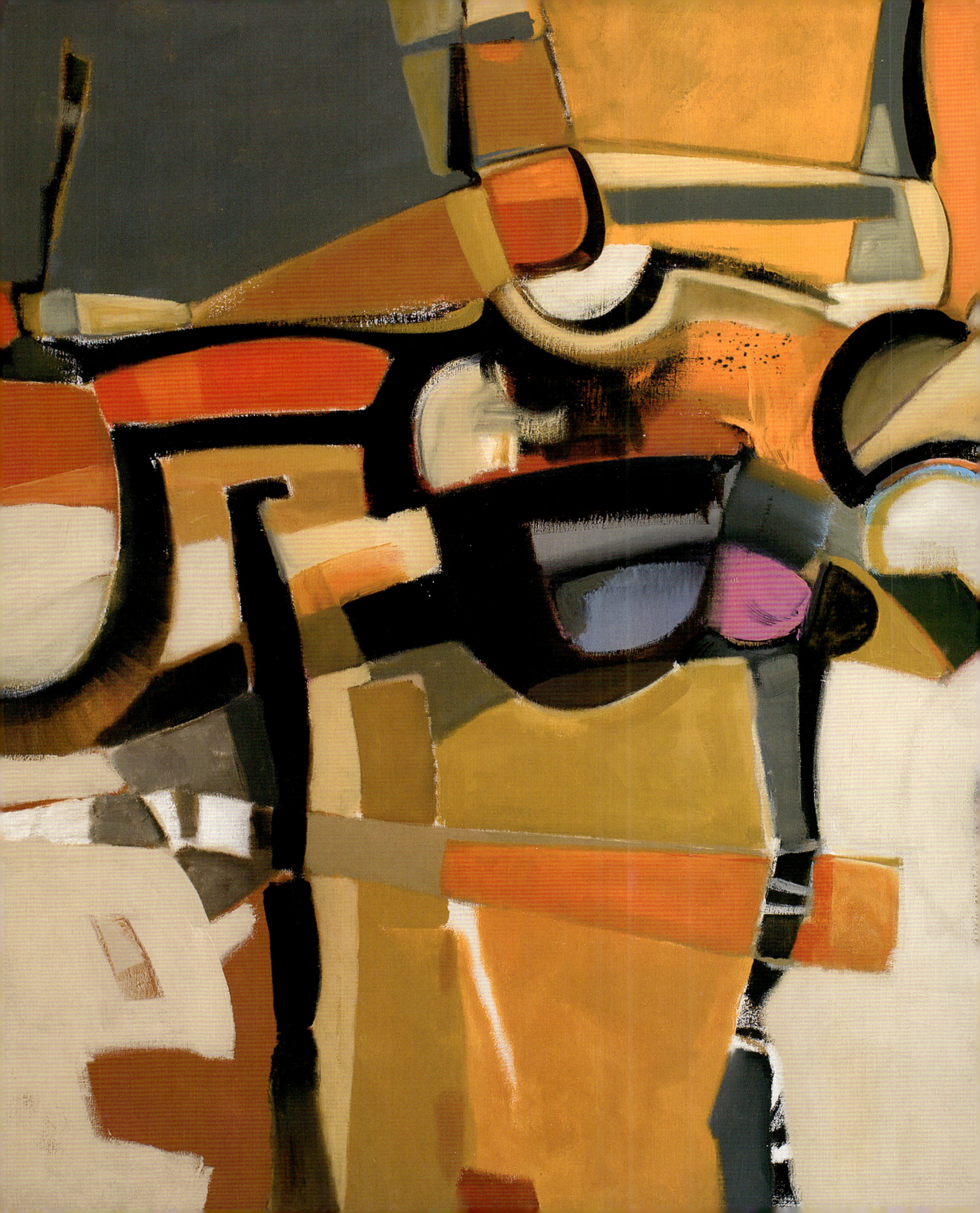

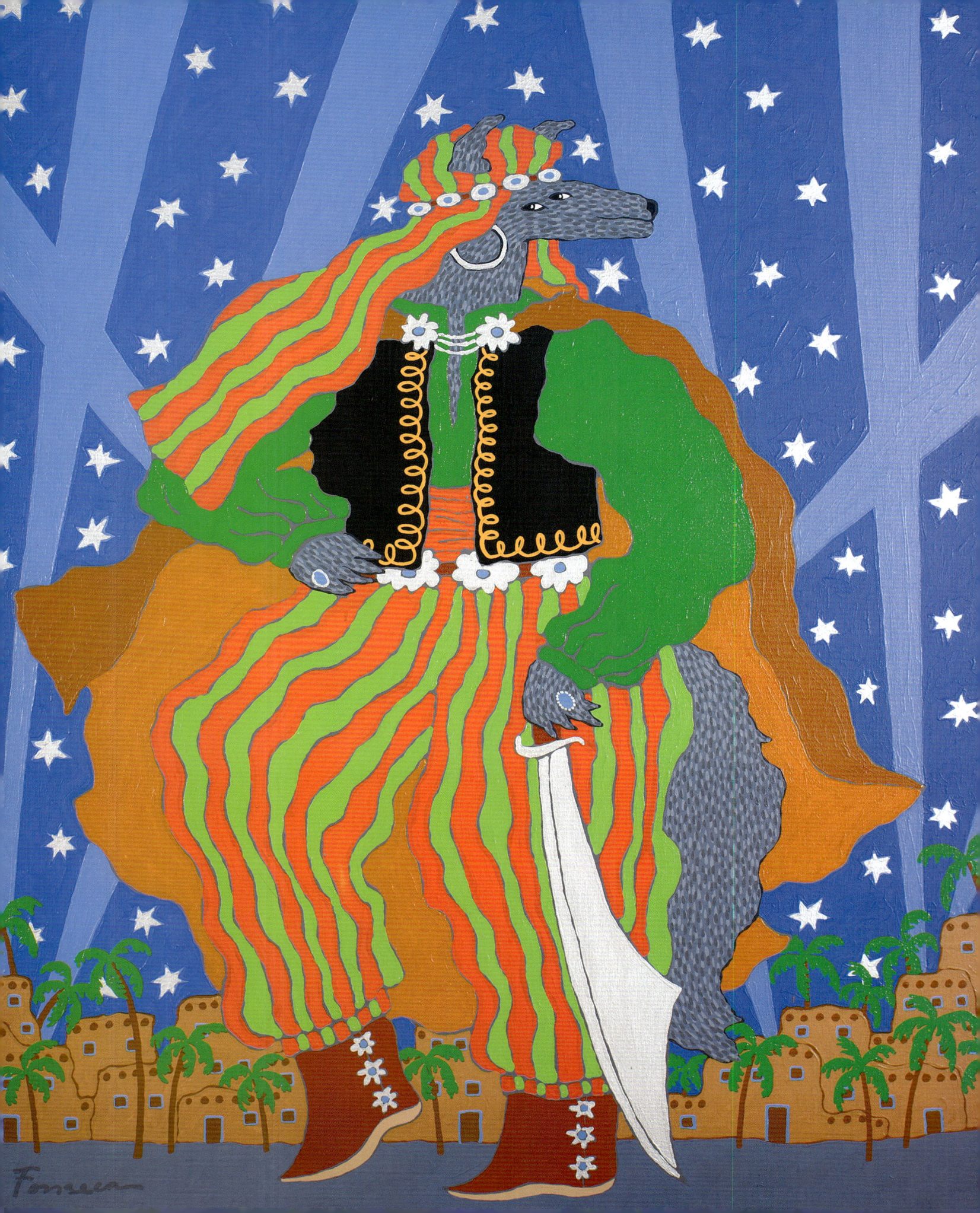

remembered especially for the punk and California funk aesthetic of his popular Coyote series, which embodied indigenous epistemology through the trope of the trickster. Humor was serious business for Fonseca, as witnessed in his acrylic painting *Coyote Doin' a Rudolph Valentino* (1985), in which the irreverent and polymorphous Coyote appears in the guise of silent cinema heartthrob Rudolph Valentino in *The Sheik* (1921), except that the searchlights in the starry sky illuminate not Hollywood but a Pueblo. More than a clever visual pun, this painting treats trickster consciousness in terms of masquerade and culture crossing, even as it plays with notions of celebrity glamour. It shares with *Love at First Bite* (mixed media, 1980) the dialectic between high art and camp/kitsch, as well as Fonseca's love of pattern and decoration. Coyote and Rose, the two carnivorous paramours of *Love at First Bite,* who appear frequently in his work, together formed a single *doppelganger*—Fonseca's alter ego. Represented in a faux-folk style, for which he was legendary, Coyote and Rose are also one with the picture surface, best described as an energetic, even agitated field of gestural marks. These are but two of thirteen essential Fonseca works Bialac collected that document all the major phases of the artist's career.

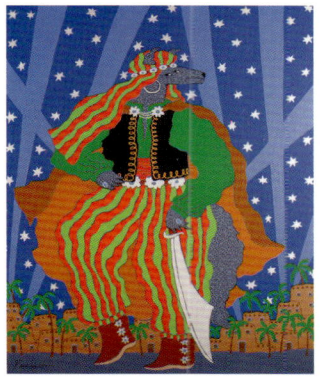

PLATE 105

HARRY FONSECA

U.S., Maidu/Native Hawaiian/
Portuguese, 1946–2006

Coyote Doin' a Rudolph Valentino, 1985

Acrylic on canvas, 60 x 48 in.

PLATE 106

HARRY FONSECA

U.S., Maidu/Native Hawaiian/
Portuguese, 1946–2006

Love at First Bite, 1980

Mixed media, 13½ x 16¼ in.

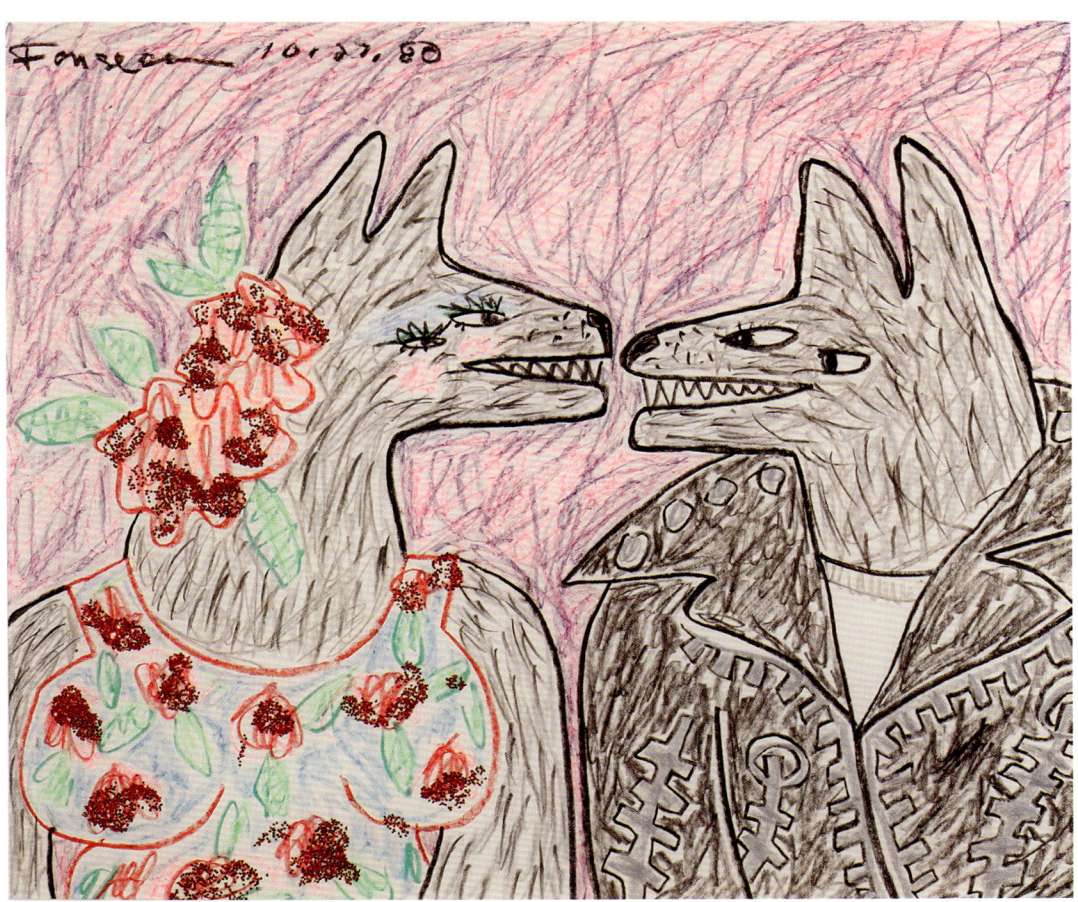

PLATE 107

JAUNE QUICK-TO-SEE SMITH

U.S., Enrolled Salish, member of

the Confederated Salish and

Kootenai Nation, Montana,

b. 1940

Charlo #23, 1985

Pastel on paper, 30 x 22 in.

Smith, a co-founder of the Gray Canyon Group in 1976, had her first solo exhibition (pastels and charcoal drawings) at the Clark Benton Gallery in Santa Fe in 1978, followed by dozens of others. Featured in a PBS film in 1980, Smith had the distinction of being in the inaugural cohort of Eiteljorg Fellows in Native American Fine Art (1999).[58] Among her works collected by Bialac are two mixed media pieces on paper: *Charlo #23* (1985) and *Summer Journey II* (1988), which combine Plains and Plateau pictography, and images of horses, birds, and other animals with intuitive gestural marks and flat, free-floating planes of color. The "overall" dispersal of forms and images in her works on paper in this period reflects both the stretching of space in Abstract Expressionism and the conceptual compositions of petroglyphs and traditional hide painting. The poetic randomness of her pictorial elements may reflect her early years as the daughter of an itinerant horse trader. Mixing a sensitivity to color in nature with Expressionist distortion, Smith thus synthesizes Aboriginal and modernist modes of art, which she has always acknowledged. As early as 1980 she self-described as a "bridge maker," one who made modern by pushing and pulling space and by drawing inspiration from Native art (including cave painting and the work of Oscar Howe) and such modernists as Paul Klee, Robert Rauschenberg, and Diebenkorn.[59]

Like Smith, Whitehorse earned an advanced degree in art at the University of New Mexico, was active in the Gray Canyon Group, and has a distinguished national and international exhibition history. Included in the Bialac Collection are selections from Whitehorse's acclaimed Kin' Nah' Zin' series, which marked her emergence as an exhibiting artist. In 1994 she recalled that these complex works on paper from the early 1980s were actually the best pieces she had ever done, because they were abstract, nonfigurative, and non-narrative, and therefore liberated from both translating and storytelling.[60] Process oriented and highly personal, such works as *Kin'nah'zin' #122* (1981) are based on memories of her home at Standing Ruins (as it is known in English): "I guess it has to do with growing up where I did at Kin-nah' zin, with just silence, with just space, with just listening to what was there in nature, the song of birds, the wind blowing through the trees. I grew up with the calmness and . . . that comes through in the work."[61] But the meditative calm and transcendent beauty viewers often identify in the series result from an elaborate, if intuitive, process, which critics noted at the outset. In an early review, Joseph Traugott wrote in *Artspace,* "'The Kin' Nah' Zin' series is a continuing exploration into the interrelationships of form and technique. The process of making these works is almost constructivist in nature. Initial geometric color-forms are monoprinted onto large sheets of paper to build the understructure of the paintings. Paint is applied to this lattice along with torn sheets of translucent Japanese paper. Such collaged surfaces result in thin veils of color which are simultaneously fractured and unified. The color-form mirrors the effect of collaged tissue so the distinctions between illusion

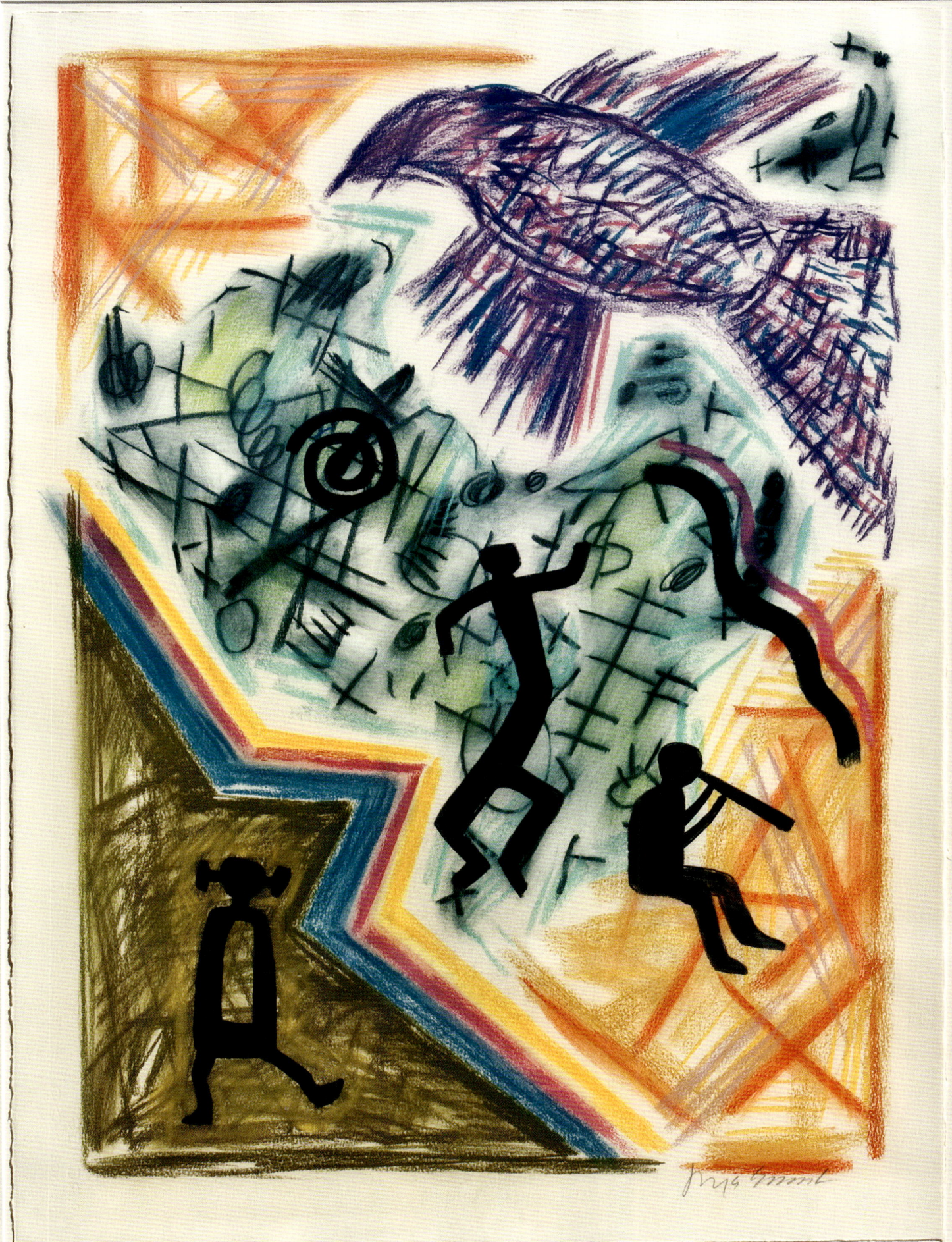

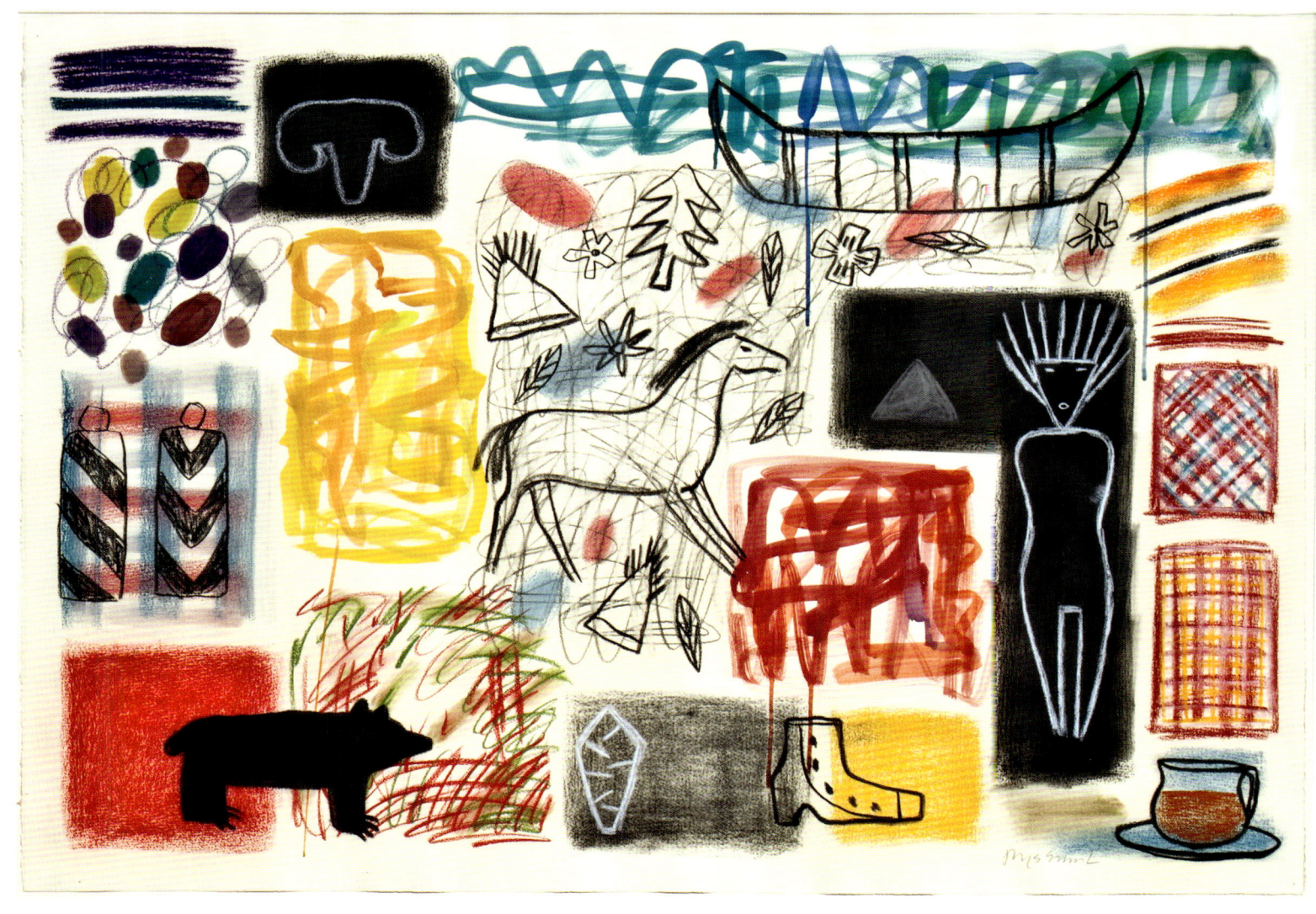

PLATE 108

JAUNE QUICK-TO-SEE SMITH

U.S., Enrolled Salish, member of the Confederated

Salish and Kootenai Nation, Montana, b. 1940

Summer Journey II, 1988

Mixed media, 30 x 40 in.

and real paper disappear."[62] The artist herself has spoken at length about her multilayered process, emphasizing the importance of drawing and the mixing of materials, and acknowledging her reliance on "Western methods and approaches in terms of modernist techniques."[63] At the same time, she refers to "ethnographic items" from Navajo culture in her art and aligns herself with her grandmother's highly personal and intuitive way of loom weaving a pattern.[64] Indeed, Whitehorse recognizes the abstract quality her work shares with her grandmother's and hopes that in "paying homage" she can build an aesthetic bridge "between not only the new and the old, but also the two cultures in which I live."[65]

PLATE 109

EMMI WHITEHORSE

U.S., Navajo, b. 1956

Kin'nah'zin #122, 1981

Mixed media, 22 × 30 in.

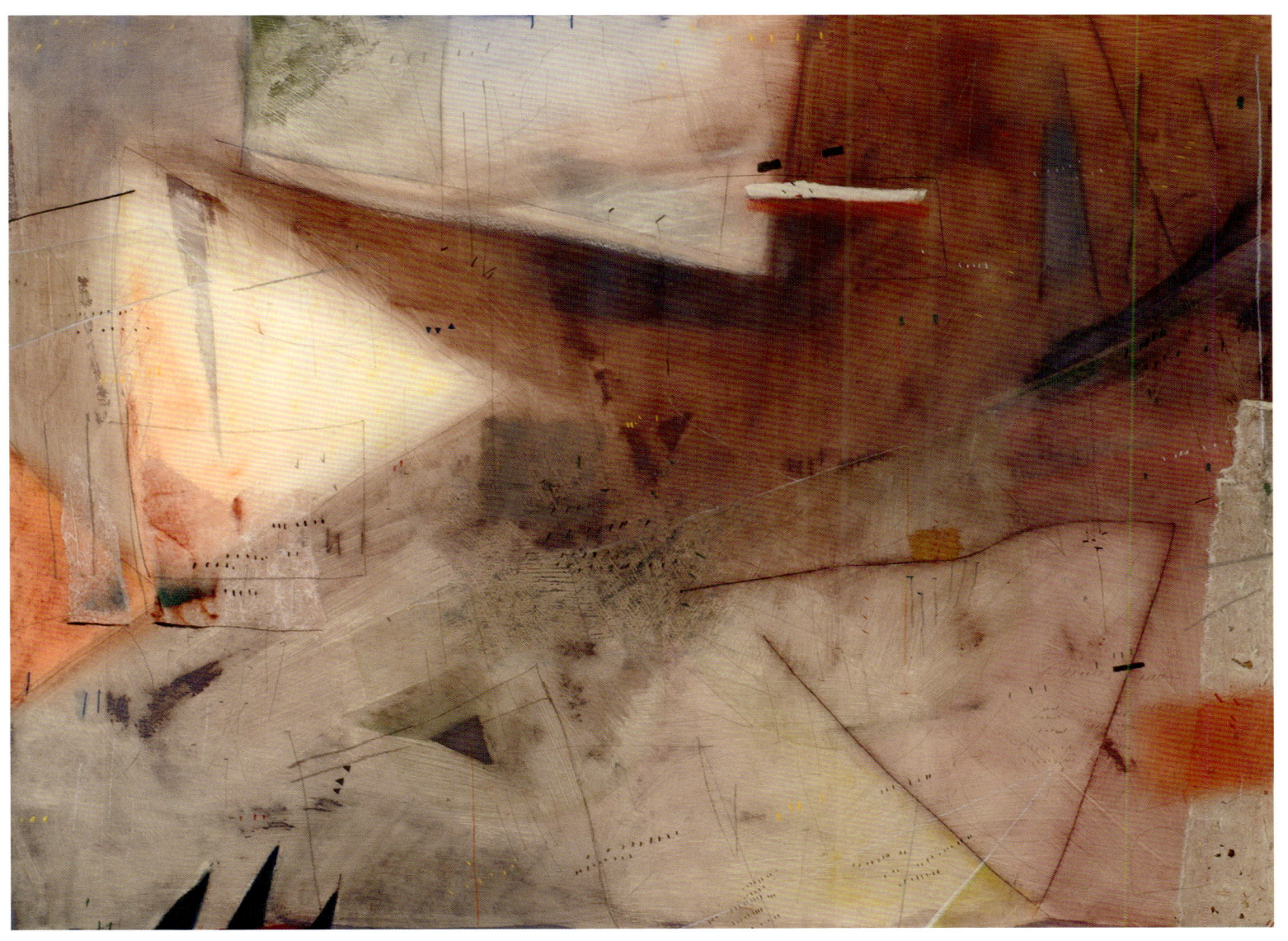

Jemison, who grew up on the Cattaraugus (Seneca) Reservation in upstate New York, has likewise been a key figure in the development of Native art since the late 1960s, when his work was first exhibited at the prestigious Tibor de Nagy Gallery in New York City (1968). In 1971 he was in a group show with Morrison, Scholder, and others at the Museum of the American Indian, and his work was published in a historic issue of *Art in America* in 1972.[66] As gallery director of the American Indian Community House in Manhattan (1978–1985), he organized dozens of exhibitions of traditional and contemporary Native art.[67] Jemison is a painter and, more recently, a filmmaker, and since 1985 he has been director of the Ganondagan State Historic Site, a restored Seneca village. His major intervention into preconceived notions of what contemporary indigenous art could or should be was the Paper Bag series he began in 1980. This critically acclaimed body of work is represented in the Bialac Collection by *Strawberry Dance—Paperbag Series* (mixed media, 1982), which was exhibited at, and published by, the Philbrook Art Center in 1986.[68] The premise was deceptively simple: paint and collage the surfaces of handmade or manufactured brown paper bags, drawing inspiration from both modern (Kurt Schwitters, Robert Rauschenberg) and Native American sources (Seneca beaded bags, Lakota parfleches, and Cree birch bark objects). Like other modernist maneuvers, Jemison saw his bags "as testing the limits of acceptability." As he wrote in 1986, "The paper bag is a part of a consumer society that views paper and, by extension trees also, as expendable, and in which 'nature' itself is incorporated into the commodity market."[69] He also noted that his paper bags result from "seeing in the real world a moment or idea that seems important and then trying to capture that from memory."[70] This returns us to the vitality, specificity, and decorative energy of *Strawberry Dance,* which was surely triggered by experiencing a traditional Haudenosaunee (Iroquois) summer dance. Simultaneously artful and examples, perhaps, of Arte Povera, Jemison's bags are meant nonetheless to transcend "purely aesthetic concerns . . . to make statements about being Seneca." It requires "objective and constant thought," he wrote, "to rise above the mundane, the coarse, and thereby sense the special and meaningful aspects of our heritage."[71]

TO HIS CREDIT, BIALAC has continuously acquired older and newer work, simultaneously establishing the historical foundation of the collection even as he freshened it with many of the latest developments. Indeed, it is impressive to note how early in their careers he has been willing to collect the work of younger artists who are creating challenging and inspiring works of art. In closing, then, I want to consider five fascinating examples that testify to the diversity of Bialac's taste and his uncanny ability to be as cutting edge a collector as are the artists whose work he collects. Diego Romero's *Bar Flys* (etching, 1995) is a classic example of an inventive style of

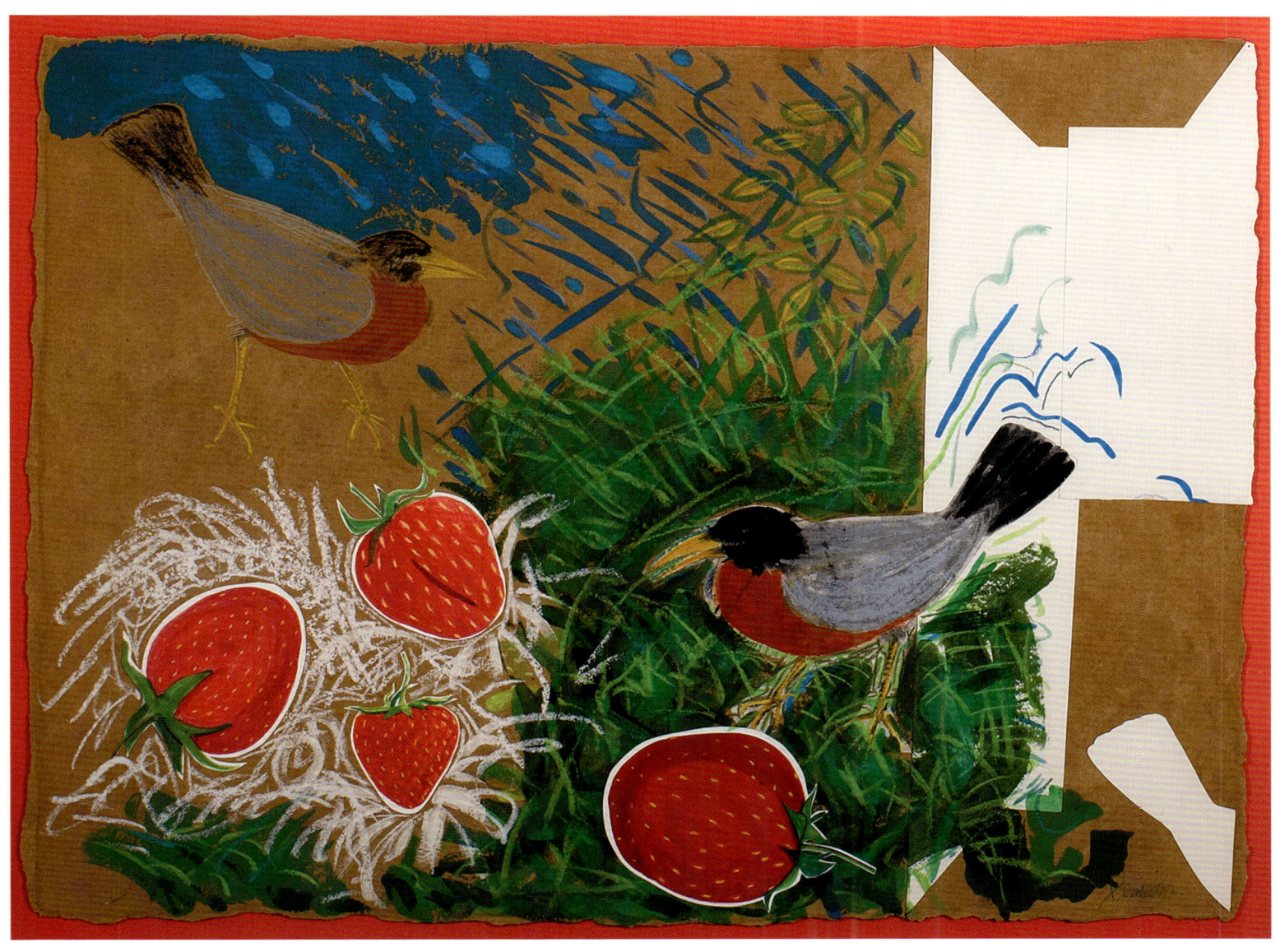

PLATE 110

GERALD PETER JEMISON

U.S., Seneca, b. 1945

Strawberry Dance—Paperbag Series, 1982

Collage, mixed media, 31 x 23 in.

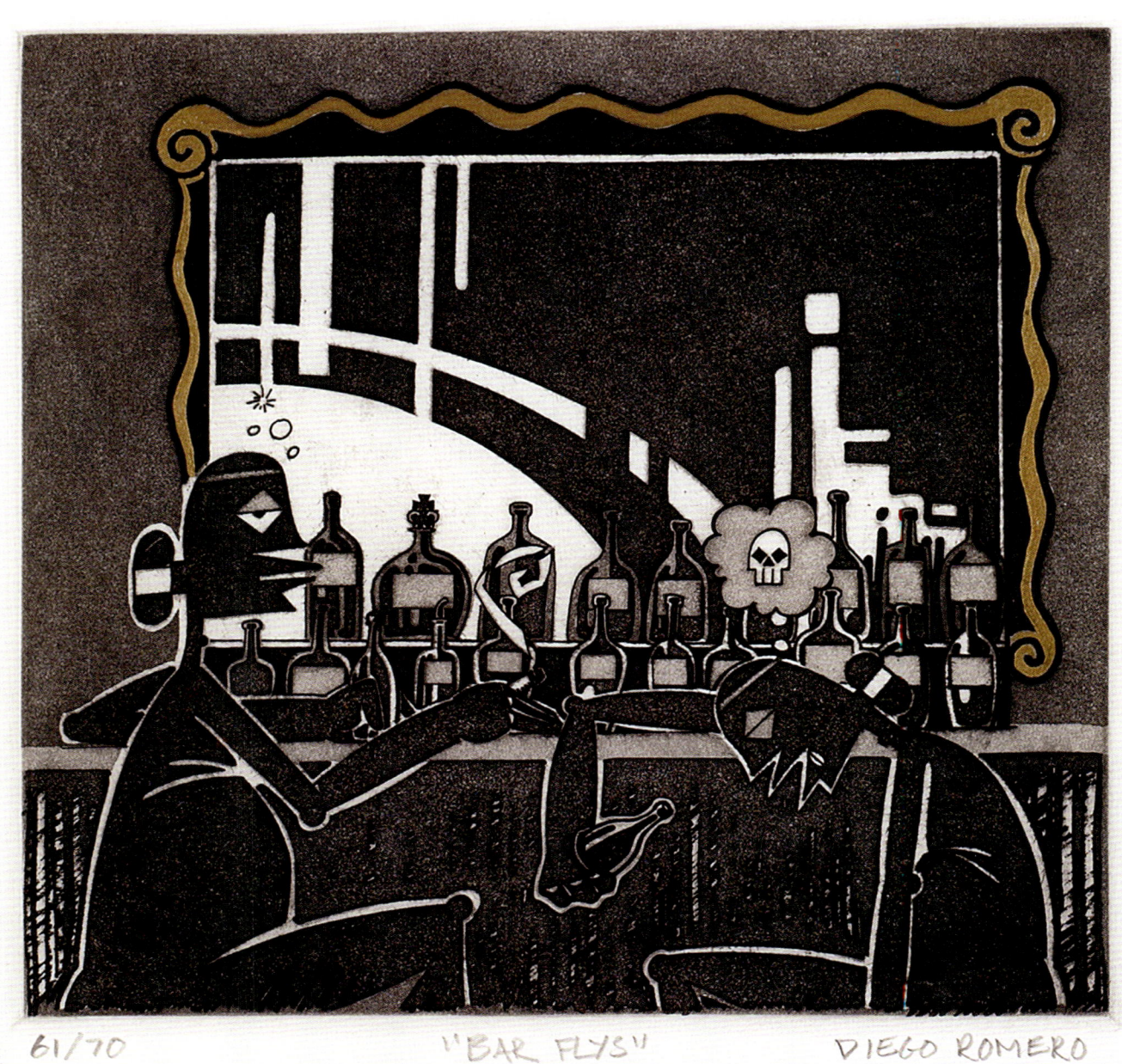

61/70   "BAR FLYS"   DIEGO ROMERO

PLATE 111

DIEGO ROMERO

U.S., Cochiti Pueblo, b. 1964

Bar Flys, 1995

Etching, 9 x 9¼ in.

representation (often seen on his painted pottery) that combines the influence of comic books and Mimbres decoration with Greek black figure vase-painting style to offer ironic critiques on postcontact history from a postcolonial point of view. A Cochiti artist who earned an MFA at UCLA in 1993, Romero's imagery is consistently tough and funny. The Kwakwaka'wakw painter, photographer, and installation artist Marianne Nicolson earned an MFA at the University of Victoria, but such works as *Climbing the Tree of Life* (acrylic on wood, 1999) are informed by the cultural knowledge shared with her by traditional elders. The "decorative" (symbolic) border of the painting refers to both traditional button blankets and the "big house," which unifies an individual, a family, and a community.[72] The coppers at the four corners of the central image represent cultural wealth, while the text in her language amplifies the duality of life and death embodied in the tree of life at center: "Children climb over me up the Tree of Life into Heaven."[73] This large (58- x 66- x 3-inch) dramatic and complex painting—so traditional and so contemporary—was featured in the first *Eiteljorg Fellowship* exhibition in 1998.

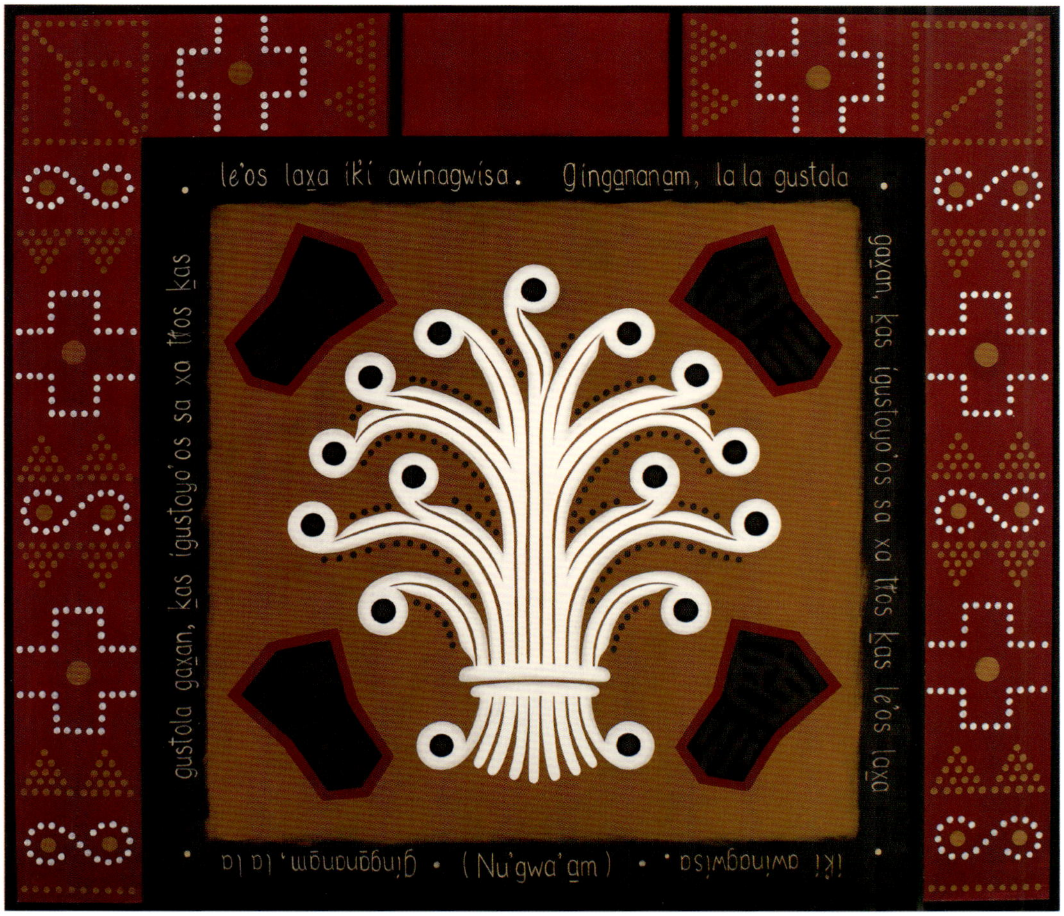

PLATE 112

MARIANNE NICOLSON

Canada, Dzawada'enuxw of the Kwakwaka'wakw First Nations, b. 1969

Climbing the Tree of Life, 1999

Acrylic on wood, 56 x 64 in.

Other artists, including Jeffrey Gibson (Mississippi Choctaw, Cherokee), Jeanette Katoney (Navajo), and Tony Abeyta (Navajo), share Nicolson's interest in the intersection in visual art of land, nature, and history. Gibson, who was educated at the Art Institute of Chicago and the Royal College of Art in London, has been exhibited widely in Europe and the United States. An "aesthetic scientist," Gibson experiments with materials and processes to generate hybrid works of art, such as *Tricks and Unusual Gestures* (mixed media, 2004). Simultaneously sculpture and painting, the work is mostly flat but articulated with sumptuous textures. Its admixture of kitschy decoration and organic imagery suggestive of the primeval lagoon results in a ripe, exotic beauty that is appealing and unsettling. *Tricks and Unusual Gestures,* which forms part of a larger body of work exhibited at the National Museum of the American Indian, was based on Erasmus Darwin's *Zoonomia: Or The Laws of Organic Life* (1794). As the artist has noted, "I wanted to compare, for myself, the power dynamics and politics found in contemporary society to the power dynamics and species survival found nature. This is of course channeled through abstraction and then the added adornment of the pigmented silicone (I was looking at the kitsch factor of whimsies from the Niagara Falls region at the turn of the century and raised beadwork). I wanted to push adornment into something with conceptual content just beyond decoration."[74] Indeed, *Tricks and Unusual Gestures*—which is decidedly high concept, engaged with the history of science, and which crosses biology with art history—typifies many of the experimental, high quality painted reliefs Gibson created between 2004 and 2006.[75] In the intervening years he has created large site-specific installations with found objects and made paintings using spray paint and serigraphy.

Katoney, a Navajo artist who studied at the IAIA and now lives at Hardrock, Arizona, on the Navajo Reservation, makes abstractions "rooted in the natural world."[76] Inspired by her mother, the weaver Alice Katoney, and the sand painter Joe Ben, Jr., Katoney conceives her art as "a way of prayer."[77] Her *Song for Corn* (mixed media, 2007) belongs to a series of pictorial abstractions incorporating sand, an influence from the physical and cultural environment on the Navajo Reservation where she grew up, near Dinnebito, Arizona: "The earth is female in Navajo, so the sand gives me, as a female Navajo artist, a great connection from which to develop artistic expression."[78] Working in pastels, prismacolors, or oil, Katoney investigates rug designs, ancient rock art images, and Navajo symbols of nature and its processes in a typically Navajo way, emphasizing beauty, balance, and harmony. An award-winning painter (at the Santa Fe Indian Market and at the Red Earth Festival in Oklahoma City, for example), Katoney's thoughtful synthesis of modernist techniques and Aboriginal subject matter and spirituality is a twenty-first-century continuation of a tradition begun by her predecessor, Apie Begay, more than a hundred years ago.

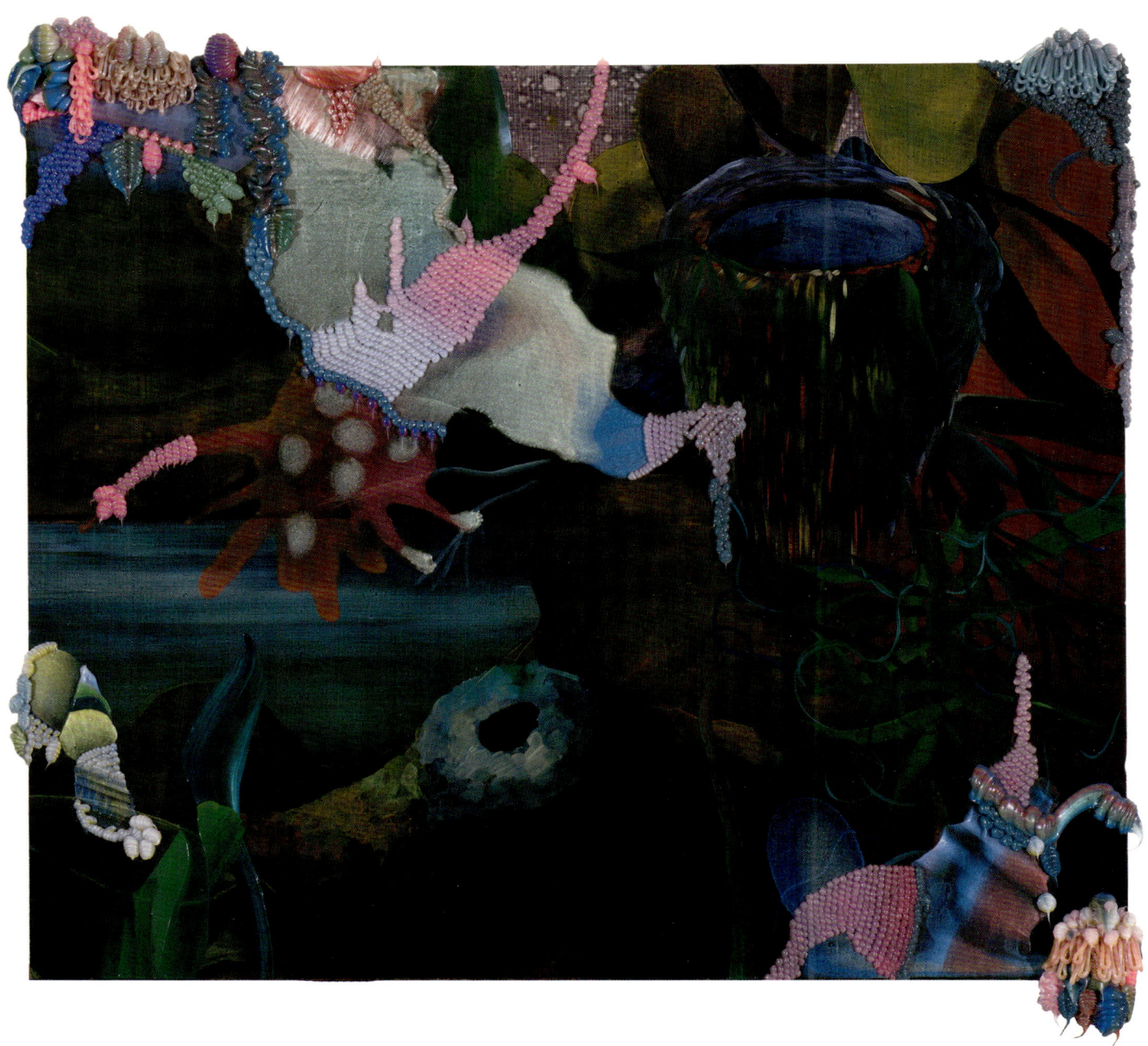

PLATE 113

JEFFREY GIBSON

U.S., Mississippi Choctaw/Cherokee, b. 1972

Tricks and Unusual Gestures, 2004

Acrylic, oil, and pigmented silicone, 17½ x 19½ in.

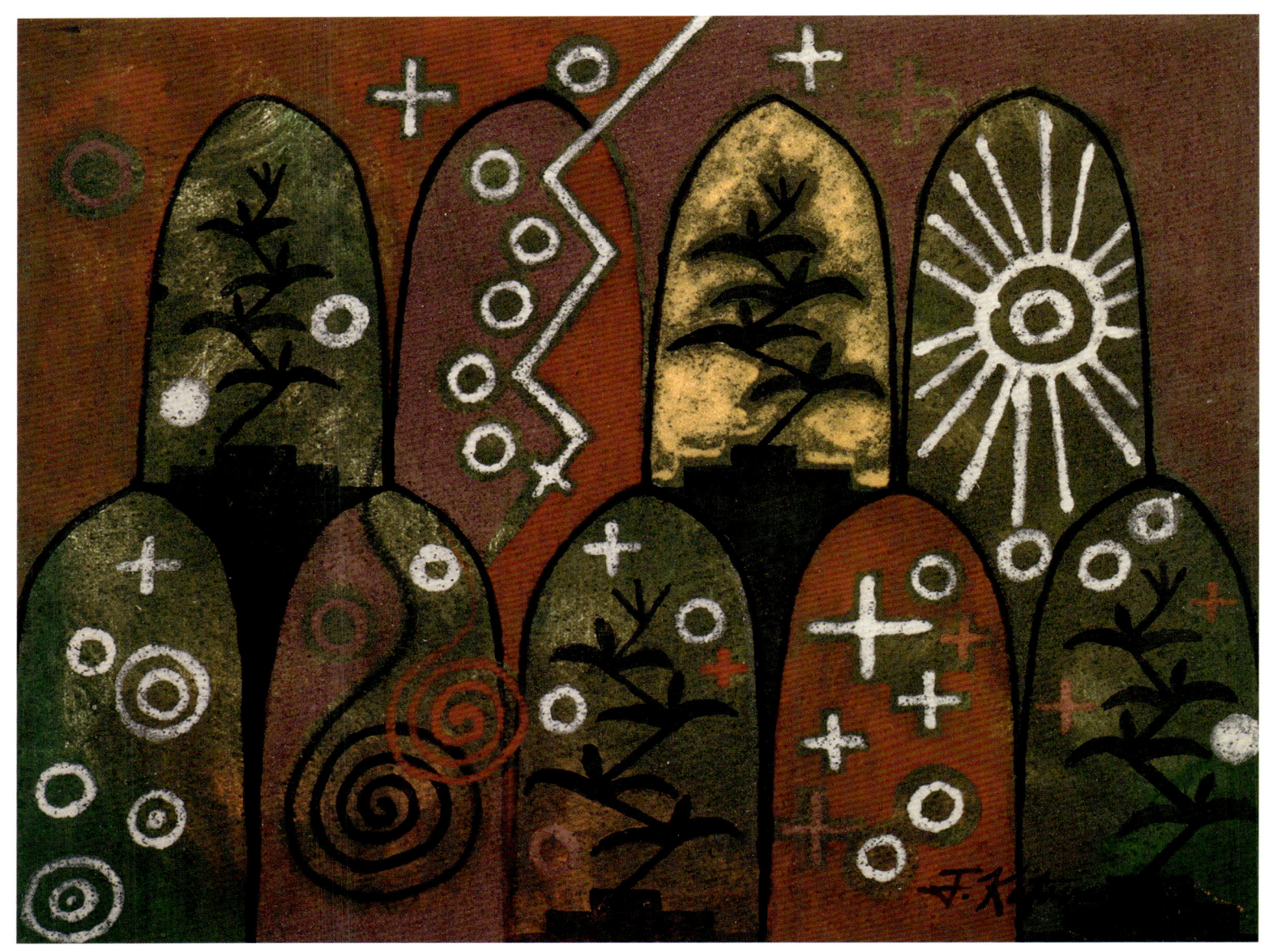

PLATE 114

JEANETTE KATONEY

U.S., Navajo, b. 1967

Song for Corn, 2007

Natural pigments on canvas, 11 x 14 in.

Similarly, like his father, Narciso, before him, Tony Abeyta makes contemporary art informed by both Aboriginal and Euro-American traditions. Well educated, traveled, and exhibited, he is a much celebrated and admired painter, whose work has been collected by museums in the Southwest and on the East Coast, mirroring his ability to negotiate without struggle the difference between regionalist and urban art cultures.[79] He has recalled with clarity growing up in Gallup, New Mexico, near the Navajo and Zuni reservations, with the Acoma and Laguna pueblos not far away. Not surprisingly, then, southwestern land and its attendant visual culture feature prominently in his often telluric work. At times he has used sand, for example, to evoke pictography or cave paintings.[80] Abeyta's *Seed Simply Emerging* (2008), which was included in *Underworlderness,* his solo exhibition at the Heard Museum (2008–2009), is a large, bold yet subtle mixed media work about the dialogue between earth, sky, and plants.

The central panel, a charcoal and ink wash drawing on paper, features a complex quasi-abstract iconography that suggests the growth of spores, seeds, roots, and plants in the "dark murky waters of a subterranean realm."[81] The side panels, which are more lyrical and decorative, symbolize river patterns and work to quietly frame and focus the biomorphic drama evolving in the center. Abeyta seeks in *Seed Simply Emerging* to visualize for us a "mysterious subconscious realm rich in nutrients," as well as a concept of cultural emergence, based on Navajo creation stories. The poetic statement he wrote about the piece for the *Underworlderness* exhibition is instructive in this regard.

There are so many magical things invisible to our eyes. Nature has every answer to an ailing world. Medicinal herbs emerge from seedlings, plants grow to pollinate other plants and life continues with frenetic celebration in this drawing. The flanking panels . . . are made from clay beads and polished micaceous black clay. The beads recollect moments from my childhood where ants would carry Anasazi beads from the subterranean world to the surface of their piles of gravel. I could see some artifact of the underworld basking in the sun's glow. At night I imagined them glowing like constellations on their glittering sacred mound.[82]

Some viewers will see the kinship between Abeyta's organic forms and those in the work of both Whitehorse and Terry Winters, artists for whom he has immense respect. He has noted a kinship between his process and that of the Spanish Surrealist Joan Miro: the invention of botanical shapes, the channeling of archetypical information, and thus the initiation of a dialogue with antiquity.[83]

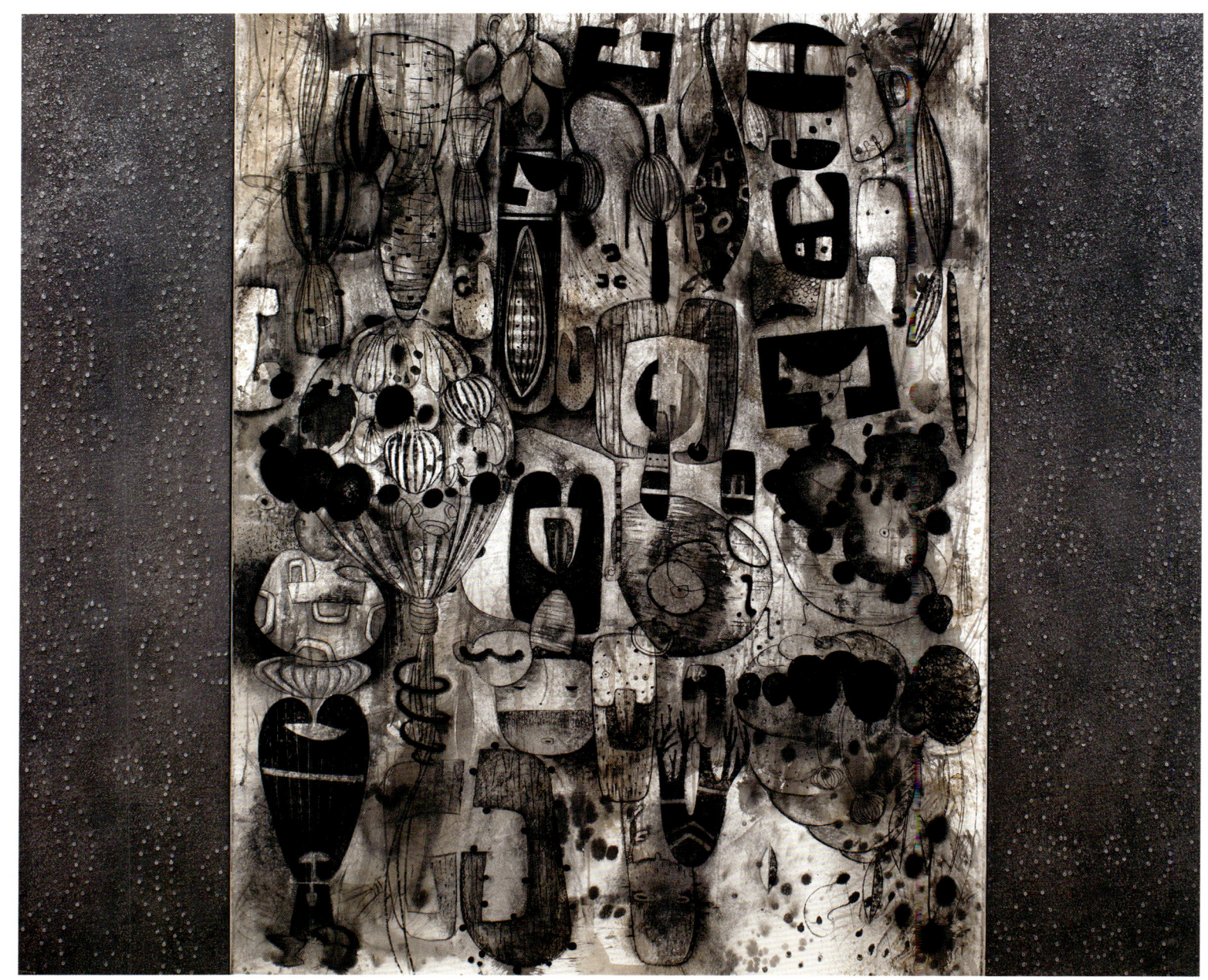

PLATE 115

TONY ABEYTA

U.S., Navajo, b. 1965

Seed Simply Emerging, 2008

Mixed media, 64½ x 70 in.

Abeyta, like Apie Begay a century ago, has made contemporary art using Yei'bichai as subject matter. And just as Chapman recognized immediately the significance of Begay's drawings, when Bialac saw *Seed Simply Emerging* being installed, he envisioned it as a twenty-first-century addition to his wide-ranging collection. Bialac and Abeyta are good friends, who respect each other's contribution to Native art history. Indeed, Bialac has befriended many of the artists represented in his collection, which Abeyta has described as "an artifact of his friendships with artists."[84] And just as Bialac is a visionary collector, with eclectic taste in nineteenth-, twentieth-, and twenty-first-century art, Abeyta is an equally visionary artist, one who stands here as a symbol of multiple generations of modern Native American artists whose work, although deeply informed by tradition, has sought to reflect the present and shape the future.

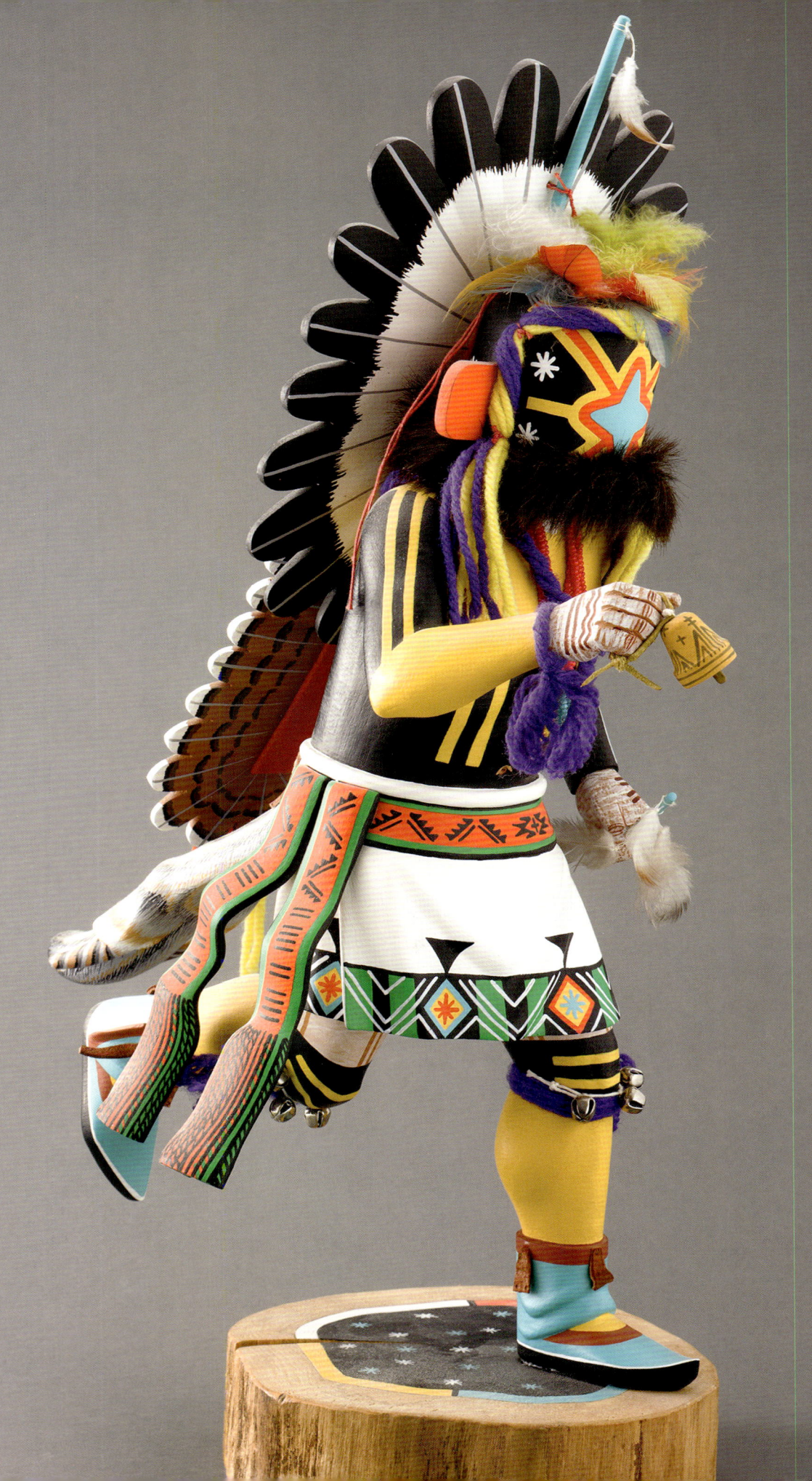

5 | Kachina Dolls

TRADITION AND INNOVATION

Mark Andrew White

JAMES T. BIALAC BEGAN his collection of American Indian art in the early 1960s with the purchase of a Hopi kachina doll from dealer Tom Bahti of Bahti Indian Arts in Tucson. The purchase eventually led to a collection of approximately 1,000 kachina dolls from many of the most celebrated carvers of the twentieth century, such as Alvin "Makya" James and Henry Peter Shelton. Bialac developed close personal and professional relationships with many of the carvers and worked regularly with organizations that promoted carving, such as the Hopi Cultural Center and Hopi Arts & Crafts.

Although the Bialac Native American Art Collection includes a number of kachina dolls created before World War II, most date from postwar, when the dolls became an increasingly marketable art form, closer in many respects to sculpture than to their original purpose as religious icons. Kachina dolls (*katsina tithu*) are a venerated tradition in Hopi culture and are traditionally a gift to a young girl by a male relative in the guise of kachinas (*katsinam*), spirits that represent natural phenomena and unseen forces in the cosmos of the Hopi.[1] According to Barton Wright, a

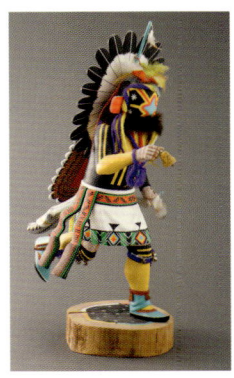

PLATE 116

PETER "HOYESVA" SHELTON, JR.

U.S., Hopi Pueblo, 1920–1992

Star Chaser, c. 1960s–1980s

Cottonwood root, paint, 20 in.

kachina doll "was and is a visual prayer from Hopi men to unmarried girls, one designed to form an alliance between the young women and the Kachina spirits to enhance the well-being of the former."[2] Hopi girls could play with the dolls but were generally instructed to hang them on the wall as physical expressions of religious beliefs. Most *katsina tithu* in the early twentieth century were characterized by an emphasis on the head, which was out of proportion to a smaller and somewhat columnar body, with the arms folded across the chest or held at the side.

Kachina dolls occasionally entered museum and private collections before the twentieth century, but the tourist market for dolls did not develop until the Fred Harvey Company's Indian Department began marketing them at the Louisiana Purchase Exposition in St. Louis in 1904.[3] The Museum of Northern Arizona's *Hopi Craftsman Exhibition,* which began in 1930, also encouraged Hopi kachina carvers to produce for the market. As market demand increased following World War II, carvers introduced innovations in size, carving, and materials. Kachina dolls began to increase in size, probably to take advantage of an established market practice that priced by the inch, and they became more articulated, with the carvers using poses suggestive of the kachina dances. During this time, carver Peter Shelton introduced acrylic paints, which provided vivid coloration. Dolls of this type were made for the market and cannot be termed *katsina tithu,* since they were not given in ceremonies. In this regard, kachina dolls of this period may be considered figural sculpture.

PLATE 117

ARMAND FRITZ

U.S., Hopi Pueblo, b. 1949

Tusunhomitsi (Warrior Mouse)
and Family Performing
the Hopi Pueblo
Butterfly Dance, c. 1990s

Cottonwood root, paint, 6¼ in.

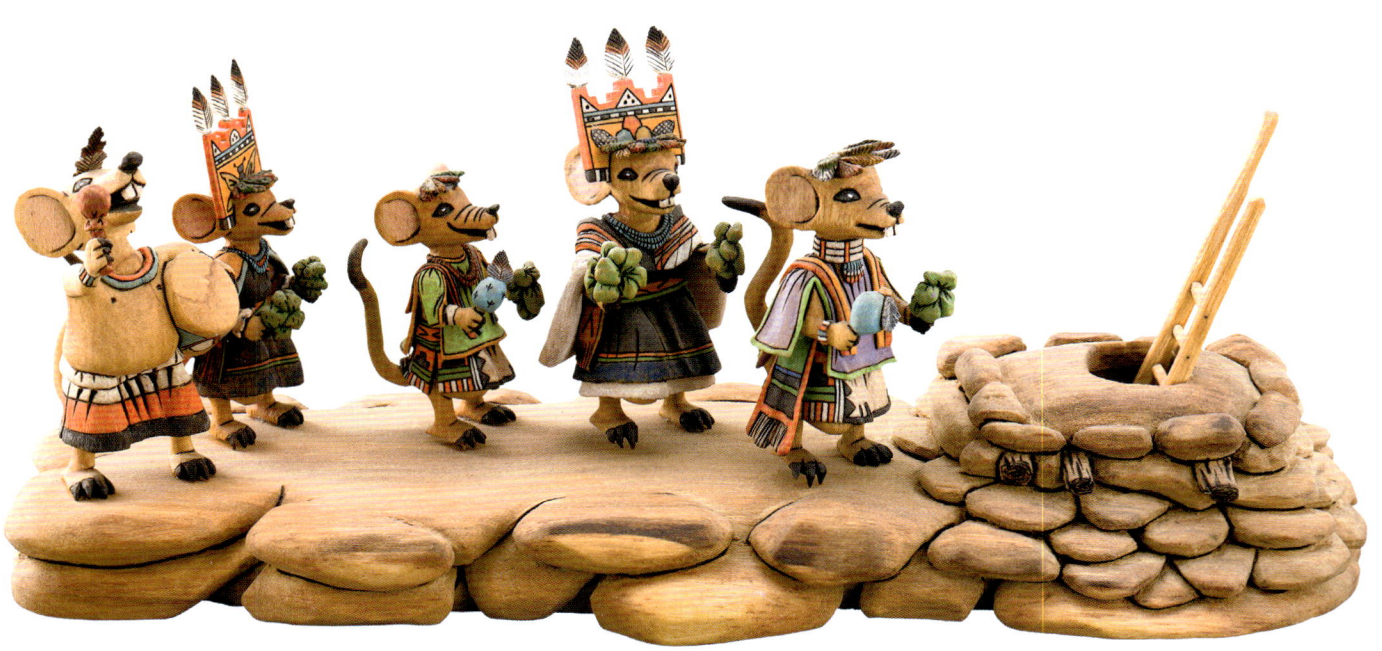

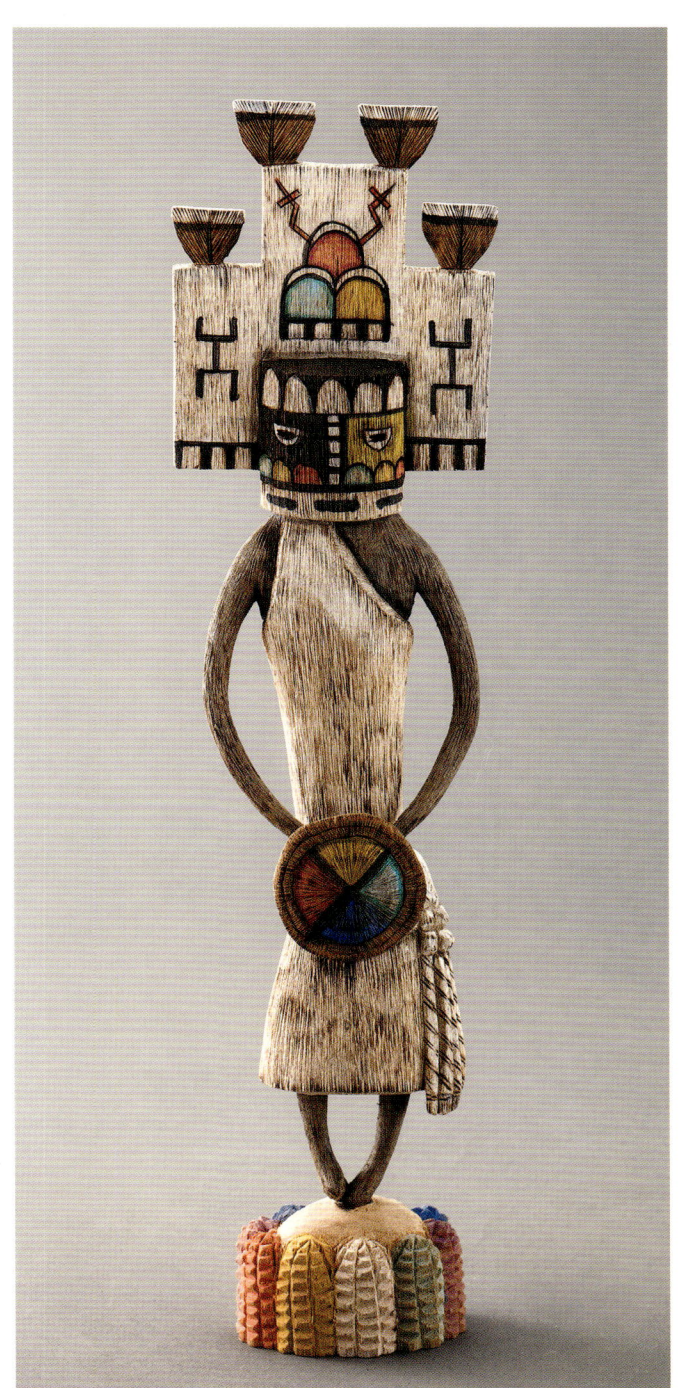

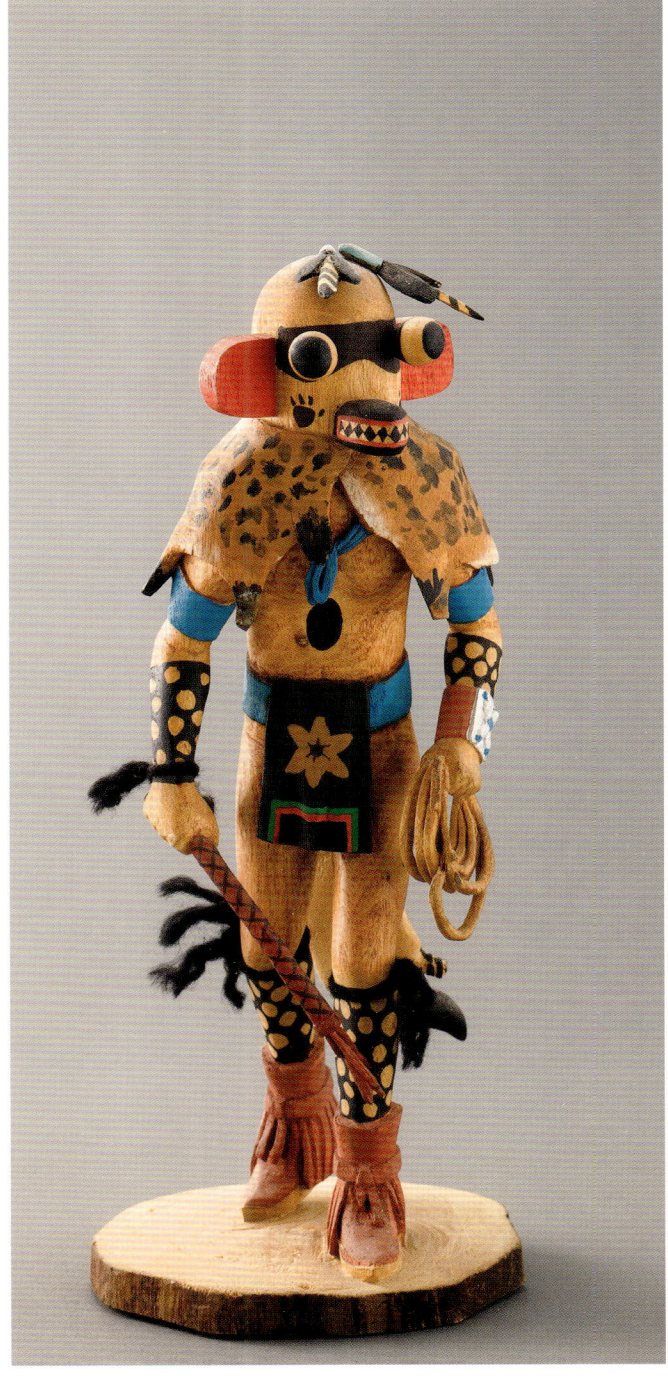

PLATE 118

AARON J. FREDERICKS

U.S., Hopi Pueblo, b. 1964

Cumulous Cloud Maiden on a Colorful Corn Base, 2008

Cottonwood root, stain, kaolin, 11¾ in.

PLATE 119

BRIAN HONYOUTI

U.S., Hopi Pueblo, b. 1947

Tokotsi (Wildcat) Kachina, 1974

Cottonwood root, paint, stain, 11½ in.

During the 1960s, when Bialac began collecting kachina dolls, a tendency toward realism also prevailed among carvers. Alvin "Makya" James not only carved the dolls to correct anatomical proportions, but also employed active poses, creating a demand for realism in kachina doll carving that remains a vital stylistic tendency in the market. James also used cloth, rawhide, and other materials that enhanced the naturalism of the kachina doll. Carvers such as Leon Dallas and Brian Honyouti have continued this tradition of the "action kachina."

The increasing demand for realism in the market prompted some carvers to return to prewar carving forms. Bendrew Atokuku, Dion Dashee, Ryon Polequaptewa, Fred Ross, and Manfred Susunkewa, among others, employed the old proportions and forms as an homage to earlier traditions. Other carvers responded to the realism of the 1960s–1970s by moving closer to abstract sculpture. The Artist Hopid, formed in 1973, had introduced modernist abstraction as a means of depicting kachinas, and even though the group directed its efforts chiefly to painting and sculpture, its example proved instructive for kachina carvers. Aaron J. Fredericks and other carvers have used forms rarely seen in older styles.

These innovations and developments in kachina carving since World War II are represented in the Bialac collection, and the significant breadth and depth of the collection constitutes an invaluable resource for the scholarly study of Hopi kachina carving traditions.

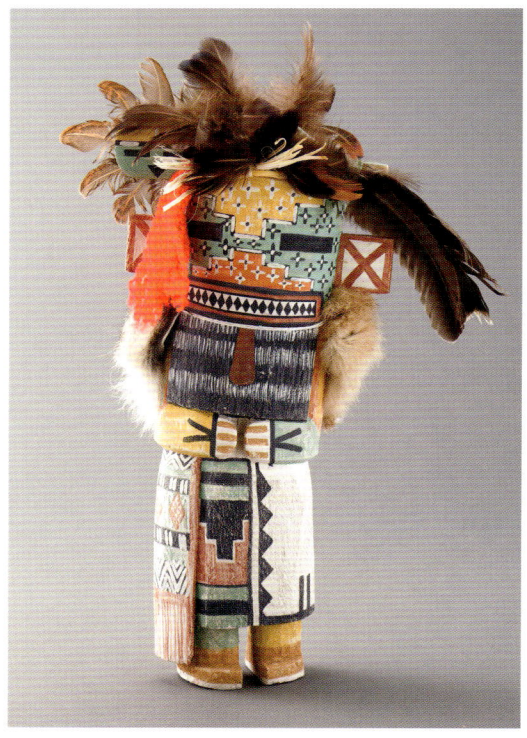
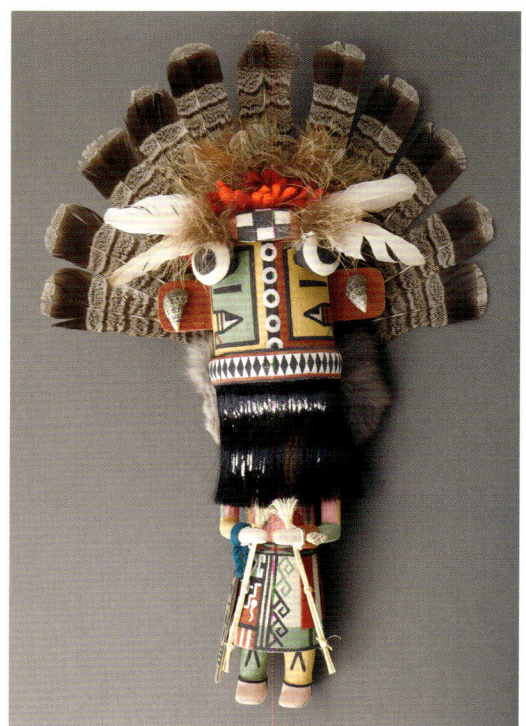

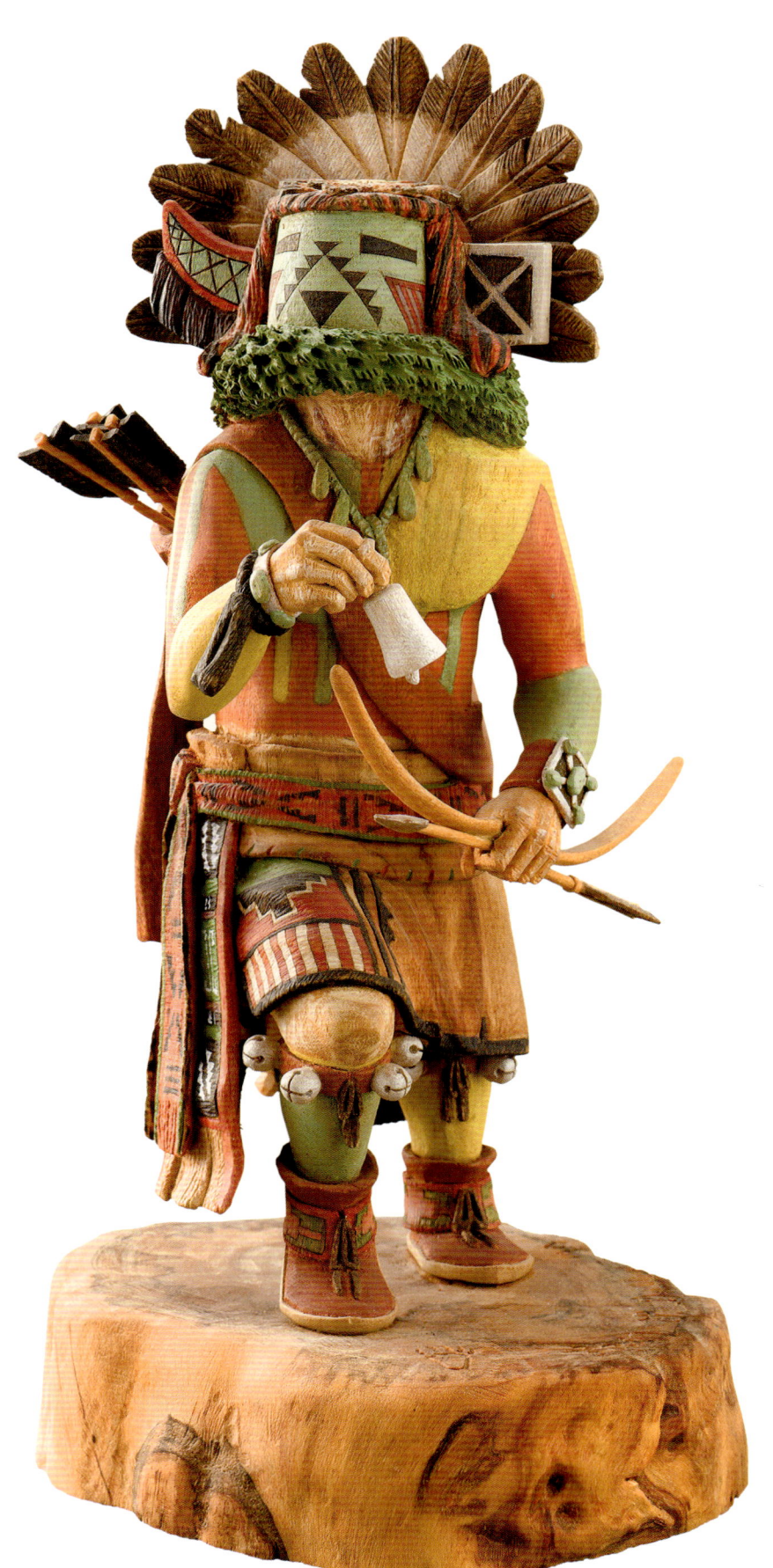

PLATE 122

LEON DALLAS

U.S., Hopi Pueblo, b. 1960

Neyaksola (Supai Uncle) Katsina, 1990

Cottonwood root, paint, and feathers,

13¼ in.

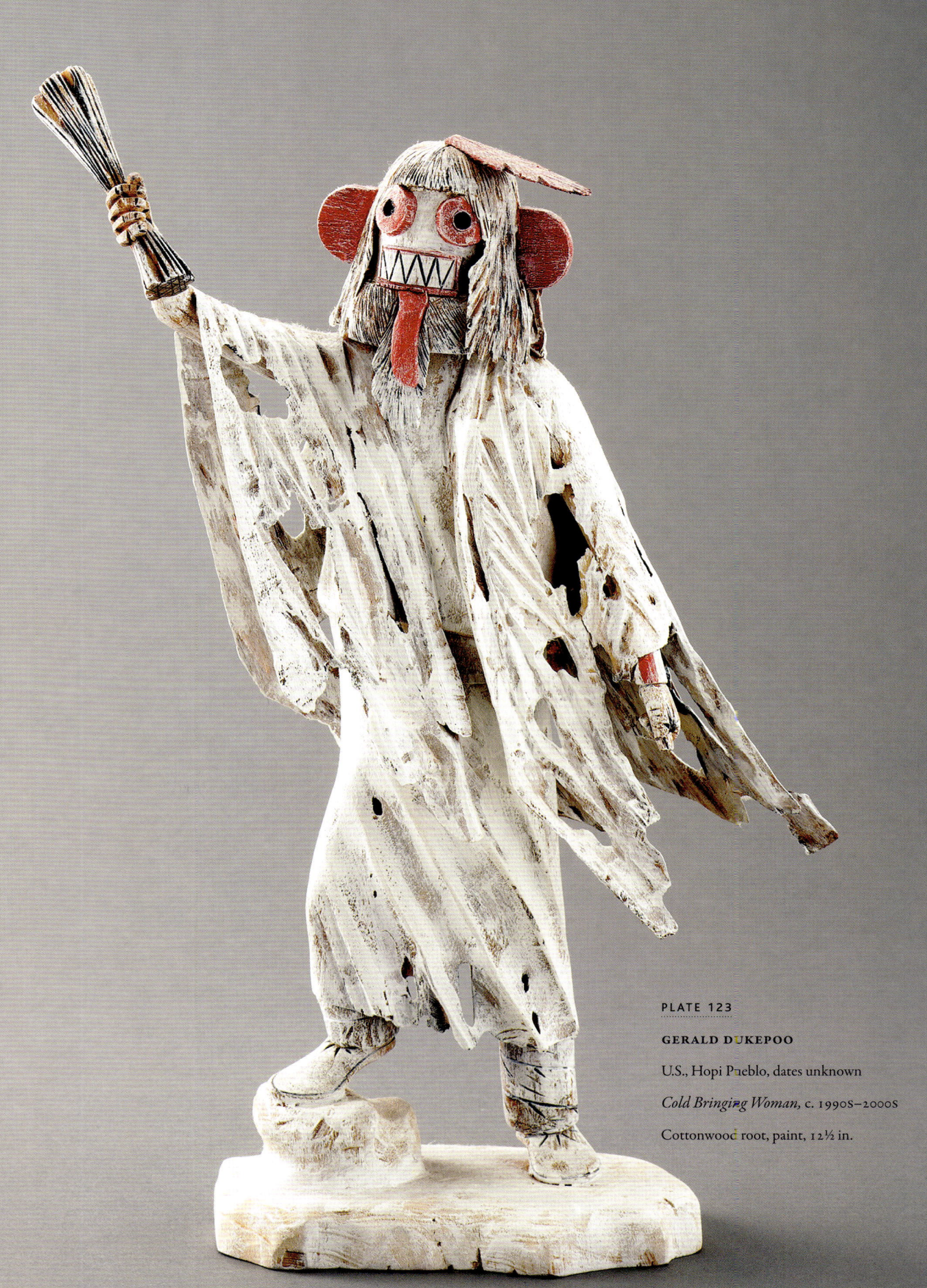

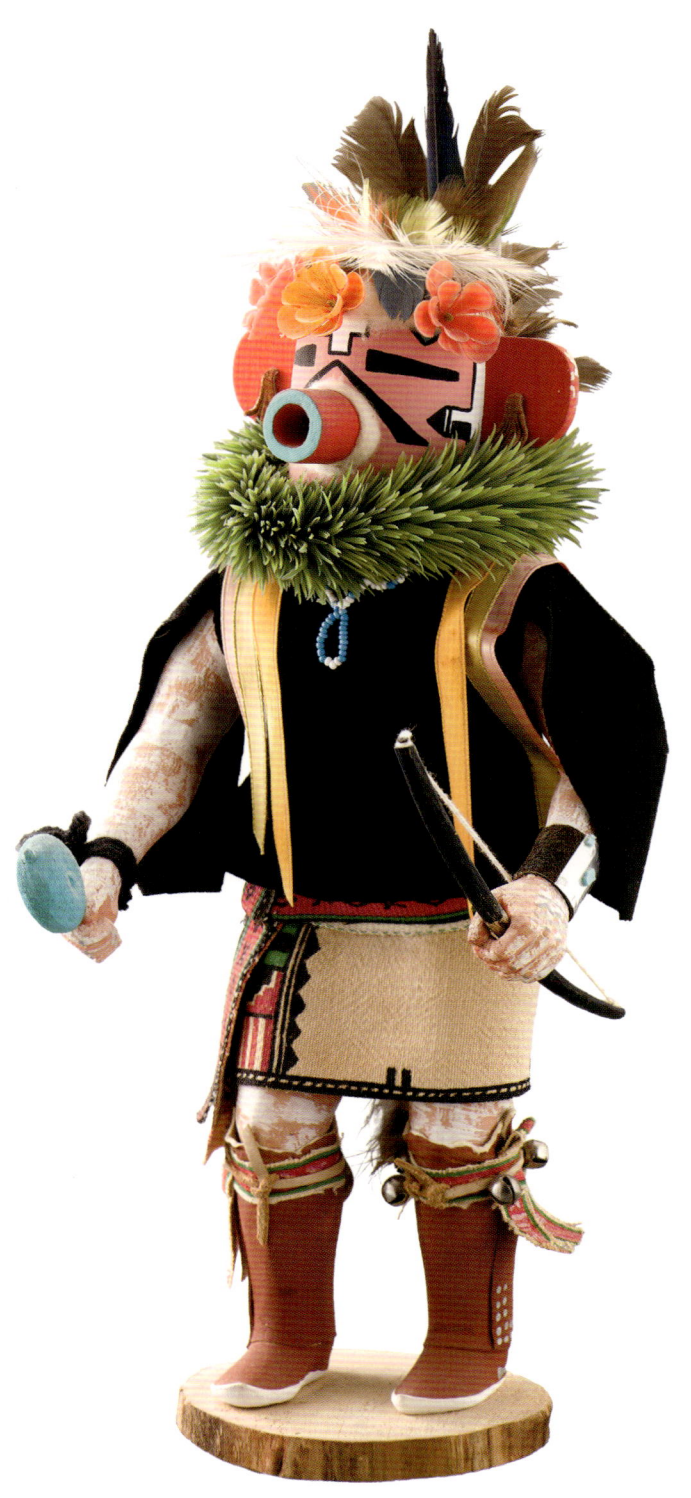

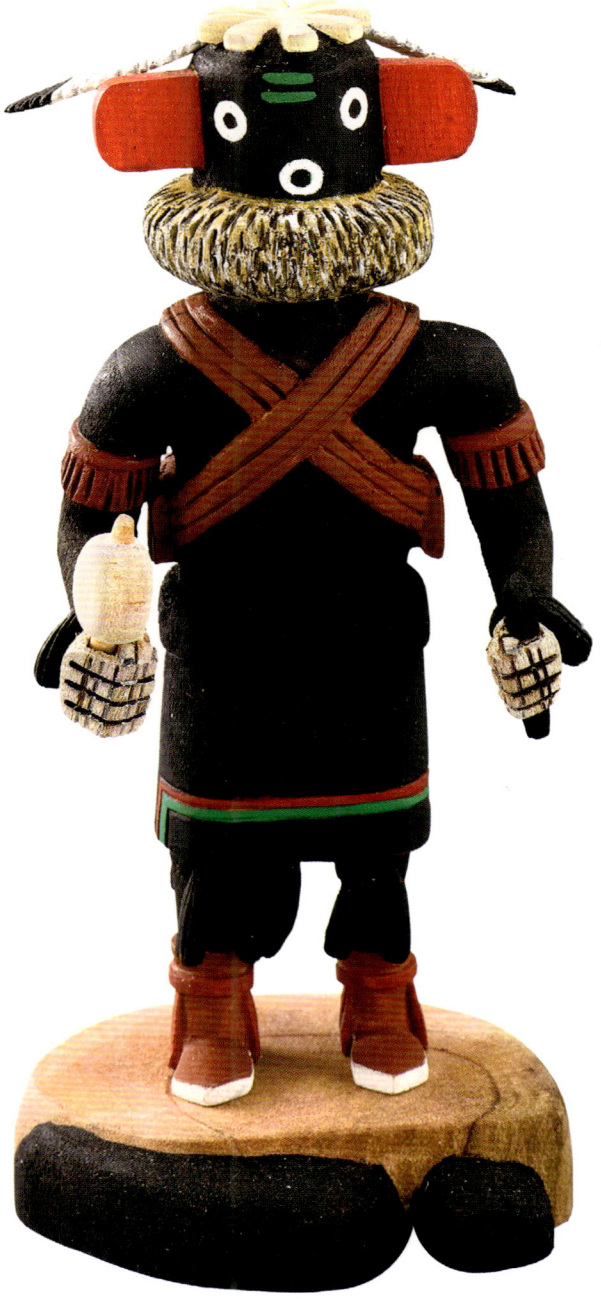

PLATE 124

GORMAN DAVID

U.S., Hopi Pueblo, dates unknown

Navan (Velvet Shirt) Katsina, 1970–80s

Cottonwood root, paint, 16½ in.

PLATE 125

CARLTON HARVEY, SR.

U.S., Hopi Pueblo, dates unknown

Coal Katsina, n.d.

Cottonwood root, paint, 6 in.

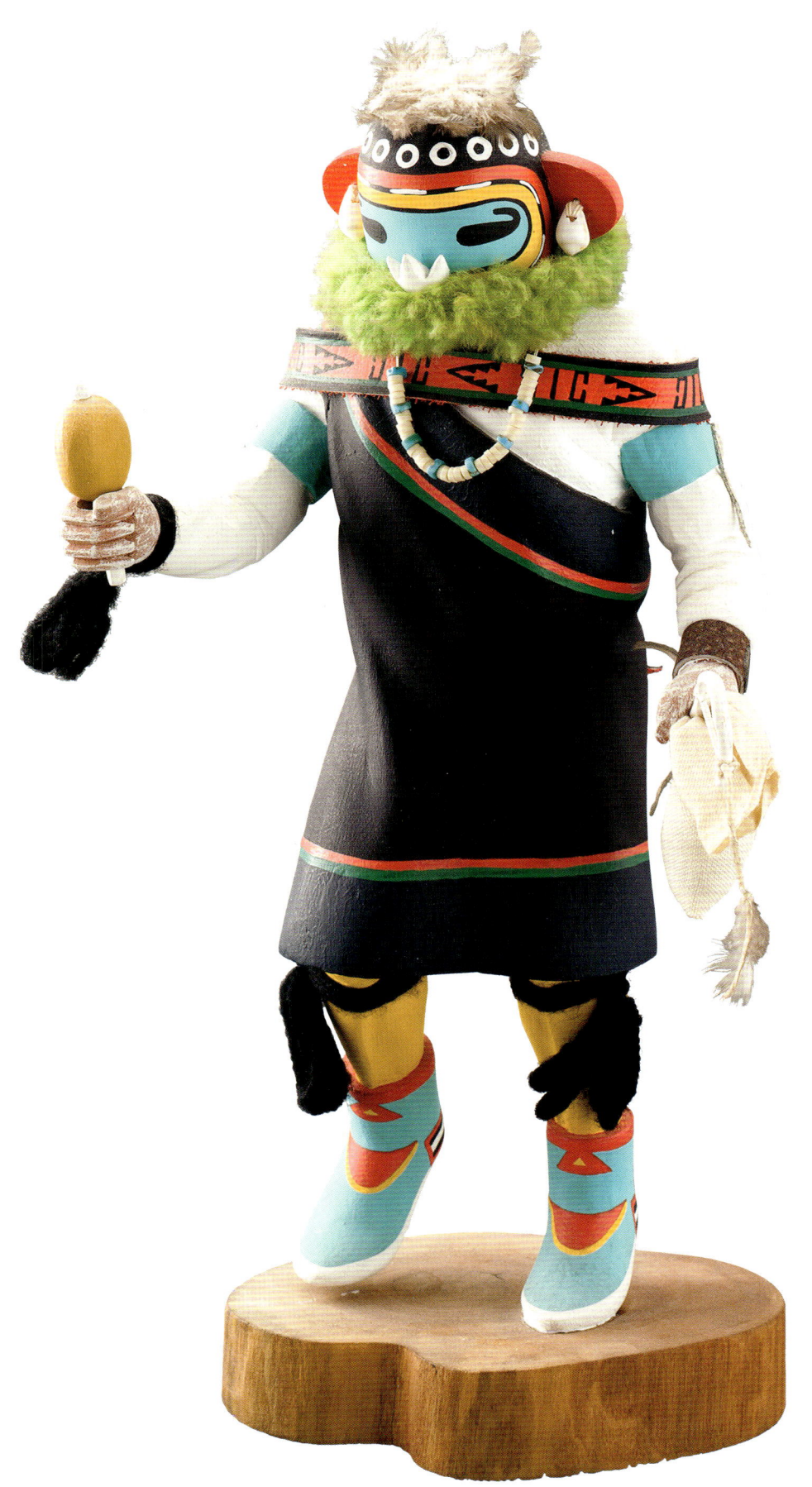

PLATE 126

ALVIN "MAKYA" JAMES, SR.

U.S., Hopi Pueblo, 1936–c. 2003

Kwasai-taga (Skirt Man) Katsina, 1968

Cottonwood root, paint, 13½ in.

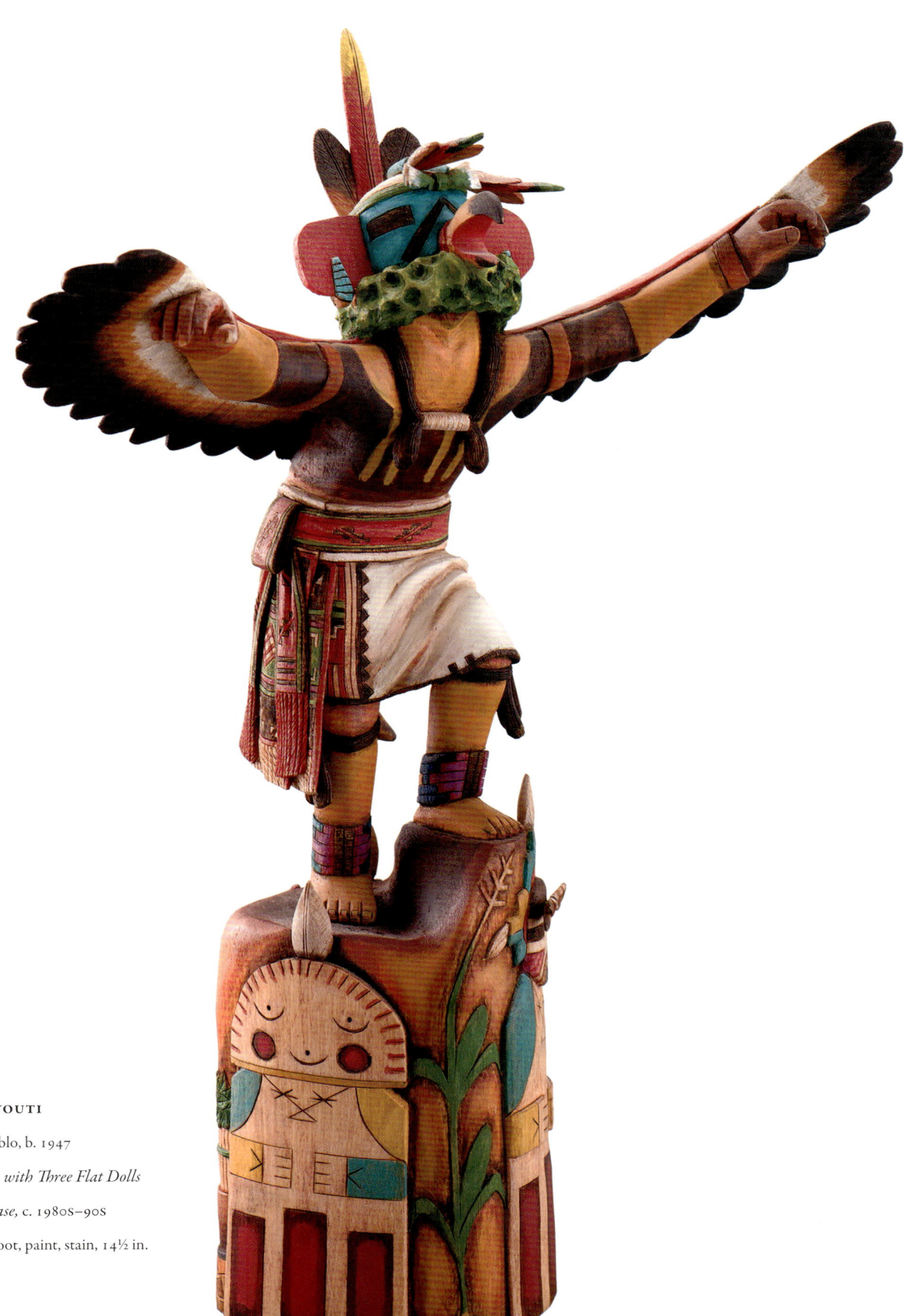

PLATE 127

BRIAN HONYOUTI

U.S., Hopi Pueblo, b. 1947

Eagle Kachina with Three Flat Dolls

Carved into Base, c. 1980s–90s

Cottonwood root, paint, stain, 14½ in.

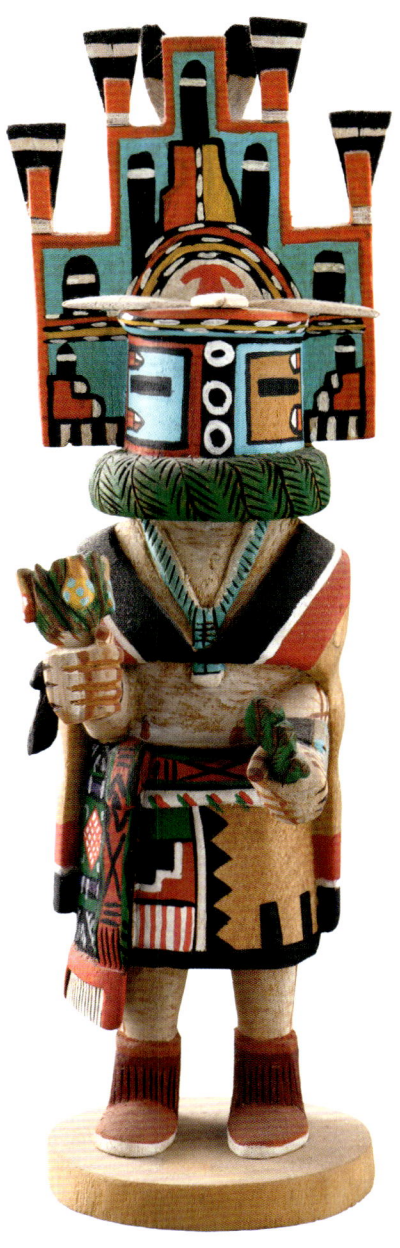

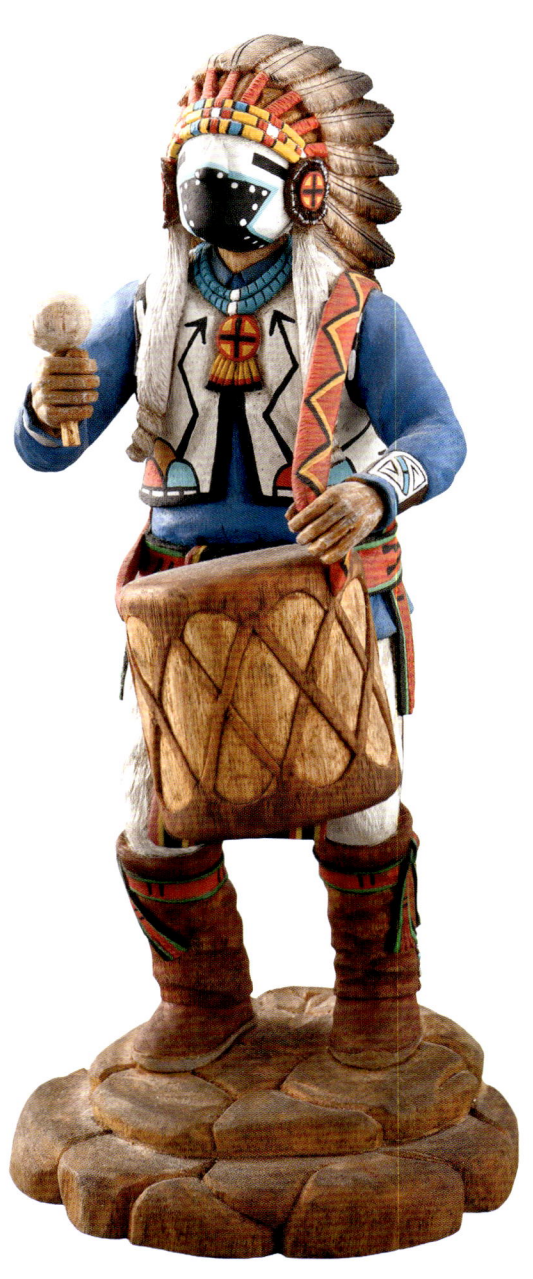

PLATE 128

SHIRLEY ADAMS

U.S., Hopi Pueblo, b. c. 1920s

Hemis Katsina, c. 1980s

Cottonwood root, paint, 13½ in.

PLATE 129

MAURICE TAWESA NUTUMYA

U.S., Hopi Pueblo, dates unknown

Comanche Drummer, c. 1980s–90s

Cottonwood root, paint, stain, 9½ in.

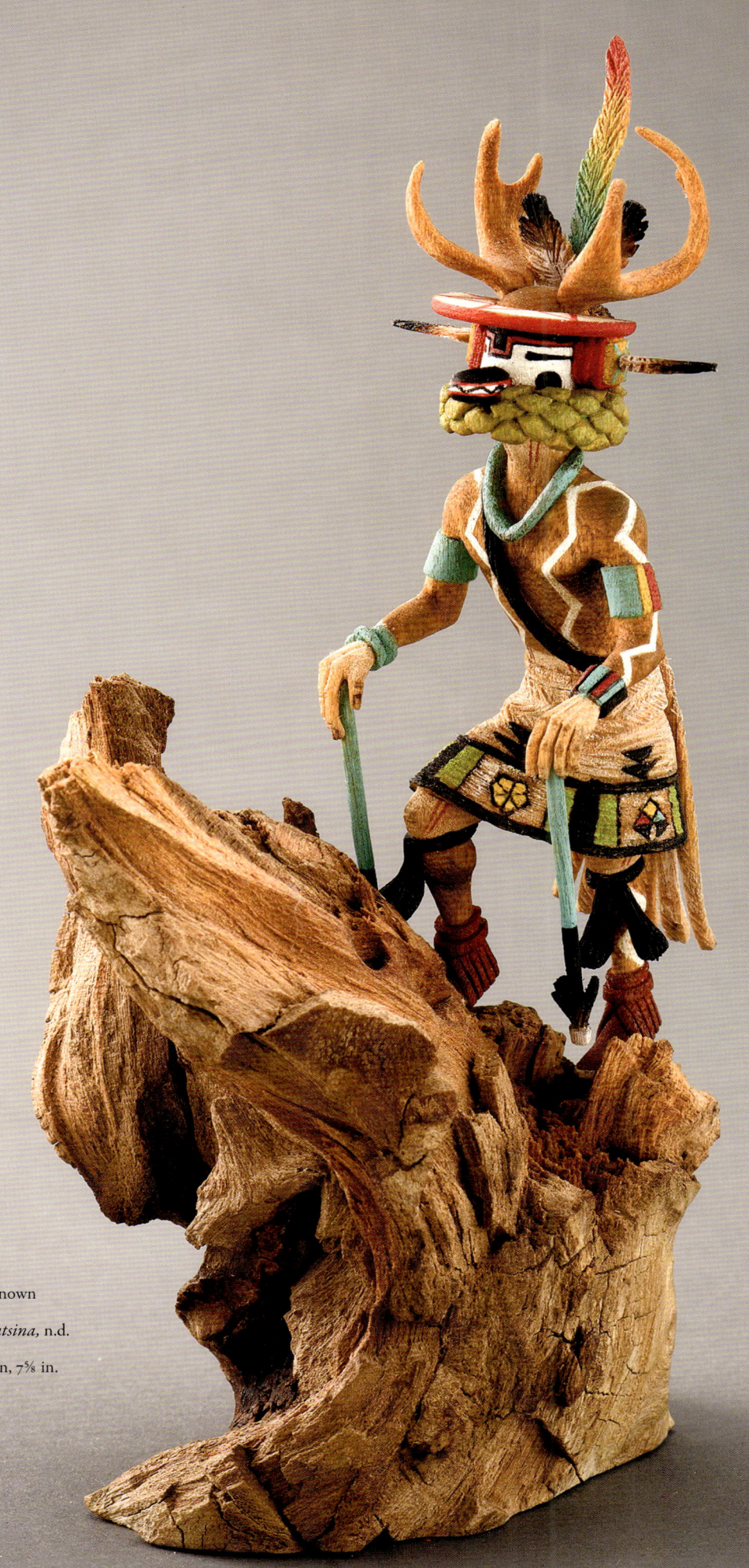

PLATE 130

ADRIAN C. POLEAHLA

U.S., Hopi Pueblo, dates unknown

Sowi'ingwkatsina (Deer) Katsina, n.d.

Cottonwood root, paint, stain, 7⅝ in.

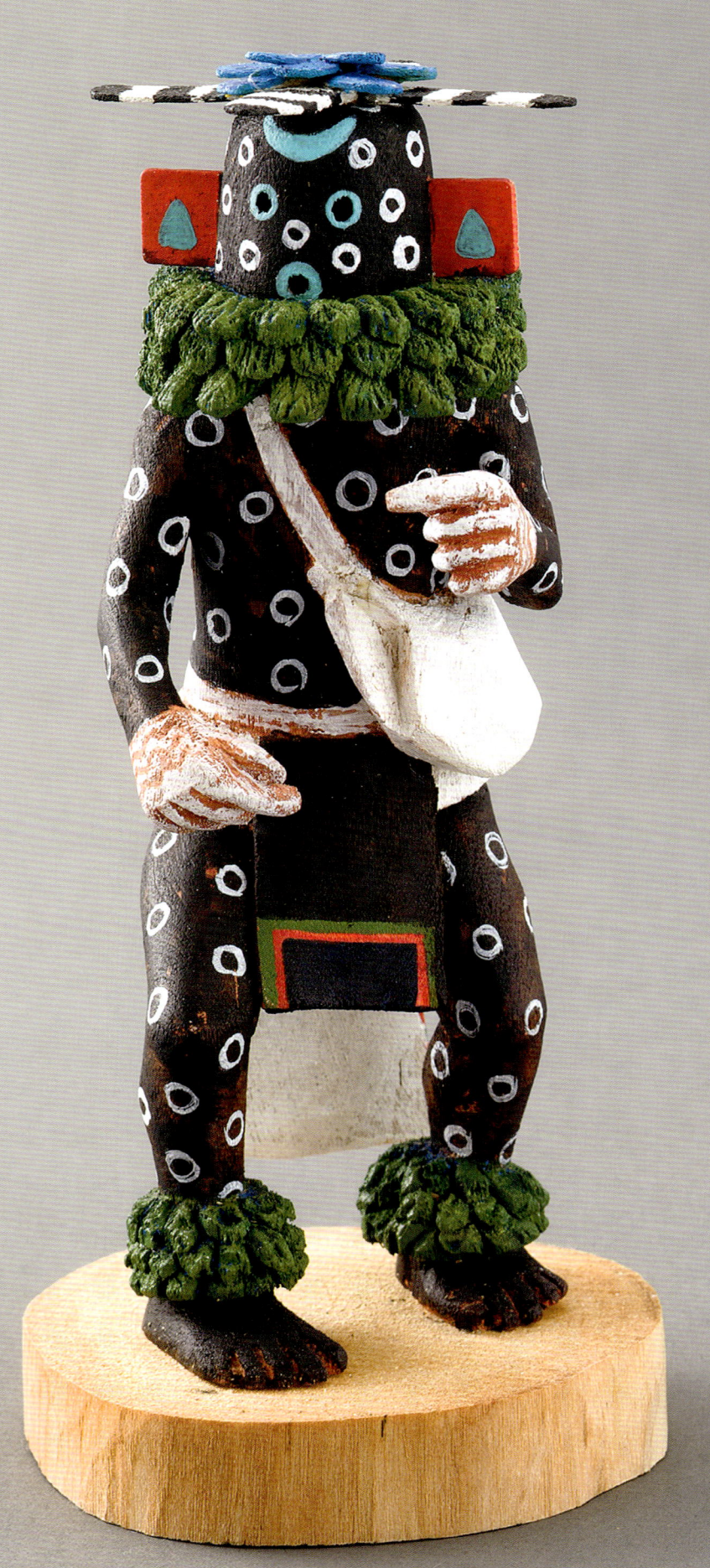

PLATE 131

NEIL DAVID, SR.

U.S., Hopi Pueblo, b. 1944

Parch Corn Boy, 1998

Cottonwood root, paint, 7½ in.

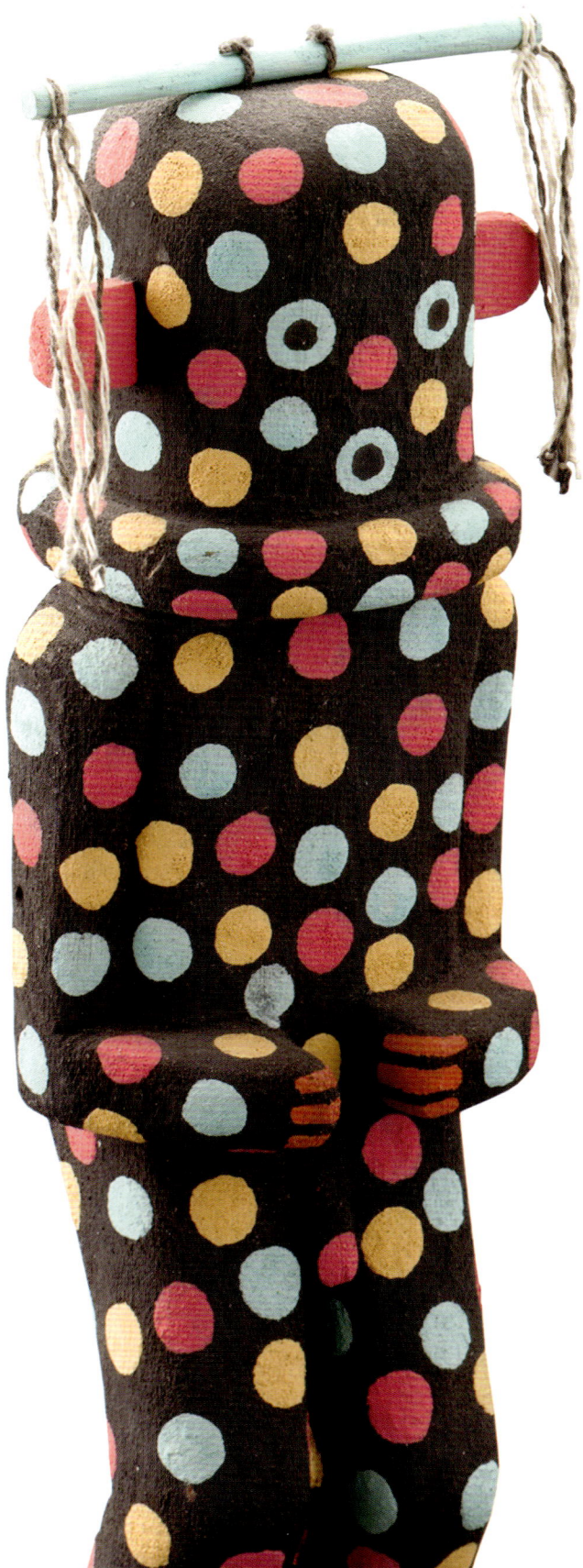
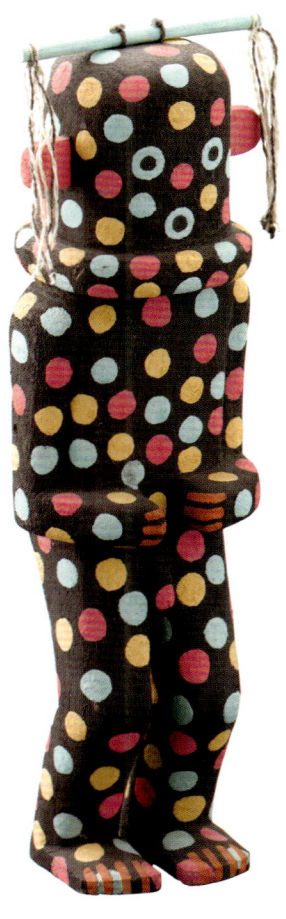

PLATE 132

FRED ROSS

U.S., Hopi Pueblo, b. 1973

Shulawitsi, c. 2000

Cottonwood root, paint, yarn, 10¾ in.

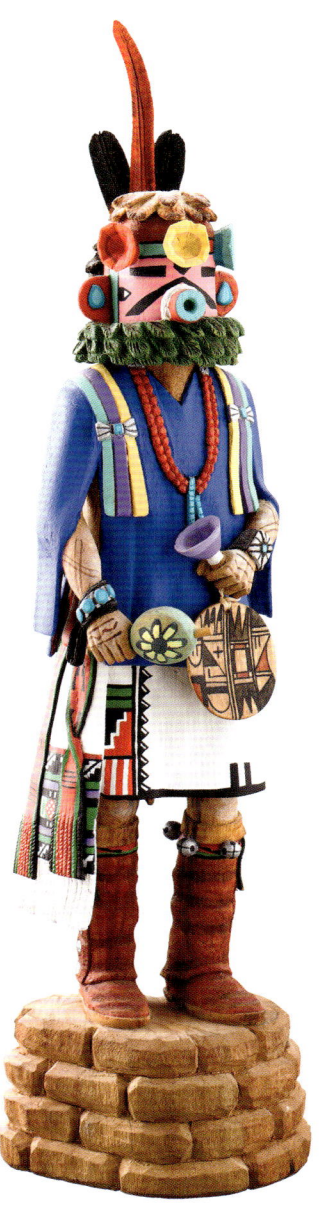

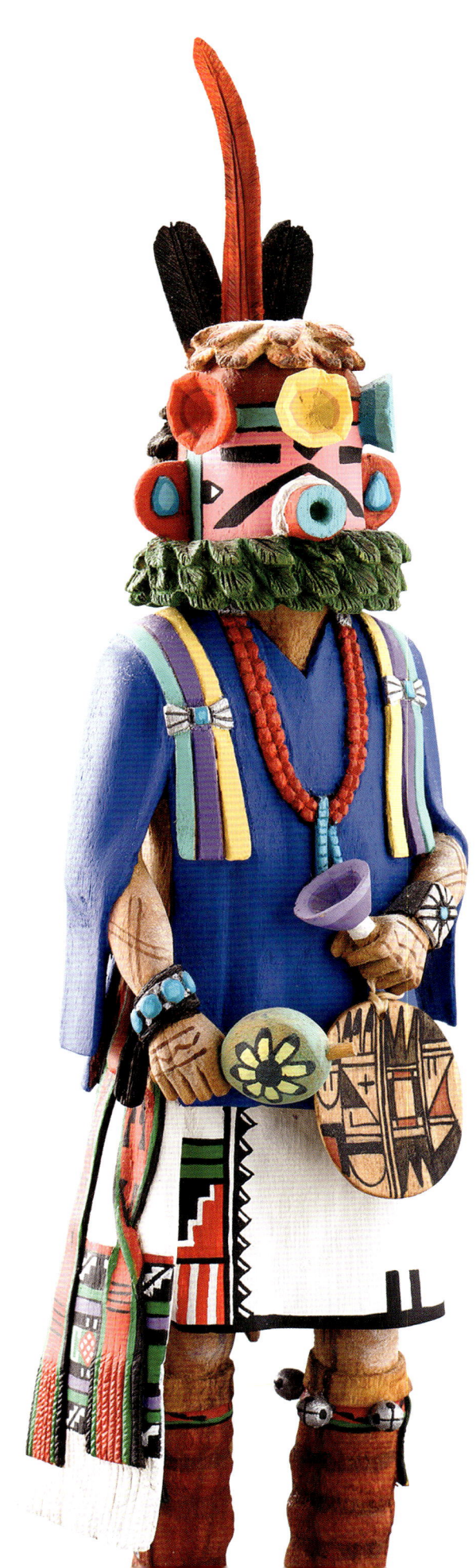

PLATE 133

ORIN POLEY

U.S., Hopi Pueblo, b. 1942

Navan (Velvet Shirt) Katsina, n.d.

Cottonwood root, paint, cloth, and

leather, 15 in.

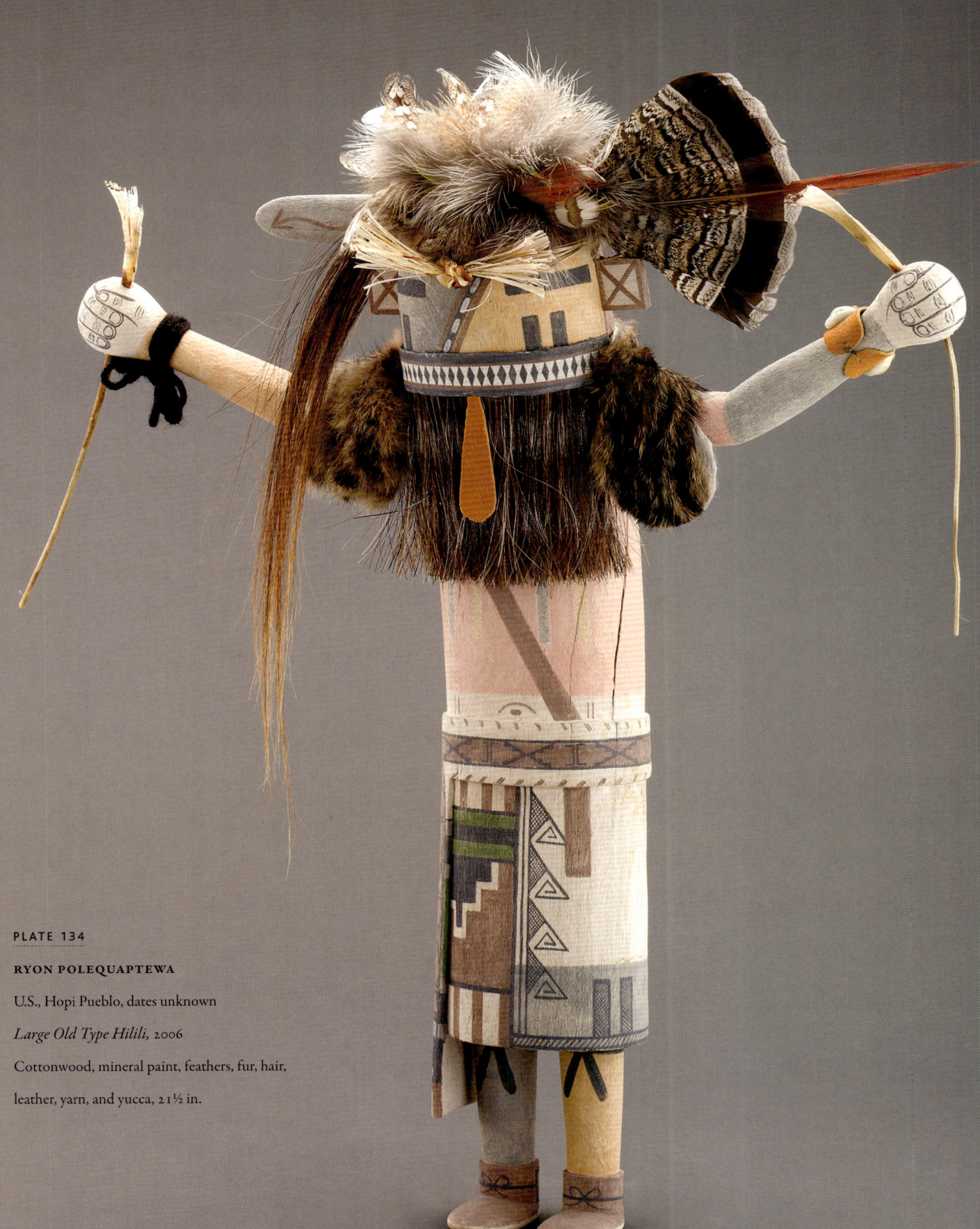

PLATE 134

RYON POLEQUAPTEWA

U.S., Hopi Pueblo, dates unknown

Large Old Type Hilili, 2006

Cottonwood, mineral paint, feathers, fur, hair,

leather, yarn, and yucca, 21½ in.

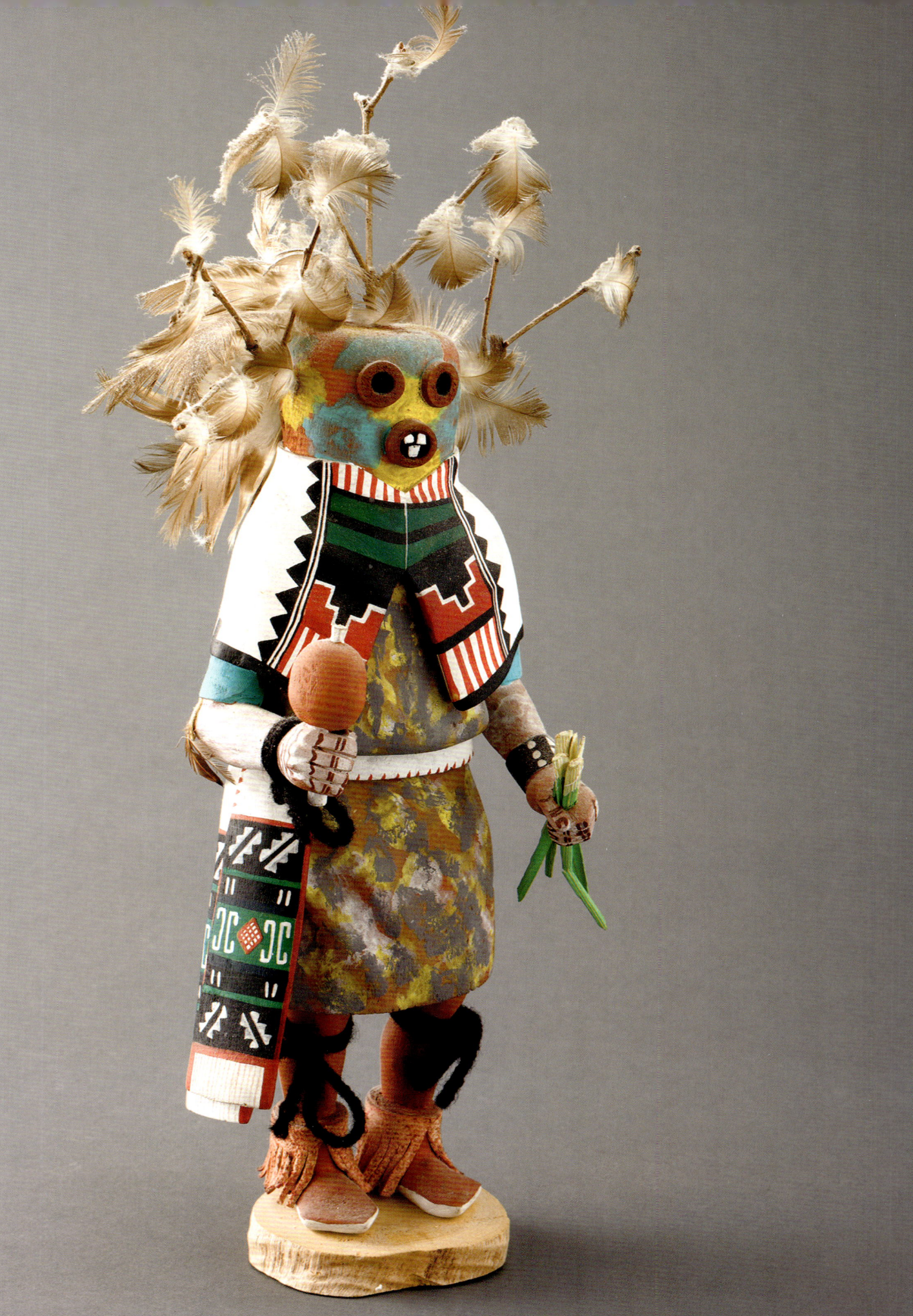

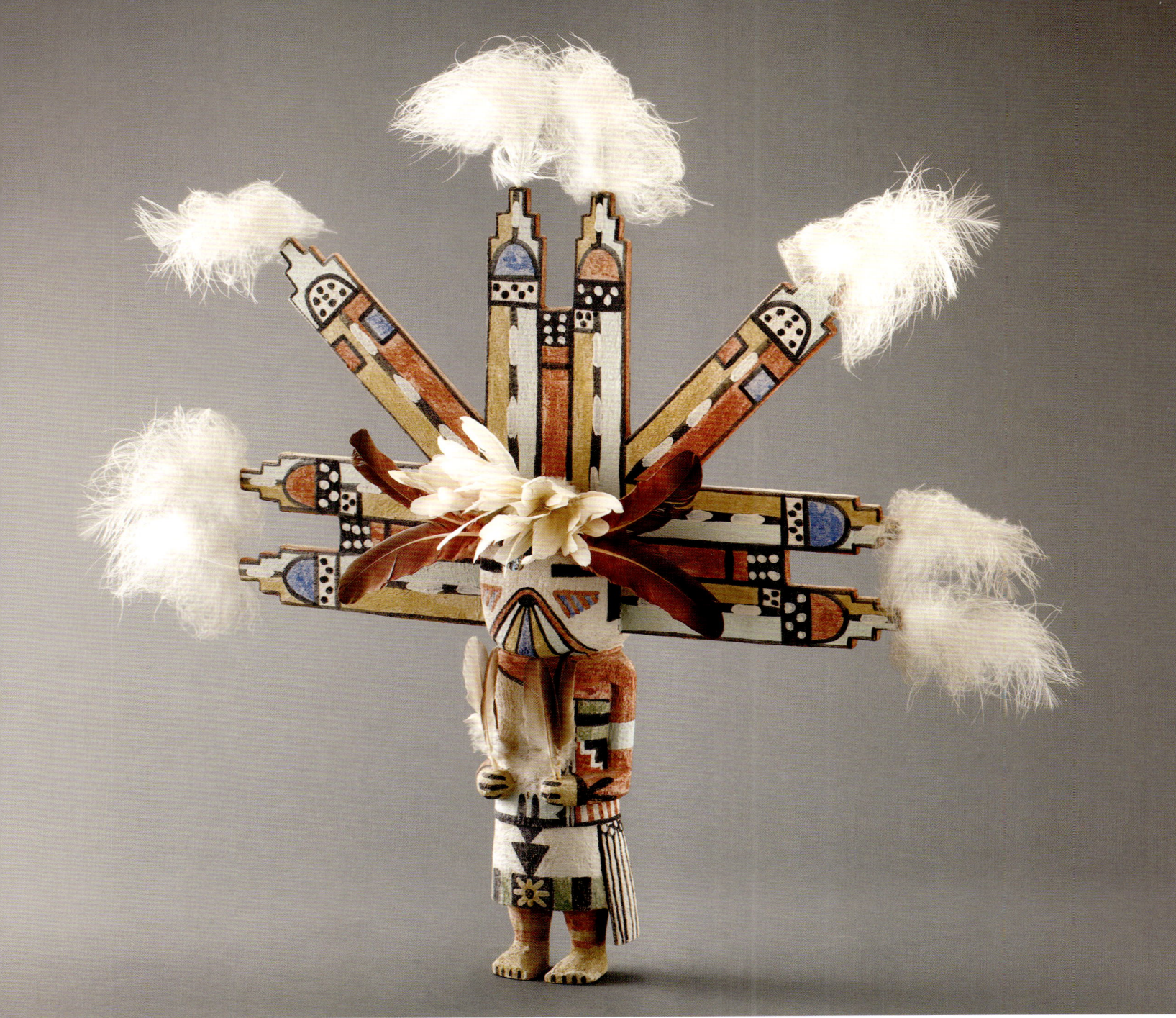

PLATE 135

MARY SHELTON

U.S., Hopi Pueblo, dates unknown

Masau, c. 1960s–1980s

Cottonwood root, paint, feathers, stick,

and yarn, 14 in.

PLATE 136

MANFRED SUSUNKEWA

U.S., Hopi Pueblo, b. 1940

Old Type Palhik Mana, c. 1990

Cottonwood root, mineral paint, feathers, shell,

and string, 20½ in.

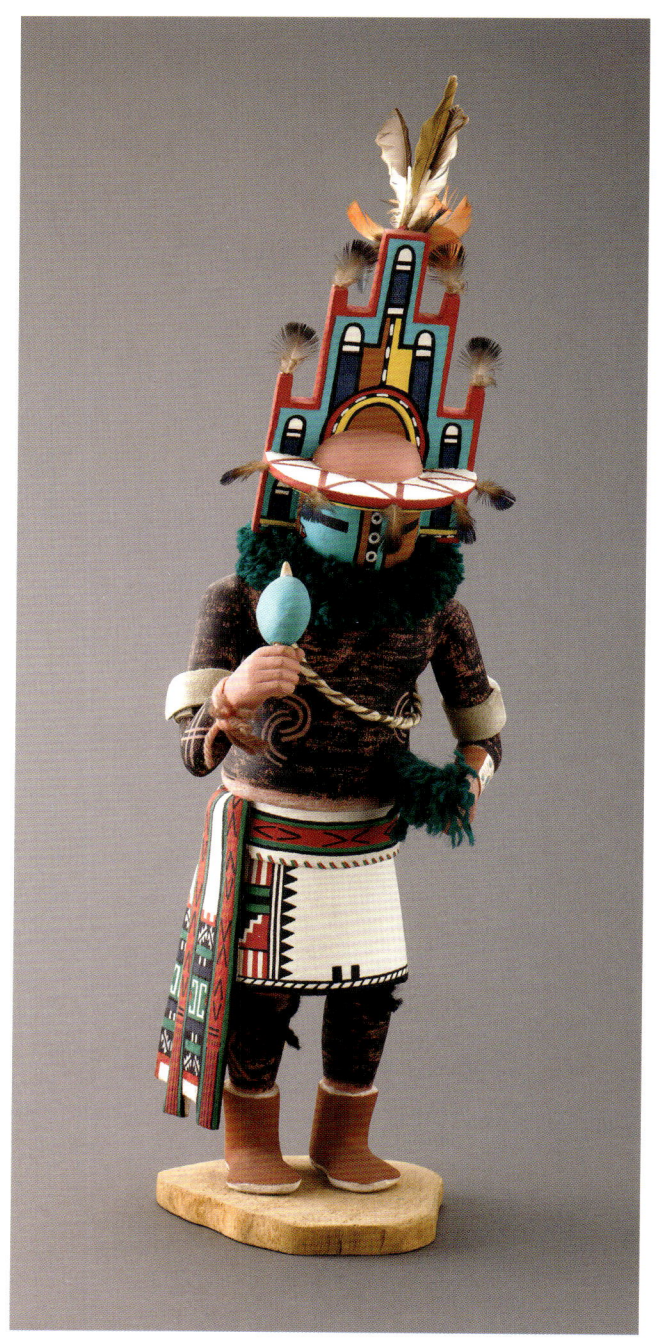

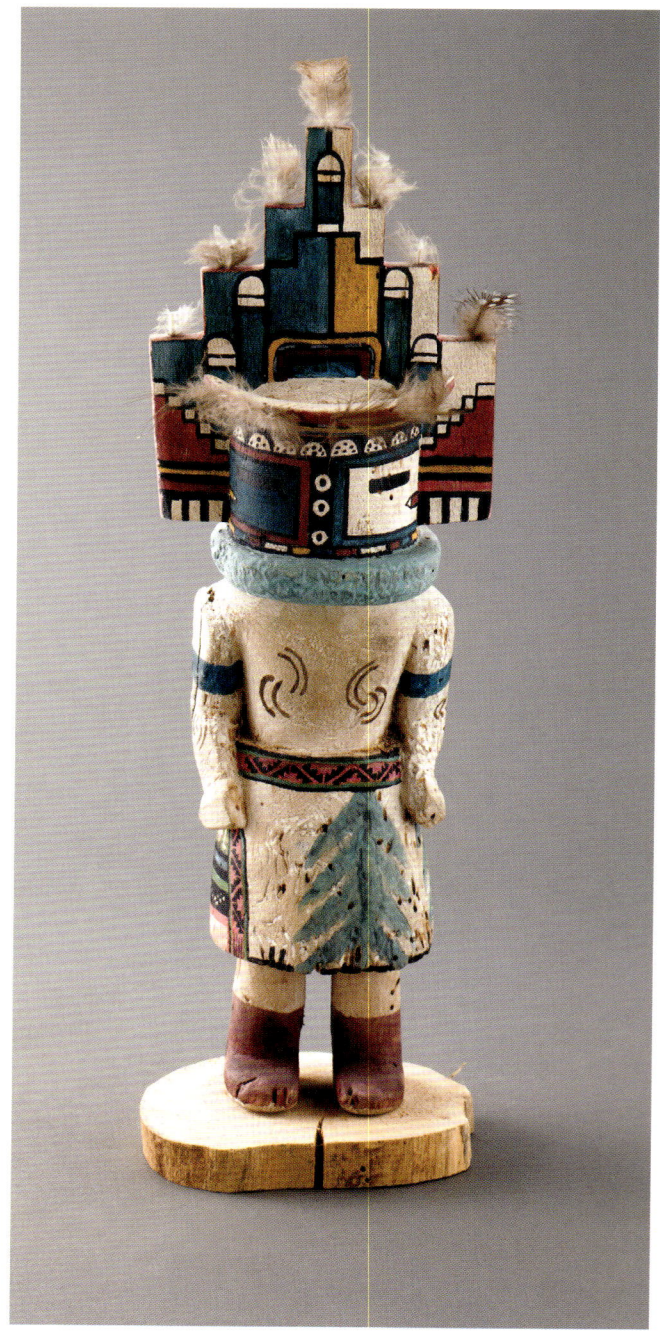

PLATE 137

HENRY PETER SHELTON

U.S., Hopi Pueblo, b. 1929

Niman kachina, c. 1960s–1980s

Cottonwood root, paint, feathers,

and yarn, 19¾ in.

PLATE 138

UNKNOWN

U.S., Hopi Pueblo

Hemis Katsina, n.d.

Cottonwood root, paint, 15 in.

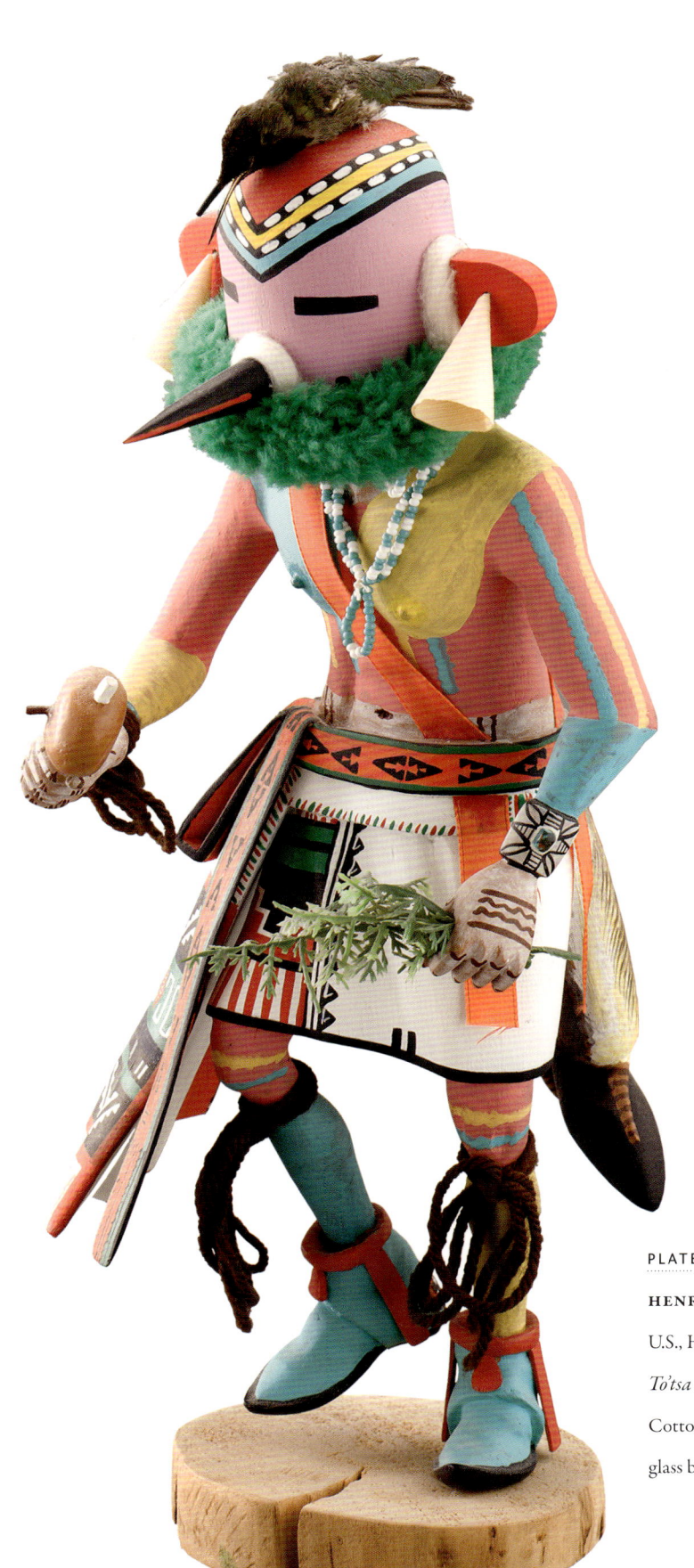

PLATE 139

HENRY PETER SHELTON

U.S., Hopi Pueblo, b. 1929

To'tsa (Hummingbird) Katsina, c. 1960s–1980s

Cottonwood root, paint, feathers, cornhusk, cotton, felt,

glass beads, plastic, and yarn, 15 in.

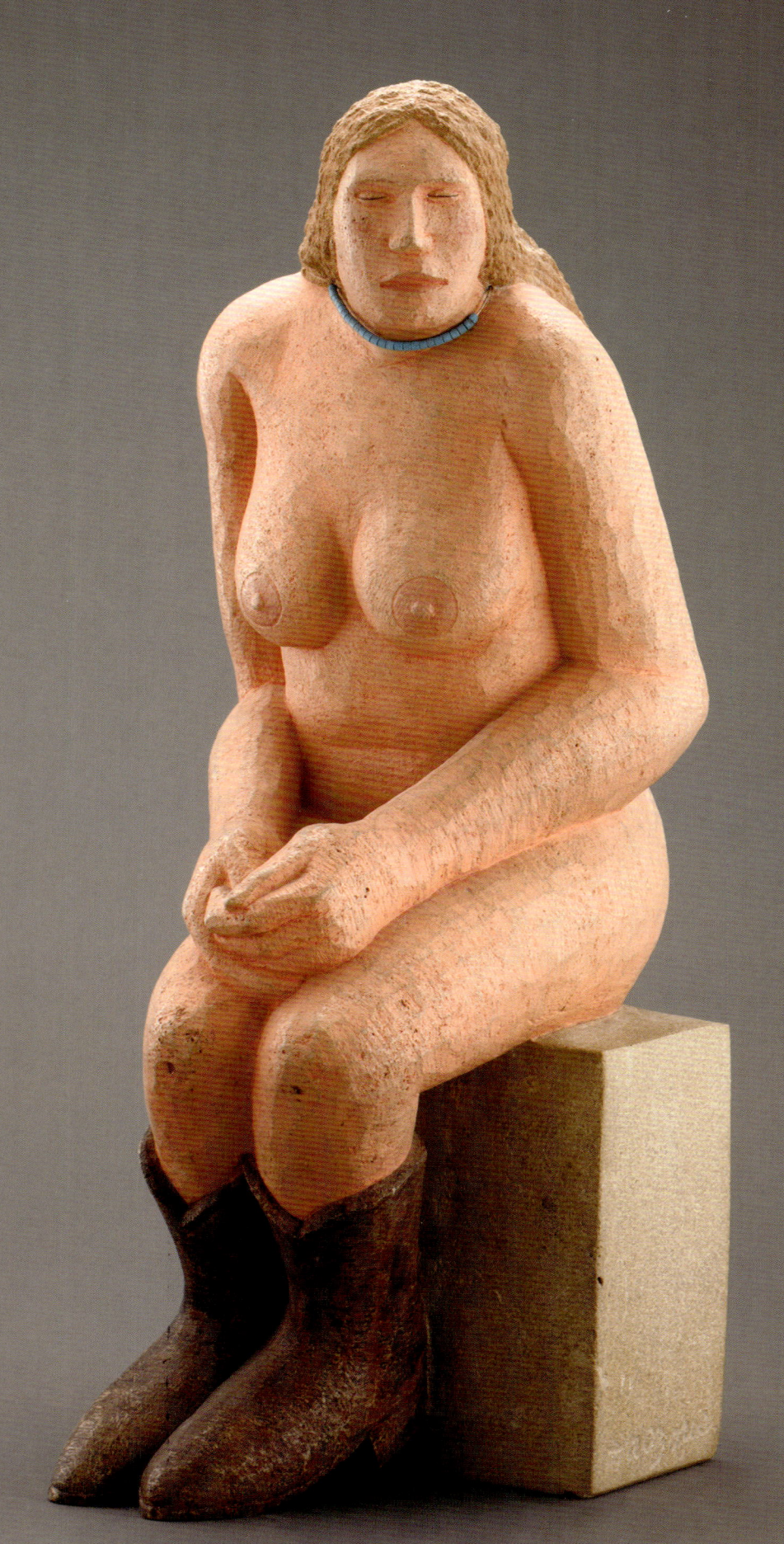

6 | Outside the Frame

THREE-DIMENSIONAL ART

Christina E. Burke

IN ADDITION TO PAINTINGS AND KACHINAS, the Bialac Collection boasts a significant group of nearly six hundred three-dimensional works of art created by Native artists throughout the twentieth century. Included among these are pieces by such luminaries as Mary Juan (Maricopa), Allan Houser (Apache), and Charles Loloma (Hopi). Although most of these works are from the southwestern United States, there are also important pieces from the Southeast, Northwest Coast, Arctic, and other areas. The group is notable for the high quality and incredible diversity of the art, which speaks to the craftsmanship and creativity of the artists as well as to the eye of the collector. The collection includes rattles, jewelry, ceramic vessels and figures, sculpture, baskets, carved fetishes, textiles, and other objects such as drums, flutes, fans, masks, toys, and even coin banks. What binds these divergent pieces together is that they are firmly rooted in the indigenous community—and in its cultural, religious, and artistic traditions—from which their makers came. For the purposes of this chapter, the work is divided into two groups. The first includes rattles, baskets, ceramic vessels, and textiles, and the second, ceramic figures, sculpture,

PLATE 140

ROBERT HAOZOUS

U.S., Chiricahua Apache/
Navajo, b. 1943

Nude with Cowboy Boots, n.d.

Limestone, paint, turquoise,

19½ x 6⅓ x 9 in.

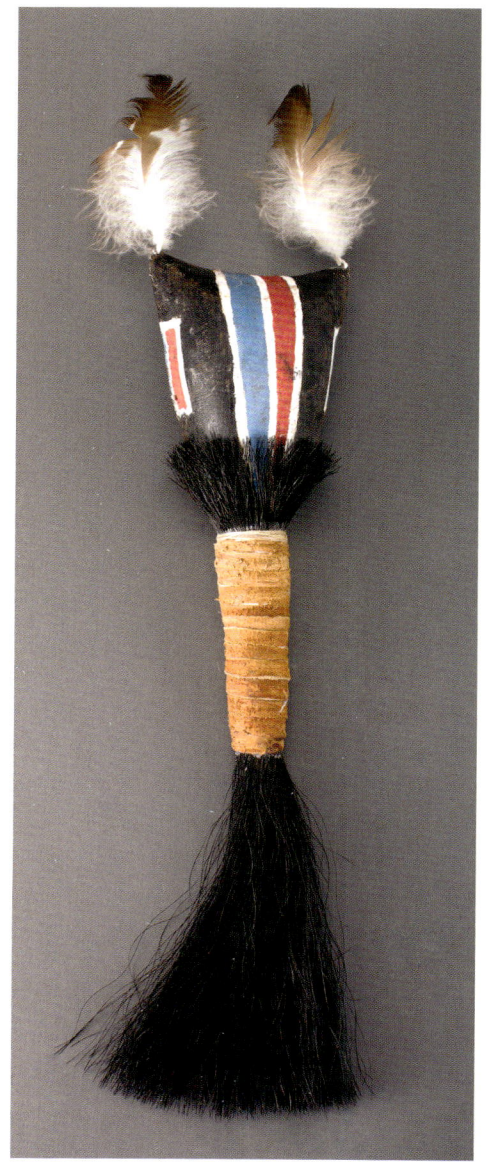

and jewelry. Although both groups feature traditional and contemporary styles, the former is generally more traditional in both material and form. The latter group is more figurative, regardless of media.

For Native people, rattles are more than just instruments used to create music for entertainment; they are an integral part of ceremonial life. Among the Pueblos of the Southwest, decorated gourd rattles are essential to the masked kachina dances that define their annual ritual cycle. This tradition is reflected in the more than ninety rattles in the Bialac Collection, including those with such kachina images as Sun Face, Pot Carrier, and Hemis.[1] The Sun Face (Dawa, or Tawa) is a powerful kachina who brings warmth and light and playfulness. The face is often ringed with flower petals or feathers emanating as rays do from the sun. The Pot Carrier, who brings water, is identified by the red-rimmed outline of a white handprint set against the black background of the face. The Hemis rattle features not only painted decoration, but also a tableta headdress carved from wood and decorated with paint and feathers. The tableta is worn by dancers during the Home Dance, when kachinas leave the human world of the Pueblo and return to their home in the mountains.

Unlike the Pueblo rattles made of hollow gourds, a Navajo rattle in the collection (plate 141) is formed from rawhide attached to a wood handle and decorated. Its aesthetic power is in its simplicity of construction and design, as it is marked with bold stripes of black, blue, and red, outlined in white. Such rattles are used in sings, ceremonies conducted to restore the health and well-being of an individual, family, or community as a whole. Sings are led by religious leaders who have memorized extensive complex chants, accompanied by rattles, to bring blessings or to restore harmony to the community.

Other rattles are less traditional, including a ceramic piece (plate 146) by Cherokee artist Bill Glass and a Hopi coiled basketry rattle (plate 144) by Annabelle Nequatewa. The ceramic piece is characteristic of Glass's style, known for its bold, graphic images—in this case an eagle head—created with glazes. The basketry rattle is a type of weaving from the Hopi community Second Mesa.[2] This work is created from a variety of materials, including coils of beargrass wrapped with dyed strands of yucca, which are here woven to create a zigzag pattern in black and red.

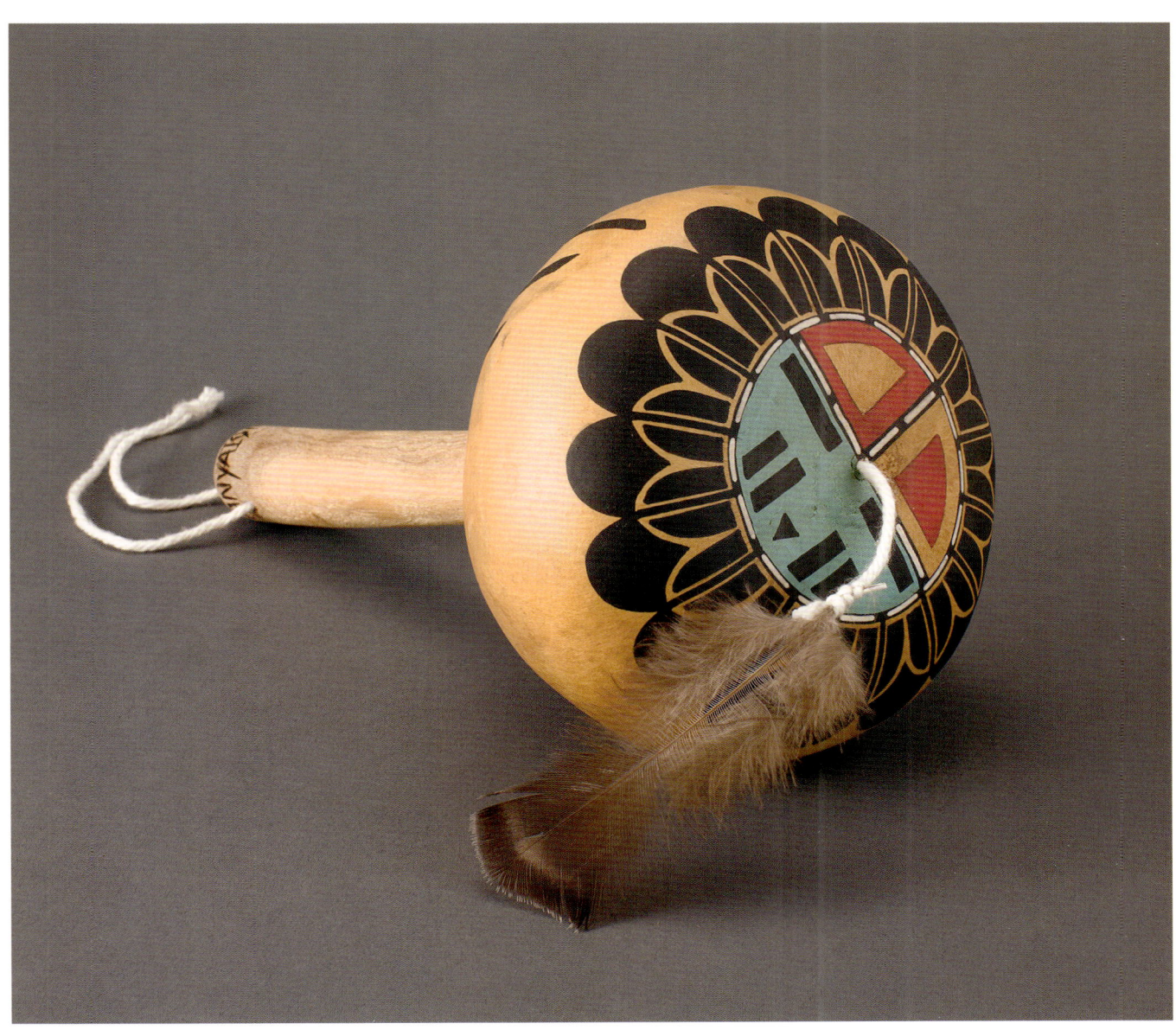

PLATE 142

ADKIN KUWANYAIOMA

U.S., Hopi Pueblo, b. 1960

Rattle (Sun Face), late twentieth century

Gourd, paint, feathers, string, and wood, 8½ in.

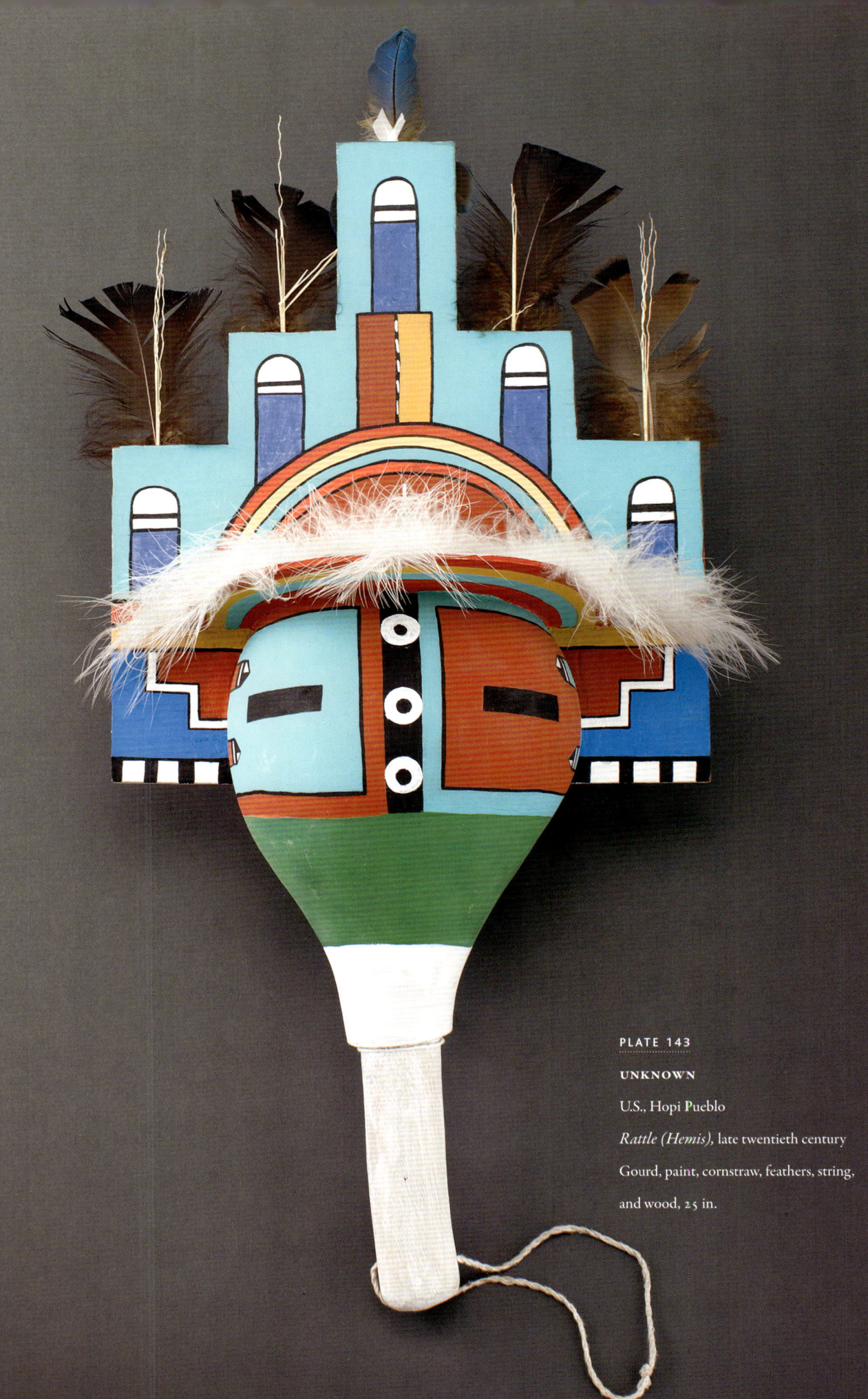

PLATE 143

UNKNOWN

U.S., Hopi Pueblo

Rattle (Hemis), late twentieth century

Gourd, paint, cornstraw, feathers, string,

and wood, 25 in.

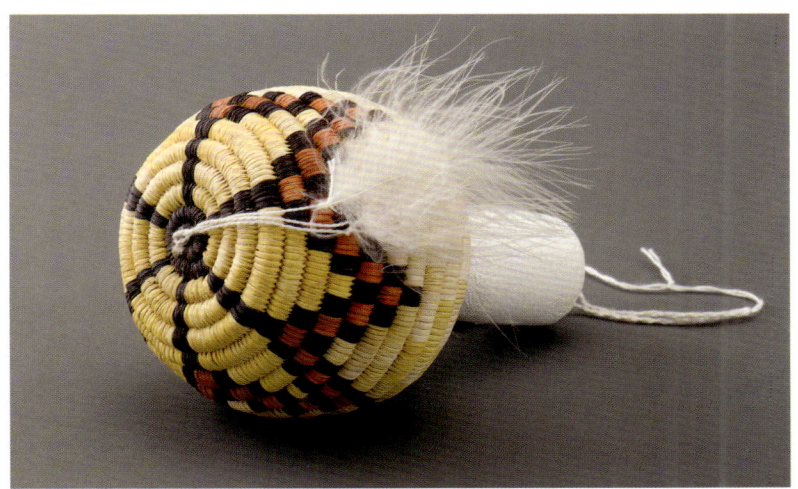

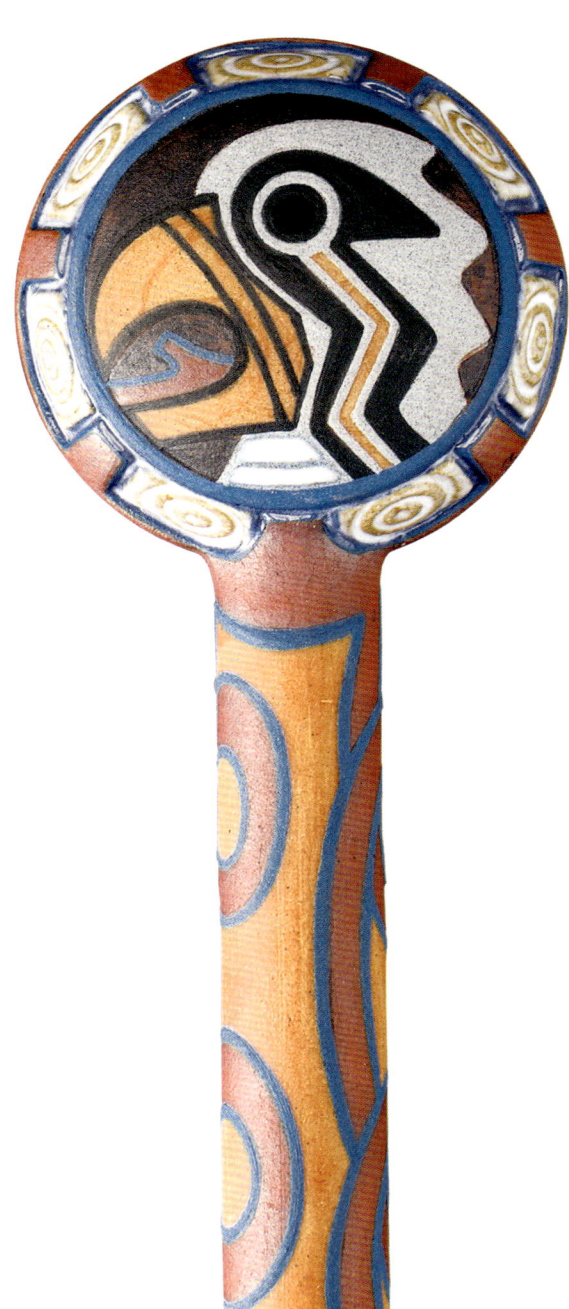

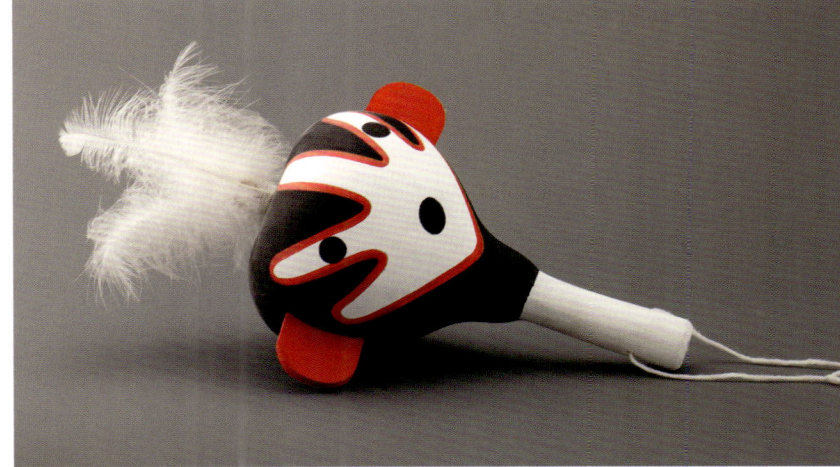

This type of woven artistry is seen in both basketry and textiles, which feature examples of distinctive cultural styles using particular materials, forms, and designs. Among the nearly thirty baskets are a Hopi wicker plaque characteristic of pieces from Third Mesa, as well as a coiled basket with kachinas (plate 151), by Joyce Ann Saufkie, which, like the coiled rattle, is from Second Mesa. Although similar in form and use, these baskets differ in both materials and weaving techniques. Wicker plaques are plaited with a simple weave of warp binding together weft. Coiled basketry involves bundling together a cylinder of materials, like beargrass, which is then wrapped and sewn onto existing coils with strands of yucca. One of the remarkable aspects of this and other pictorial baskets is that the imagery is sewn into the piece during construction and not added afterward. This means that the artist must plan ahead and be mindful of the details of color, pattern, and design as she weaves the piece, especially one as complex as this, which boasts geometric designs, animals, and multicolored kachina figures, including Crow Mother.

Two other baskets are wonderful examples of figurative pieces. The *Lidded Turkey Effigy Basket* is typical of those made for non-Native collectors by Coushatta weavers from the Southeast (Alabama and Louisiana). Constructed of pinecone petals and raffia, these animal figures became very popular in the 1940s and '50s.[3] Another figurative basket is *Horsehair Coiled Basket* (Mouse). Miniature baskets of horsehair are another popular item among collectors, who prize them for the extreme attention to detail required to work with such fine material.

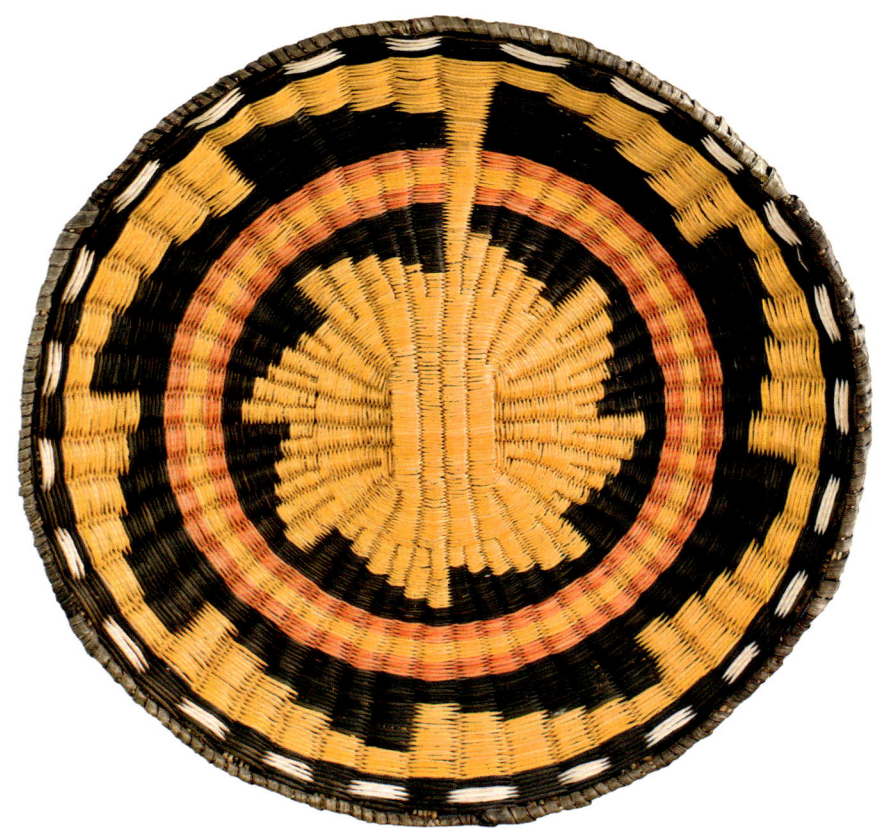

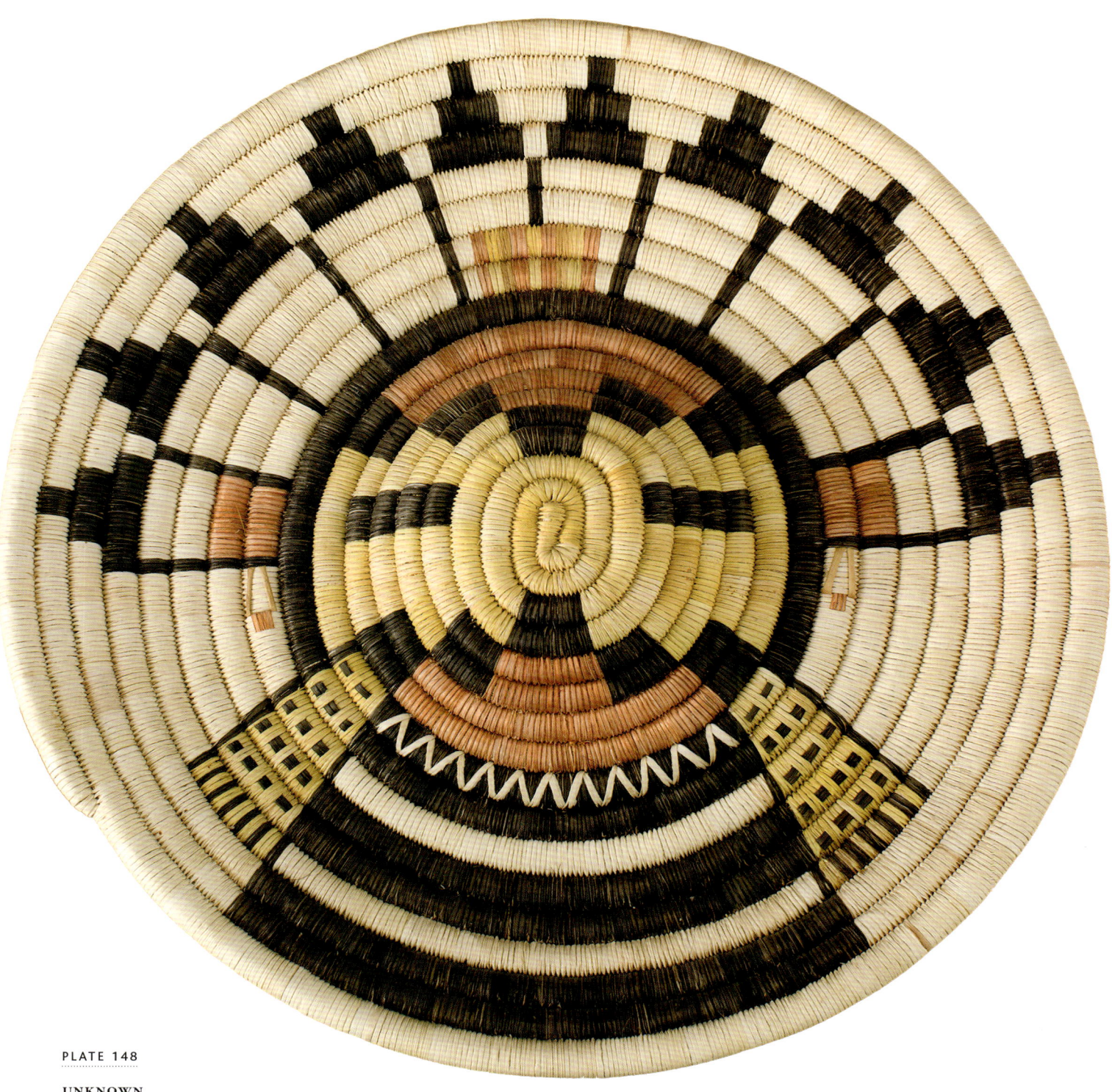

PLATE 148

UNKNOWN

U.S., Hopi Pueblo

Coiled Plaque with Katsina Face, c. 1960s

Natural, dyed, and bleached yucca on beargrass, 1½ × 13 in.

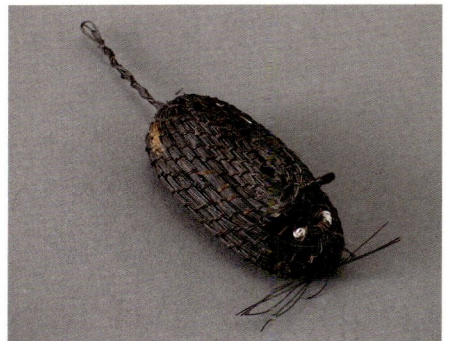

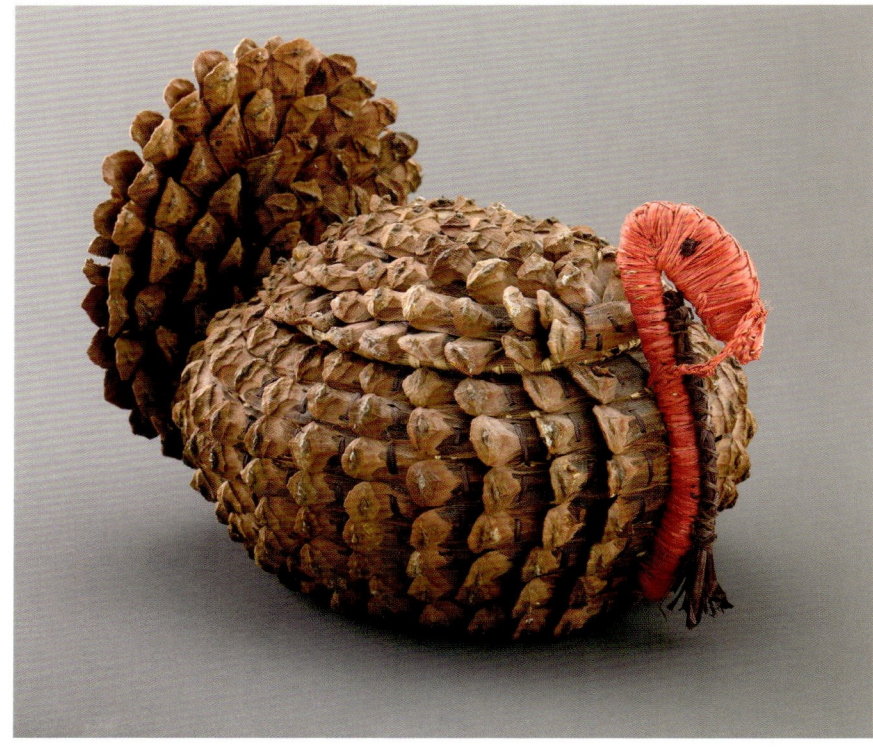

Weaving of cotton cloth is a long tradition in the Southwest, but when the Spanish brought sheep to the New World, loom weaving of wool quickly became an important art form for the Navajos.[4] Among the weavings in the Bialac Collection, two in particular stand out as illustrating important styles of Navajo textiles. One is a chief's blanket (plate 152), a traditional style of broad stripes alternating in black, red, and white, so named because these kinds of blankets have always been objects of great prestige for wealthy and powerful people. This is a revival of a Second Phase blanket, originally produced during the mid-nineteenth century.

In contrast to the bold geometric designs of the chief's blanket, a pictorial weaving by Loretta Begay depicts a complex scene with many figures participating in a Yei'bichai dance. During this ceremony, dances are performed and chants sung to restore health and harmony to the community.[5] In the background is the Navajo landscape, marked by majestic mesas, while to the left is a hogan, a traditional eight-sided home. This type of pictorial textile is sought by collectors and museums alike because of the degree of skill required to weave the intricate imagery, and because of the appeal of a particular scene. What makes this piece unique and whimsical are the cars that surround the group of dancers. Such a juxtaposition of traditional ceremony and modern life might seem incongruous, but it documents the contemporary reality for many Native people.

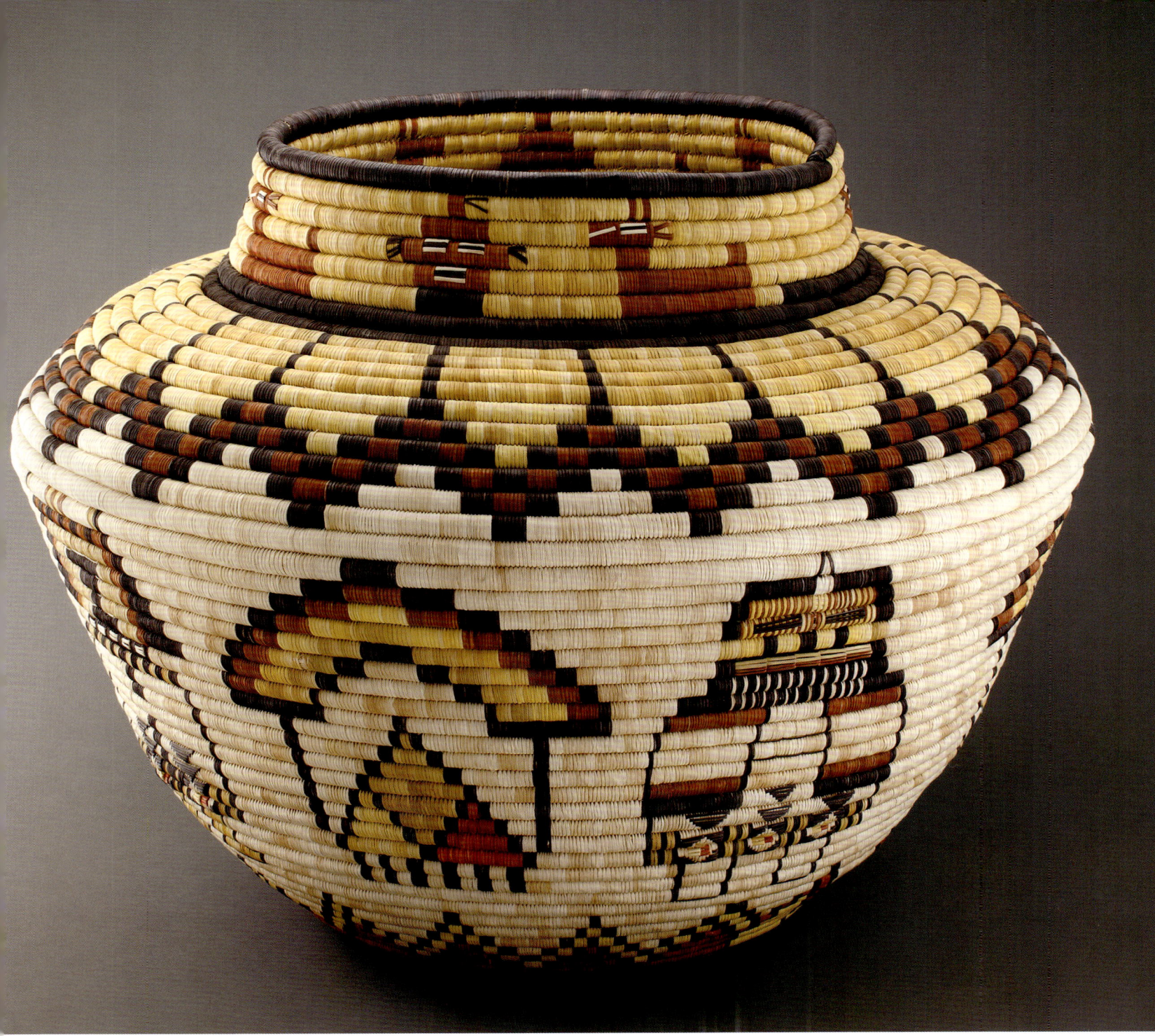

PLATE 151

JOYCE ANN SAUFKIE

U.S., Hopi Pueblo, dates unknown

Coiled Olla Basket with Katsinas, n.d.

Natural, dyed, and bleached, 20 x 25 in.

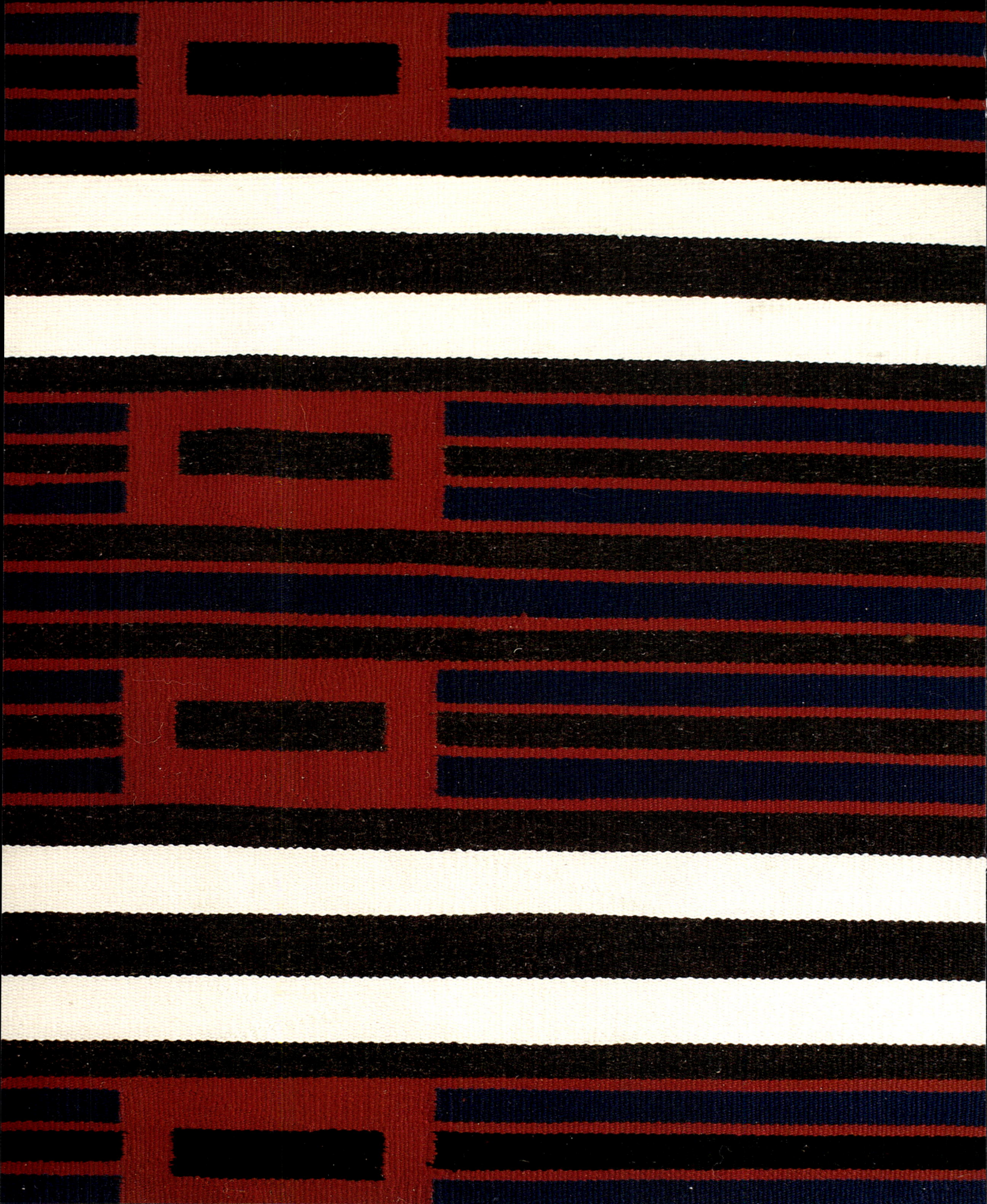

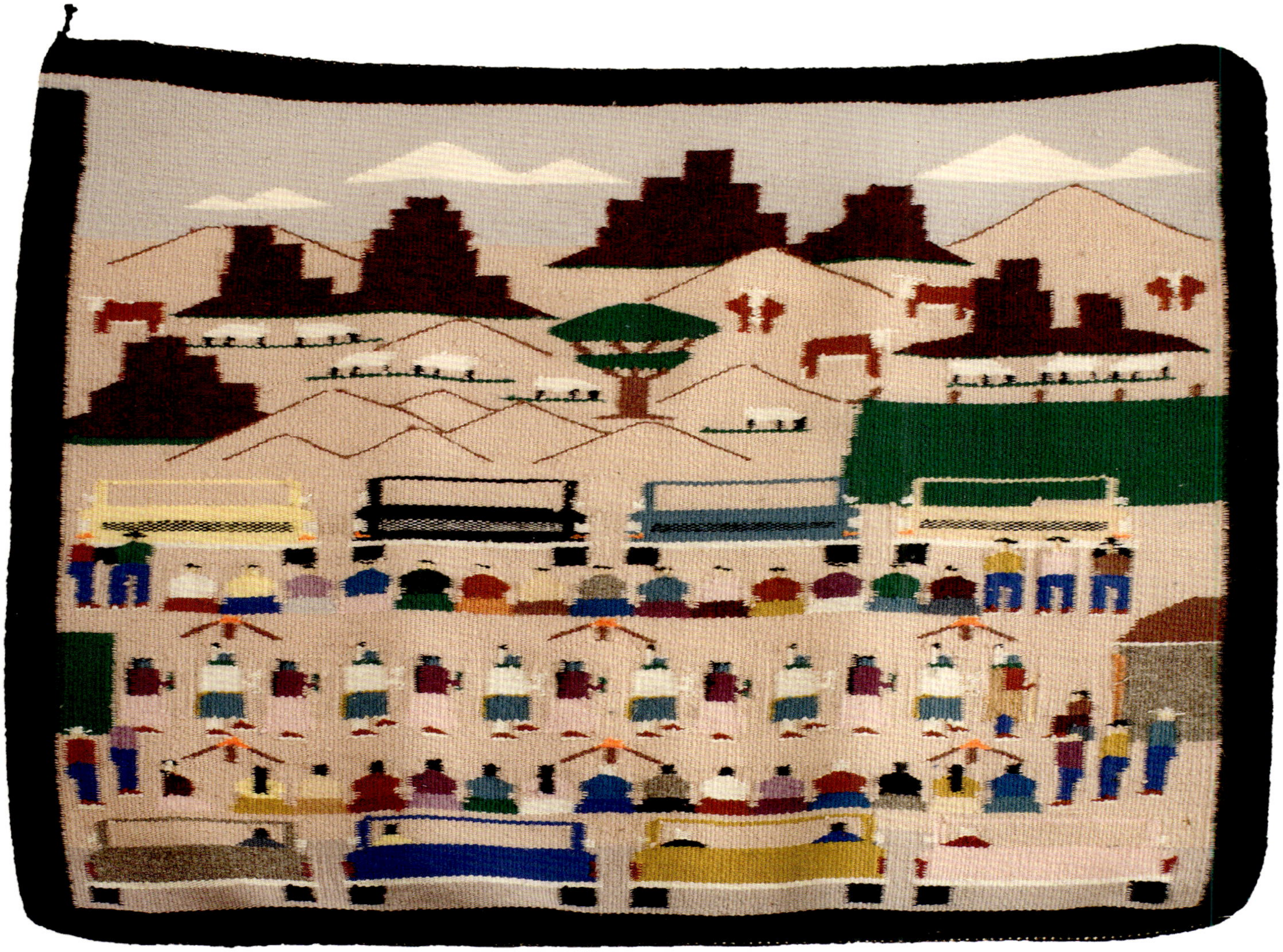

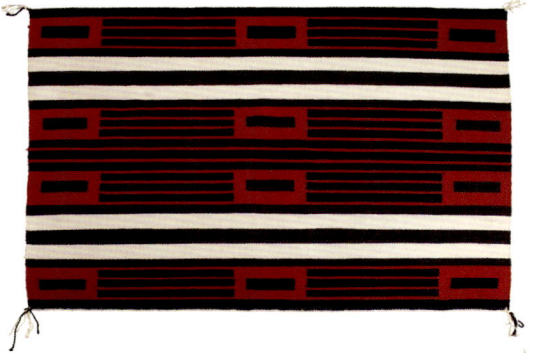

PLATE 152

UNKNOWN

U.S., Navajo

Chief's Blanket, n.d.

Natural and dyed handspun wool,

45½ x 35 in.

PLATE 153

LORETTA BEGAY

U.S., Navajo, dates unknown

Pictorial Weaving, c. 1990s

Natural and dyed wool, 24 x 29 in.

Close to ninety ceramic vessels round out the grouping of traditional three-dimensional arts in the Bialac Collection. Pottery is an ancient art form, and nowhere is this more true than in the Southwest, where tribal ceramic traditions date back centuries. Each Pueblo has a distinctive style of pottery marked by particular forms, decorative techniques, and imagery, created from natural clays found in specific areas, knowledge of which is passed down in families from generation to generation. Indeed, the collection boasts the work of numerous members of the Martinez, Lewis, and Nampeyo families, among many others.[6]

Among the more traditional pots are several outstanding pieces by Mary Juan, a Maricopa potter from southern Arizona, whose work became the standard for her community. This beautiful black-on-red bowl (plate 154) is a perfect example of a hand-built and polished redware bowl, decorated with stepped geometric designs and curvilinear forms painted with mesquite sap. Not only is it a classic piece of Maricopa pottery, but few continue this type of work today, so Juan's piece stands as a testament to a tradition that has not been carried into the twenty-first century. Another example of traditional pottery is a red-on-redware piece made by artist Gilbert Atencio (San Ildefonso), a nephew of potter Maria Martinez. Although best known for his painting, Atencio made pottery and jewelry, too. This vessel is painted with the ever-present Avanyu figure, the mythical feathered serpent who brings rain to the parched desert. In addition to those pots from the Rio Grande pueblos is a stellar example of Hopi pottery by Rachel Sahmie Nampeyo. This large polychrome buffware cylinder is elegantly painted with traditional Hopi stylized bird designs. Its size, shape, and exacting detail define it as a masterpiece of ceramic art.

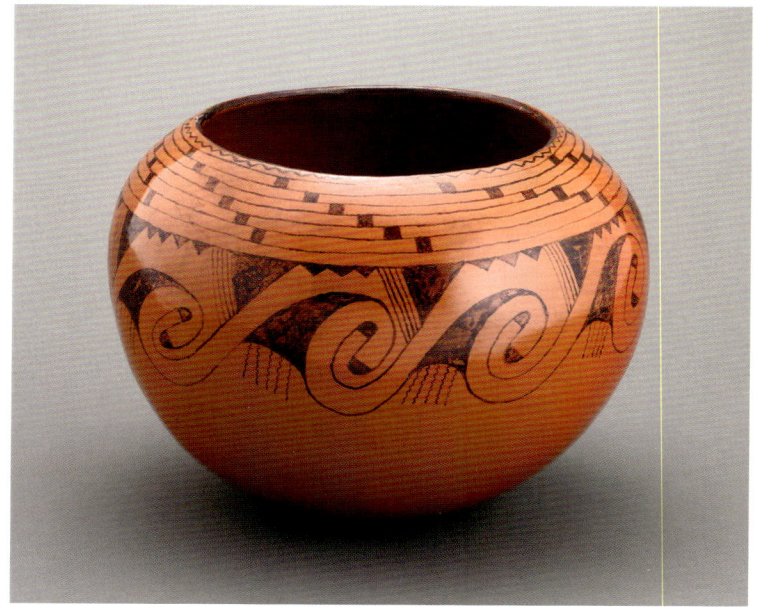

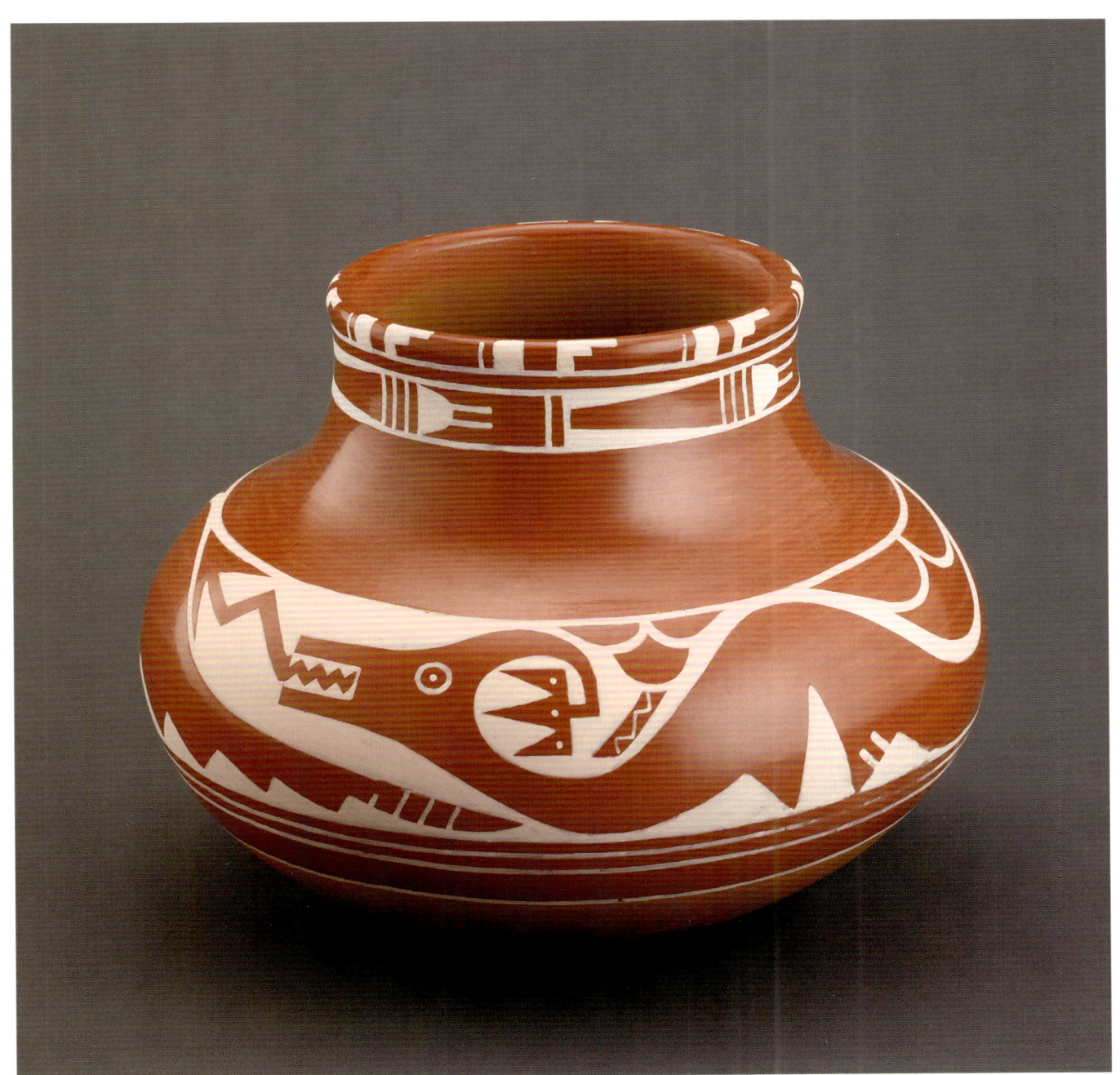

PLATE 155

GILBERT ATENCIO

U.S., San Ildefonso Pueblo, 1930–1995

Red-on-Redware Vessel (Avanyu), 1970s

Earthenware, 7 x 8 in.

PLATE 156

RACHEL SAHMIE NAMPEYO

U.S., Hopi Pueblo, b. 1956

Polychrome Cylinder Vase, c. 1980

Earthenware with mineral/vegetal paints,

17 x 5½ in.

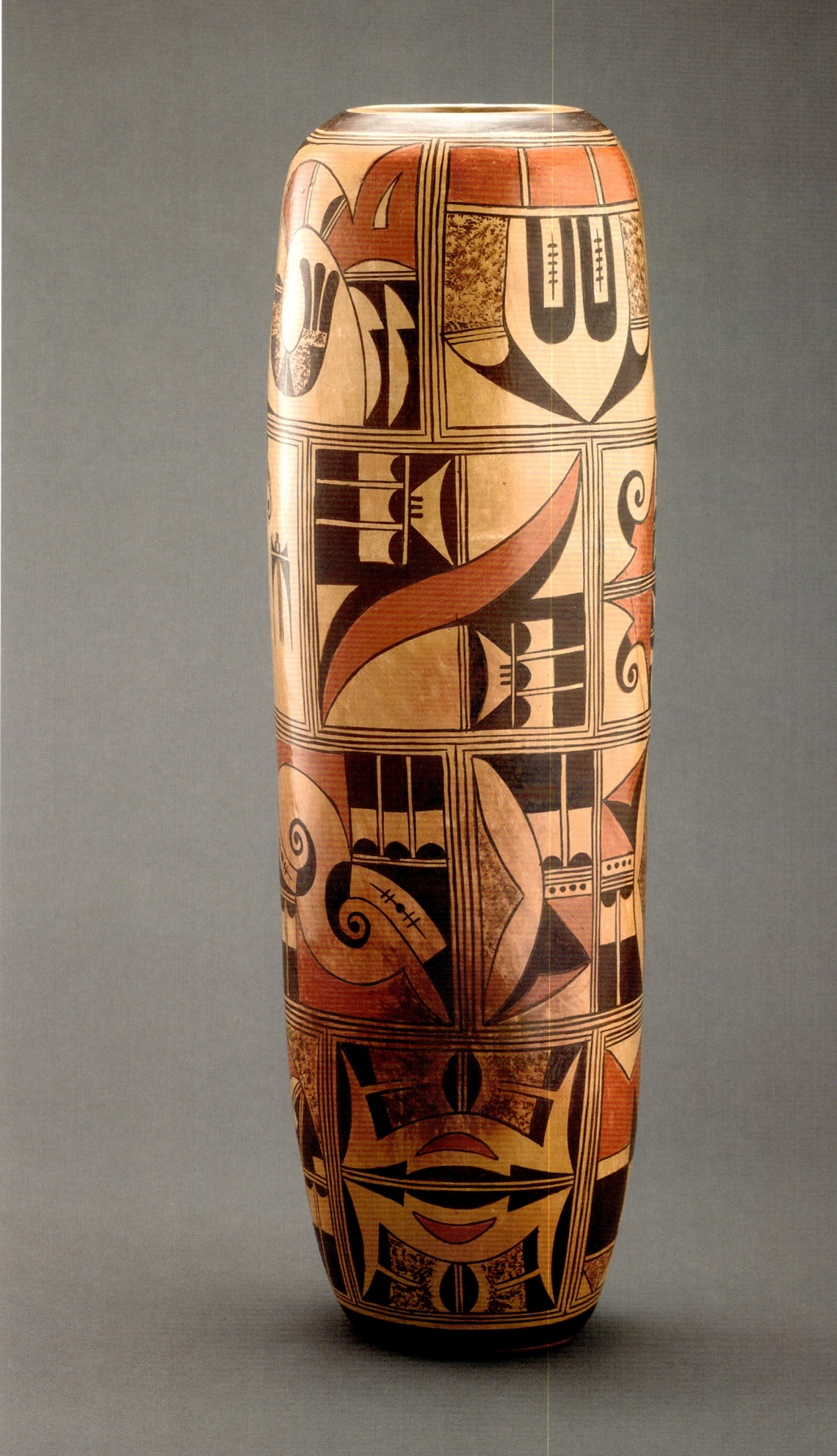

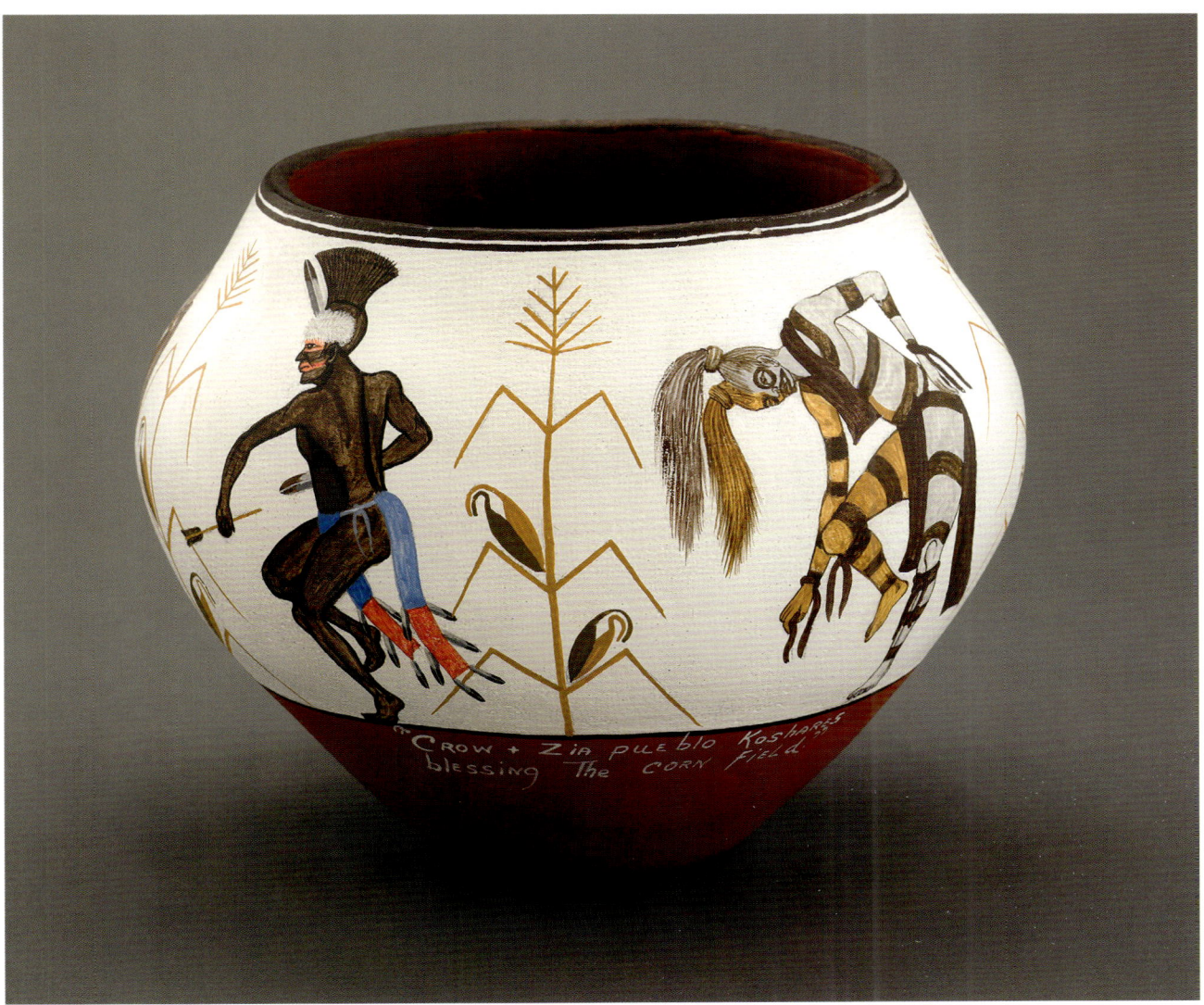

Pieces in contemporary styles are also in abundance. There are several collaborative works by husband-and-wife team Sofia and Rafael Medina (Zia), including a polychrome olla painted with several dancers, including Koshares, or ritual clowns. Although the image is traditional, the materials (acrylic paint) and realistic style are quite contemporary. Work by Santa Clara artist Tammy Garcia offers a different style of decoration altogether. Her piece is a redware seed pot with deeply carved bird designs. What is so striking is the contrast between the highly polished surface and the matte finish of the carved recesses. This type of bold imagery is typical of Santa Clara ceramics, but the style is distinctive to Garcia. In addition to pottery, she is now translating such designs into bronze sculpture.

PLATE 157

SOFIA AND RAFAEL MEDINA

U.S. Zia Pueblo, Sofia: b. 1932;
Rafael: 1929–1998

Polychrome Jar/Olla
with Dancers, 1971

Earthenware and acrylic paint,
7 x 8 in.

PLATE 158

TAMMY GARCIA

U.S., Santa Clara Pueblo, b. 1969

Carved Redware Seed Jar, n.d.

Earthenware, 3 x 4½ in.

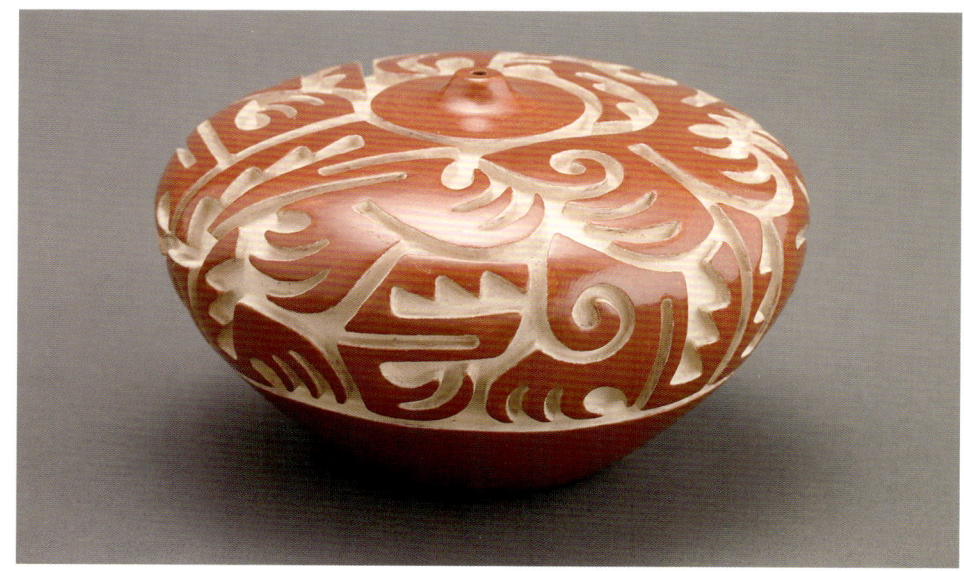

The ceramic figures in the collection offer even more diversity of material and style. Among the more traditional pieces is one by Annie Fields (Mojave), whose female figure (plate 162) is formed and painted with native clays. The figure is then adorned with clothing and a classic Mojave woven bead collar to further identify her with her community in western Arizona. Michael Kanteena (Laguna) draws on the past but brings it into the present with his long-necked deer figure. The style is inspired by images found on ancient Mimbres pottery, recognizable for its graphic human and animal figures painted in black and white. In this piece, Kanteena brings that prehistoric Flat Style to life by adding a third dimension to its form. Tony Da's beautiful bear figure shows the legacy of his grandmother, Maria Martinez, and father, Popovi Da, as well as his own unique style. Here, he highlights textures by carving and etching the piece, adding embellishments of inlaid turquoise. And for something completely different—the work of Anita Fields (Osage) is characterized by stylized forms with matte finishes in contrasting black and white.

These figures are a perfect transition to discussion of the three dozen sculptures in the Bialac Collection, which encompass many materials—from stone to bronze to ceramics—created by artists from across North America. They include traditional stone carvings by Canadian Inuit artist David Ikutaaq, whose female figure is a wonderful example of work from the Arctic. The clean lines and solid body of the figure are distinctively northern, as is the material (basalt).[7] Also from the north are sculptures in glass and in wood by Preston Singletary (Tlingit) and John Hoover (Aleut), respectively. Singletary is known for his unique execution of Northwest Coast material culture in glass, which he uses to create boxes, masks, and rattles, which were historically carved from wood.

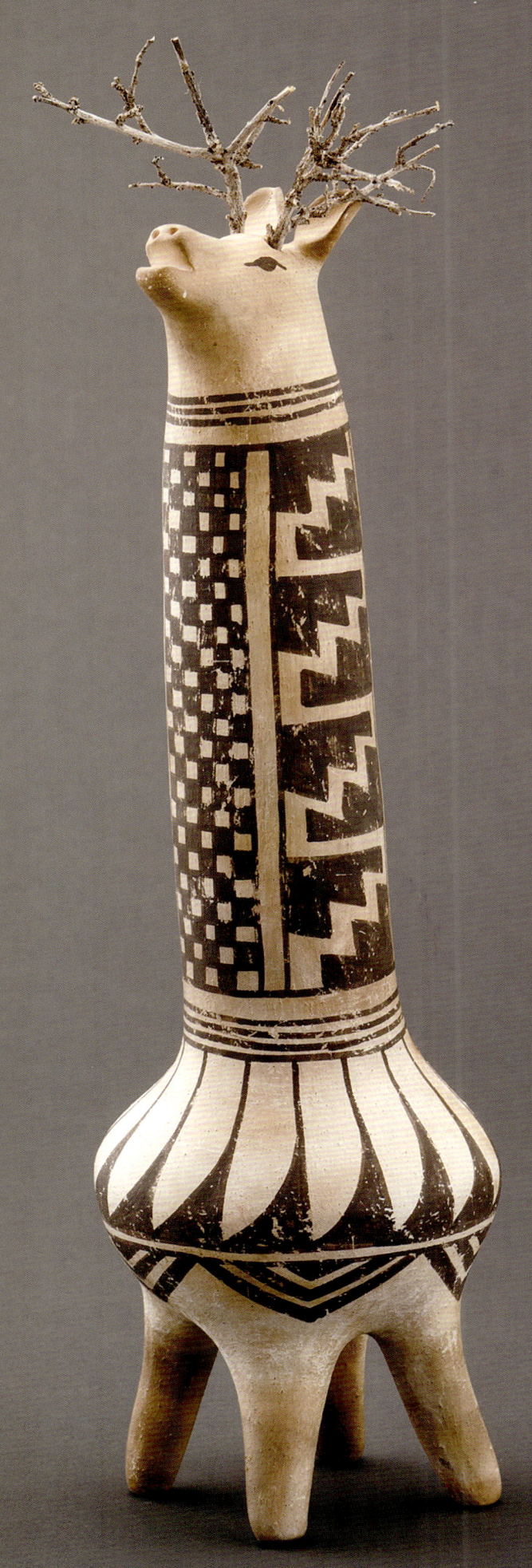

PLATE 159

MICHAEL KANTEENA

U.S., Laguna Pueblo, b. 1959

Long-necked Mimbres Deer Figure, 2009

Black-on-white earthenware, 11 x 3¼ in.

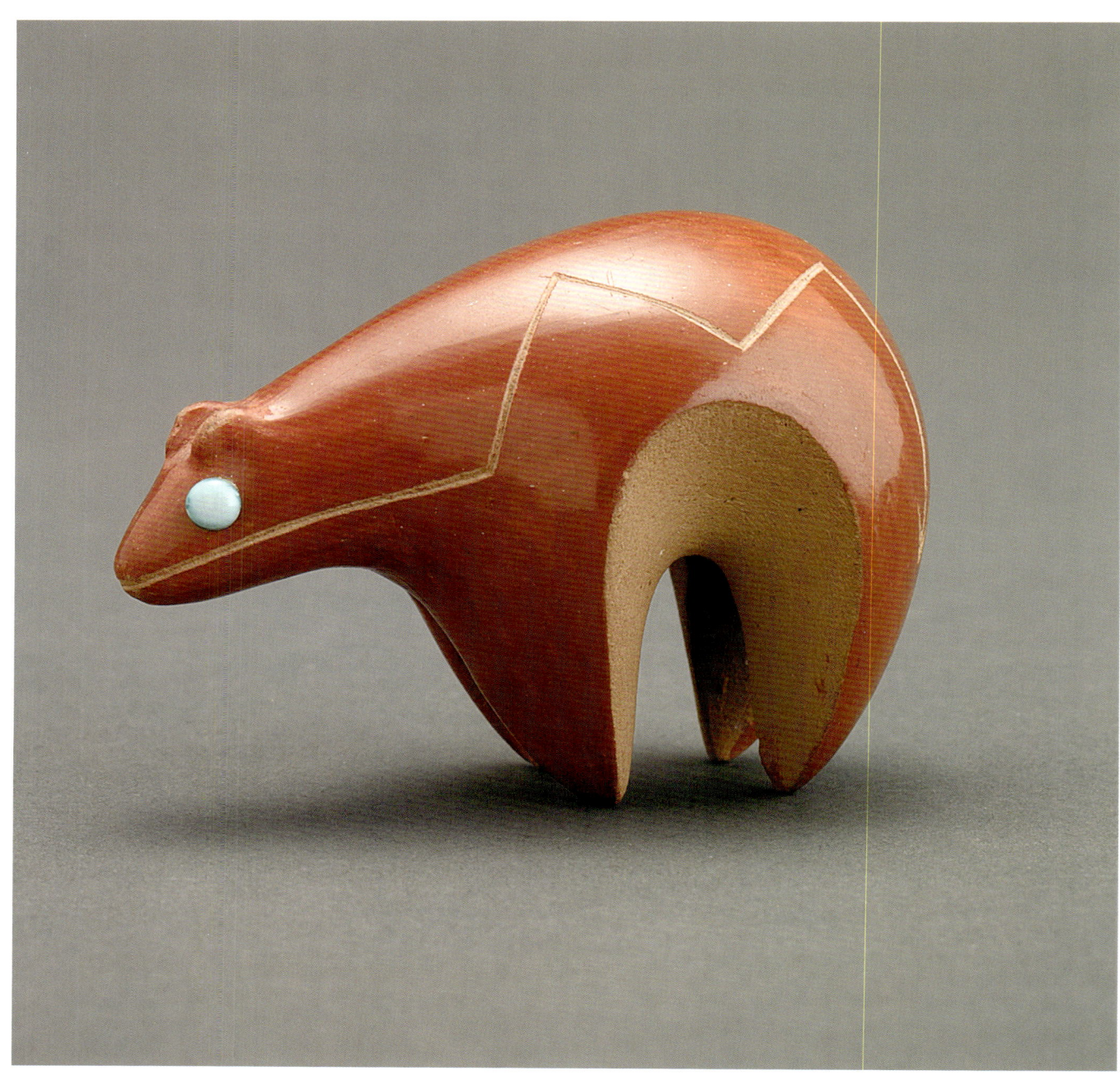

PLATE 160

ANTHONY EDWARD "TONY" DA

U.S., San Ildefonso Pueblo, 1921–1971

Polished Red Bear (with Heartline), 1970s

Earthenware with turquoise, 1¾ x 2⅝ x 1½ in.

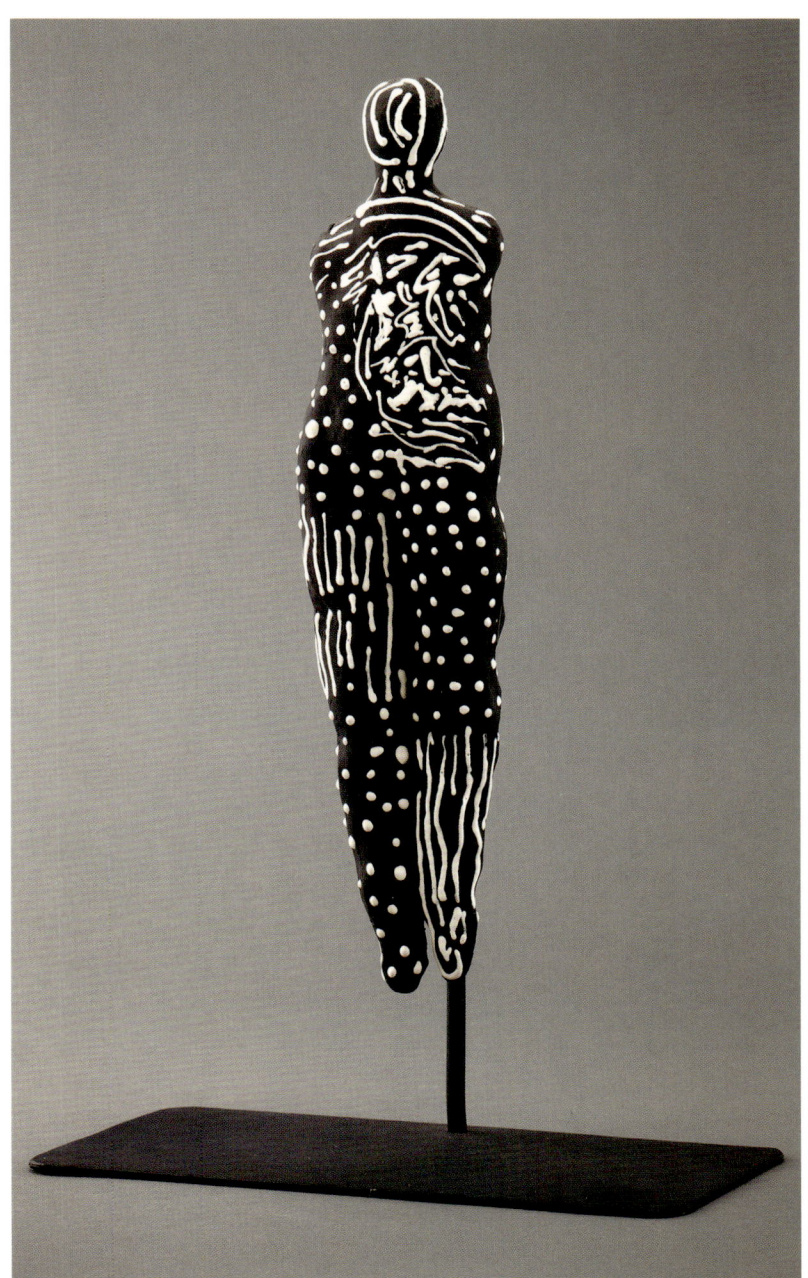

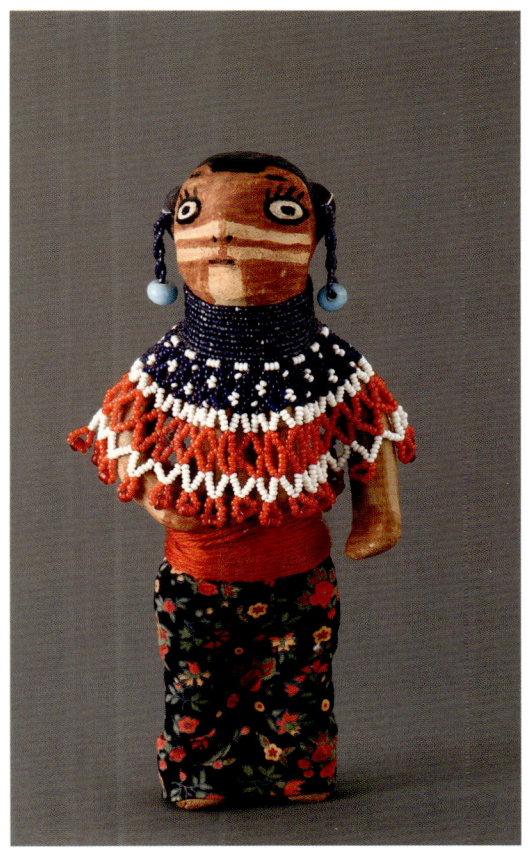

PLATE 162

ANNIE FIELDS

U.S., Mojave, 1884–1971

Female Ceramic Mojave
Figure, c. 1960

Earthenware with oxides,

cloth, and beads, 8 in.

PLATE 161

ANITA FIELDS

U.S., Osage/Muskogee (Creek), b. 1951

Clay Figure I, 2009

Earthenware, oxides, and slip, 12½ × 3 × 1¾ in.

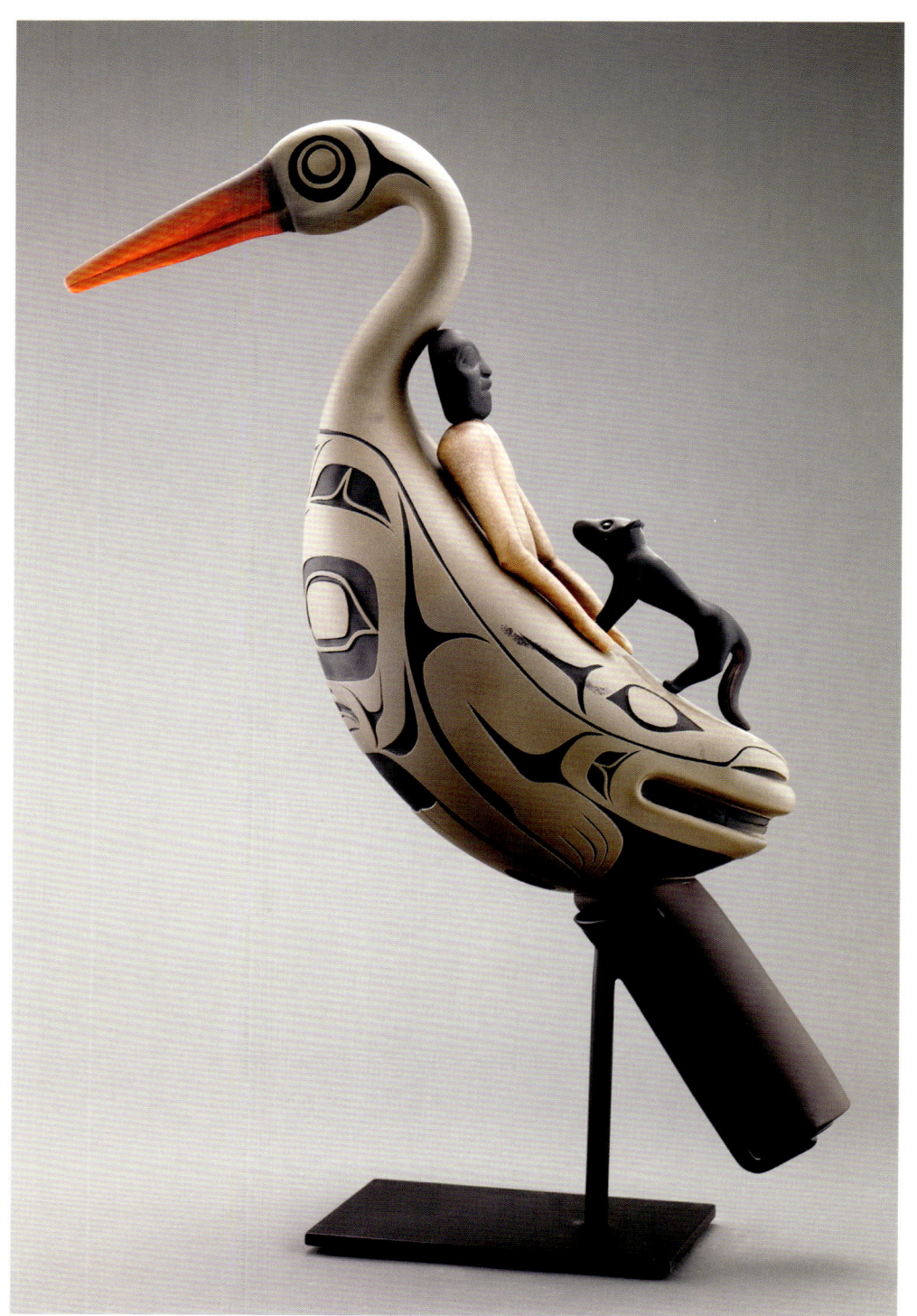

PLATE 163

PRESTON SINGLETARY

U.S., Tlingit, b. 1963

Oystercatcher Rattle, 2006

Blown, fabricated, and

etched glass, 22 x 15½ x 6½ in.

PLATE 164

DAVID IKUTAAQ

Canada, Inuit, 1924–1984

Standing Woman, n.d.

Basalt, 8½ x 6¾ x 6¼ in.

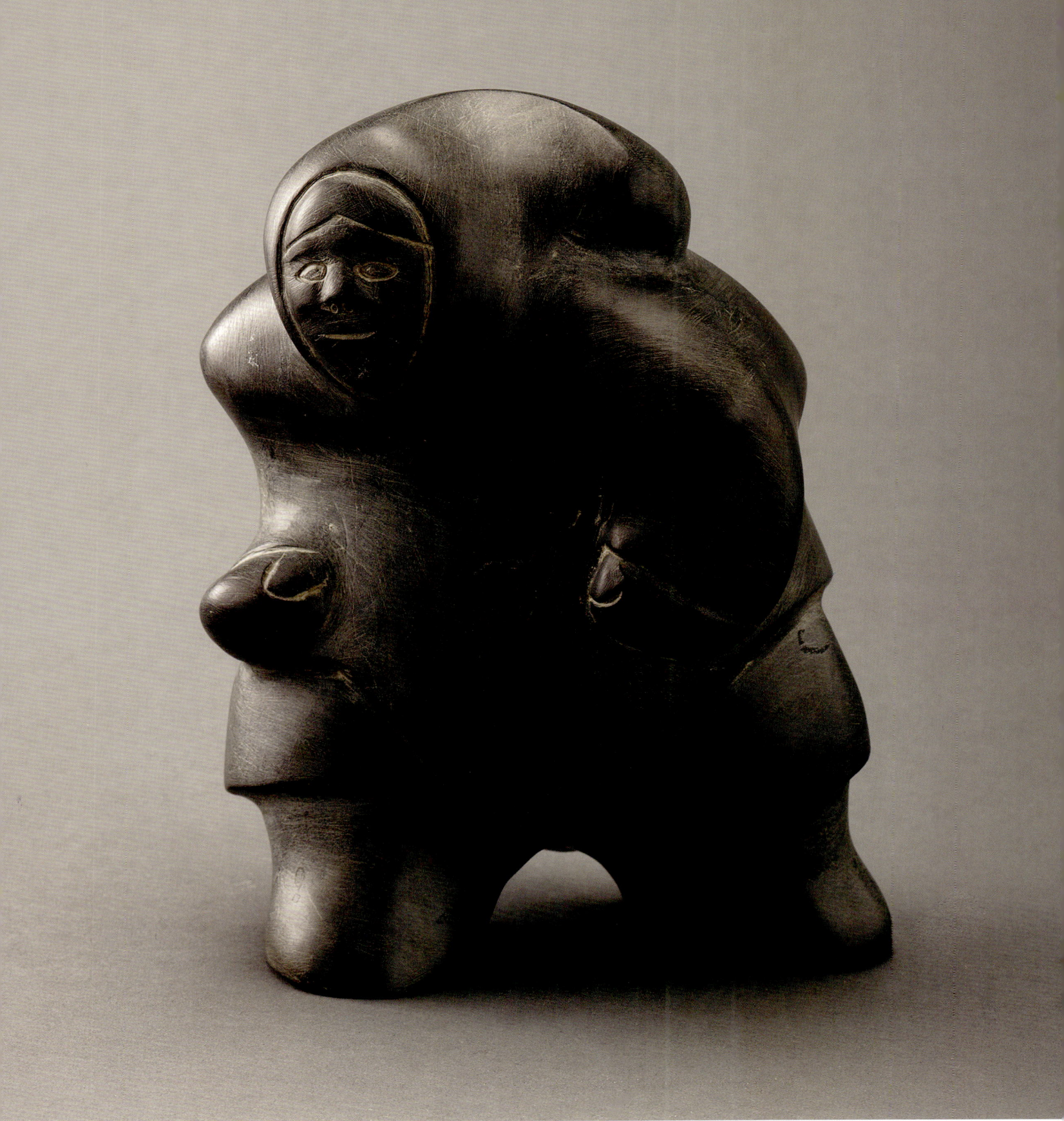

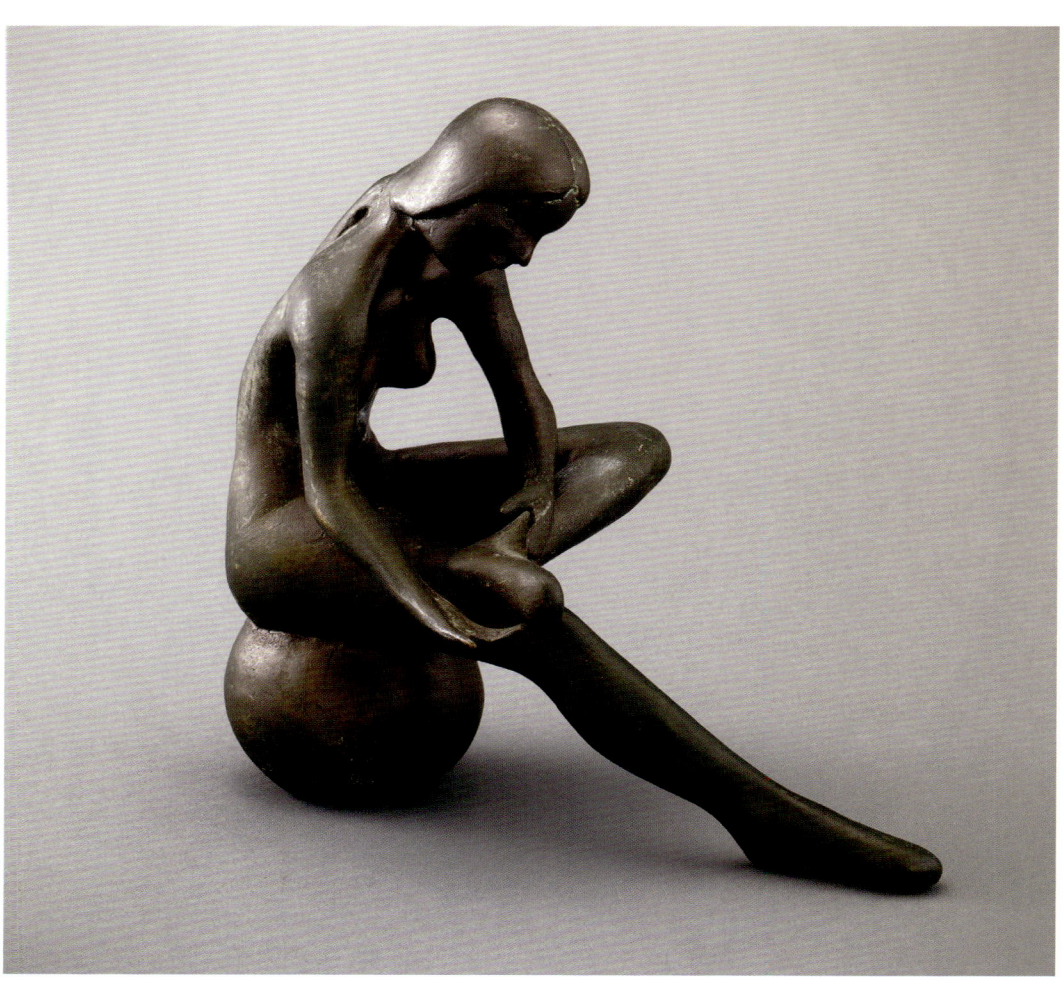

Aleut artist John Hoover translated traditional stories and aesthetics into contemporary sculpture. In *Shaman Catching a Soul,* he carves cedar into a triptych that opens to reveal sinuous elongated figures, illustrating the story of a shaman who travels to the spirit world to retrieve a soul that has become dissociated from its body. Allan Houser, the world-famous Apache sculptor, has created a classic image of a gaan, or mountain spirit dancer.[8]

Not all the sculptures in the collection are of rituals or ceremonial objects, however. Santa Clara artist Michael Naranjo has sculpted a bronze figure engaged in a daily and intimate ritual of bathing, titled *Morning.* And Robert Haozous (Apache), son of Allan Houser, turns on the humor with his *Nude with Cowboy Boots* (n.d., plate 140). This limestone sculpture depicts a seated woman who is naked except for her turquoise necklace and cowboy boots. Finally, Roxanne Swentzell (Santa Clara) works in clay to create her spirited figure, who is escaping her everyday life by reading a book.

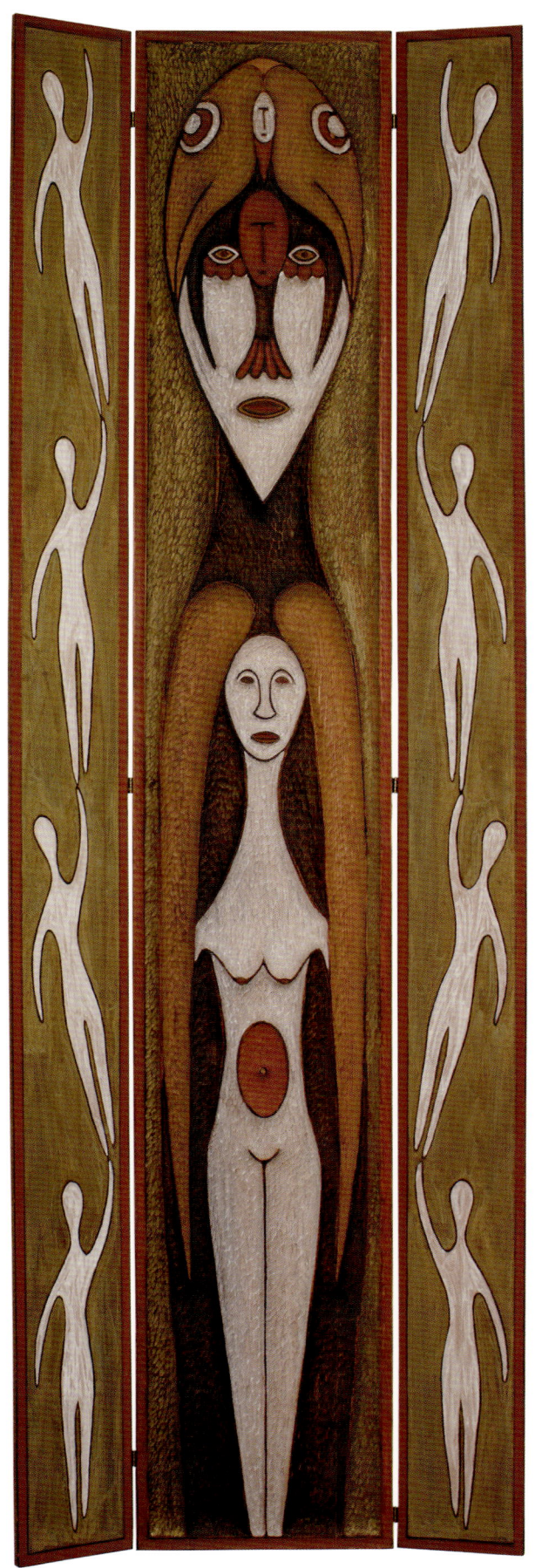
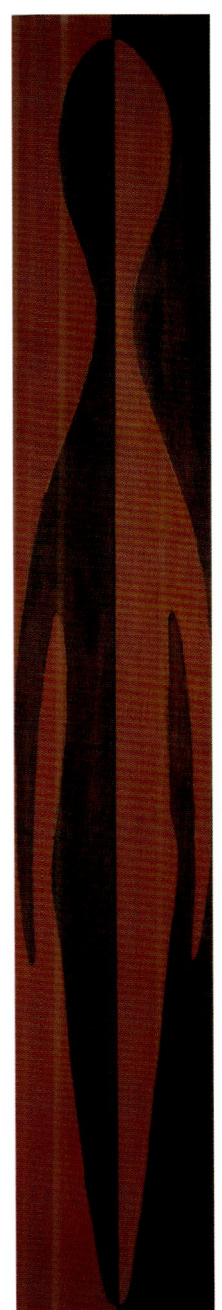

PLATE 166

JOHN HOOVER

U.S., Aleut, 1919–2011

Shaman Catching a Soul, 1978

Cedar and stain, 71½ x 23¾ in.

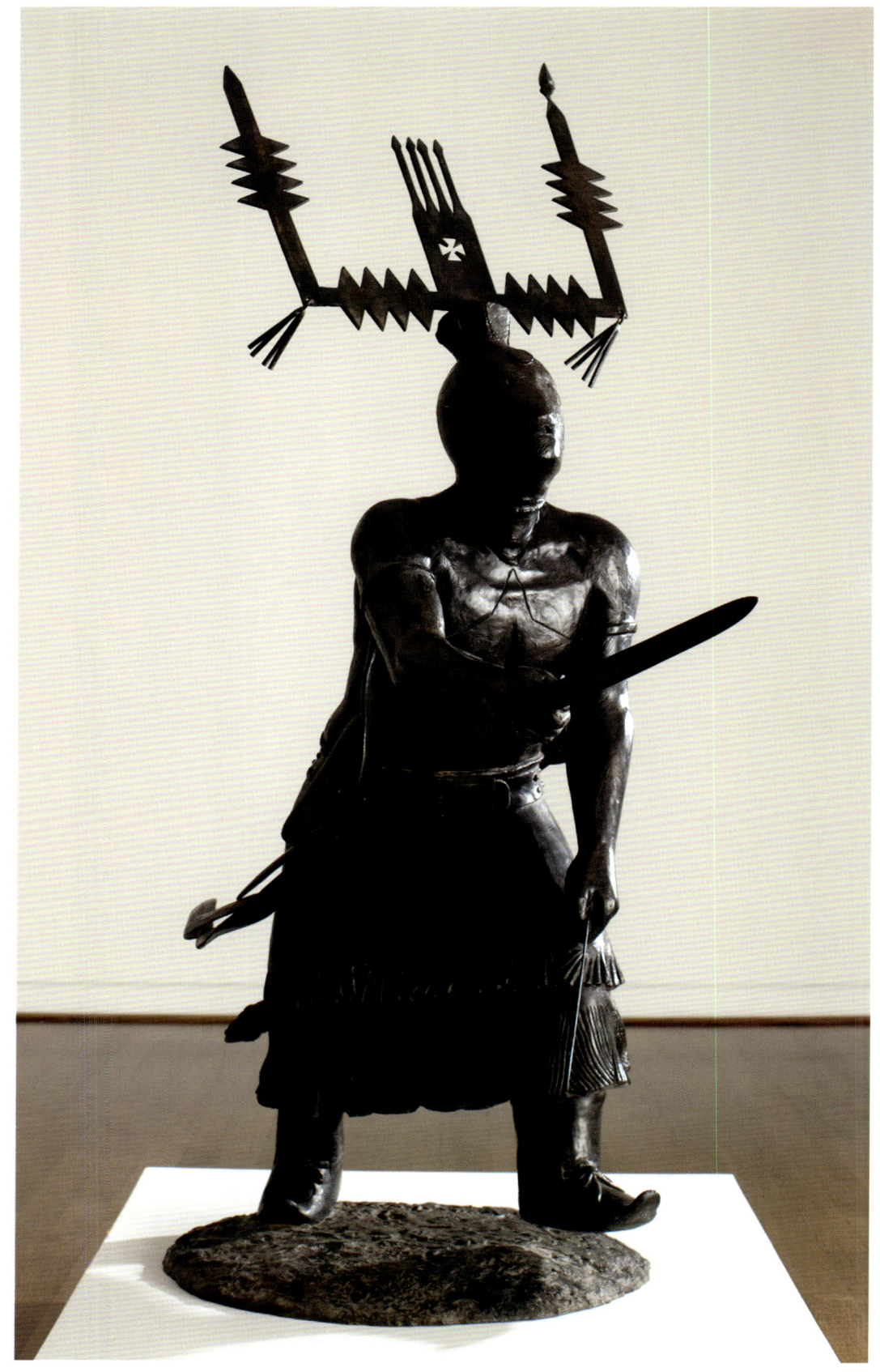

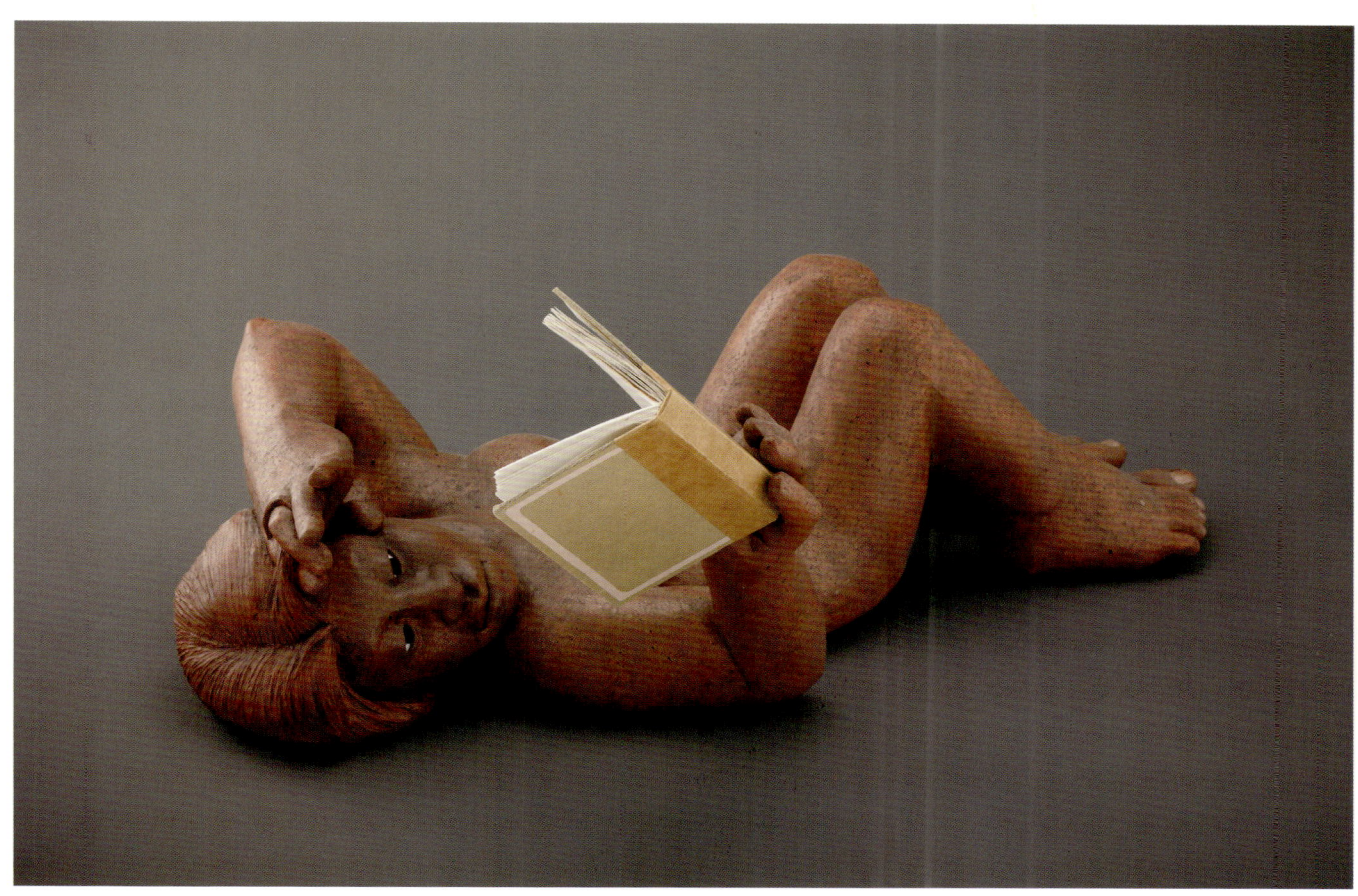

PLATE 167

ALLAN HOUSER

U.S., Chiricahua Apache, 1919–1994

Dance of the Mountain Spirits I, 1989

Cast bronze, 65½ x 56 x 26 in.

© Chiinde LLC

PLATE 168

ROXANNE SWENTZELL

U.S., Santa Clara Pueblo, b. 1962

Another World, n.d.

Earthenware with oxides and paper, 10½ x 24 x 16 in.

The last category, and one of the largest, is jewelry and carved fetishes. This group also includes both classic examples of tribally specific techniques and imagery (like the Navajo squash blossom necklace) as well as contemporary and even abstract interpretations of these traditions.[9] Many pieces depict such Pueblo kachinas as Shalako, Knifewing, and Koshare.[10] Others have realistic images of animals and the natural world, such as the night sky.[11] Figurative details in these intricate pieces are achieved with fine lapidary work using various materials (stone, shell, coral, etc.) set in complex inlay to create an image.

Jewelers use various techniques, including casting and overlay, to create more abstract pieces. Examples of such bold design include a chiseled buckle by Navajo jeweler Gibson Nez, a tufa-cast bracelet by Larry Golsh (Pala Mission), and an overlay buckle by Hopi artist Michael Kabotie. Other jewelers use unique styles of inlay to add the dimension of color to their compositions, as in rings by two Hopi jewelers, Roger Tsabetsaye and Charles Loloma. The former features turquoise, coral, and jet, which have been cut and incised to create a miniature abstract composition. The latter piece by master jeweler Loloma is a classic example of his unique inlay style. The piece is created by shaping elongated slivers of stone, shell, wood, and ivory set side by side.[12]

The Bialac Collection illustrates an array of artistic traditions and the ever-changing styles of three-dimensional Native art. From rattles used in ceremonies and baskets and pottery made with ancient techniques and designs, to bronze and glass sculptures created as art for art's sake, the work demonstrates the remarkable creativity of artists from across North America.

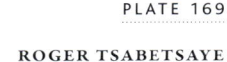

PLATE 169

ROGER TSABETSAYE

U.S., Zuni Pueblo, b. 1941

Ring (Mosaic—Inlay), 1970s

Sterling silver, turquoise, coral, and jet, ¾ x 1 in.

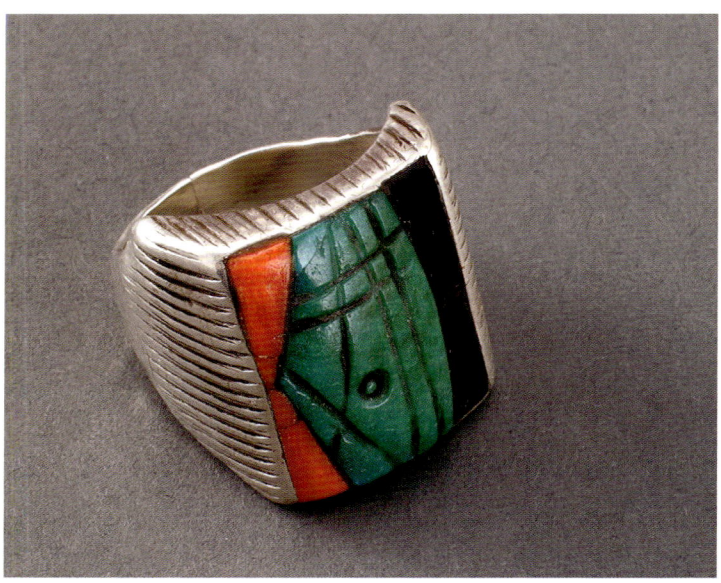

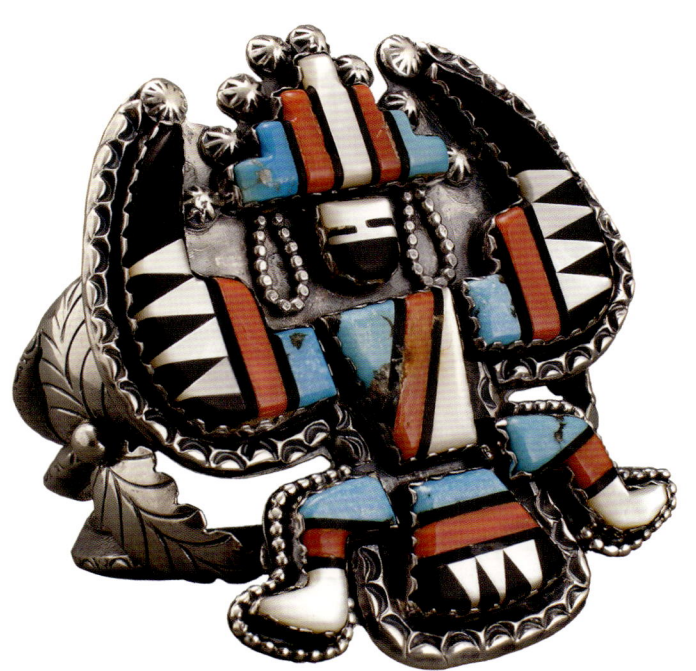

PLATE 170

UNKNOWN

U.S., Zuni Pueblo

Bracelet (Zuni Knifewing—Inlay), 1970s

Sterling silver, turquoise, coral, 3 in.

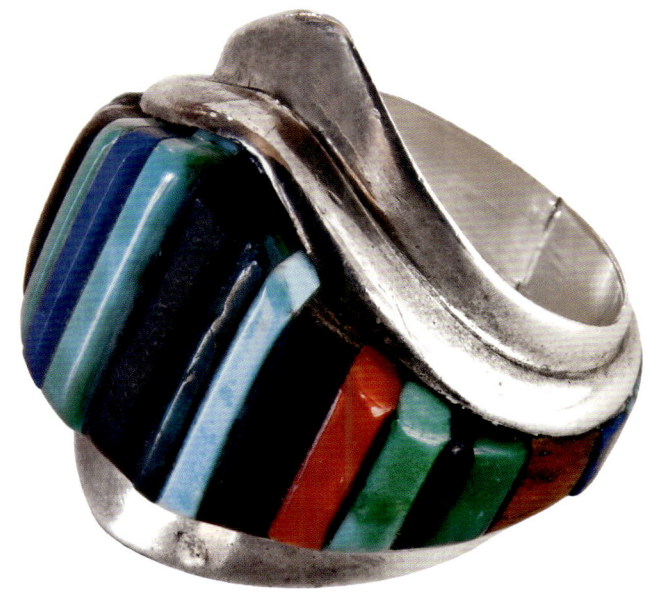

PLATE 171

CHARLES LOLOMA

U.S., Hopi Pueblo, 1921–1991

Ring ("Shape" Ring—Inlay), late 1970s–early 1980s

Sterling silver, turquoise, coral, lapis lazuli, malachite, ironwood,

ebony, and shell, 1 x 1⅛ in.

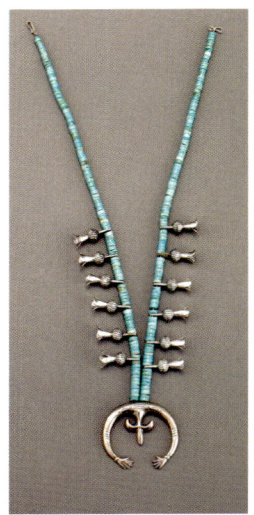

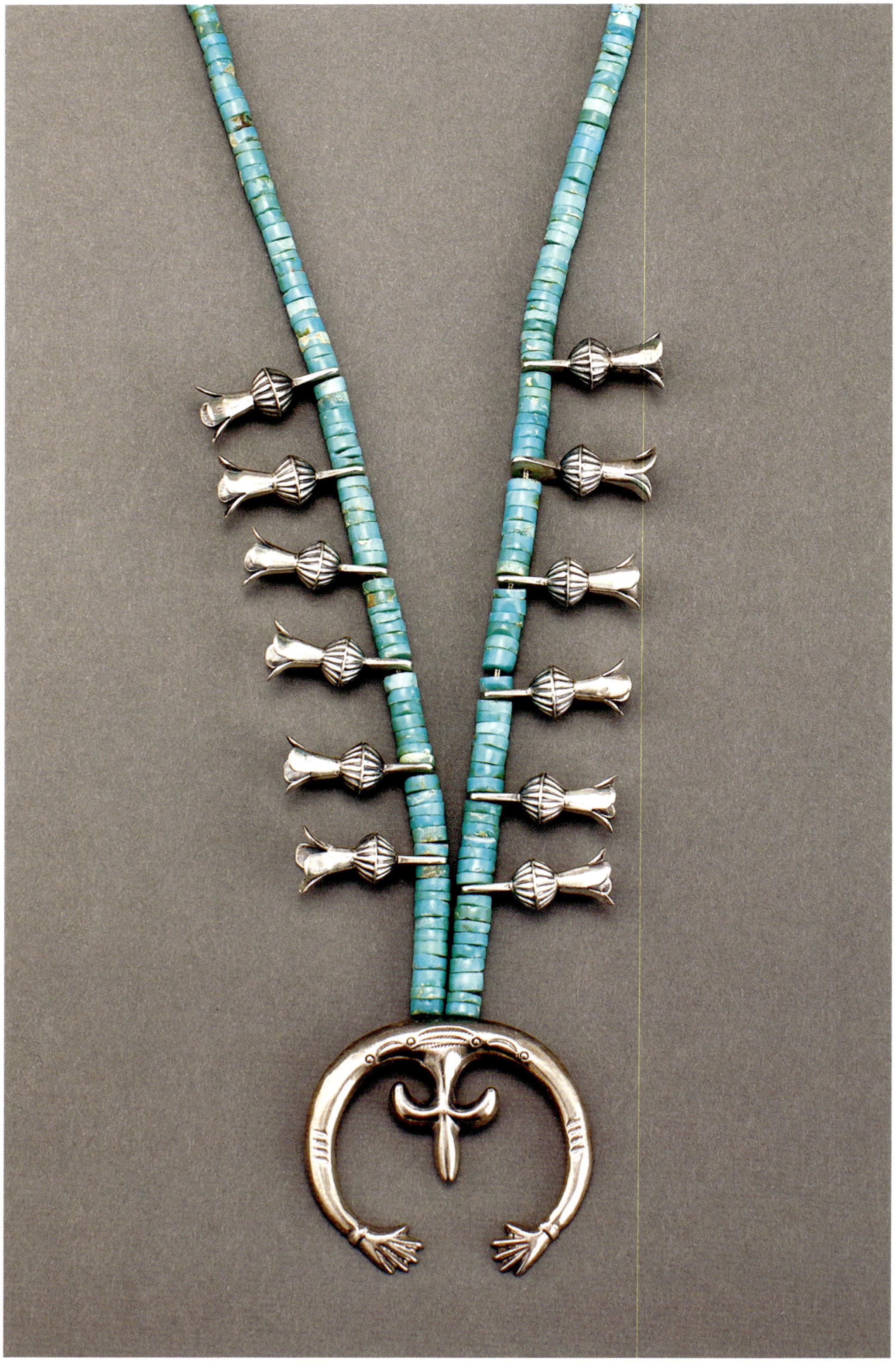

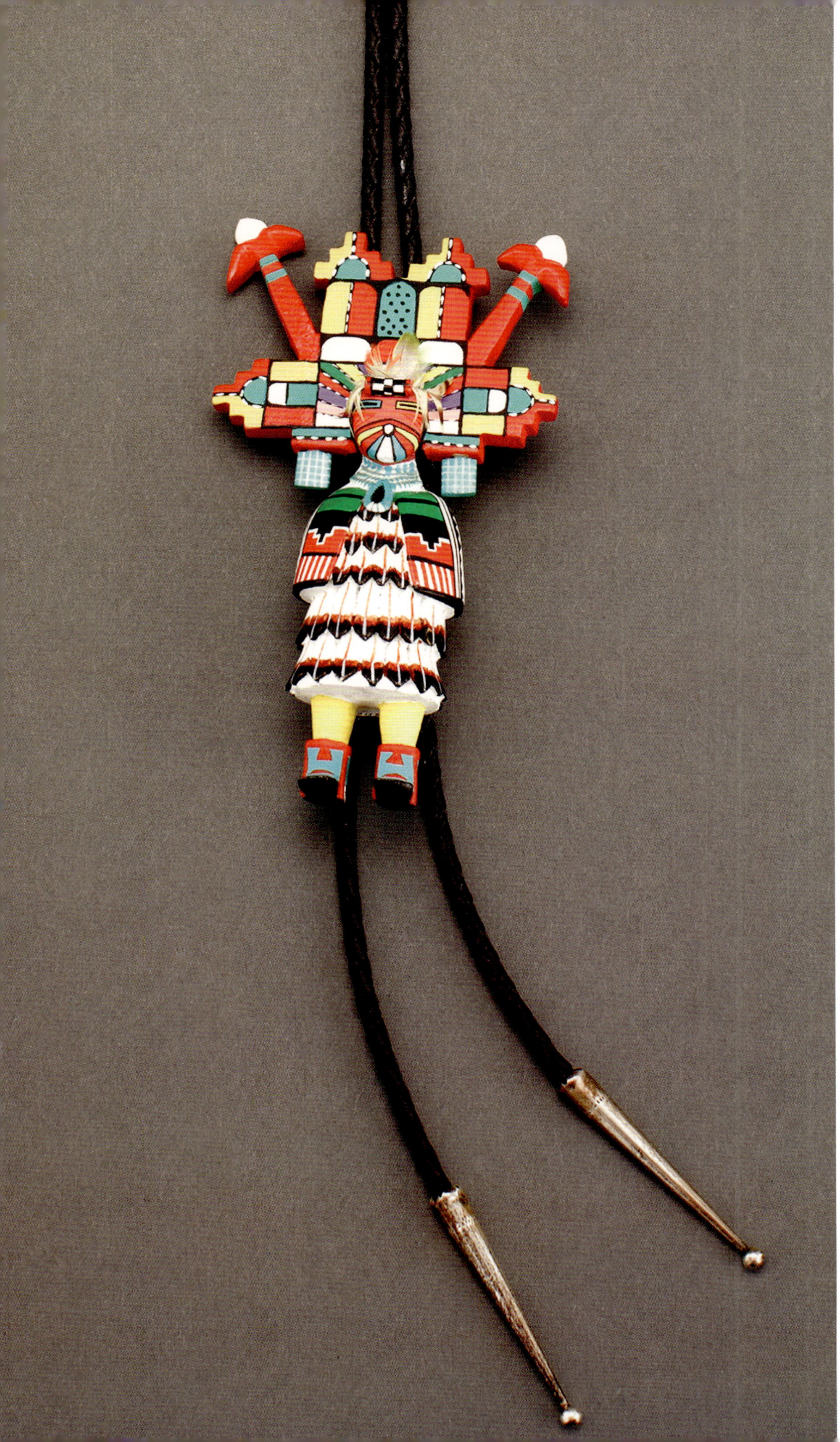

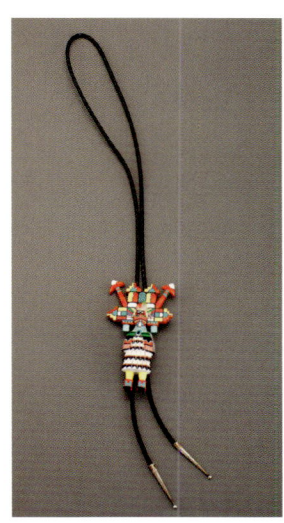

PLATE 173

MARY SHELTON

U.S., Hopi Pueblo, dates unknown

Bolo (Shalako), n.d.

Cottonwood root, paint, metal,

and leather, 4¾ x 2⅝ in.

189

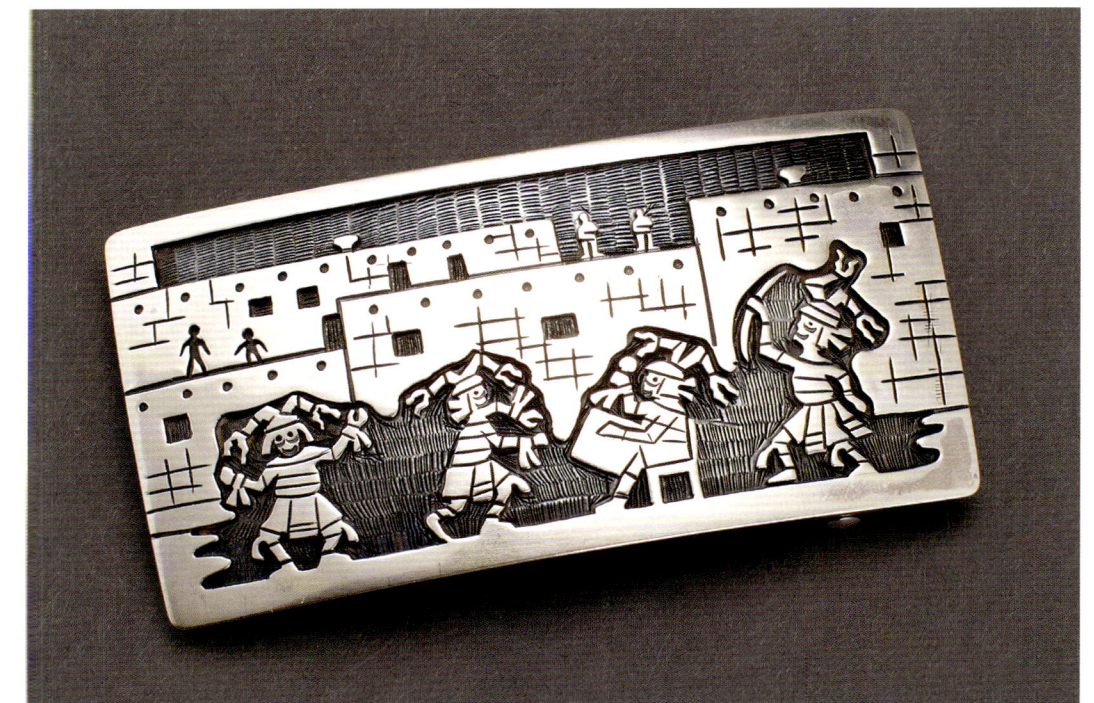

PLATE 174

RAYMOND KYASYOUSIE

U.S., Hopi Pueblo,

dates unknown

Buckle (Clowns Dancing—
Overlay), 1980s

Sterling silver, 1½ x 3 in.

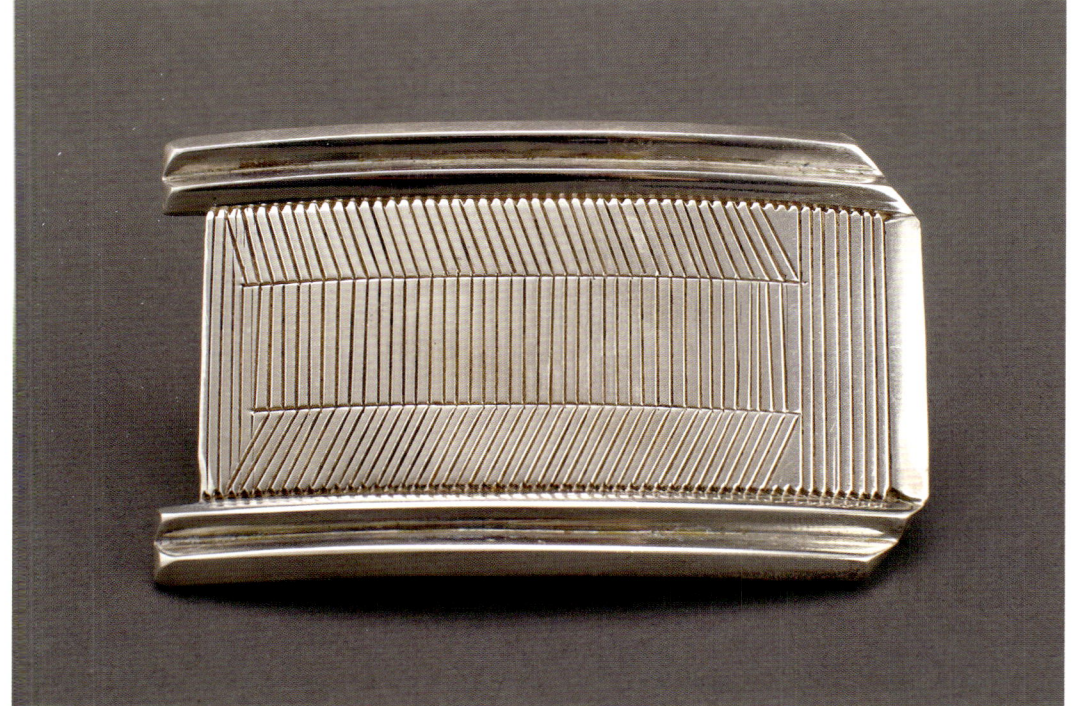

PLATE 175

GIBSON NEZ

U.S., Navajo/Jicarilla Apache,

1947–2007

Buckle (Linear Pattern), 1970s

Sterling silver, 1⅞ x 3 in.

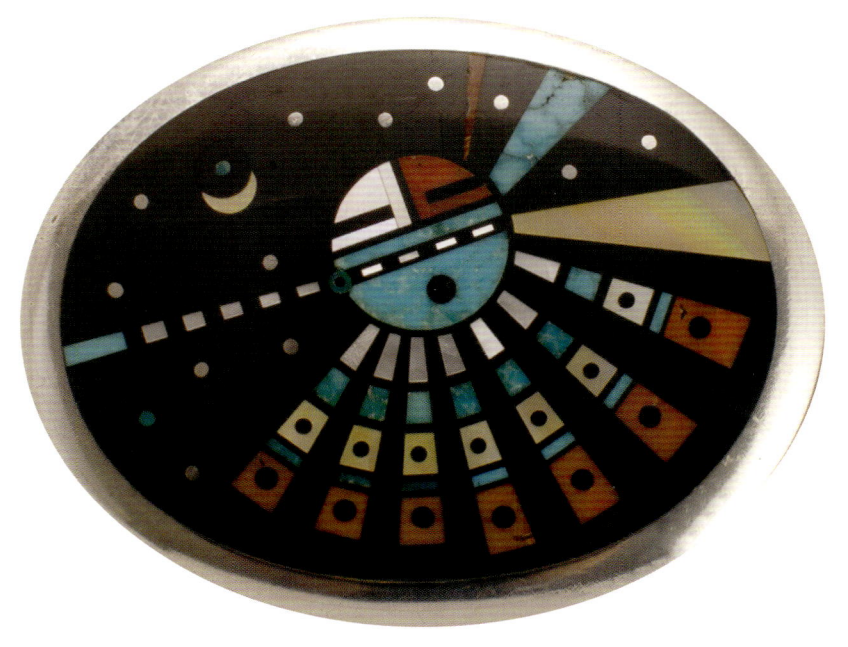

PLATE 176

JESSE MONONGYA

U.S., Navajo/Hopi Pueblo, b. 1952

Buckle (Night Sky—Inlay), 1970s

Sterling silver, turquoise, coral,

mother of pearl, jet, 2¼ x 2½ in.

PLATE 177

HELEN AND LINCOLN ZUNIE

U.S., Zuni Pueblo: Helen, 1929–2008;

Lincoln, b. 1927

Buckle (Horse—Inlay), 1970s

Sterling silver, turquoise, coral, 3 x 4⅛ in.

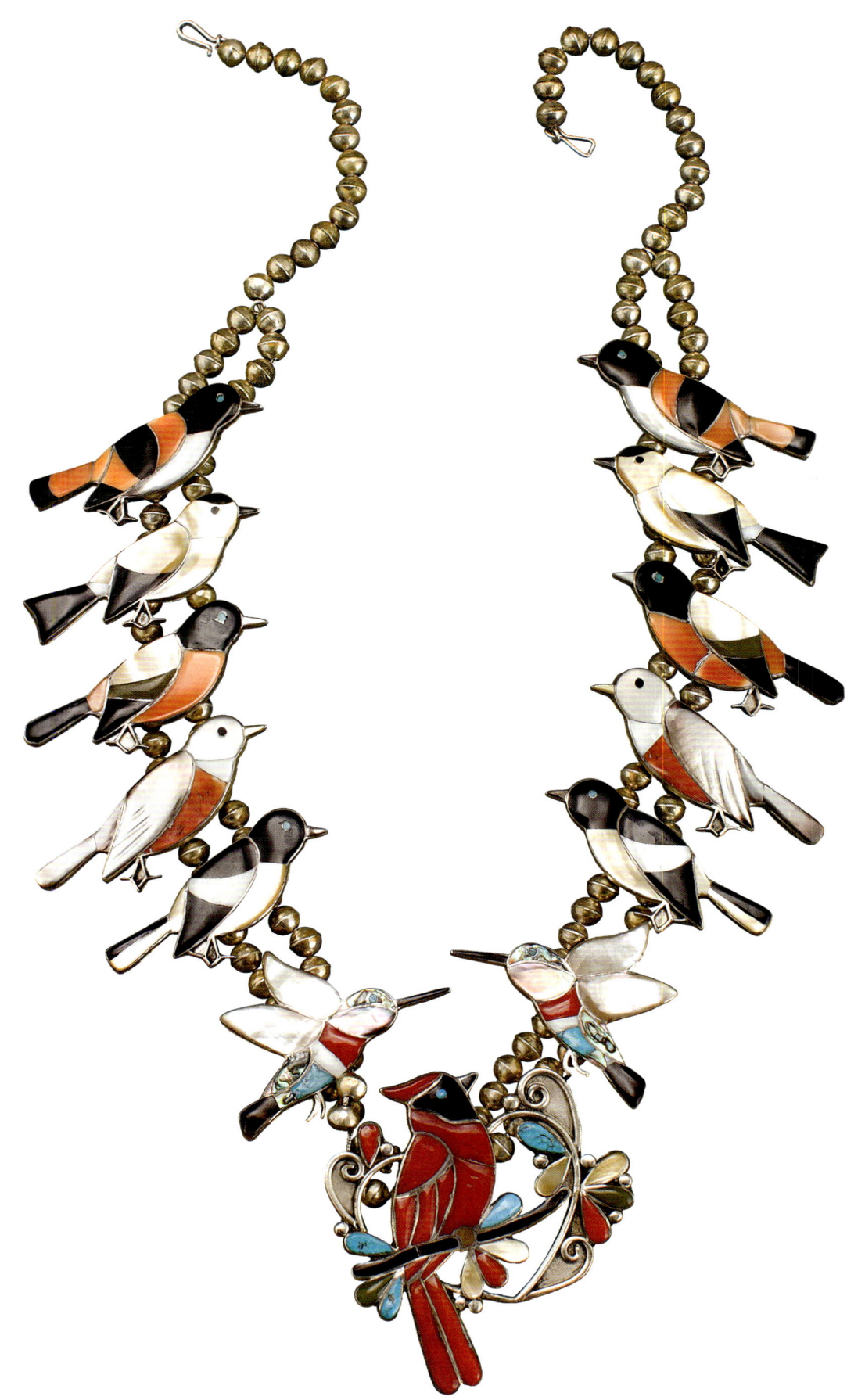

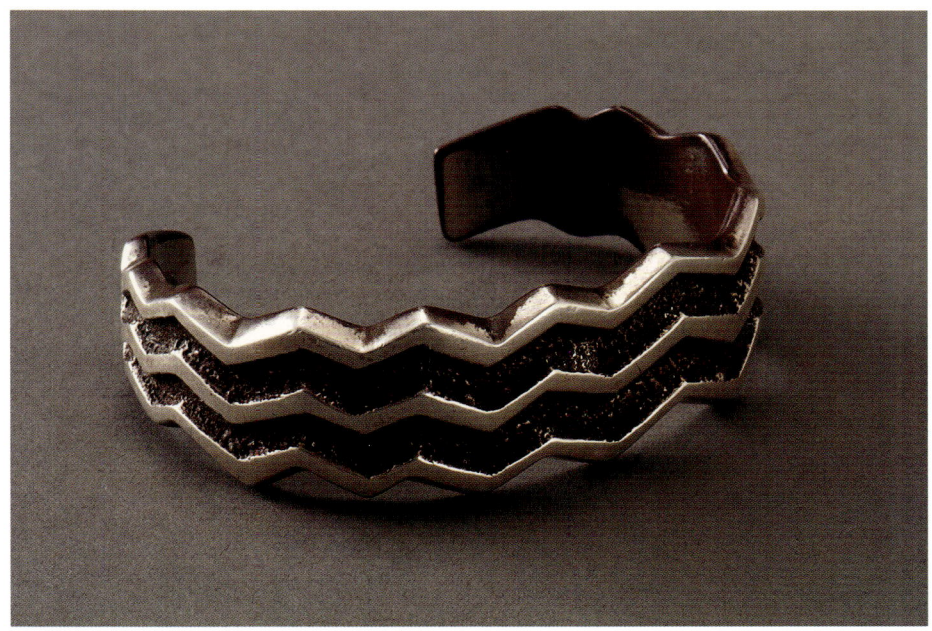

PLATE 179

LAWRENCE G. GOLSH

U.S., Pala Band Luiseño/Cherokee,

b. 1942

Bracelet (Tufa Cast), 1980s

Sterling silver, ¾ x 2⅝ x 2 in.

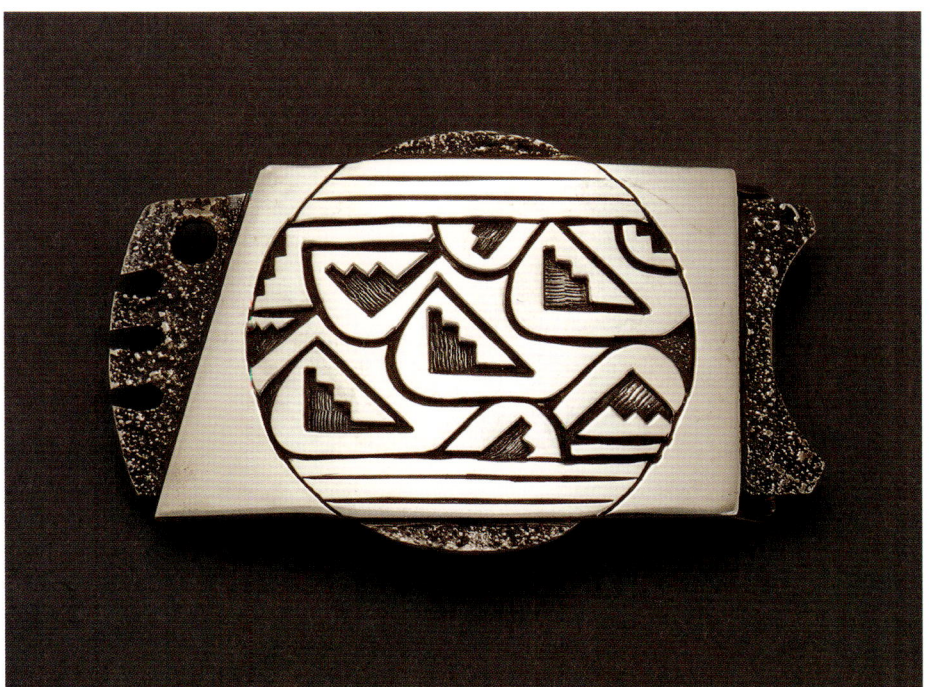

PLATE 180

MICHAEL KABOTIE

U.S., Hopi Pueblo, 1942–2010

Buckle (Stepped Design—Overlay),

1980s

Sterling silver, 1⅞ x 2⅞ in.

PLATE 178 (FACING)

DENNIS AND NANCY EDAAKIE

U.S., Zuni Pueblo: Dennis, 1931–2008;

Nancy, b. 1937

Necklace (Birds—Inlay), 1965–1970

Sterling silver, turquoise, coral, 30 in.

OVERLEAF (ALSO PLATE 15, P. 28)

HELEN HARDIN (TSA-SAH-WEE-EH)

U.S., Santa Clara Pueblo, 1943–1984

Winter Awakening of the O-khoo-wah, 1972

Acrylic on board, 15 x 30 in.

© The Helen Hardin Estate

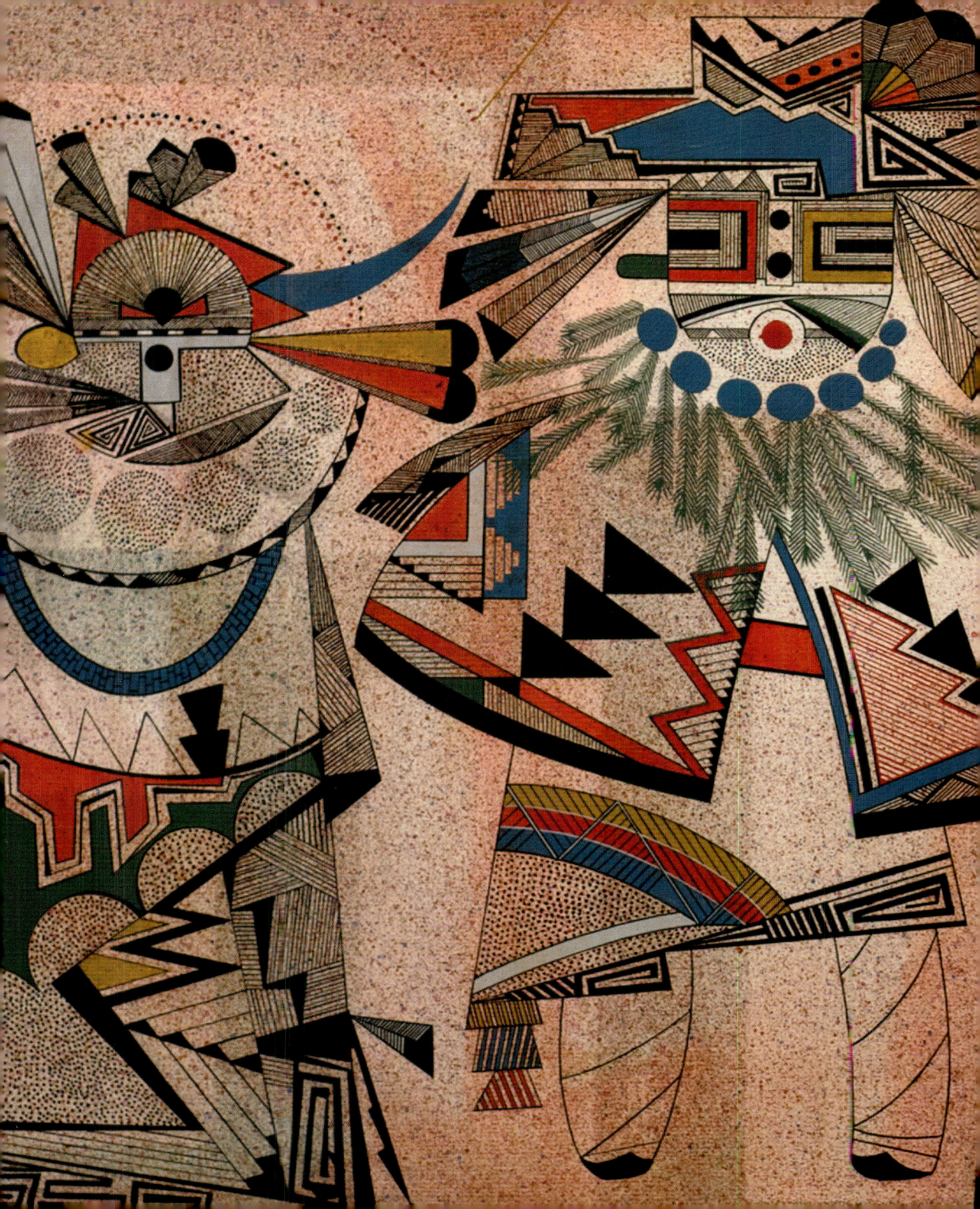

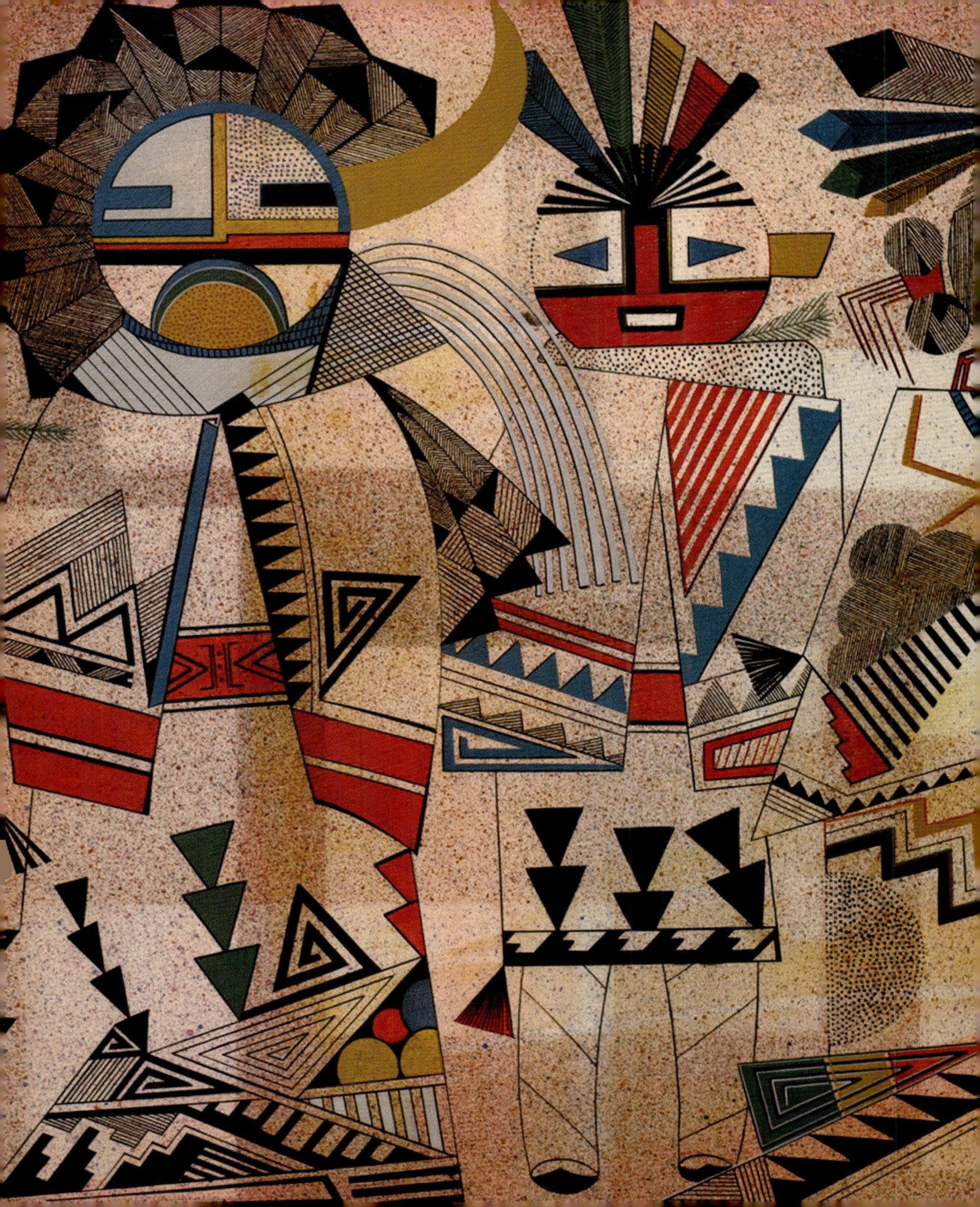

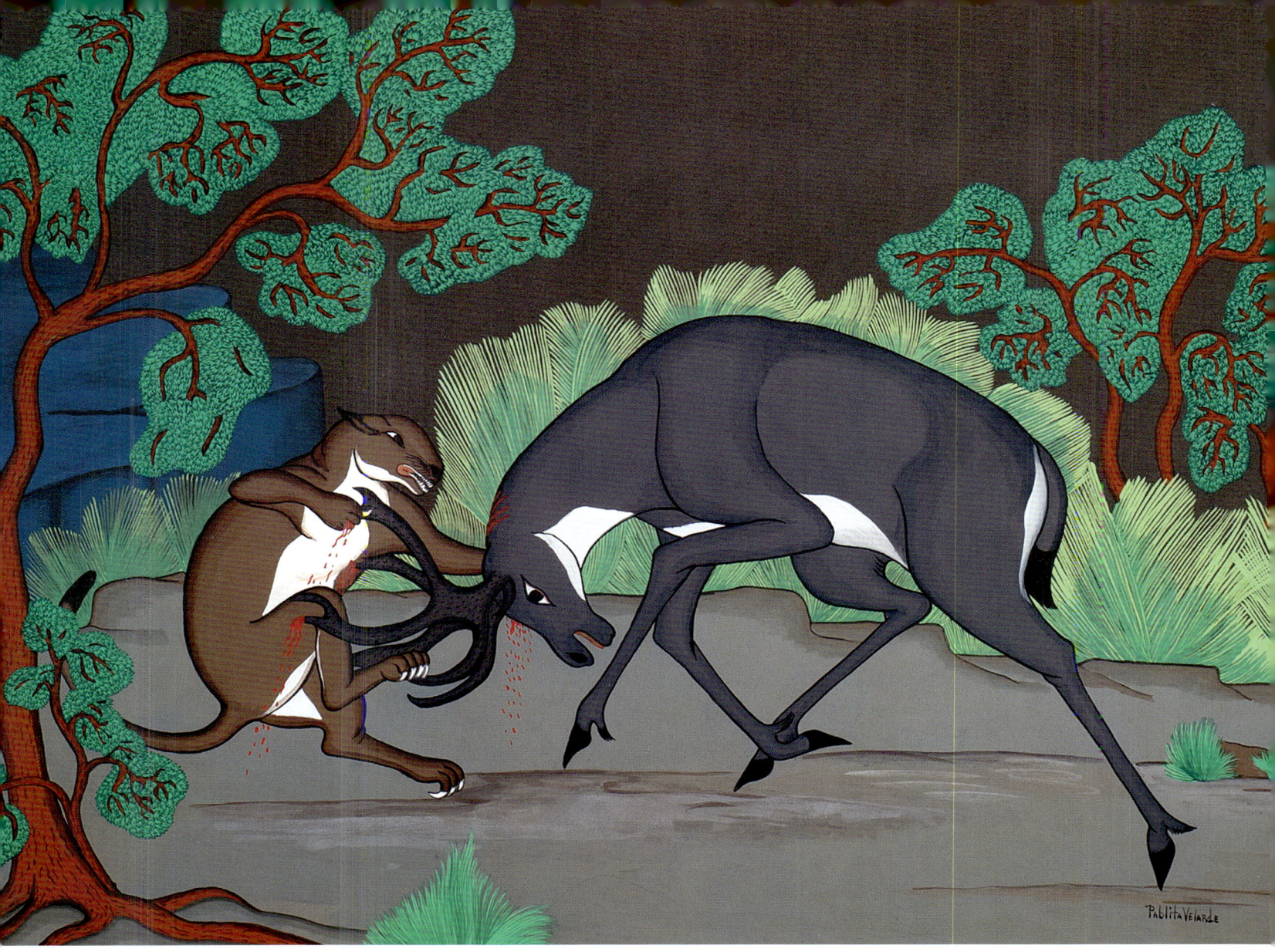

PLATE 181

PABLITA VELARDE

U.S., Santa Clara Pueblo, 1918–2006

The Battle, 1958

Watercolor on paper, 14¾ x 19½ in.

Courtesy of Margarete Bagshaw,

Golden Dawn Gallery

Notes

CHAPTER 1: JAMES T. BIALAC: A LASTING LEGACY

1. This essay is based on a series of interviews that I conducted with James Bialac between June and October 2011.

2. Bialac interview by Mark White, May 18, 2010.

3. Ibid.

4. Clara Lee Tanner, *Southwest Indian Painting: A Changing Art,* 2nd ed. (Tucson: University of Arizona Press, 1973); Patricia Janis Broder, *Hopi Painting: The World of the Hopis* (New York: Brandywine Press, 1978), and *Earth Songs, Moon Dreams: Paintings by Native American Women.* (New York: St. Martin's Press, 1999); Jerry Jacka and Lois Essary Jacka, *Art of the Hopi: Contemporary Journeys on Ancient Pathways* (Flagstaff, Ariz.: Northland, 1998), and *Enduring Traditions: Art of the Navajo (*Flagstaff, Ariz.: Northland, 1994); Tom Bahti and Mark Bahti, *Southwestern Indian Ceremonials*, rev. ed. (Flagstaff, Ariz.: KC Publications, 1997); Barton Wright, *Clowns of the Hopi: Tradition Keepers and Delight Makers* (Flagstaff, Ariz.: Northland, 1994), and *Hopi Kachinas The Complete Guide to Collecting Kachina Dolls* (Flagstaff, Ariz.: Northland, 1977); Gerhard Hoffman, ed., *Indianische Kunst Im 20 Jahrhundert/Indian Art in the 20th Century* (New York: Te Neues, 1985).

5. Jeanne Snodgrass King, *Drawn from Memory: The James T. Bialac Collection of American Indian Art* (Phoenix, Ariz.: Heard Museum, 1996), 1.

CHAPTER 2: JAMES T. BIALAC AND THE PATRONAGE OF AMERICAN INDIAN ART

This essay could not have been possible without the advice and assistance of my colleagues Christina Burke, Diana Pardue, W. Jackson Rushing III, and Christy Vezolles. I am also indebted to Jim Bialac for the countless hours he spent graciously narrating the history of his collection.

1. Clara Lee Tanner, *Southwest Indian Painting: A Changing Art*, 2nd ed. (Tucson: University of Arizona Press, 1973), 442.

2. The *Scottsdale National* divided its categories by media, although it had a special category for "experimental" art. Paul F. Huldermann, "Scottsdale—A New Focal Point in Indian Art," in *New Dimensions in Indian Art*, ed. Byron Harvey III (Scottsdale: Arizona: Scottsdale National Indian Arts Council, 1965), 23. The Philbrook, by contrast, initially characterized contemporary work as "non-traditional styles of painting" in its *Fourteenth Annual National Competition American Indian Painting and Sculpture* in 1959, and in 1960 as "symbolic and new styles of painting." Eventually, the museum separated entries into classifications of "regional paintings," "special category," and "sculpture." Modern or contemporary paintings were placed in the "special category," which was "designed to recognize new trends in American Indian art; abstractions, symbolic designs, or methods of painting which use European-derived shading and perspective. All works based on an Indian theme." *Fourteenth Annual National Competition American Indian Painting and Sculpture,* May 5–May 31, 1959, Philbrook Art Center, Tulsa, Oklahoma, n.p.; *Fifteenth Annual National Competition American Indian Painting and Sculpture,* May 3–June 2, 1960, Philbrook Art Center, n.p.; and *Nineteenth Annual American Indian Artists Exhibition,* May 5–May 31, 1964, Philbrook Art Center, n.p.

3. The House of Six Directions was named for the six directions in Puebloan cosmology: north, south, east, west, up, and down. Eugene L. Controtto, "This Business of Selling Indian Applied Arts. . . . " *Desert* 24, no. 9 (September 1961): 18–21.

4. Tanner, *Southwest Indian Painting*, 443.

5. Paul F. Huldermann, "Our Story," *Tenth Annual Scottsdale National Indian Art Exhibition*, February 27–March 7, 1971, 3.

6. *Third Annual Scottsdale National Indian Art Exhibition*, February 29–March 8, 1964, n.p.

7. "Indian Art Exhibit Opens at Hotel Here," unidentified newspaper, February 1963, Native American Artists Resource Collection, Heard Museum.

8. Paul F. Huldermann, "New Chapter in Scottsdale Cultural History Forecast," unidentified newspaper, February 1963, Native American Artists Resource Collection.

9. "Indian Art Timely," unidentified newspaper, February 1963, Native American Artists Resource Collection.

10. Joy L. Gritton, *The Institute of American Indian Arts: Modernism and U.S. Indian Policy* (Albuquerque: University of New Mexico Press, 2000), 2.

11. Maggie Wilson, "Movable Goals Bring Success to 'Liberated' Triple-Winner," *Arizona Republic*, March 28, 1973, 35.

12. Swazo won the San Francisco Art Festival Merit Award with *Council of the Corn Maidens* in 1969. Hinds grew up in San Francisco, with adopted parents, and began his career painting Bay Area abstractions. When he turned to American Indian subjects, his modernist style often led to rejections from conservative juries at the Philbrook and the *Intertribal Ceremonial* in Gallup. The acceptance of experimental styles at the *Scottsdale National* led Hinds to observe that "an Indian artist no longer needs to stick to one medium, one style, flat two-dimensional stuff. He can progress in any direction his talent and training take him." He also questioned the perceived prohibition against abstraction in American Indian art and claimed, "We invented abstractions." Maggie Wilson, "Indian Artist 'Rebel' Is Far from Tesuque," *Scottsdale Daily Progress Weekender* 7, no. 18 (March 4, 1967): 1.

13. "Scottsdale Indian Arts Exhibition a Sellout," *Arizona Republic*, April 1, 1972, 43.

14. Joan Hale, "The James T. Bialac Collection: Amerindian Paintings and Graphics," March 1967, Heard Museum.

15. Other significant acquisitions in 1966–1967 included Gerald Nailor's *Navajo Debutante* (1938, plate 2), Jerome Tiger's *War Party* (n.d., plate 184), Quincy Tahoma's *The Navajos in Pursuit* (1948, plate 182), and Pablita Velarde's *The Battle* (1958, plate 181). The Velarde was purchased from John Tanner at the same time as the Tsihnahjinnie.

16. Clara Lee Tanner, *The James T. Bialac Collection of Southwest Indian Paintings* (Tucson, Arizona: Arizona State Museum, 1967), n.p. Tanner articulated her arguments more clearly in the introduction to *Southwest Indian Painting* and discussed the influence of both the *Scottsdale National* and IAIA on American Indian art (443–44).

17. Tanner, *Southwest Indian Painting*, 179, 186, and 316.

18. Ibid., 3.

19. Tanner, *The James T. Bialac Collection of Southwest Indian Paintings*, n.p.

20. Brody included Romando Vigil's *Deer Dance*, which Bialac had acquired in 1969. J. J. Brody, *Indian Painters and White Patrons* (Albuquerque: University of New Mexico Press, 1971), 84. Three paintings that were included in Dunn's book eventually entered Bialac's collection: Oscar Howe's *An Early Painting* (1935), Nor-my-se-ye's *Zuni Fire Dancer* (c. 1920), and Leo Reano's *Antelope Hunt*, all of which were acquired in the 1990s. Dorothy Dunn, *American Indian Painting of the Southwest and Plains Areas* (Albuquerque: University of New Mexico Press, 1968), 262, 279, 295, and 348.

21. Bialac, interview with Christy Vezolles, June 14, 2011.

22. "Artist Hopid," www.kabotie.com/Pages/artisthopid.html, accessed September 19, 2011.

23. Personal communication from Bialac to author, September 1, 2011.

24. W. Jackson Rushing III, "Authenticity and Subjectivity in Post-War Painting: Concerning Herrera, Scholder, and Cannon," in Rennard Strickland and Margaret Archuleta, *Shared Visions: Native American Painters and Sculptors in the Twentieth Century* (Phoenix, Arizona: The Heard Museum, 1991), 16.

25. Scholder quoted in Werner Gundersheimer, Frank H. Goodyear, Jr., and Paul J. Karlstrom, *Fritz Scholder: Paintings* (Tucson, Ariz.: Nazraeli Press, 2001), 12.

26. Jamake Highwater, *Song of the Earth: American Indian Painting* (Boston: New York Graphic Society, 1976), 117. Highwater fraudulently claimed Cherokee and Blackfoot ancestry, and his ethnicity was publicly challenged in 1984 by Joseph B. DeLaCruz, president of the National Congress of American Indians, and journalist Jack Anderson.

27. "Indianness" had been of great concern following the creation of IAIA and the *Scottsdale National,* but many of the cited scholars tackled the subject in the early 1980s. For example, Wade, in the introduction to *The Arts of the North American Indian*, explained that the purpose of the exhibition and catalogue was to "look both forward and back, seeking the fundamental

principles underlying the vast sweep of American Indian art," but with the recognition that such definition was a decidedly "Western" view. The catalogue raised numerous questions regarding American Indian art, including where such ethnic qualifications were still acceptable. Edwin L. Wade, et al., *The Arts of the North American Indian: Native Traditions in Evolution* (New York: Hudson Hills Press, 1986), 17. In answer to lingering concerns over the use of contemporary styles by American Indian artists, Highwater argued that it was not style but conception that best expressed the ethnicity of the artist: "What is 'Indian' about Indian painting is not the depiction of *Indian scenes* but the mentality that underlies the whole process by which the work of art comes into existence. And that characteristic mentality is also capable of drastic and modernist change without any necessary loss of its 'Indianness.'" Highwater, *The Sweet Grass Lives On: Fifty Contemporary North American Indian Artists* (New York: Lippincott and Crowell, 1980), 19. Silberman considered American Indian painting, regardless of style, "a spiritual affirmation of Indianness." Arthur Silberman, *100 Years of Native American Painting* (Oklahoma City: Oklahoma Museum of Art, 1978), 13.

28. In 2004, Bialac acquired Gerald Peter Jemison's *Strawberry Dance—Paperbag Series* (1982, plate 110), which had been included in Wade, *The Arts of the North American Indian*, 270.

29. Joel Harnett, "Treasure Hunt of the Senses," *Native Peoples* 13, no. 6 (September/October 2000): 50.

30. For a discussion of Hoover's exhibition at the Heard, see Julie Decker, *John Hoover: Art and Life* (Seattle: University of Washington Press, 2002), 43.

31. Postcard from Dorothy Jean Ray to Bialac, July 30, 2005, James T. Bialac curatorial files, Fred Jones Jr. Museum of Art, University of Oklahoma, Norman. Ray sent photocopies of the pieces she offered for sale, along with descriptions and anecdotal information about the works in question. She noted that *Eskimo Igloo* was drawn when Moses was living in Nome in 1964, and that *Walrus Hunters* was based on a story he had heard from Assesuk (Jimmy Killigivuk). The hunt took place in the vicinity of Cape Lisburne, Point Lay, or the north side of Point Hope.

32. Dorothy Jean Ray, *Graphic Arts of the Alaskan Eskimo*, Native American Arts 2, Indian Arts and Crafts Board, 1969, 76–77. The etching depicts a polar bear and cub below a map of the Seward Peninsula. The border includes drawings copied after engravings from old drill bows.

33. Ray called *Potlatch Dance* "one of my all-time favorites." Letter from Ray to Bialac, December 15, 2002.

CHAPTER 3: NATIVE AMERICAN PAINTING: SCHOOLS, STYLES, AND MOVEMENTS

1. For those unfamiliar with and interested in the role of such patrons in the commercialization of an ethnic art, see J. J. Brody, *Indian Painters and White Patrons* (Albuquerque: University of New Mexico, 1971), and *Pueblo Indian Painting: Tradition and Modernism in New Mexico, 1900–1930* (Santa Fe: School of American Research Press, 1997); Bruce Bernstein and W. Jackson Rushing III, *Modern by Tradition: American Indian Painting in the Studio Style* (Santa Fe: Museum of New Mexico Press, 1995); Dorothy Dunn, *American Indian Painting of the Southwest and Plains Areas* (Albuquerque: University of New Mexico Press, 1968); Edwin L. Wade, "The Ethnic Art Market and the Dilemma of Innovative Indian Artists," in *Magic Images: Contemporary Native American Art*, ed. Edwin L. Wade and Rennard Strickland (Norman: University of Oklahoma Press, 1981), and *The Arts of the North American Indian* (New York: Hudson Hill Press, 1986); John Anson Warner, *Paradigms of Twentieth Century Native American Painting* (Osaka, Japan: Kansai University of Foreign Studies Publication, 1994), and *Contemporary Canadian Native Art: Newly Emerging Art Styles* (Osaka, Japan: Kansai Gaidai University, 1996).

2. Brody, *Pueblo Indian Painting*, 3. These documented paintings, purchased by Frank Cushing, James Stevenson, and others, are in the collection of the National Anthropological Archive, National Museum of Natural History.

3. Warner, *Contemporary Canadian Native Art*.

4. John O'Brian, ed., *Clement Greenberg: The Collected Essays and Criticism*, vol. 1 (Chicago: University of Chicago Press, 1993), 117.

5. Margaret Dubin, "Sanctioned Scribes: How Critics and Historians Write the Native American Artworld," in *Native American Art in the Twentieth Century*, ed. W. Jackson Rushing III (London: Routledge, 1999), 157.

6. McMaster, "Towards an Aboriginal Art History," in *Native American Art in the Twentieth Century*, ed. W. Jackson Rushing III (London: Routledge, 1999), 83.

7. Robert Hughes, *Culture of Complaint: The Fraying of America* (London: Oxford University Press, 1993), 7.

8. Personal correspondence, Cohoe, August 27, 1981.

9. Tom Hill, and Richard W. Hill, Sr., eds. *Creation's Journey: Native American Identity and Belief* (Washington, D.C.: Smithsonian Institution Press, National Museum of the American Indian, 1994).

CHAPTER 4: MAKING MODERN: SELECTED PAINTINGS, DRAWINGS, AND PRINTS

1. Kobena Mercer, ed., *Cosmopolitan Modernisms* (Cambridge, Mass., and London: MIT Press and the Institute of International Visual Arts, 2005), 7.

2. Marit Munson, ed., *Kenneth Chapman's Santa Fe: Artists and Archaeologists, 1907–1931: The Memoirs of Kenneth Chapman* (Santa Fe: School for Advanced Research, 2007), 40, and see the photograph of Apie Begay posing with his works on paper, 41.

3. Ibid., 40.

4. J. J. Brody, *Indian Painters and White Patrons* (Albuquerque: University of New Mexico Press, 1971), 73–74; Clara Lee Tanner, *Southwest Indian Painting: A Changing Art* (Tucson: University of Arizona Press, 1957, 2nd printing 1980), 66.

5. Patrick D. Lester, *The Biographical Directory of Native American Painters* (Tulsa: SIR Publications, 1995), 52.

6. Ann Hedlund, e-mail to the author June 4, 2011, where she notes also that a slightly different reading, 'Naakai din'e," would signify Apie Begay's membership in the Mexican clan. It's worth noting that in the photograph of Begay taken by Chapman (see note 2), he does, in fact, look Mexican.

7. D. Y. Begay, in conversation with the author, June 11, 2011.

8. Leland Wyman, "Navajo Ceremonial System," in *Handbook of North American Indians*, vol. 10, ed. Alfonso Ortiz (Washington, D.C.: Smithsonian Institution, 1983), 546.

9. Fred Kabotie and Bill Belknap, *Fred Kabotie: Hopi Indian Artist* (Flagstaff: Museum of Northern Arizona Press, 1977), 28, and cf. J. J. Brody, *Pueblo Indian Painting: Tradition and Modernism in New Mexico, 1900–1930* (Santa Fe: School of American Research Press, 1997), 82–83.

10. Kabotie and Belknap, *Fred Kabotie,* 8.

11. Brody, *Pueblo Indian Painting*, 86.

12. For Kabotie and the recreation of Awatovi murals, see W. Jackson Rushing III, *Native American Art and the New York Avant-Garde* (Austin: University of Texas Press, 1995), 110–11.

13. Brody, *Pueblo Indian Painting*, 72.

14. Ibid., 85.

15. See Frank Hamilton Cushing, *Zuni Folk Tales* (New York: Alfred A. Knopf, 1931), 93–104; Matilda Coxe Stevenson, "The Zuni Indians," *23ʳᵈ Annual Report of the Bureau of American Ethnology* (Washington, D.C.: Government Printing Office, 1904), 94–102.

16. Stevenson, "The Zuni," plates 13 and 14.

17. Brody, *Pueblo Indian Painting*, 120.

18. *Kolowisi Water Serpent Puppet*, www.brooklynmuseum.org/opencollection/objects/129018/Kolowisi_Water_Serpent_Puppet, accessed June 8, 2011.

19. Bruce Bernstein, "Julian and Maria Martinez," in *St. James Guide to Native North American Artists*, ed. Roger Matuz (New York: St. James Press, 1998), 361–62. Maria Martinez is represented in the FJJMA by thirty-seven objects, many of which were made in collaboration with various family members, including her husband, Julian.

20. Brody, *Pueblo Indian Painting*, 47, 146.

21. See also Tse-Ye-Mu (Romando Vigil), *Bird with Fertility Symbols* (1924) in Dorothy Dunn, *American Indian Painting of the Southwest and Plains Area* (Albuquerque: University of New Mexico Press, 1968), 203, figure 81.

22. Brody, *Pueblo Indian Painting*, 146.

23. See the poet and art collector Alice Corbin Henderson's recollection of Tonita Peña's memory of Esther Hoyt in Dunn, *American Indian Painting*, 203.

24. Tanner, *Southwest Indian Painting*, 133.

25. Dunn, *American Indian Painting*, 210–11.

26. On the support of her husband, Epitacio Arquero, in resisting pressure from Cochiti elders to cease painting images of ceremonial dancers, see Lisa Roberts, "Tonita Peña," in *St. James Guide*, 447.

27. Pablita Velarde, quoted in Sally Hyer, "Pablita Velarde: The Pueblo Artist as Cultural Broker," in *Between Indian and White Worlds: The Cultural Broker*, ed. Margaret Connell Szasz (Norman: University of Oklahoma Press, 1994), 279–80.

28. Marsden Hartley, "Tribal Esthetics," *The Dial* 65 (November 1918), 400.

29. On the Bursum Bill and the politics of exhibiting Pueblo watercolors on the East Coast in the early 1920s, see David W. Penney and Lisa A. Roberts, "America's Pueblo Artists: Encounters on the Borderlands," in *Native American Art in the Twentieth Century: Makers, Meanings, Histories*, ed. W. Jackson Rushing III (New York and London: Routledge, 1999), 32–33.

30. Rushing, *Native American Art*, 97.

31. See Dunn, *American Indian Painting*, 218–23, and Rosemary Ellison, "Introduction," in *Contemporary Plains Indian Painting*, ed. Myles Libhart (Anadarko: Oklahoma Indian Arts and Crafts Cooperative, 1972), 14–19. For Lois Smoky, see Marla Redcorn, "Lois Smoky," in *St. James Guide*, 528–29. See also Oscar B. Jacobson, *Kiowa Indian Art* (Nice, France: l'Edition d'Art C. Szwedzicki, 1929), and Janet C. Berlo, "The Szwedzicki Portfolios of American Indian Art, 1929–1952, Part I," *American Indian Art Magazine* 34 (February 2009): 37–39.

32. Weston La Barre, *The Peyote Cult* (New York: Schocken Books, 1969), 109.

33. See Daniel C. Swan, *Peyote Religious Art: Symbols of Faith and Belief* (Jackson: University Press of Mississippi, 1999), ix.

34. Daniel C. Swan, e-mail to the author, June 14, 2011.

35. See Jamake Highwater, *Song from the Earth* (Boston: New York Graphic Society, 1976), 64.

36. Swan, *Peyote Religious Art*, 64.

37. Dunn, *American Indian Painting*, 280, 300.

38. For Raymond Jonson's Native-inspired primitivism, see Rushing, *Native American Art*, 79–85. On Herrera, see my essay "Modern by Tradition: The 'Studio Style' of Native American Painting," in *Modern by Tradition*, ed. Bruce Bernstein and W. Jackson Rushing III (Santa Fe: Museum of New Mexico, 1995), 61–73.

39. Dorothy Dunn, "The Art of Joe Herrera," *El Palacio* 59 (December 1952): 367.

40. W. Jackson Rushing III, "Authenticity and Subjectivity in Post-War Painting: Concerning Herrera, Scholder, and Cannon," in *Shared Visions: Native American Painters and Sculptors in the Twentieth Century*, ed. Margaret Archuleta and Rennard Strickland (New York: New Press for the Heard Museum, 1991), 13.

41. Brody, *Indian Painters*, 152. See also Guy Monthan and Doris Monthan, "Ha-So-De: One of the First Individualists," *American Indian Art Magazine* 1 (Summer 1976): 34–39.

42. Other key works in the collection by independent modernists active in the 1960s include John Hoover (Aleut), *How the Mosquitoes Were Formed* (1960, plate 35); Joseph Senungetuk (Inupiat), *Abstract Man and Birds* (1966, plate 44); and Patrick Swazo Hinds (Tesuque Pueblo), *Council of the Corn Maidens* (1969, plate 18).

43. Marilee Jantzer-White, "Patrick DesJarlait," *St. James Guide*, 158.

44. W. Jackson Rushing III, *Allan Houser: An American Master* (New York: Harry N. Abrams, 2004), 22–23.

45. On emplacement in DesJarlait's work, see Bill Anthes, *Native Moderns: American Indian Painting, 1940–1970* (Durham: Duke University Press, 2006), 90, 113–16.

46. "George Morrison Debut," *Art Digest* 22 (May 1, 1948): 19. Thanks to my colleague Mark White for sharing this review with me.

47. W. Jackson Rushing III, "Modern Spirits: The Legacy of Allan Houser and George Morrison," in *Essays on Native Modernism: Complexity and Contradiction in American Indian Art* (Washington, D.C., and New York: National Museum of the American Indian, Smithsonian Institution, 2006), 57, and Evan Maurer et al., *Morrison's Horizon*, exhibition catalogue (Minneapolis, Minn.: Minneapolis Institute of Art, 1998).

48. Fritz Scholder, "Scholder on Scholder: A Self-Interview," *American Indian Art Magazine* 1 (Spring 1976): 50.

49. Rushing, "Authenticity and Subjectivity," 16. For the

founding of the IAIA, see Joy L. Gritton, *The Institute of American Indian Arts* (Albuquerque: University of New Mexico Press, 2000).

50. On Scholder, Postmodern irony, and the mass media, see Joseph Traugott, "Native American Artists and the Postmodern Cultural Divide," *Art Journal* 51 (Fall 1992): 36–43.

51. See www.mourlot.com for a history of the studio and its founder, Fernand Mourlot.

52. See Tally Richards, "Indian in Paris," *American Indian Art Magazine* 2 (Spring 1977): 48.

53. The Anishinabe artist Robert Houle has made Catlin's importation to Paris of Ojibwe people the subject of an exhibition seen in both Paris and Canada; see Robert Houle et al., *Robert Houle's Paris/Ojibwa*, exhibition catalogue (Peterborough, Ontario: Gallery of Peterborough, 2011).

54. Joan Frederick, *T. C. Cannon: He Stood in the Sun* (Flagstaff: Northland Publishing, 1995), 45.

55. On Cannon's stylistic sources and the layers of art historical referents in his work, see Rushing, "Authenticity and Subjectivity," 17–18.

56. Cf. Rushing, "Modern Spirits," 60.

57. See Thomas Hoving, *The Art of Dan Namingha* (New York: Harry N. Abrams, 2000), 21–29.

58. See Amy Trevelyan, "Jaune Quick-to-See Smith," in *Contemporary Masters: The Eiteljorg Fellowship for Native American Fine Art*, vol. 1 (Indianapolis: Eiteljorg Museum of American Indians and Western Art, 1999), 50–54.

59. See Smith's comments in Highwater, *Song from the Earth*, 180, where she speaks thoughtfully of balancing male and female polarities, as well as ancient and contemporary ones.

60. Emmi Whitehorse in Lawrence Abbott, *I Stand in the Center of the Good: Interviews with Contemporary Native American Artists* (Lincoln: University of Nebraska Press, 1994), 291.

61. Ibid., 298.

62. Joseph Traugott, "Emmi Whitehorse: Kin' Nah' Zin,'" *Artspace* 6 (Summer 1982): 40.

63. Whitehorse in Abbott, *I Stand in the Center of the Good*, 286; see also 287 on process.

64. Ibid., 288–89.

65. Emmi Whitehorse, in Phoebe Farris, "Emmi Whitehorse," *St. James Guide*, 624.

66. Lloyd E. Oxendiene, "23 Contemporary Indian Artists," *Art in America* 60 (July/August 1972): 58–69.

67. See Abbott, *I Stand in the Center of the Good*, 87.

68. See Gerhard Hoffman, "Native American Art in the Context of Modern and Postmodern Art," in *The Arts of the North American Indian*, ed. Edwin L. Wade (New York: Hudson Hills Press in Association with Philbrook Art Center, 1986), 270.

69. Peter Jemison, "The Paper Bag Works," in *Ni' Go Tlunh A Doh Ka* (*We Are Always Turning Around on Purpose*), exhibition catalogue (Old Westbury: Amelie A. Wallace Gallery, State University of New York, 1986), 22.

70. Ibid.

71. Ibid.

72. See Andrea Walsh, "Marianne Nicolson," in *Contemporary Masters*, 30, and "Marianne Nicolson Speaks," in *Reservation X: The Power of Place in Aboriginal Contemporary Art*, ed. Gerald McMaster (Seattle: University of Washington Press and Canadian Museum of Civilization, 1998), 100.

73. Walsh, "Nicolson," 30.

74. Jeffrey Gibson, e-mail to the author, July 21, 2011.

75. See, for example, Kate Morris, "Places of Emergence: Painting Genesis," in *Off the Map: Landscape in the Native Imagination*, ed. Kathleen Ash Milby (Washington, D.C., and New York: NMAI Editions, Smithsonian Institution, 2007), 47–63.

76. Katherine L. Chase, *Indian Painters of the Southwest: The Deep Remembering* (Santa Fe: School of American Research Press, 2002), 55.

77. Jeanette Katoney, quoted in ibid.

78. Ibid.

79. See his comments at http://tonyabeytastudio.com, accessed July 26, 2011.

80. See his comments in Gerhard Hoffman and Gisela Hoffman, "Tony Abeyta," *St. James Guide*, 5.

81. Tony Abeyta, in conversation with the author, July 31, 2011.

82. Tony Abeyta, artist statement, *Underworldness* exhibition, 2008.

83. Tony Abeyta, in conversation with the author, July 31, 2011.

84. Ibid.

CHAPTER 5: KACHINA DOLLS: TRADITION
AND INNOVATION

1. There are various accepted spellings for the term "kachina." "Kachina," "katchina", and "katsina" are in regular usage. The Hopi use "katsina" as the closest phonetic equivalent to their pronunciation of the word.

2. Barton Wright, "The Drift from Tradition," in *Katsina: Commodified and Appropriated Images of Hopi Supernaturals,* ed. Zena Pearlstone (Los Angeles: University of California Los Angeles Fowler Museum of Cultural History, 2001), 146. Hopi carver Alph Secakuku has stated, "We believe [kachina dolls] are personifications of the katsina spirits, originally created by the katsinam in their physical embodiment." Alph H. Secakuku, *Following the Sun and Moon: Hopi Kachina Tradition* (Flagstaff, Arizona: Northland Publishing, 1995), 4.

3. For a discussion of early Euro-American encounters with kachina dolls, see Marsha C. Bol, "Early Euro-American Ethnographers and the Hopi Tihu," in *Katsina,* ed. Pearlstone, 132–41.

CHAPTER 6: OUTSIDE THE FRAME:
THREE-DIMENSIONAL ART

1. In Pueblo religion, kachinas are spirit beings central to traditional cosmology and ritual practices. There are hundreds of kachinas, which vary from community to community, each representing an ancestor, natural phenomenon, or essence or force in the universe. For an overview, see White (this volume); E. Charles Adams, *The Origin and Development of the Pueblo Katsina Cult* (Tucson: University of Arizona, 1991); Barton Wright, *Hopi Kachinas: The Complete Guide to Collecting Kachina Dolls* (Flagstaff, Ariz.: Northland Publishing, 2000).

2. For a discussion of Hopi basketry, see Lydia L. Wycoff, "Southwest," in *Woven Worlds: Basketry from the Clark Field Collection at the Philbrook Museum of Art,* ed. Lydia L. Wycoff (Tulsa, Okla.: Philbrook Museum of Art, 2001), 31–47.

3. This basket is very similar in construction and style to one by Maggie Poncho (Coushatta) in the Philbrook Museum of Art. See J. Marshall Gettys, "Southeast," in *Woven Worlds: Basketry from the Clark Field Collection at the Philbrook Museum of Art,* ed. Lydia L. Wycoff

(Tulsa, Okla.: Philbrook Museum of Art, 2001), 173–91.

4. See Eulalie H. Bonar, *Woven by the Grandmothers: Nineteenth Century Navajo Textiles from the National Museum of the American Indian* (Washington, D.C.: Smithsonian Institution, 1996), and Joe Ben Wheat, *Blanket Weaving in the Southwest* (Tucson: University of Arizona, 2003).

5. During these ceremonies, Navajo people don masks representing Yei, or Holy People, the spirit beings central to Navajo cosmology and ritual practice. For an overview, see Gladys A. Reichard, *Navajo Religion: A Study of Symbolism* (New York, New York: Pantheon, 1950), and Gary Witherspoon, *Language and Art in the Navajo Universe* (Ann Arbor: University of Michigan, 1977).

6. There are many excellent sources on Pueblo pottery; see, for example, Rick Dillingham, *Fourteen Families in Pueblo Pottery* (Albuquerque: University of New Mexico, 1994), and Stephen Trimble, *Talking with the Clay: The Art of Pueblo Pottery in the 21st Century* (Santa Fe, N.Mex.: School of American Research, 1997).

7. See George Swinton, *Sculpture of the Eskimo* (London: C. Hurst, 1972).

8. See W. Jackson Rushing III, *Allan Houser: An American Master* (New York: H.N. Abrams, 2004).

9. For an overview of Native jewelry, see Diana F. Pardue, *Contemporary Southwestern Jewelry* (Phoenix, Ariz.: Heard Museum, 2007), and Dexter Cirillo, *Southwestern Indian Jewelry: Crafting New Traditions* (New York, New York: Rizzoli, 2008).

10. Mary Shelton's bolo tie is basically a miniature kachina figure made from carved and painted cottonwood.

11. The son of renowned jeweler Preston Monongye, Jesse Monongye has developed his own style of exquisitely detailed inlay, such as shown in *Buckle (Night Sky—Inlay)*. See Lois Sherr Dubin, *Jesse Monongya: Opal Bears and Lapis Skies* (New York: Hudson Hills Press, 2002).

12. For an in-depth discussion of Loloma's life and work, see Martha Hopkins Struever, *Loloma: Beauty Is His Name* (Santa Fe, N.Mex.: Wheelwright Museum, 2005).

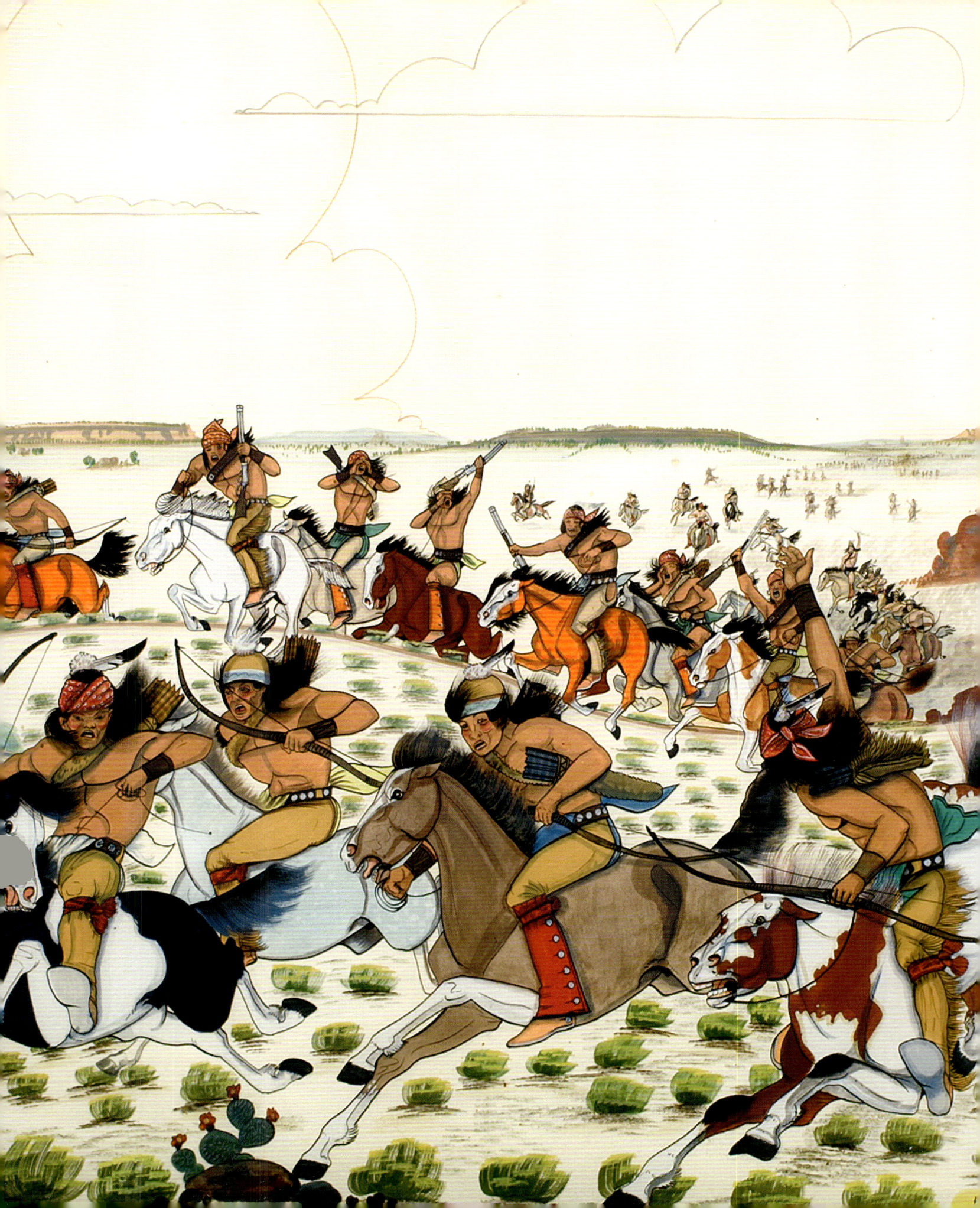

Bibliography

Abbott, Lawrence. *I Stand in the Center of the Good: Interviews with Contemporary Native American Artists*. Lincoln: University of Nebraska Press, 1994.

Adams, E. Charles. *The Origin and Development of the Pueblo Katsina Cult*. Tucson: University of Arizona, 1991.

Anthes, Bill. *Native Moderns: American Indian Painting, 1940–1970*. Durham: Duke University Press, 2006.

Bahti, Tom. *Southwestern Indian Ceremonials*. Flagstaff, Ariz.: KC Publications, 1970.

Bahti, Tom, and Mark Bahti. *Southwestern Indian Ceremonials*. Rev. ed. Flagstaff, Ariz.: KC Publications, 1997.

Berlo, Janet C. "The Szwedzicki Portfolios of American Indian Art, 1929–1952, Part I." *American Indian Art Magazine* 34 (February 2009): 37–39.

Bernstein, Bruce. "Julian and Maria Martinez." In *St. James Guide to Native North American Artists*, edited by Roger Matuz, 361–62. New York: St. James Press, 1998.

Bernstein, Bruce, and W. Jackson Rushing III. *Modern by Tradition: American Indian Painting in the Studio Style*. Santa Fe: Museum of New Mexico Press, 1995.

Bol, Marsha C. "Early Euro-American Ethnographers and the Hopi Tihu." In *Katsina: Commodified and Appropriated Images of Hopi Supernaturals*, edited by Zena Pearlstone, 132–45. Los Angeles: University of California Los Angeles Fowler Museum of Cultural History, 2001.

Bonar, Eulalie H. *Woven by the Grandmothers: Nineteenth Century Navajo Textiles from the National Museum of the American Indian*. Washington, D.C.: Smithsonian Institution, 1996.

Broder, Patricia Janis. *Earth Songs, Moon Dreams: Paintings by Native American Women*. New York: St. Martin's Press, 1999.

———. *Hopi Painting: The World of the Hopis*. New York: Brandywine Press, 1978.

Brody, J. J. *Indian Painters and White Patrons*. Albuquerque: University of New Mexico, 1971.

———. *Pueblo Indian Painting: Tradition and Modernism in New Mexico, 1900–1930*. Santa Fe, N.Mex.: School of American Research Press, 1997.

Burlin, Natalie Curtis. *The Indians' Book: An Offering by the American Indians of Indian Lore*. New York: Harper and Brothers, 1907.

Chase, Katherine L. *Indian Painters of the Southwest: The Deep Remembering*. Santa Fe: School of American Research Press, 2002.

Cirillo, Dexter. *Southwestern Indian Jewelry: Crafting New Traditions*. New York: Rizzoli, 2008.

Controtto, Eugene L. "This Business of Selling Indian Applied Arts." *Desert* 24, no. 9 (September 1961): 18–21.

Cushing, Frank Hamilton. *Zuni Folk Tales*. New York: Alfred A. Knopf, 1931.

Decker, Julie. *John Hoover: Art and Life*. Seattle: University of Washington Press, 2002.

Dillingham, Rick. *Fourteen Families in Pueblo Pottery*. Albuquerque: University of New Mexico, 1994.

Dubin, Lois Sherr. *Jesse Monongya: Opal Bears and Lapis Skies*. New York: Hudson Hills Press, 2002.

Dubin, Margaret, "Sanctioned Scribes: How Critics and Historians Write the Native American Artworld," in *Native American Art in the Twentieth Century*, ed. W. Jackson Rushing III, 149–66. London: Routledge, 1999.

Dunn, Dorothy. *American Indian Painting of the Southwest and Plains Areas*. Albuquerque: University of New Mexico Press, 1968.

———. "The Art of Joe Herrera." *El Palacio* 59 (December 1952): 367.

Ellison, Rosemary. "Introduction." In *Contemporary Plains Indian Painting*, edited by Myles Libhart, 14–19. Anadarko: Oklahoma Indian Arts and Crafts Cooperative, 1972.

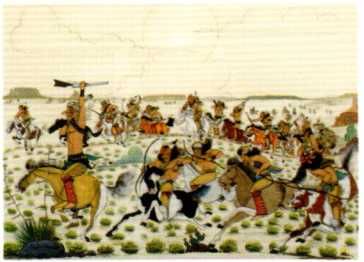

PLATE 182

QUINCY TAHOMA

U.S., Navajo, 1920–1956

The Navajos in Pursuit, 1948

Watercolor on paper 18 x 27 in.

Erickson, John T. *Kachinas: An Evolving Hopi Art Form?* Phoenix: Heard Museum, 1977.

Ewers, John C. "Early White Influence upon Plains Indian Painting: George Catlin and Carl Bodmer among the Mandan, 1832–34." *Smithsonian Miscellaneous Collections* 134, no. 7. Washington D.C.: Smithsonian Institution, 1957.

Farris, Phoebe. "Emmi Whitehorse." In *St. James Guide to Native North American Artists*, edited by Roger Matuz, 622–25. New York: St. James Press, 1998.

Frederick, Joan. *T. C. Cannon: He Stood in the Sun.* Flagstaff: Northland Publishing, 1995.

"George Morrison Debut." *Art Digest* 22 (May 1, 1948): 19.

Gettys, J. Marshall. "Southeast." In *Woven Worlds: Basketry from the Clark Field Collection at the Philbrook Museum of Art,* edited by Lydia L. Wycoff, 173–91. Tulsa, Okla.: Philbrook Museum of Art, 2001.

Gombrich, Ernst W. *The Sense of Order: A Study in the Psychology of Decorative Art.* Ithaca: Cornell University Press, 1978.

Grey, Samuel L. *Tonita Peña.* Albuquerque, N.Mex.: Avanyu, 1990.

Gundersheimer, Werner, Frank H. Goodyear, Jr., and Paul J. Karlstrom. *Fritz Scholder: Paintings.* Tucson, Ariz.: Nazraeli Press, 2001.

Hartley, Marsden. "Tribal Esthetics." *Dial* 65 (November 1918): 400.

Highwater, Jamake. *Song from the Earth: American Indian Painting.* Boston: New York Graphic Society, 1976.

———. *The Sweet Grass Lives On: Fifty Contemporary North American Indian Artists.* New York: Lippincott and Crowell, 1980.

Hill, Rick. *Creativity Is Our Tradition: Three Decades of Contemporary Indian Art at the Institute of American Indian Arts.* Santa Fe, N.Mex.: Institute of American Indian and Alaska Native Culture and Arts Development, 1992.

Hill, Tom, and Richard W. Hill, Sr., eds. *Creation's Journey: Native American Identity and Belief.*

Washington, D.C.: Smithsonian Institution Press, National Museum of the American Indian, 1994.

Hoffman, Gerhard, ed. *Indianische Kunst im 20 Jahrhundert.* Munchen: Prestel, 1985.

Hoffman, Gerhard, ed. *Indianische Kunst Im 20 Jahrhundert/Indian Art in the 20th Century.* New York: Te Neues, 1985.

———. "Native American Art in the Context of Modern and Postmodern Art." In *The Arts of the North American Indian*, ed. Edwin L. Wade, 257–82. New York: Hudson Hills Press in Association with Philbrook Art Center, 1986.

Hoffman, Gerhard, and Gisela Hoffman. "Tony Abeyta." In *St. James Guide to Native North American Artists*, edited by Roger Matuz, 3–5. New York: St. James Press, 1998.

Houle, Robert, et al. *Robert Houle's Paris/Ojibwa.* Exhibition catalogue. Peterborough, Ontario: Gallery of Peterborough, 2011.

Hoving, Thomas. *The Art of Dan Namingha.* New York: Harry N. Abrams, 2000.

Hughes, Robert. *Culture of Complaint: The Fraying of America.* London: Oxford University Press, 1993.

Hulderman, Paul F. "Scottsdale—A New Focal Point in Indian Art." In *New Dimensions in Indian Art*, edited by Byron Harvey III, 20–26. Scottsdale, Ariz.: Scottsdale National Indian Arts Council, 1965.

Jacka, Jerry, and Lois Essary Jacka. *Art of the Hopi: Contemporary Journeys on Ancient Pathways.* Flagstaff, Ariz.: Northland, 1998.

———. *Beyond Tradition: Contemporary Indian Art and Its Evolution.* Flagstaff, Ariz.: Northland, 1988.

———. *Enduring Traditions: Art of the Navajo.* Flagstaff, Ariz.: Northland, 1994.

Jacobson, Oscar B. *Kiowa Indian Art.* Nice, France: l'Edition d'Art C. Szwedzicki, 1929.

Jantzer-White, Marilee. "Patrick DesJarlait." In *St. James Guide to Native North American Artists*, edited by Roger Matuz, 158. New York: St. James Press, 1998.

Jemison, Peter. "The Paper Bag Works." In *Ni' Go Tlunh A Doh Ka* (*We Are Always Turning Around on Purpose*). Exhibition catalogue, 22. Old Westbury: Amelie A. Wallace Gallery, State University of New York, 1986.

Kabotie, Fred, and Bill Belknap. *Fred Kabotie: Hopi Indian Artist*. Flagstaff: Museum of Northern Arizona Press, 1977.

King, Charles S., and Richard L. Spivey. *The Life and Art of Tony Da*. Tucson, Ariz.: Rio Nuevo, 2011.

King, Jeanne Snodgrass. *Drawn from Memory: The James T. Bialac Collection of American Indian Art*. Phoenix, Ariz.: Heard Museum, 1996.

La Barre, Weston. *The Peyote Cult*. New York: Schocken Books, 1969.

LaPena, Frank, and Janice T. Driesbach, eds. *The Extension of Tradition: Contemporary Northern California Native American Art in Cultural Perspective*. Sacramento, Calif.: Crocker Art Museum, 1985.

Lester, Patrick D. *The Biographical Directory of Native American Painters*. Tulsa, Okla.: SIR Publications, 1995.

Lippard, Lucy R. *Mixed Blessings: New Art in a Multi-Cultural America*. New York: Pantheon Press, 1990.

Manley, Ray, and Clara Lee Tanner. *Ray Manley's Collecting Southwestern Indian Arts and Crafts*. Tucson, Ariz.: Ray Manley Publishing, n.d.

———. *Ray Manley's Hopi Kachinas*. Tucson, Ariz.: Ray Manley Photography, n.d.

Maurer, Evan, et al. *Morrison's Horizon*. Exhibition catalogue. Minneapolis, Minn.: Minneapolis Institute of Art, 1998.

McMaster, Gerald R. "The New Tribe: Critical Perspectives and Practices in Aboriginal Contemporary Art." Diss., Universiteit van Amsterdam, 1999.

———. "Towards an Aboriginal Art History." In *Native American Art in the Twentieth Century: Makers, Meanings, Histories*, edited by W. Jackson Rushing III, 81–96. London: Routledge Press, 1999.

Mercer, Kobena, ed. *Cosmopolitan Modernisms*. Cambridge, Mass., and London: MIT Press and the Institute of International Visual Arts, 2005.

Monthan, Guy, and Doris Monthan. "Ha-So-De: One of the First Individualists." *American Indian Art Magazine* 1 (Summer 1976): 34–39.

Morris, Kate. "Places of Emergence: Painting Genesis." In *Off the Map: Landscape in the Native Imagination*, ed. Kathleen Ash Milby, 47–53. Washington, D.C., and New York: NMAI Editions, Smithsonian Institution, 2007.

Munson, Marit, ed. *Kenneth Chapman's Santa Fe: Artists and Archaeologists, 1907–1931: The Memoirs of Kenneth Chapman*. Santa Fe, N.Mex.: School for Advanced Research, 2007.

New, Lloyd Kiva. *Future Directions in Native American Art*. Santa Fe, N.Mex.: Institute of American Indian Arts, 1972.

O'Brian, John, ed. *Clement Greenberg: The Collected Essays and Criticism*. Vol. 1. Chicago: University of Chicago Press, 1993.

Oxendine, Lloyd E. "23 Contemporary Indian Artists." *Art in America* 60 (July/August 1972): 58–69.

Pardue, Diana F. *Contemporary Southwestern Jewelry*. Phoenix, Ariz.: Heard Museum, 2007.

Pearlstone, Zena. *Katsina: Commodified and Appropriated Images of Hopi Supernaturals*. Los Angeles: Fowler Museum, UCLA, 2001.

Penney, David W., and Lisa A. Roberts. "America's Pueblo Artists: Encounters on the Borderlands." In *Native American Art in the Twentieth Century: Makers, Meanings, Histories*, edited by W. Jackson Rushing III, 32–33. New York and London: Routledge, 1999.

Ray, Dorothy Jean. *Aleut and Eskimo Art: Tradition and Innovation in South Alaska*. Seattle: University of Washington Press, 1981.

———. *Graphic Arts of the Alaskan Eskimo*. Native American Arts 2. Washington, D.C.: Indian Arts and Crafts Board, 1969.

Redcorn, Marla. "Lois Smoky." In *St. James Guide to Native North American Artists*, edited by Roger Matuz, 528–29. New York: St. James Press, 1998.

Reichard, Gladys A. *Navajo Religion: A Study of Symbolism*. New York, New York: Pantheon, 1950.

Richards, Tally. "Indian in Paris." *American Indian Art Magazine* 2 (Spring 1977): 48.

Roberts, Lisa. "Tonita Peña." In *St. James Guide to Native North American Artists*, edited by Roger Matuz, 445–47. New York: St. James Press, 1998.

Rushing, W. Jackson, III. *Allan Houser: An American Master*. New York: Harry N. Abrams, 2004.

———. "Authenticity and Subjectivity in Post-War Painting: Concerning Herrera, Scholder, and Cannon." In *Shared Visions: Native American Painters and Sculptors in the Twentieth Century*, edited by Rennard Strickland and Margaret Archuleta, 12–21. Phoenix, Ariz.: Heard Museum, 1991.

———. "Modern By Tradition: The 'Studio Style' of Native American Painting." In *Modern By Tradition*, edited by Bruce Bernstein and W. Jackson Rushing III, 61–73. Santa Fe: Museum of New Mexico, 1995.

———. "Modern Spirits: The Legacy of Allan Houser and George Morrison." In *Essays on Native Modernism: Complexity and Contradiction in American Indian Art*, 53–66. Washington, D.C., and New York: National Museum of the American Indian, Smithsonian Institution, 2006.

———. *Native American Art and the New York Avant-Garde*. Austin: University of Texas Press, 1995.

Rushing, W. Jackson, III, ed. *Native American Art in the Twentieth Century: Makers, Meanings, Histories*. London: Routledge Press, 1999.

Schaaf, Gregory. *Hopi Katsina: 1,600 Artist Biographies, ca. 1840-Present*. Santa Fe, N.Mex.: Center for Indigenous Arts and Cultures Press, 2008.

Schaafsman, Polly, ed. *Kachinas in the Pueblo World*. Albuquerque: University of New Mexico Press, 1994.

Scholder, Fritz. *Indian Kitsch*. Flagstaff, Ariz.: Northland, 1979.

———. *Rot-red*. Munich: Nazraeli Press, 1995.

———. "Scholder on Scholder: A Self-Interview." *American Indian Art Magazine* 1 (Spring 1976): 50.

Secakuku, Alph H. *Following the Sun and Moon: Hopi Kachina Tradition*. Flagstaff, Ariz.: Northland Publishing, 1995.

———. *Hopi Kachina Traditions: Following the Sun and Moon*. Flagstaff, Ariz.: Northland Publishing and the Heard Museum, 1995.

Secakuku, Susan. "Katsinam in Hopi Life." In *Convergence Magazine*, Autry National Center (Winter 2008): 30–31.

Silberman, Arthur. *100 Years of Native American Painting*. Oklahoma City: Oklahoma Museum of Art, 1978.

Stevenson, Matilda Coxe. "The Zuni Indians." In *23rd Annual Report of the Bureau of American Ethnology*, 94–102. Washington, D.C.: Government Printing Office, 1904.

Struever, Martha Hopkins. *Loloma: Beauty Is His Name*. Santa Fe, N.Mex.: Wheelwright Museum, 2005.

Swan, Daniel C. *Peyote Religious Art: Symbols of Faith and Belief*. Jackson: University Press of Mississippi, 1999.

Swinton, George. *Sculpture of the Eskimo*. London: C. Hurst, 1972.

Tanner, Clara Lee. *The James T. Bialac Collection of Southwest Indian Paintings*. Tucson: University of Arizona Press, 1968.

———. *Southwest Indian Painting: A Changing Art*. 2nd ed. Tucson: University of Arizona Press, 1973.

Taylor, Joshua C., et al. *Fritz Scholder*. New York: Rizzoli International, 1982.

Traugott, Joseph. "Emmi Whitehorse: Kin' Nah' Zin'." *Artspace* 6 (Summer 1982): 40–41.

———. "Native American Artists and the Postmodern Cultural Divide." *Art Journal* 51 (Fall 1992): 36–43.

Trevelyan, Amy. "Jaune Quick-to-See Smith." In *Contemporary Masters: The Eiteljorg Fellowship for Native American Fine Art*, vol. 1, 50–54. Indianapolis: Eiteljorg Museum of American Indians and Western Art, 1999.

Trimble, Stephen. *Talking with the Clay: The Art of Pueblo Pottery in the 21st Century.* Santa Fe, N.Mex.: School of American Research, 1997.

Wade, Edwin L. "The Ethnic Art Market and the Dilemma of Innovative Indian Artists." In *Magic Images: Contemporary Native American Art*, edited by Edwin L. Wade and Rennard Strickland, 9–17. Norman: University of Oklahoma Press, 1981.

Wade, Edwin L. "The Ethnic Art Market in the American Southwest, 1880–1980." In *Objects and Others: Essays on Museums and Material Culture*, edited by George W. Stocking, Jr., 167–91. Madison, Wisc: University of Wisconsin Press, 1985.

Wade, Edwin L., ed. *The Arts of the North American Indian.* New York: Hudson Hill Press, 1986.

Walsh, Andrea. "Marianne Nicolson." In *Contemporary Masters: The Eiteljorg Fellowship for Native American Fine Art*, vol. 1, 26–30. Indianapolis: Eiteljorg Museum of American Indians and Western Art, 1999.

———. "Marianne Nicolson Speaks." In *Reservation X: The Power of Place in Aboriginal Contemporary Art*, ed. Gerald McMaster, 99–101. Seattle: University of Washington Press and Canadian Museum of Civilization, 1998.

Washburn, Dorothy K., ed. *Hopi Kachina Spirit Life.* San Francisco: California Academy of Sciences, 1980.

Warner, John Anson. *Contemporary Canadian Native Art: Newly Emerging Art Styles.* Osaka, Japan: Kansai Gaidai University, 1996.

Warner, John Anson. "The Individual in Native American Art: A Sociological View." In *The Arts of the North American Indian*, edited by Edwin L. Wade, 171–202. New York: Hudson Hill Press, 1986.

Warner, John Anson. *Paradigms of Twentieth Century Native American Painting.* Osaka, Japan: Kansai University of Foreign Studies Publication, 1994.

Wheat, Joe Ben. *Blanket Weaving in the Southwest.* Tucson: University of Arizona, 2003.

Witherspoon, Gary. *Language and Art in the Navajo Universe.* Ann Arbor: University of Michigan, 1977.

Wright, Barton. *Clowns of the Hopi: Tradition Keepers and Delight Makers.* Flagstaff, Ariz.: Northland, 1994.

———. "The Drift from Tradition." In *Katsina: Commodified and Appropriated Images of Hopi Supernaturals*, edited by Zena Pearlstone, 146–57. Los Angeles: University of California Los Angeles Fowler Museum of Cultural History, 2001.

———. *Hopi Kachinas: The Complete Guide to Collecting Kachina Dolls.* Flagstaff, Ariz.: Northland, 1977.

———. *Hopi Kachinas: The Complete Guide to Collecting Kachina Dolls.* Flagstaff, Ariz.: Northland, 2000.

Wycoff, Lydia L. "Southwest." In *Woven Worlds: Basketry from the Clark Field Collection at the Philbrook Museum of Art,* edited by Lydia L. Wycoff, 31–47. Tulsa, Okla.: Philbrook Museum of Art, 2001.

Wyman, Leland. "Navajo Ceremonial System." In *Handbook of North American Indians*, vol. 10, edited by Alfonso Ortiz, 536–57. Washington, D.C.: Smithsonian Institution, 1983.

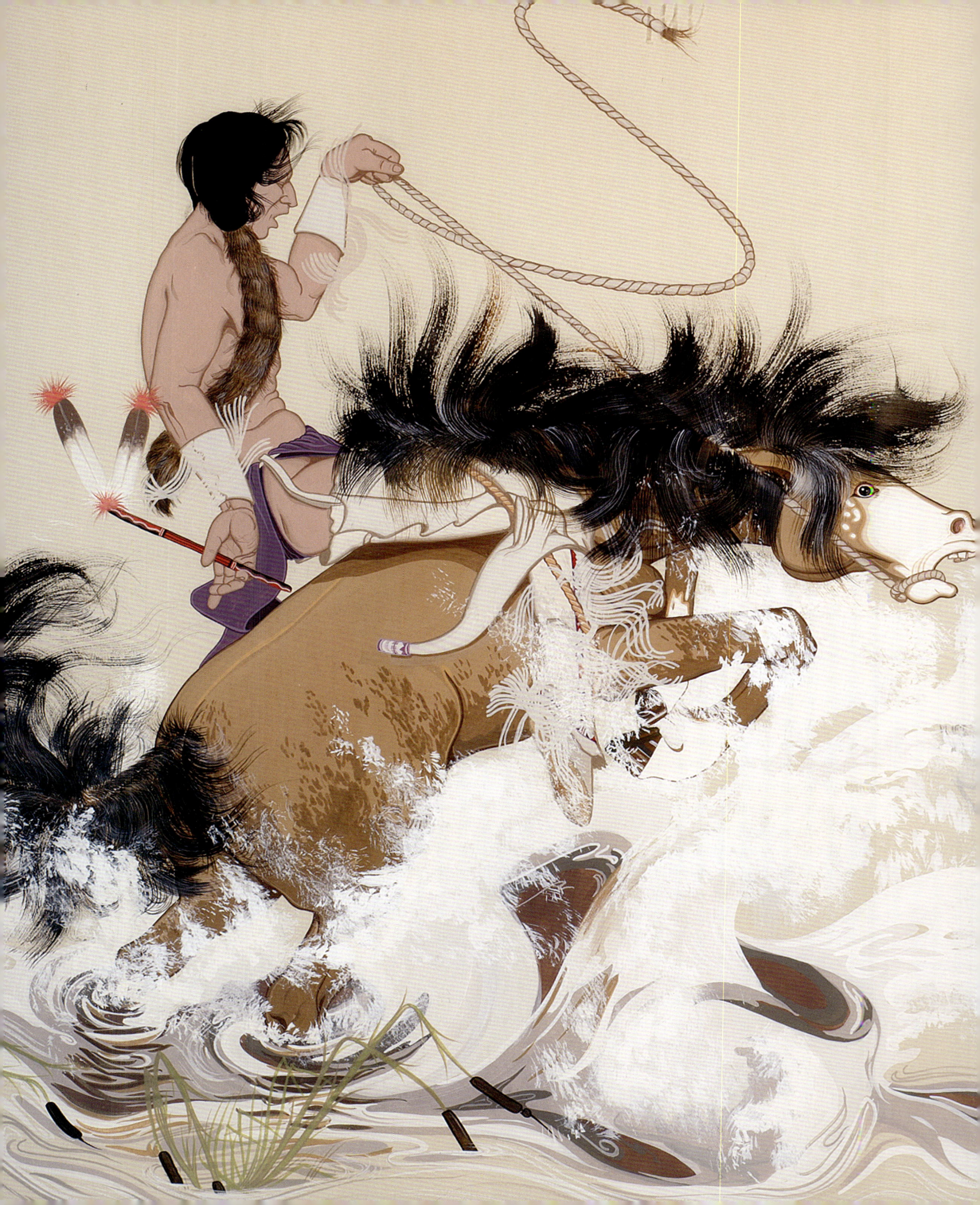

Contributors

CHRISTINA E. BURKE is Curator of Native American and Non-Western Art at the Philbrook Museum of Art.

W. JACKSON RUSHING III is Eugene B. Adkins Presidential Professor of Art History and Mary Lou Milner Carver Chair in Native American Art at the University of Oklahoma School of Art and Art History.

RENNARD STRICKLAND is Distinguished Professor Emeritus at the University of Oregon School of Law.

CHRISTY VEZOLLES is an accredited member of the American Society of Appraisers, with expertise in American and European fine art, as well as American Indian art.

EDWIN L. WADE has held positions at the School of American Research; Peabody Museum, Harvard University; Philbrook Museum of Art: and the Museum of Northern Arizona. He is currently president of the consulting firm El Otro Lado, which focuses on profit and nonprofit cultural policy development.

MARY JO WATSON is Director of the School of Art and Art History at the University of Oklahoma and Curator of Native American Art at the Fred Jones Jr. Museum of Art.

MARK ANDREW WHITE is the Eugene B. Adkins and Chief Curator at the Fred Jones Jr. Museum of Art.

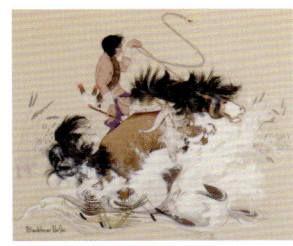

PLATE 183
BLACKBEAR BOSIN
U.S., Kiowa/Comanche,
1921–1980
Challenge, 1959
Watercolor on paper, 22 x 26 in.

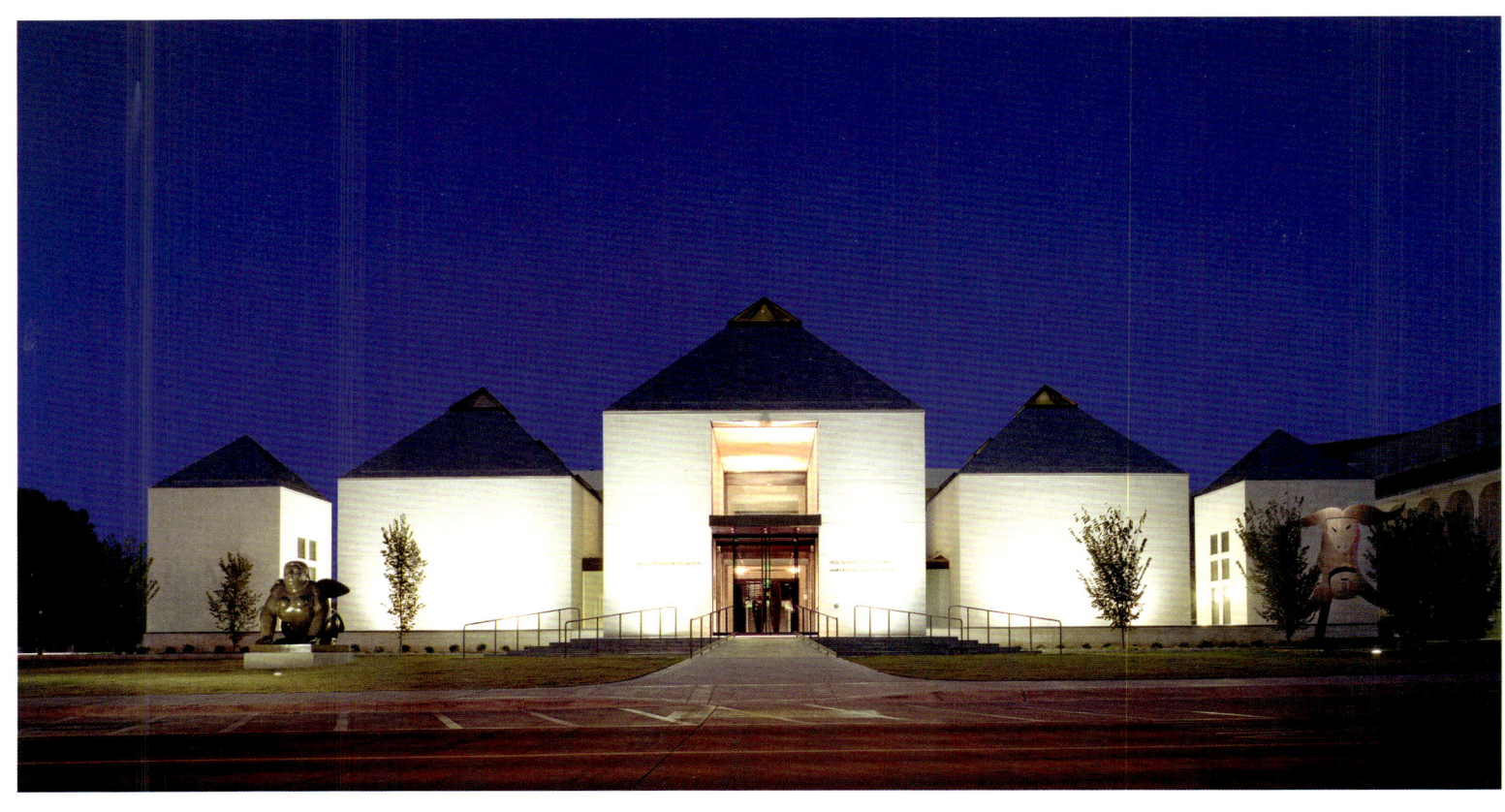

FRED JONES JR. MUSEUM OF ART
UNIVERSITY OF OKLAHOMA

Over the years, the permanent collection of the Fred Jones Jr. Museum of Art has grown exponentially through the generosity of donors such as Max Weitzenhoffer and Jerome M. Westheimer, Sr. In 1996, with an initial gift of $1 million from Mrs. Fred Jones, OU President David L. Boren and First Lady Molly Shi Boren spearheaded the successful fundraising campaign to acquire the important collection of the late Richard H. and Adeline J. Fleischaker, which is composed primarily of Native American and Southwestern art. Today, the Fred Jones Jr. Museum of Art is one of the finest university art museums in the United States. Strengths of the nearly 16,000–object permanent collection (including the approximately 3,300-object Eugene B. Adkins Collection and the more than 4,000-object James T. Bialac Collection) are the Weitzenhoffer Collection of French Impressionism, twentieth-century American painting and sculpture, traditional and contemporary Native American art, art of the American West, ceramics, photography, contemporary art, Asian art, and graphics from the sixteenth century to the present. Temporary exhibitions are mounted throughout the year that explore the art of various periods and cultures.

GHISLAIN D'HUMIÈRES

After studying history and art history at the Sorbonne in Paris, Ghislain d'Humières became a specialist in eighteenth-century furniture for Sotheby's London, and then transferred to New York. He became the director of the jewelry department at Christie's of Los Angeles and then transferred to Christie's in Geneva, where he was in charge of international clients from Europe and South America. In 2004, the Fine Arts Museum of San Francisco hired him as assistant director in charge of the opening of the new de Young Museum. Following that appointment, d'Humières joined the University of Oklahoma as the Wylodean and Bill Saxon Director of the Fred Jones Jr. Museum of Art, where he has overseen the construction of the Stuart Wing, which opened in 2011.

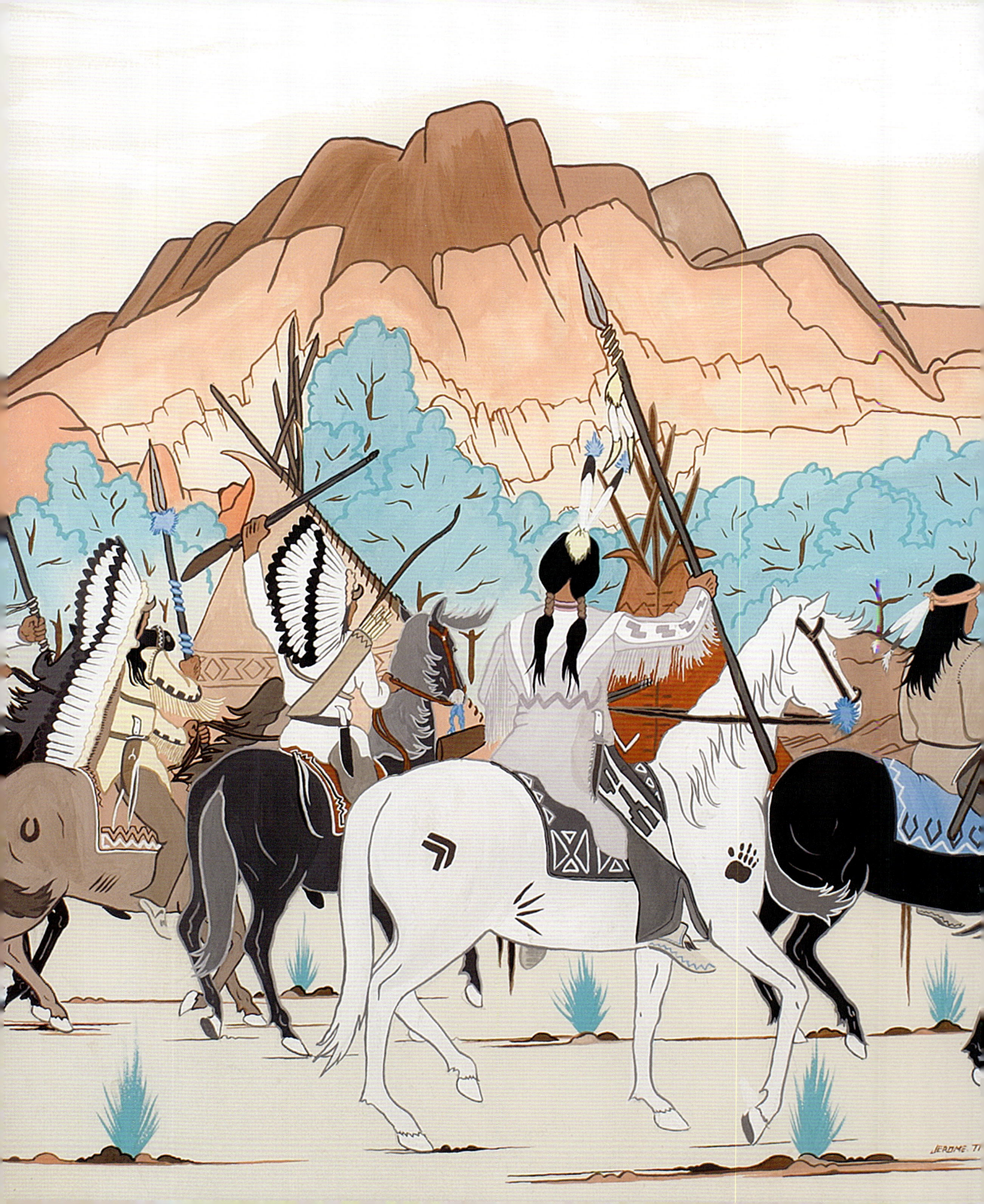

Index

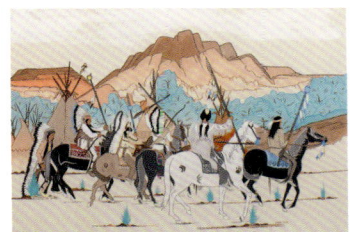

PLATE 184
JEROME TIGER
U.S., Creek/Seminole,
1941–1967

War Party, n.d.
Watercolor on paper,
18½ × 26½ in.

Copyedited by Melanie Mallon
Indexed by Heather Laskey

Book design by Carol Haralson
Set in Garamond Premier Pro with Poplar display
Image prepress by University of Oklahoma Printing Services

Printed by Everbest Printing, China, through FourColour Imports, Louisville, Kentucky
Printed on 157 gsm Gold East Matte